The Open Economy
and
the World Economy

THE OPEN ECONOMY AND THE WORLD ECONOMY

A Textbook
in International Economics

John Williamson

Basic Books, Inc., Publishers   New York

Library of Congress Cataloging in Publication Data

Williamson, John, 1937–
　The open economy and the world economy.

　Includes bibliographies and index.
1. International economic relations. I. Title.
HF1411.W564　1983　　337　　82-24463
ISBN: 0-465-05287-8

To Denise

Contents

III

Macroeconomics

Contents

IV

Development

V

World Economy

Contents

Preface

FOR MANY YEARS I had a firm intention never to write a textbook. My resolve began to waiver after I started to teach in Brazil. I soon discovered that textbooks necessarily played a larger role than I had been accustomed to accord them—not just because of the difficulties my students had in understanding what I was saying (that in principle being in Portuguese) but also because of the limited library facilities and the amount of material that had not been translated. I next discovered that the course I wanted to teach was not very similar to any of the existing texts. Every term's evolution of the course simply served to accentuate the differences, until the time finally arrived when I came to entertain the hope that I had evolved a course from which a wider audience might benefit.

In trying to explain why I was dissatisfied with existing international economics texts and what I have tried to do differently, there is a danger of sounding churlish. It is not my intention to disparage my predecessors. All the successful textbooks deal admirably with at least a part of the field; otherwise, they would not have been successful. I have drawn on them, in part consciously and, no doubt in a larger measure than I realize, unconsciously as well. Part of the difference also represents the advance of time more than anything else: I doubt whether I would have written so much on capital flows a decade ago, and I certainly could not have covered the asset market approach to the exchange rate.

The main innovations of the book can be grouped in six areas.

Coverage. In addition to the traditional staples of the Heckscher-Ohlin model, commercial policy, customs unions, the theory of the balance of payments (or is it the balance of trade?), fixed versus floating exchange rates, and the international monetary system, there are treatments of intraindustry trade, international capital flows, alternative approaches to the theory of floating exchange rates, the international capital market, proposals for a new international economic order, and global macroeconomics. Obviously one cannot hope to be comprehensive, and I have virtually omitted two significant areas. One is international industrial economics (the product cycle and direct investment), which is a sufficiently distinct field to merit separate treatment. The other is migration, where there is little that positive economic analysis has to offer.[1] With those two exceptions, I have aimed to introduce virtually all important areas, including recent developments.

Small Economy Assumption. To make room for so much new material, something had to give. Teaching in the Southern Hemisphere inspired the adoption of a major simplification that has a minimal cost in terms of relevance for the majority of students: namely, abandonment of the traditional two-country model in favor of the simpler case of the small country that trades with an outside world large enough to be treated as parametric. Since most countries are indeed small in the relevant technical sense, students from most countries will find the simpler model to be the one that they will normally need to use. However, a number of chapters also contain short addenda which deal with the large-country case, so as to provide a link to the literature. Students from large countries, by which one means especially the United States, will find those addenda serve an additional function, of giving them an insight into the extra complications that they need to bear in mind to understand the position of their own country.

World Economy Section. A potential trouble with the small economy approach is that it avoids treating those issues of interdependence that determine what drives the world economy as a whole. I hope that the danger of neglecting those issues has been averted by including a substantial section specifically analyzing the functioning of the world economy. This two-stage treatment—first analyzing how the individual unit reacts to the parametric whole, then considering what the sum total of those individual reactions implies for the operation of the system—is familiar enough to economists from microeconomic theory and seems ripe for exploitation in the international context.

Simple Models. Another way that I have sought to simplify is by selecting the simplest models that are able to make the points which need to be made. There are various criteria for selecting models, depending on the purpose for which the model is to be used: for example, a model to be used for econometric estimation or for projection and simulation needs qualities like realism and comprehensiveness. But models in textbooks are there to help students gain an understanding of how the world works, not to provide

---

1. People emigrate when they are allowed to and when their expected earnings in their potential alternative residence compensate for the costs and deprivation (of family and familiar environment) of moving. There is not a shadow of a doubt that international earnings differentials are currently so large as to stimulate the maximum flow permitted by the receiving countries—or, actually, rather more than the legally permitted maximum! Explaining migration therefore requires explaining what determines the immigration limits set by the receiving countries, and economics has nothing much to offer in that direction.

blueprints for a model to estimate in their Master's thesis. For the former purpose, simplicity is a virtue: a 2 × 2 model is better than an $n \times n$ model because one can understand what is going on in it. Not only should models be simple, but there is also virtue in familiarity: production possibility curves or *IS/LM* get my vote in preference to weird concoctions that have never made it outside the trade literature. When first introduced, even familiar models are described from first principles, although in a sufficiently succinct way as to be more suitable for the student who has already met them and merely needs his memory jogged than for the student to whom they are completely new.

An Applied Economics Approach. When I left graduate school I was a representative young economist in yearning to contribute to the progress of pure theory. Five years later I went to work in the U.K. Treasury and very soon I discovered that there is something both more fun and more rewarding than laboring to produce a model sufficiently differentiated to make the world take note of one's existence: to wit, to be faced with real live problems and confronted with the decision as to what model to throw at them. I once heard a distinguished economist lament the fact that we have lots of models instead of just one. What rubbish! The world is a complicated place, and any one model would therefore either be ridiculously inadequate or totally unwieldy. What the applied economist needs is not a single model but a rich choice, with a sense of the relationship between different models and of the considerations that are relevant to deciding which one should be applied in a particular context.

It may be that this is difficult to teach, but it seems to me that we hardly try. This book contains discussions of the circumstances which make one model applicable rather than another, of the real-world implications of models and of how worldly events can be interpreted in models, and of the stylized facts[2] about model parameters—all based on a conviction that models are there to be used, not to provide aesthetic pleasure nor to compete against Latin as a source of mental gymnastics. So far as I am concerned, a theoretical construct whose real world counterpart I cannot identify when I read about it in the newspapers is of no more interest than a set of facts undisciplined by a theoretical perspective.

A Hint of History. My historian friends have normally considered me mildly philistine, and I am not quite sure whether my endeavors to provide a historical slant will not confirm them in this opinion instead of redeeming

---

2. By a "stylized fact" economists mean a characterization of what they perceive to be the essential factual aspects of the normal case. For example, it is a stylized fact that import propensities are bigger for small countries than for large ones. That does not mean that the proposition would hold in every pair-wise comparison, but it does imply that it is a strong regularity with important implications.

me in their eyes. Be that as it may, I am sure that it is in principle a good idea to provide an introductory sketch of how the world economy got to be where it is today, and this therefore provides the topic of the first chapter. I have tried also to give some idea of how economic theory has evolved, and of the pressures that influenced its evolution, rather than just plucking models out of thin air. In addition, I indicate brief biographical details of the economists whose work is studied.[3]

The book is organized in five parts. The first, which is restricted to a single chapter, provides the historical background. The second part is devoted to the "pure" or microeconomic theory of trade, and also of investment. The third part deals with balance of payments theory, or the macroeconomics of the open economy. Part IV explores the international dimensions of economic development. The final part studies the world economy.

The primary audience to whom this book is directed is the one-year advanced undergraduate course in international economics. I have taught the bulk of the material in the book at one time or another in the one-semester course that I gave in Rio de Janeiro, but was never able to cover anything close to the entire contents. The natural way to use the book in a one-semester course would be to concentrate on parts II and III, omitting some topics like customs unions and floating exchange rates that, though interesting and important, are not central to understanding the remainder. This should leave time for the instructor to pick at least one topic from part IV or V which reflects the particular interest of the class. I also hope that the book will find a role in graduate-level courses, though I imagine that many graduate courses will wish to use a more mathematical work in parallel.

It remains to acknowledge my many debts: to my family for forbearance and to former teachers, colleagues, conferees, and students for stimulation. By name I single out Fritz Machlup, who taught me at Princeton University from 1960 to 1963; Charles Kindleberger, with whom I taught at the Massachusetts Institute of Technology in 1967; J. J. Polak, under whom I worked in the International Monetary Fund from 1972 to 1974; and the late Fred Hirsch, my colleague at Warwick University from 1975 to 1977. I owe a very particular debt to those friends who took the trouble to read certain chapters and offer me comments which eliminated at least some of my errors: Willem Buiter, John Chipman, William R. Cline, Benjamin J. Cohen, Max Corden, Carlos Diaz Alejandro, Avinash Dixit, and Paul Krugman. To these and the many others who have stimulated and disciplined my thought in international economics, I am grateful.

3. The nationality of economists born in the United States is not mentioned explicitly.

I

INTRODUCTION

THIS introductory part of the book contains only one chapter, the aim of which is to provide a minimal historical background for the study of international economics. The material is sufficiently nontechnical to be read with profit even by students whose professor prefers to plunge straight into theory.

1

Historical Perspective

GROSS world product (GWP), measured properly on the basis of purchasing power comparisons,[1] amounted to around $13 trillion in 1980. When the modern economic world started to emerge some 220 years ago, real GWP was perhaps 4 percent of that. World population has multiplied in the interim between five and six times, from some 800 million souls to around 4.5 billion, while on average output per head has increased almost as much. That average conceals a range from stagnation or worse in some traditional societies to increases of over 2500 percent in some of the richest economies like Sweden or Kuwait. The variation in income per head among countries is enormously larger than it was before economic development got under way—which was, in historical terms, not long ago.

About a fifth of world expenditure is now directed at goods (or services) produced abroad: certainly a much higher proportion than 220 years ago, when trade was largely limited to modest quantities of luxury goods, nota-

1. The most common method of adding up GDP figures to form an international aggregate is to multiply each country's GDP expressed in its national currency by its exchange rate against some common currency (in practice the U.S. dollar). This procedure suggests a 1980 GWP of something over U.S. $11 trillion. However, this method yields a severe and systematic underestimate of the income of the poorer countries, for reasons explained in chapter 10.2. The alternative involves making detailed comparisons of purchasing power in different countries, as has now been done by the U.N.-sponsored International Comparisons Project headed by Irving Kravis at the University of Pennsylvania. The estimate quoted in the text is based on an extrapolation of the results yielded by that project (Kravis, Heston, and Summers, 1982, chapter 8).

bly sugar and spices, and slaves. In those days foreign factor income, migration, tourism, and international investment, let alone the international flow of technical knowledge or the production of multinational companies, were all negligible. Economic interdependence, like development, is a historically recent phenomenon.

The purpose of this book is to enhance understanding of the causes and consequences of that interdependence. We start our study by a sketch of the joint evolution of interdependence and development.

1.1 To 1815

Prior to the late eighteenth century there was little objective reason to suppose that life would ever be anything other than "nasty, brutish and short" for the vast majority of mankind. Technical advances had been occurring sporadically for hundreds or even thousands of years, but they led to lasting benefits for no more than a small dominant minority. The majority was everywhere imprisoned on the Malthusian treadmill where any addition to output was quickly overtaken by population growth. It has been estimated that total income in the most progressive country, Britain, was growing at an average rate of 2.6 percent per *decade* before 1745 (Deane and Cole, 1969, p. 79). Such rates do not offer much hope of breaking out of the historical norm of underdevelopment.

The prospect of permanent stagnation first began to lose its apparent inevitability with the Industrial Revolution that slowly gathered force in Britain after 1760. Based on technical progress in textile manufacturing, coal mining, iron smelting, and the harnessing of steam, industrialization concentrated workers in factories and towns that were linked together by canals. Various answers have been given as to why industrialization started when and where it did. Some have tended to regard the series of inventions that launched large-scale industry as more or less an accident, which happened to give British capitalists the chance to dominate foreign competition and accumulate capital. Others have placed primary emphasis on the human capital factor, the availability of engineers and entrepreneurs: the German economist-sociologist Max Weber (1864–1920) linked the emergence of the entrepreneurial spirit to the Protestant ethic. Others again have pointed to external factors, such as the riches plundered from Bengal in the Seven Years' War (1756–63) and the foreign markets ripe for exploitation by whoever first pulled together the capital to exploit the technical advances

4

that would have been feasible anywhere. Sir Arthur Lewis (b. 1915), the Barbadian economist and economic historian who won the Nobel Prize in 1979, has argued that the decisive factor was the progressivity of British agriculture, which both released manpower for the factories and created a demand for their production.

Be that as it may, what is clear is that by the beginning of the nineteenth century Britain was securely on the way to becoming the world's first industrial country. It was in fact not until well into the century that the proportion of the labor force in agriculture was surpassed by that in industry, but the pace of technical advance and industrial expansion was sustained and built up a cumulative force that Walter Rostow (b. 1916) christened the "take-off" into self-sustaining growth. It was a long time before working-class living standards started to rise, but eventually the demand for labor by the modern sector became strong enough to support rising real wages. This in turn induced a fall in the birth rate and the gradual evolution of a developed society in the sense that we now use the term.

1.2 Pax Britannica, 1815–1914

Industrialization started to spill over from its British homeland soon after the beginning of the century of near-peace. Before 1850 it was already well underway in Belgium, France, and the United States. After that date it spread to Germany, Italy, Japan, Scandinavia, and Russia (this includes most of the countries presently classified as industrialized). Development with little industrialization, based on the export of primary products to satisfy the growing needs of the industrial "center" countries, took off in what became known as the "countries of recent settlement:" Canada, Australia, New Zealand, South Africa, and the Southern Cone (Argentina, Chile, Uruguay). Growth without much development, involving the export of primary products but on a scale too small and with too few repercussions on the rest of the economy to overcome Malthusian forces and lead to take-off, occurred at widely scattered places throughout the tropics.

International trade has often been called the engine of nineteenth-century growth. The markets for the expanding output of British industry were primarily foreign markets. By 1854 Britain was exporting over 20 percent of its gross national product (GNP) and the British share of world exports of manufactures was more than 40 percent (Deane and Cole, 1969, p. 33). Exports were important also in sustaining demand in the newly industrializing countries of midcentury—Belgium, France, and the United States. They were quite central to the expansion of the areas of recent settlement in the second half of the century. Without the laissez faire policies of the industrial center and the dramatic fall in transport costs following the spread of railways after 1860 and the large-scale introduction of steamships after 1870, the export-led growth that occurred would have been quite impossible.

There were, however, some countries in which protection to promote import substitution played a role complementary to or more important than that of export expansion. Germany provides the best-known and clearest case, but infant-industry protection was important also in the United States, Japan, Italy, Austria-Hungary, and Russia. Where development was based on industrialization, it was typically aided in the early stages by a degree of protection.

Trade was by no means the only way in which international factors impinged on national growth rates. Unprecedented numbers of migrants moved from Europe to the United States and the lands of recent settlement and also, sometimes less voluntarily, from China and India to tropical countries with low population densities and exploitable natural resources, like Malaya, Mauritius, and Kenya. On the other hand, the flow of slaves from Africa to the Americas finally ceased. Capital, overwhelmingly in the form of long-term fixed-interest bonds, flowed in vast quantities from the older industrial countries of Western Europe, Britain, and France to the developing countries of the periphery like the United States, Russia, and the areas of recent settlement and the tropics. After the turn of the century Britain was exporting some half of its savings, or 7 percent of its GNP— an equivalent flow from the United States today would be of the order of $200 billion per annum!

For the last third of the nineteenth century, the world was also increasingly integrated by virtue of its monetary system. Gold had long been used to provide the basis of the coinage in certain countries, but it was only after about 1870 that gold triumphed over silver and the gold standard became the international norm. The gold standard involved countries defining their currencies in gold (thus maintaining fixed exchange rates among themselves), holding gold reserves with which to settle deficits with one another, and often using gold coins as well. This system made it easy to settle international debts and thus facilitated the growth of international trade. Orthodoxy also held that the system ensured balance of payments adjustment since a country losing gold would contract its money supply and this would create pressures of progressively greater intensity toward the restoration of a surplus (see chap. 8.1). The gold base of the monetary system did mean that extensive gold discoveries (Colorado and California in the 1840s, South Africa in the 1890s) tended to produce periods of inflation, while other periods witnessed downward pressure on prices and considerable distress in trade, but countries sticking to a fixed gold parity were spared major, substantial inflations. The gold base prevented governments doing much to combat crises, which were often quite sharp, but at least were rarely prolonged.

It is worth asking why industrialization did not spread even more rapidly during this Golden Age and, in particular, why it barely affected the tropical countries. One reason is certainly the prevalence of colonialism: India, for example, which was industrially quite advanced at the start of the nineteenth century, could not protect its industries because of British control. The textile industry survived on the basis of cheap labor, but other industries were slow to develop. However, even at the height of colonialism there were many countries that were not constrained as India was and most made even less progress. Explanations tend to come back to that same set of factors invoked to explain why Britain was the first country to industrialize: the primitive state of tropical agriculture, which denied a local market to aspiring industrialists; the retention of political power in the hands of landowners with a vested interest in buying cheap imports rather than promoting industrialization; and the lack of technical education and entrepreneurial drive.

1.3 The Age of Crises, 1914–45

The confident, if still not universal, economic progress of the nineteenth century was rudely shattered by the outbreak of the First World War in 1914. Free trade, free movement of persons, free movement of capital, and the gold standard were progressively replaced in the combatant countries by whatever controls and restrictions were judged expedient to the pursuit of total war.

The war wrought unprecedented physical, as well as human, destruction on the European continent. It led to the downfall of the tsarist regime and its replacement by the world's first Communist government in the Soviet Union. This new government renounced Russian debts, thus annihilating a large part of France's accumulated foreign wealth. Britain fared little better, realizing a large part of her stock of foreign assets and undertaking large debts to finance the war. Countries outside Europe suffered a shortage of imported manufactures and coal from their traditional European suppliers; while this created inconvenience at the time, it also provided a boost to industrialization in the form of import substitution in a whole range of peripheral countries.

When the carnage was finally over and the world went back to making peace in 1919, the dominant economic aim was that of restoring prewar normality. Exporters sought their old export markets—but found in many cases that they no longer existed. Capital mobility was restored; however, capital no longer flowed from Britain and France to capital-poor developing countries, but from the new dominant world power, the United States, to (above all) war-ravaged Germany. An attempt was made to restore the gold standard, even with unchanged parities on the part of the United States and Britain, despite the intervening—and *differential*—inflation, thus condemning Britain to high unemployment throughout the 1920s. Countries like Germany and some of the new states of Eastern Europe (Poland, Austria, and Hungary) suffered the world's first experiences of unambiguous hyperinflation. At least when they finally stabilized, they pegged their exchange rates at competitive levels, thus getting the chance to share in the fleeting prosperity of the late 1920s.

The whole unrealistic attempt to restore the *status quo ante* was finally shattered in the economic whirlwind of the depression into which the world plunged after 1929. Unemployment mounted to unprecedented levels of 20 percent or 30 percent or even more as banks failed, debts were renounced, capital markets dried up, the gold standard was abandoned, competitive devaluation became a vogue, and protectionism triumphed. The countries that did least badly out of the 1930s were those (Germany, Britain, Brazil) that jumped most quickly on the bandwagon of economic nationalism and renounced most decisively the old orthodoxy of the gold standard, combining depreciation and protectionism with the sort of expansionary measures subsequently rationalized by Keynes. Their gains were in part at the expense of those who stuck longest to the gentlemanly rules of a bygone age and gamely imported the unemployment being exported by the beggar-my-neighbor policies of the more ruthless (to use the phrase of the English economist Joan Robinson, b. 1903).

Nationalism and economic collapse fanned the flames that led once more to total war in 1939. To all participants except infantry soldiers, the Second World War proved even more devastating than the first. But even while the fighting was at its peak, there was this time a determination to plan a postwar world conducive to prosperity and development which would give peace a chance. Almost a year before the war ended, a historic conference met at Bretton Woods, New Hampshire, and agreed to establish two international organizations designed to supervise the emergence of a liberal international economic order: the International Monetary Fund (IMF) (see chap. 15), intended to deal with monetary questions, and the International Bank for Reconstruction and Development, or World Bank (see chap. 14.3), whose purpose was to promote a flow of long-term loans for purposes of reconstruction and development to replace the international capital market that had vanished in the Great Depression. Plans were also in hand to create an International Trade Organization to prevent future commercial warfare such as had occurred in the 1930s (see chap. 13). The Soviet Union participated in the Bretton Woods conference, and there were hopes that after the war she would not retreat into virtual isolation from the world economy as she had during the interwar period.

1.4 The Great Boom, 1945–73

Those hopes were quickly dashed. The Soviet Union did not join the Bretton Woods organizations but instead set about creating Communist governments in Eastern Europe under the umbrella of the Red Army. Relations between East and West quickly deteriorated into the Cold War, to the point where the victory of the Chinese Communists in 1949 was interpreted in the West as a simple extension of Russian power. Postwar reconstruction proved even more painful and took much longer than had been expected and would no doubt have been more difficult still had not the Cold War goaded the United States into an unprecedently generous aid program for Western Europe—the European Recovery Program, or the Marshall Plan as it is more popularly known. The Cold War looked like escalating into a third world war with the Berlin blockade of 1949 and the Korean War of 1950–53. At the time it seemed like an extension of the age of crises.

In retrospect, 1950 was the darkest hour before the dawn. Political confrontation began to relax, almost imperceptibly until the death of Stalin in 1953. As relaxation occurred, it became apparent that the hard years of reconstruction had been well spent in preparing a solid base for future growth. Liberalization of intra-European trade under the auspices of the Organization for European Economic Cooperation (OEEC) and with the stimulus of the European Payments Union (EPU) yielded major benefits in terms of increased efficiency, growth, and welfare. By the mid-1950s the period of reconstruction was over and the biggest boom in world history was recognizably under way. The recovery was formalized by the declaration of currency convertibility made jointly by the leading European countries at the end of 1958 and by the subsequent transformation of the OEEC into the Organization for Economic Cooperation and Development (OECD).

Between 1960 and 1973, when the boom ended under the twin pressures of accelerating inflation and the first major oil price increase, GWP grew by something like 5.5 percent per annum. This may be compared with the estimated growth of British output of 2.5 percent per *decade* in the early eighteenth century or with a growth of probably something over 1.5 percent per annum in GWP in the previous great period of world expansion from the 1860s to 1914.[2] The spurs to this growth may be found in unprecedented technological dynamism, cheap energy, expansion of education, rather successful application of Keynesian concepts of economic management, and increasing interdependence. Costs to the growth became evident in terms of increasing pollution and environmental destruction, as well as accelerating inflation in the later stages, but the general view was that such ills were curable with enough attention (and resources) and that the main causes for concern were the danger that expansion might some day be halted by resource constraints and the inadequate participation of some countries in the fruits of growth.

In fact, while many countries fretted about being left behind—from the United States worrying about Sputnik to the developing countries (LDCs) who complained of an ever-widening gap—the growth was extraordinarily generally dispersed. As the technologically leading country with the least opportunities for shifting resources out of low-productivity traditional sectors to high-productivity modern sectors, it was not at all surprising that the United States should grow slower than most other countries; but she grew faster than her own past record. Europe, stimulated by the formation of the European Economic Community (EEC) in 1958, continued right into the early 1970s to grow at rates that were initially regarded as a freak maintainable only while making up ground lost during the war. Japanese growth was without historical precedent, over 10 percent per annum from 1960 to 1973 and still accelerating till the late 1960s, thus taking the country from the stage of semiindustrialization to affluence in a mere quarter century. The Communist countries experienced growth that, even if not quite as rapid as the outpacing of capitalism suggested by the official statistics, was undoubtedly fast. Nor were the developing countries as a group left behind. Their growth got under way more slowly, in part because there was no past leeway to catch up as in the war-torn industrialized countries, in

2. This very rough estimate is based on my combination of the growth rates for the main progressive countries cited by Kuznets (1956, p. 13), together with guesstimates for the remainder.

10

part because economic development rarely became a priority until political independence had been achieved, and perhaps in part because too many developing countries pursued an import substitution strategy appropriate for the economic warfare of the 1930s rather than the export promotion strategy possible in a world boom (see chap. 11). But get under way it did, so that their average growth rate overtook that of the developed countries in the late 1960s. The crossover in per capita growth came only after 1973, but it too is now an established fact. Of course this growth was unequally distributed, with the oil exporters enjoying a privileged position even before 1973 and East Asia and Latin America doing substantially better than South Asia and Africa. Nevertheless, for the first time in history, growth became the global norm.

Trade became once more, as it had been in the nineteenth century but had ceased to be during the Age of Crises, an engine of growth. Obviously increased export demand cannot explain the growth of the system as a whole, since the world is a closed economy, but for individual countries the stimulus provided by external demand was typically central to their being caught up in the general expansion. The volume of world trade multiplied almost four times between 1955 and 1973. The most dynamic components were interchange of manufactures *among* the developed countries, stimulated by regional trade liberalization, especially within the EEC, and general tariff reduction under the auspices of the General Agreement on Tariffs and Trade (GATT) (see chap. 13); the export of oil by those countries blessed with abundant supplies; and, in the later years, exports of relatively unsophisticated manufactures by some of the developing countries to the developed countries. Exports of primary products other than oil continued to suffer cyclical fluctuations in price, and demand was relatively stagnant between the Korean boom in the years 1950 to 1951 and 1973.

Capital mobility also played an important role in generating growth. Initially the major forms of international capital flows were aid and World Bank lending to the developing countries, and direct foreign investment by multinationals (mainly with a United States base) in both developed and developing countries. This last form of lending first emerged in the late nineteenth century, became important with the emergence of differentiated products incorporating technical and managerial know-how as the new growth industries of the interwar period, and perhaps reached its apogee in the 1950s. The distinctive characteristic of direct investment (see chap. 6.5) is that the investor retains managerial control and thus makes available on an equity basis intangible capital (patents, know-how, trademarks, etc.) rather than just cash. It is because of this that the share of output controlled by multinationals has been able to continue growing in recent years despite

11

rather stagnant flows of finance: most investment is now financed by retained earnings or local borrowing, but the decisive advantage provided by transnationality, the ability to draw upon a pool of intangible capital generated by other members of the group in the outside world, is still present. Foreign borrowing, on the other hand, increasingly took the form of bank credits, typically from the Eurodollar market that, to general surprise, started to emerge in the late 1950s (see chap. 14.1). For ten years or so the borrowers from this new international capital market were overwhelmingly from the developed countries, but LDC borrowing also began on a significant scale in the late 1960s.

As the European boom ran up against labor constraints in the late 1960s, it was sustained by an influx of *gastarbeiter* (guest workers) from the Mediterranean area. Emigrants' remittances suddenly became a major source of foreign exchange for an increasing number of countries. Nor was this temporary migration the only form of international mobility of persons to assume economic importance: increasing affluence led to a boom in tourist expenditures.

Throughout these years of unprecedented and almost uninterrupted prosperity, there were voices warning of the fragility of the good times. The reasons given varied, from the insidious effects of inflation to the danger of a new depression, from strangulation by pollution to the exhaustion of key natural resources or the inadequacy of food production, from the breakdown of the international monetary system to revolutionary explosion—not to mention the threat of nuclear war. The prophets of doom could not all be right about the precise shock that would bring the boom to an end, but they were correct in warning that it would not go on forever. One can identify three major factors that in the event contributed to a decisive slowdown which started in 1974.

1. A marked acceleration in inflation. This gathered pace slowly through the 1960s, received renewed impetus from the deficit financing of the Vietnam War in the United States and, to a lesser extent, from French appeasement of the 1968 quasi-revolution and from increased expenditures on such worthy aims as pollution control. The inflation was generalized by the attempt to hold together the pegged exchange-rate system inherited from Bretton Woods and finally got out of hand during the massive simultaneous world boom of 1973 with its rocketing primary product prices. To combat the inflation, policy had already turned severely restrictive in the major industrial countries before the end of 1973.

2. The long-predicted breakdown of the Bretton Woods system occurred in stages: the two-tier gold market in 1968, United States renunciation of gold convertibility of the dollar in 1971, and finally the abandonment of pegged exchange rates in favor of floating in early 1973. In that year it also

became apparent that the attempt to agree on a successor system to that designed at Bretton Woods was going to fail.

3. Following the Arab-Israeli War of October 1973, the Organization of Petroleum Exporting Countries (OPEC) quadrupled the oil price and thereby transferred something like 2 percent of GWP from the consumers to the producers of oil. The immediate effect was to intensify both inflation and recession, as well as to create balance of payments disequilibria of unprecedented size and add to the general uncertainty (see chap. 17).

1.5   Post–1974

Only historians, who have the advantage of hindsight, should try to characterize historical periods by giving them labels. Something very basic changed in the 1973 to 1974, but it is not yet clear where the world is now heading, so we will not try to characterize the post–1974 epoch.

The major characteristics of this recent period are most easily described by way of contrast to the preceding one. The first point to make is that growth has slowed down quite markedly, to an average rate of growth of GWP of approximately 3 percent per annum. This deceleration has not, however, been uniform. It has been much greater in the developed countries (including the Communist countries) than in the developing world. Within the latter, performance has also varied markedly: the Middle East has, not surprisingly, done well; South Asia (the Indian subcontinent) has also actually done better than before; East Asia has held up well; Latin America and the Mediterranean have clearly not been advancing as fast as before, but the overall performance remains respectable; while Africa has seriously fallen back. Even though population growth has also begun falling in most developing countries, per capita income growth has in general slowed down; this is the first such reverse for a significant period since the end of the Second World War.

The causes of the reduction in growth are still a matter of dispute. Demand has been held significantly slacker in the developed countries in the interest of combating inflation. It seems that in many countries labor was not willing to accept the lowering of the real wage that would have been necessary if capitalists were to find it profitable to continue employing as many workers as before, given that more of the gross product was diverted to the oil producers. This placed the authorities in a position where they had to choose between higher unemployment and explosive inflation. However, the significantly better performance of the developing countries may be taken as evidence that supply-side factors are also important, and, in particular, that the approach to economic maturity has exhausted opportunities for easy growth in Europe and Japan (as they had previously been exhausted in North America). To the extent that that is correct, it implies that growth would have fallen off even without the shocks that broke the boom at the end of 1973. There is also wide agreement that higher energy prices have played a role in slowing growth, by diverting resources from manufacturing investment where the incremental capital-output ratio (ICOR) is low to the energy sector where the ICOR is high; but there is no consensus on how important a factor that is. Many other factors, like inflation, taxes, and environmental protection legislation, have also been blamed.

The second major point is that the world economy has been far less stable since 1973 than it was over the preceding twenty years. Inflation has been much higher and more variable (both across countries and over time). The 1975 recession was much sharper than anything previously experienced in the postwar period, while the subsequent (1976–78) recovery was much weaker, at least outside the United States, and did not suffice to restore employment to levels that had become accepted as normal. Balance of payments surpluses and deficits were substantially larger, in proportion to GWP, and were also more variable, especially though not solely as a reflection of changes in the real oil price, which shot up again in the period 1979 to 1980. Exchange rates fluctuated quite wildly at times. Finally, economic management lost that quality of consistency imparted by the dominance of Keynesian orthodoxy in the 1950s and 1960s and was torn between monetarism and short-run Keynesian expediency.

Third, there have been signs of some quite important changes in trade flows. Intratrade in manufactures among the developed countries and exports of oil have ceased to be the most dynamic elements of world trade. That role has been taken over by manufactured exports by the developing countries, in particular to other developing countries (especially but not only oil exporters), and by exports of temperate agricultural products. The success of the newly industrializing countries (NICs)—Brazil, Korea, Taiwan, etc.—in increasing manufactured exports to the industrial countries was despite some recrudescence of protectionism there, which affected particularly the products imported from the NICs. These trends have led to increasing diversification in the pattern of trade. It is still true that developing countries are net exporters of primary products and net importers of manufactures and that the reverse is true for industrialized countries; but those net flows are a shrinking proportion of the gross flows. Furthermore, income level is even less closely associated with whether countries are net exporters of primary products rather than manufactures than it used to be:

not only because some (by no means all) oil exporters are rich but also because some of the richest developed countries (like Australia and New Zealand) remain primary-product exporters while the NICs are now predominantly exporters of manufactures. What remains true is that most of the desperately poor countries are still overwhelmingly exporters of nonoil primary products, though even there Egypt, India, and Indonesia provide important exceptions.

Trade in services is much more important relative to trade in goods than is commonly realized, amounting to some 25 percent of all trade. The two largest items in the varied collection that constitutes trade in services are tourism and income on capital. The direction of tourism is heavily influenced by geographic-climatic factors: especially by rich people looking for convenient sun (North Americans to the Caribbean, Europeans from the dark north to the Mediterranean). Income on capital (profits and interest) is generated by past investments and loans. Thus the creditor countries are the United States and parts of Europe, while the developing countries, other than the oil exporters with the largest accumulated financial wealth, tend to be in deficit. One other invisible flow has become very important to many countries in recent years—the flow of remittances by emigrants to their families in their countries of origin. In addition to the flow from Northern Europe to the Mediterranean that was already important in the 1960s, but has flattened out since then, two other flows have become important in the last decade: from the United States to the Caribbean and, even more, from the oil exporters of the Persian Gulf area to the surrounding Islamic states. The extreme case is the Yemen Arab Republic, which earns about a *thousand times as much* from emigrants' remittances as from exports!

Capital flows have also changed in an important way since 1973. Specifically, the large net flow has been from oil exporters to the OECD countries, who act as financial intermediaries in lending funds to the developing countries. Of course, there are much larger gross flows (especially among the OECD countries), there are some direct flows from OPEC to the developing countries, and the OPEC net lending is not even approximately equal to developing-country borrowing every year. But the stylized fact is that OPEC indirectly lends its current surplus to the developing countries. The indebtedness of the latter has increased rapidly. In another way the pattern of capital flows has *not* changed since the late 1960s: it remains dominated by bank loans, with both direct investment and bonds playing secondary roles. Accordingly the Eurodollar and now Asiadollar markets have continued to expand rapidly.

A final characteristic of the period since 1973 is that the world has got by without any set of agreed rules governing international monetary conduct. Exchange rates have floated, the gold price has gone on a roller

15

coaster, payments adjustment has occurred or been postponed, all without any formal rules of international conduct, so that many have spoken of an "international monetary nonsystem."

1.6 Summary

Economic development and increasing economic interdependence have evolved simultaneously since the modern economic world started to emerge in the late eighteenth century. This is not an accident: development is fostered by interdependence in a range of ways, involving trade (export-led growth and increased allocative efficiency), capital flows, migration, and the transfer of technology. Both the periods of great world prosperity, in the late nineteenth century and after the Second World War, were marked by a functioning international system that enabled individual countries to grow by integrating themselves into the world economy. By contrast, a sick international system such as that of the 1930s makes it far more difficult for the component nations to prosper.

1.7 Bibliography

Presumably most students will already have done a course that covers the economic history of their own country: if not, it should be a priority to read a general treatment of that subject.

A stimulating discussion of the question why some countries developed while others did not is to be found in W. Arthur Lewis, *The Evolution of the International Economic Order* (Princeton: Princeton University Press, 1978). The classic treatment of the role of trade as the engine of growth in the late nineteenth century is to be found in Ragnar Nurkse's 1959 Wiksell Lectures entitled *Patterns of Trade and Development* (Stockholm: Almquist and Wiksell, 1959, and New York: Oxford University Press, 1967). Although Rostow's book has been much criticized, especially because of its zeal in attempting to force diverse historical experiences into the common mold of five stages of economic growth, the idea of the take-off into sustained growth still merits attention: see Walter W. Rostow, *The Stages of Economic Growth: A Non-Communist Manifesto* (Cambridge: Cambridge University Press, 1958). For a good general history, see William Ashworth, *A Short History of the International Economy Since 1850*, 2nd ed. (London: Longmans, 1962).

Statistics have been taken from Phyllis Deane and W. A. Cole, *British Economic Growth, 1688–1959*, 2nd ed. (Cambridge: Cambridge University Press, 1969); Simon Kuznets, "Quantitative Aspects of the Economic Growth of Nations," *Economic Development and Cultural Change*, Oct. 1956; United Nations *Yearbook of National Accounts Statistics* (New York, 1978); and World Bank, *World Development Report* (New York, 1981). The authoritative work on the International Comparisons Project is I. B. Kravis, A. Heston, and R. Summers, *World Product and Income: International Comparisons of Real Gross Product* (Baltimore: Johns Hopkins University Press for the World Bank, 1982).

II

MICROECONOMICS

THIS PART of the book deals with what is usually called pure trade theory, or sometimes barter theory or real trade theory. There are three reasons that have led me to prefer the description *micro:* (1) this emphasizes that the analysis is conducted according to the customary rules of the game of micro theory, to wit, that macroeconomic equilibrium (full employment and payments equilibrium) is maintained; (2) it permits the inclusion of the pure theory of investment, as well as of trade; and (3) it preserves symmetry with the name of part III, for which there are even stronger reasons.

Some professors prefer to teach macro theory before micro, on the ground that the more apparent relevance of the analysis to real world problems makes it easier to motivate students. My own view is that this is outweighed by the greater importance that micro foundations have in permitting an appreciation of macro analysis, as opposed to the need to appreciate macro assumptions in order to understand micro. For those who disagree part III can be studied before part II without undue difficulty. The problem of irrelevance is best tackled by counterexample, by discussing the implications of supposed abstractions like the Stolper-Samuelson or Rybczynski theorems.

2

Comparative Advantage

THE SCIENCE of economics, like the phenomenon of economic growth, took off in the second half of the eighteenth century. At that time the conventional wisdom on foreign trade was derived from the writings of the mercantilist school. Although economists nowadays tend to hurl the epithet "mercantilist" at their opponents as a term of abuse, it is worth devoting a little time to understanding the doctrines of the school as is done in the first section of the chapter. The second section develops a model that represents the idea of *absolute advantage* as providing the basis for trade, in accordance with the ideas of the founding father of modern economics, the great Scottish economist Adam Smith (1723–90). The third section then shows that this model needs only minor reinterpretation in order to represent the far weaker condition that a country have a *comparative advantage* in production—an insight originally due to the English economist David Ricardo (1772–1823), usually counted as the founder of modern trade theory.

2.1 Mercantilism

Mercantilists argued that the attraction of trade lay in the opportunity that it offered of earning a surplus in the balance of payments. Exports are a blessing since they stimulate industry and lead to an import of the precious metals, gold and silver (which mercantilists identified with true wealth, as real estate agents in the old gold mining area of Colorado still do). Imports are a burden since they reduce the demand for the products of domestic industry and drain away bullion. The policy advice offered by mercantilists was that exports and production should be encouraged by state support and subsidies, while imports should be discouraged by protectionist restrictions, especially in industries of strategic importance.

These views are not wholly absurd. There are times when demand does fall short of the capacity to produce and hence when higher demand stemming from more exports or fewer imports is to be welcomed. There are times when a country is having difficulty balancing its overseas accounts and hence welcomes a surplus in foreign trade. Even when a country has no immediate need for the funds earned by a surplus, it may like to accumulate them with an eye to the future flexibility this gives. This was a potent consideration in the eighteenth century when a good stock of bullion enhanced a country's ability to finance foreign wars, which were a more agreeable pastime for princes than having to defend their native soil. Again,' protecting industries of strategic importance is not absurd so long as there is a probability of war. Finally, while the mercantilists erred analytically in associating a high *level* of the money supply—caused by past imports of bullion—with prosperity, the error is one shared with naive Keynesianism; both the mercantilist and the Keynesian position can be given an element of respectability by recognizing that it is the *increase* in the money supply that has stimulating effects on business.

One can therefore find situations and senses in which most of the mercantilist positions are defensible. The problem with mercantilism was that it missed the main point of what trade is about and thereby failed to recognize that its conclusions were valid only in certain cases rather than in general. As with so many other areas of economics, the main point was established once and for all by Adam Smith in his opus *The Wealth of Nations* (1776). He showed that voluntary exchange between countries brings benefits to both, without the need for one to have a surplus (or the other a deficit). This demonstration did not banish mercantilist sentiments from the world, but it did draw a sharp dividing line between the populist politicians and their like who have continued to talk in such terms to the present day and professional economists who learned to discriminate between the situations in which a surplus is a national blessing and those in which it is not.

2.2 Absolute Advantage

Adam Smith presented a very simple and intuitive theory to explain how trade could benefit both participants. He supposed that one country could produce a certain good—let us call it M and think of it as machines or manufactures—better than another country, while that second country could produce some other product X—think of it as a primary product extracted from nature—better than the first. Obviously if both countries concentrate their production on the good in which they enjoy an absolute advantage and then export that good to their trading partner, they can both consume more than if they refuse to trade. To increase consumption is the fundamental object of trading.

While it is very simple to understand Smith's argument intuitively without any formal analysis, further developments demand mastery of the analytical tools of the trade. We therefore proceed to construct a formal model that embodies the assumption of absolute advantage, using the tools of modern theory rather than the arithmetical examples that classical authors used.

Postulate two countries, U and W, with U as *us* (our country) and W the rest of the *world*. Clearly this means that country W is going to be very large relative to U. In fact, like the individual firm or consumer in a perfectly competitive market, U will be able to trade as much as it likes at the parametric prices determined by competition in W.[1]

Suppose that W has an absolute advantage in the production of M. This means that the input requirement per unit of output in the M industry is less in W than in U. Suppose also that there is only one scarce factor of production, labor, and that there are constant returns to scale. This means that it is possible to summarize the production technology in a single

1. This assumption cannot in general be *exactly* correct, except in the special case treated in this chapter where prices are determined by the "Ricardian technology" of the large country. We shall, however, continue to use the assumption in future chapters where that justification is absent. In that context, each country must have *some* influence on price—otherwise there would be no way in which price could vary in a world composed entirely of small countries! What we are essentially doing is making the empirical assumption that the national influence on world prices is sufficiently modest to be ignored as a first approximation—which appears to be a quite acceptable approximation to reality for most countries.

parameter, the quantity of labor required to produce a unit of output (an input-output coefficient). Call this parameter l_m in the home country U and $l_m{}^*$ in the foreign country W. Then the assumption that W has an absolute advantage in the production of M says that $l_m{}^* < l_m$.

Similarly, U having an absolute advantage in the production of X implies that $l_x < l_x{}^*$, where l_x and $l_x{}^*$ are respectively the home and foreign labor inputs per unit of output of X, with labor the only scarce input and constant returns to scale.

Denote the size of the labor force available in the home country U by L. Then if the whole labor force were to be devoted to the production of X, it would be possible to produce L/l_x. Similarly, if country U concentrated all its resources on the production of M, it could produce L/l_m of M. Because of the linear technology (only one scarce factor and constant returns to scale), deployment of half the labor force in X and the other half in M would result in a production level of half the maximum possible production of X *and* half the maximum possible production of M. In other words, that point would lie midway on the straight line connecting L/l_x and L/l_m. Reflection will show that any other division of the total labor force L between the X and M industries would also yield a point on the straight line connecting L/l_x and L/l_m. In other words, the production possibility curve, or transformation curve, is in the linear model a straight line, as shown in figure 2–1.

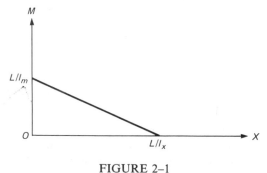

FIGURE 2–1
Transformation Curve in U

What would the equilibrium in such an economy look like if the economy were closed (that is, if there were no trade)? As usual in microeconomics, equilibrium is determined by the interaction between demand and supply factors, the latter represented by the transformation curve already con-

22

structed. We shall assume that the demand side can be represented by a social indifference curve with all the usual properties of indifference curves.[2] Such a curve is introduced in figure 2–2.

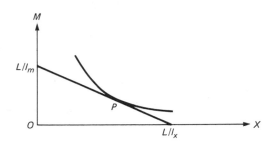

FIGURE 2–2
Equilibrium in the Closed Economy U

Obviously equilibrium would occur at point *P*, the point of production and consumption. Furthermore, the relative price of *X* has to be equal to the relative cost of production: $p_x/p_m = l_x/l_m$. Graphically, this relative price is represented by the slope of the transformation curve.[3]

So much for equilibrium in economy *U* in autarky. Consider next the situation in the large country *W*. It also will have a straightline transformation curve, with a slope equal to l_x^*/l_m^*. Since by the pattern of absolute advantage we have postulated $l_x^* > l_x$ and $l_m^* < l_m$, it is certainly true

2. This convenient assumption will be used throughout, but the reader should be aware that the assumption that preferences can be represented by a set of well-behaved social indifference curves is uncomfortably strong. The basic problem is that the quantity of additional *X* needed to maintain the utility of each consumer constant when the quantity of *M* declines by one unit will in general depend on the distribution of income between consumers. To rule this out one has to make some set of very special assumptions. For example, one may assume that tastes are both identical and "homothetic" (which means that each indifference curve is a blown-up version of each other one, that is, that the marginal rate of substitution is independent of the level of consumption). Casual observation indicates that in the real world preferences are far from identical, while the stylized fact of Engel's law suggests they are not homothetic. Alternatively, one may assume that the income distribution remains constant, or that it is adjusted optimally, for example, by a set of lump-sum taxes and transfers. Since many of the changes we wish to study involve changes in the distribution of income, while in general there is little reason to believe income distribution to be optimal, the alternative approaches are not very satisfactory either. The fact is that any attempt to deal with the ambiguities resulting from endogeneity of the income distribution would at this level impose costs in terms of obscuring the main points of the analysis that far outweighed the benefits in terms of more precise understanding. The serious student should, however, pursue the subject further, by consulting the references in the last paragraph of the bibliography.

3. The equation of the transformation curve is $l_m M + l_x X = L$. Since *L* is a constant, total differentiation gives $l_m dM + l_x dX = 0$, or $dM/dX = -l_x/l_m = -p_x/p_m$.

23

that $l_x^*/l_m^* > l_x/l_m$; that is, the transformation curve in country W is steeper than that in U. Furthermore, the slope of the transformation curve in W will represent the relative price prevailing there. But, assuming that there is free trade and zero transport costs,[4] competition will ensure that the same price prevails in both U and W. Since W is by assumption large relative to U, the price that will prevail in both countries is that determined by W's costs of production. This means that U gets the opportunity of trading with W at W's prices.

The relative price at which a country trades has a special name: the *terms of trade*. The normal concept is the *commodity terms of trade* and is measured as the price of exports divided by the price of imports. In the example analyzed here, country U will export the primary product X *ex*tracted from nature and import the *m*anufactured good M, so that the terms of trade will be represented by p_x/p_m. It may be easier to remember that X is the *ex*portable and M is the *im*portable good.

Figure 2–2 has to be modified to reflect trading possibilities to see what happens when country U is opened up to foreign trade. This is done in figure 2–3. Given that country U can buy or sell as much as it likes at the fixed terms of trade determined by production costs in the large country W, this is very simple. The terms of trade are represented by a (negative) slope, with steeper slopes representing more favorable terms of trade (that is, higher relative prices for exports). The country can trade along any line with the slope that represents the terms of trade. In particular, it can trade along PC, which is exactly what it will do. Since the economy is open to foreign trade, production and consumption do not have to coincide as they did in the closed economy. Given the terms of trade, the optimal point for production is P, since this enables the economy to reach higher consumption levels by trading up PC than would be attainable by producing at any other point on the transformation curve (let alone at any point within the production possibility frontier). U will therefore specialize in production of the good X in which it has an absolute advantage.[5]

Consumers also face prices equal to the terms of trade. Their utility is maximized where the indifference curve is tangential to the trading line, so that C represents the point of consumption. Since U is no longer producing

4. This assumption provides the polar case of complete integration of the country into the international economy, in contrast with the other polar case of complete autarky. The intermediate case of partial integration resulting from a policy of protection provides the subject matter of chap. 5.

5. It is easy to see that individual profit-maximizing producers would find it in their interest to concentrate on producing X. The value of production at the relative price given by the terms of trade will be the same at any point on a given trading line and will be greater the further that trading line is from the origin. Thus the maximum revenue that producers can earn, given that they are restricted to the triangle OPZ, is yielded by producing at the point P.

24

Comparative Advantage

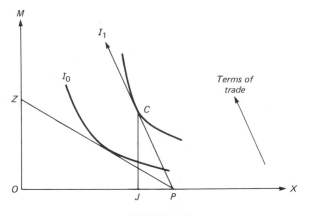

FIGURE 2–3
Equilibrium in the Open Economy U

any M, its entire consumption, equal to CJ, has to be imported. The country pays for these imports by exporting a part of its production of X equal to JP, the remainder (OJ) being consumed at home. Note that the balance of trade is zero, that is, the value of imports is equal to the value of exports.[6]

Finally, note that country U has unequivocally benefited from the opening of the economy and its consequent specialization in production of the good in which it has an absolute advantage. This can be seen by noting that the consumption point C lies on an indifference curve I_1 that is higher than I_0, the highest that is attainable under autarky.

2.3 Comparative Advantage

Was it really worth all that trouble to establish formally that a country able to produce one type of good with less resources than another can gain by concentrating on the production of that good and then exporting part of its output to buy a good that another country can make with fewer resources than would be required for domestic production?

If that case, of absolute advantage, were the only one for which the analysis held good, the answer would surely be no. But in fact it is now very easy to see that this is not true. In constructing figure 2–3, we made use of the fact that $l_x^*/l_m^* > l_x/l_m$ so that PC is steeper than PZ. We argued that

6. The value of exports is $p_x(JP)$ and that of imports is $p_m(CJ)$, while the terms of trade p_x/p_m is the slope of the trading line, that is, CJ/JP.

25

$l_x*/l_m* > l_x/l_m$ because $l_x* > l_x$ and $l_m* < l_m$. But these conditions are by no means necessary. It would be possible for $l_x* > l_x$ and $l_m* > l_m$, that is, for our country to have an absolute advantage in the production of *both* goods, but for l_x*/l_m* still to exceed l_x/l_m. In that case we would get exactly the same diagram as figure 2–3, and hence the whole analysis would remain valid: our country's producers would still have an incentive to specialize in the production of *X,* the exportation of part of which would still permit the country to buy enough *M* to make consumers better off. Or it would be equally possible for $l_x* < l_x$ and $l_m* < l_m$, that is, for our country to have an absolute *dis*advantage in the production of both goods, but as long as l_x*/l_m* still exceeded l_x/l_m, the diagram, the analysis, and the conclusions would all remain valid.

What the argument in the preceding paragraph shows is that it is not *absolute* advantage that determines the direction of and the possibility of benefiting from trade but rather *comparative* advantage. Our country has a comparative advantage in the production of *X* so long as $l_x*/l_m* > l_x/l_m$. Whenever that condition holds, our country has to give up less *M* to produce an extra unit of *X* than does country *W*. In other words, the *opportunity cost* of producing *X* is less in country *U* than in country *W*. That is enough to give *U* an incentive to produce and export *X* in return for *M,* whether it be absolutely more productive or less productive in all goods than *W*—as well as in Adam Smith's case where each country has an absolute advantage in the production of one good.

On the other hand, suppose that l_x*/l_m* were equal to l_x/l_m. Then the trade opportunity line *PC* in figure 2–3 would coincide with the transformation curve *PZ* and trade would be pointless since it would not enable consumers to achieve any higher indifference curve. That is, of course, the case in which a country has no comparative advantage to exploit. But the worst thing that can happen is that the country lacks any comparative advantage—it cannot suffer a comparative disadvantage in everything, as is sometimes implied by the economically illiterate.

There is also the possibility of $l_x*/l_m* < l_x/l_m$. In that case *U* would have a comparative advantage in the production of *M,* and figure 2–3 would need modifying to show a set of trade possibility lines flatter than the transformation curve. It is important to figure out what the equilibrium would then look like.

The addition to the argument made in this section looks very simple when the model has been set up as was done in the previous section. But of course Adam Smith and his successors did not have the benefit of modern analytical techniques—they were still arguing in verbal terms or at most with the help of arithmetical examples. It was some forty years after the publication of Adam Smith's *Wealth of Nations* before Ricardo pointed out that mutually beneficial trade required only the weak postulate of *comparative* advantage rather than the strong condition that each country have an absolute advantage in something.

2.4 Summary

Before the advent of modern economics the mercantilists argued that trade was good when it led to an export surplus. There are circumstances where countries may well wish to increase their net exports to achieve a surplus, but this misses the main point, that the exchange of products a country is good at producing for those it is not good at producing can permit given productive resources to go further in satisfying human needs. Such beneficial exchanges are possible whenever the *relative* ability to produce goods differs between countries, that is, whenever a country has a *comparative advantage*—even if it is *absolutely* more or less productive than some other country in the production of *all* goods.

2.5 Addendum: The Large Economy

The purpose of this addendum is to provide a brief sketch of the consequences of relaxing the assumption that our economy is small relative to that of the rest of the world. Suppose therefore that we have two countries of comparable size, and that U has the comparative advantage in the production of X so that its transformation curve is flatter than W's.

The assumption of comparable size allows us to add together the two production possibility curves to construct a world transformation curve as shown by GEH in figure 2–4. The point G represents the maximum possible production of X if all resources in both countries are devoted to X production; it is the sum of OP in figure 2–3 and the analagous maximum possible production of X in country W. Analagously, H represents the maximum possible production of M. Point E represents the situation in which each country specializes in production of the good in which it has a comparative advantage, so its horizontal ordinate corresponds to OP in figure 2–3 and its vertical ordinate to the maximum possible production of M in country

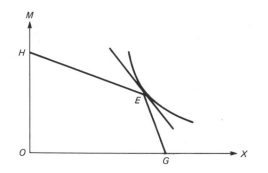

FIGURE 2–4
Equilibrium in the World Economy with Two Large Countries

W. The segment *EG* represents positions where *U* is specializing in the production of *X* while *W* produces a mixture of *M* and *X* so it has the slope of *W*'s transformation curve. Analagously, the segment *EH* has the slope of *U*'s transformation curve and shows situations where *W* is specialized in the production of *M* while *U* produces both goods. The world transformation curve is necessarily concave[7] to the origin because, for example, when the world first starts to produce some *X*, that is, to move right and down from point *H*, it first transfers productive capacity in *U* into *X* production. Since *U* has a comparative advantage in *X*, its opportunity cost —the amount of *M* that has to be sacrificed to produce an extra unit of *X*—is relatively low. Only when all *U*'s capacity has already been absorbed in *X* production, that is, after point *E*, does the world economy have to switch *W*'s resources into producing *X* and so incur the higher opportunity cost represented by the steeper transformation curve in *W*.

Suppose that it is possible to represent the sum of world consumer preferences by a well-behaved social indifference curve as drawn in figure 2–4. (This would, for example, be possible if consumer tastes were identical and homothetic not merely within but also between countries.) It is clear that there are five qualitatively different possibilities as to the form of the tangency between the highest indifference curve attainable and the world transformation curve: (1) at point *E*, as shown; (2) along the segment *EG*; (3) along the segment *EH*; (4) at point *G*; and (5) at point *H*.

In case 1, both countries specialize and the relative price of good *X*, which also happens to be country *U*'s terms of trade, lies between the

7. Concave but not strictly concave. The definition of strict concavity is that any chord joining two points in the feasible production set lies wholly in the interior of the production set. The definition of concavity is that any chord joining two points in the feasible production set lies wholly in the production set, including its frontier. In common language, a concave transformation curve is "bowed out" from the origin.

28

relative costs of U and W. Exactly where in that range it falls depends on consumer demand, that is, on the slope of the social indifference curve at point E. This is the classical case considered by Ricardo. When it holds, the situation in country U can still be represented by a diagram like figure 2–3, but with the important difference that the trade possibility line is now endogenous rather than exogenous. That is, the terms of trade open to U depend upon the distribution of its demand.

Consider the next case 2, the segment EG, where U specializes but W does not. It is easy to see that this is identical to the small economy case: U can trade with W at the fixed terms of trade determined by W's relative costs.

In case 3, the segment EH, W specializes but U does not. This produces a radical change in conclusions. As figure 2–5 shows, U modifies its production and starts to trade as a result of opening up the economy. But consumption stays at C, exactly where it was in the closed economy. All the benefits of trade go to W. But the conclusion that specialization is *necessary* to derive gains from trade is critically dependent upon the linear technology embodied in the present model, as the next chapter will show.

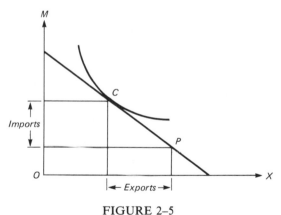

FIGURE 2–5
Trade with Nonspecialization in Economy U

Cases 4 and 5 are degenerate cases where there is no trade, and hence introducing the possibility of trade alters nothing.

Finally, the smaller country U is relative to W, the closer will be the peak E of the world transformation curve (figure 2–4) to H. This increases the probability of case 2, equilibrium on the segment EG, arising. But case 2 was exactly the same as the small country case previously analyzed (see p. 24), where it is the small country that draws all the benefit from trade, while the large country finds itself in the situation that U did in case 3. The conclusion that the large country would not benefit from trade is dependent upon the special assumptions embodied in the model. But the converse conclusion, that small countries are particularly likely to benefit from trade, is a very robust one.[8] At a pinch, large countries like the United States or Brazil could survive a blockade. For a small country like Luxembourg or Singapore, the end of trade would quickly mean a return to the Stone Age.

2.6 Bibliography

It is well worth delving into the writings of the masters who developed the ideas of absolute and comparative advantage. See Adam Smith, *An Enquiry into the Nature and Causes of the Wealth of Nations,* originally published in 1776, especially chap. 1 and 2 of bk. 4, and David Ricardo, *On the Principles of Political Economy and Taxation,* originally published in 1817, chap. 7.

An interesting topic not touched on in the present chapter is generalization of the analysis to the case of more than two goods. The idea of ranking goods according to their comparative cost ratios, so as to divide goods into those that will be exported and those that will be imported, was introduced by Gottfried Haberler, *The Theory of International Trade* (New York: Macmillan, 1937), pp. 136–40.

Treatments of the difficulties of using social indifference curves are to be found in T. D. Scitovsky, "A Reconsideration of the Theory of Tariffs," in H. Ellis and L. Metzler, eds., *Readings in the Theory of International Trade* (Homewood, Il.: Richard D. Irwin, 1950); P. A. Samuelson, "Social Indifference Curves," *Quarterly Journal of Economics,* Feb. 1956, reprinted in J. E. Stiglitz, ed., *The Collected Works of Paul A. Samuelson,* vol. 2 (Cambridge, Mass.: MIT Press, 1966), chap. 78; and J. S. Chipman, "A Survey of the Theory of International Trade: Part 2, The Neo-Classical Theory," *Econometrica,* Oct. 1965.

8. A proposition is said to be "robust" if it remains valid under a wide range of circumstances. Economists often assess the robustness of a conclusion by examining whether it holds under a variety of different plausible models.

3

Heckscher-Ohlin Model

DAVID Ricardo reasoned in terms of a one-factor model in which the product of his single factor, labor, happened to be different between countries. But it is natural to ask *why* the productivity of labor should vary. There are answers consistent with Ricardo's one-factor model—for example, such differences might be due to climatic conditions or to different levels of technology. However, an alternative explanation was suggested in the 1920s by the Swedish economists Eli Heckscher (1879–1952) and Bertil Ohlin (1899–1979) and has since become the orthodox explanation of the source of comparative advantage. The basic idea is that countries differ in their relative stocks of the different factors of production and that these differential factor supplies influence the costs of producing particular goods. For example, a country with an abundant supply of capital finds it relatively cheap to produce goods whose production requires much capital and little labor, and therefore has a comparative advantage in—and exports—such *capital-intensive* goods.

This basic idea has been much refined and explored in the past half century, in particular in a most famous series of papers by Paul Samuelson (b. 1915), the 1970 winner of the Nobel Prize in economics. This chapter presents the theory and discusses its principal implications. The analysis is largely conducted in terms of what is called the $2 \times 2 \times 2$ framework: with two factors of production, labor (L) and capital (K); two goods, still M and X; and two countries, still U (our small country) and W (the large country representing the rest of the world). As a preliminary, the front section of the chapter reviews the basic microeconomic theory of a 2×2 closed economy.

31

3.1   Equilibrium in the Closed Economy

The starting point for analysis of production is the isoquant diagram (see fig. 3–1). An isoquant is the locus of combinations of factors of production that can efficiently produce a given level of output of a certain good, for example, X. It is the production-side analogue of the indifference curve, which shows the locus of combinations of two consumer goods that will induce a given level of satisfaction for a certain consumer. The isoquant diagram thus has input of the two factors, L and K, on the two axes. With a neoclassical technology of continuous substitution between L and K, each isoquant is smooth and convex to the origin as in figure 3–1A. With Leontief-type fixed coefficients, each isoquant has the right-angled form shown in figure 3–1B. With two Leontief-type fixed coefficient production processes available for the same good, each isoquant would have three linear segments as shown in figure 3–1C: the sloping segment represents combinations of the two production processes represented by the two corners. Obviously with more processes available one would get more segments on the isoquant, ultimately tending to approach the neoclassical formulation with many processes.

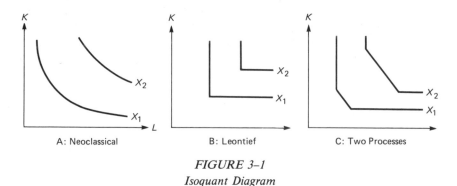

FIGURE 3–1
Isoquant Diagram

In the case of constant returns to scale, or a linear homogeneous production function, a single isoquant tells everything there is to know about the production side of the economy. Once the isoquant is known for some output level X_1, the isoquant for any other output level X_2 can be calculated by seeking points (X_2/X_1) as far from the origin as those on the isoquant X_1. Figure 3–1 shows a second isoquant, $X_2 = 2X_1$, which implies that the input of both factors is always double that on the X_1 isoquant. The assumption of constant returns to scale will be made throughout this chapter. How reasonable an assumption is it? For parts of manufacturing industry, it is quite acceptable. Existing plants can normally be duplicated or expanded at approximately constant costs, at least beyond some minimum size. But in resource-based industries, including agriculture, it is not uncommon to find decreasing returns to scale. And in quite a few manufacturing industries, most notably aircraft production (where learning by doing is important), large parts of engineering (those using batch production methods), and the chemical and other process industries (where it matters that the volume of containers expands more rapidly than their surface area as size increases), evidence indicates that normal-sized plants have unexhausted economics of scale. Nevertheless, the case of constant returns to scale provides a natural benchmark; it is easier to learn the analysis by studying this case and subsequently to modify it when there is reason to believe that returns to scale are either increasing or decreasing.

It is possible to study the production equilibrium of an economy (with two goods and two factors) by bringing together the two isoquant diagrams for the two goods in a diagram called the Edgeworth box, named after its inventor, the English neoclassical economist Francis Edgeworth (1845–1926). The sides of the box represent the quantities of the two factors of production available to the economy in question. Figure 3–2 shows the length of the box representing the quantity of labor L available to U and its height representing the quantity of capital K. Now insert the isoquant diagram of export good X starting from the bottom left-hand corner, that is, from the origin O_x. The diagram is simply reproduced from figure 3–1A. Industry M also has an isoquant diagram, which can also be inserted in the Edgeworth box. In this case, however, it must be flipped over and placed with its origin at O_M in the top right-hand corner. An isoquant representing a higher level of production of M lies further from O_M, which of course means that it is closer to O_x.

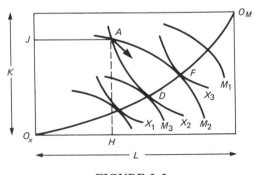

FIGURE 3–2
Edgeworth Box

Consider a typical point in the Edgeworth box, such as point A. That point represents a certain allocation of the given supplies of the two factors of production between the two industries: O_XH of L to industry X and the remainder of the L to industry M; and O_XJ of K to industry X with the remainder to industry M. Looking at industry X's isoquants, we can see that the quantities O_XH of L and O_XJ of K are sufficient to produce an output X_2 of X. Similarly, the remaining quantities of L and K have to be looked at from the standpoint of M's isoquant map with the origin at O_M. It can be seen that they would permit production of M_2 of M. In general, then, any point in the Edgeworth box represents a specific division of the available factor supplies between the two industries and, hence, specific output levels of the two goods. It is assumed that the supplies of both factors are fully utilized, that is, that full employment prevails.

Does point A represent an "efficient" division of the factors of production in the sense of a division that cannot allow a higher output of one type of good without sacrificing output of the other? No, since by reallocating K from industry X to industry M and L from industry M to industry X, we can move down in the direction indicated by the arrow and reach higher isoquants for *both* goods. This process can continue until the point where the isoquants are tangential to one another. After that point any further progress toward the lower right-hand corner would involve moving to lower isoquants of both goods. Hence the set of efficient production points are those, like D and F, where the isoquants are tangential to one another. These points of tangency can be joined up, as shown in the diagram, to form the *contract curve* running from O_X to O_M.

As drawn, the contract curve is convex toward the lower right-hand corner. This is not an accident, but represents an important assumption about technology: that the X industry is intensive in L. The meaning of X being L-intensive is shown in figure 3–3A. This diagram shows representative isoquants for both the X and M industries. It is not true that the X industry *must* employ more L (per unit of K) than the M industry: at point D the M industry's labor-capital ratio (measured by the flatness of the ray from the origin to point D) is higher than that of the X industry at point F. But comparing points D and F is not comparing like with like. If relative factor prices, which are represented by the slope of the isocost line BD, were to give the M industry an incentive to pick the factor combination represented by D, they would give the X industry an incentive to pick the factor combination represented by A rather than F. That is, X being intensive in L means that for *given factor prices* X will always have an incentive to produce with a higher L/K ratio than will M. Now it can be seen why X being intensive in L implies that the contract curve in figure

3–2 must lie below the diagonal. For any given factor prices, the L/K ratio is higher in X than in M, which is precisely what is implied by lying below the diagonal.

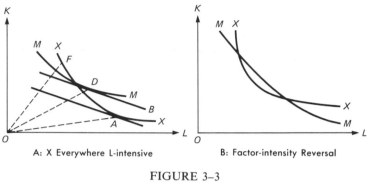

A: X Everywhere L-intensive   B: Factor-intensity Reversal

FIGURE 3–3
Factor Intensity

If isoquants never cross, the same industry is everywhere L-intensive (and the other is everywhere K-intensive). However, one cannot rule out a priori the possibility shown in figure 3–3B where the isoquants cross— that one industry is L-intensive at one set of factor prices and the other L-intensive at a different set of factor prices. In the case shown, X is L-intensive when the price of labor relative to capital is high and K-intensive when the price of labor relative to capital is low. In fact, it seems that factor-intensity·reversals do sometimes occur—for example, the production of rice is labor intensive in Thailand but capital intensive in Texas. For the moment we shall simply assume away factor-intensity reversals, but it will be necessary to return later and explore some of their implications.

The next step in the analysis is to derive the production possibility curve —a construct first introduced into trade theory in 1930 by the Austrian-born economist Gottfried Haberler (b. 1900). In the one-factor model (see fig. 2–1) studied in the previous chapter, this was a straight line. In the neoclassical two-factor model with possibilities of substitution in production used in this chapter, it is a downward-sloping and concave-to-the-origin curve as shown in figure 3–4. This can be seen by recognizing that since the production possibility curve is defined as the curve showing the maximum possible output of one good for given levels of production of the other, it represents all those combinations of outputs found along the contract curve in the Edgeworth box (see fig. 3–2). Thus the point X_{max} in figure 3–4 shows the maximum possible output of X, which occurs when all

35

resources are devoted to X production, which is represented by the point O_M in figure 3–2; X_{max} is in fact the value of the X isoquant at the upper right-hand corner of the Edgeworth box. Similarly, M_{max} represents the value of the M isoquant at the point O_x in the Edgeworth box where all resources are devoted to M production. The point Y corresponds to a point like D on the contract curve of the Edgeworth box. It definitely lies outside the straight line joining X_{max} and M_{max}, because a point like Z on that line corresponds in the Edgeworth box to a point on the diagonal joining O_X and O_M, and we know that when the two industries have different factor intensities, the contract curve does not coincide with the diagonal. Hence it is possible to produce more of both commodities than at Z by reallocating K to M production and L to X production to yield a point Y consistent with a concave production possibility curve (ppc). This argument can be repeated to show that the ppc is everywhere concave, as shown. The argument can be used, for example, to show that the point on the ppc corresponding to point F in the Edgeworth box must lie outside the straight line connecting Y and X_{max} in figure 3–4.

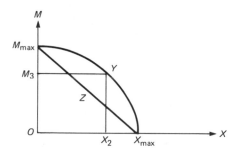

FIGURE 3–4
Neoclassical Production Possibility Curve

Naturally different assumptions about the nature of technology lead to different shapes of the ppc. Two interesting special cases are shown in figures 3–5 and 3–6. In the former, technology is assumed to have the form $X = f(L)$, $M = g(K)$; the production of X uses only labor and that of M uses only capital. The X isoquants are therefore vertical lines and the M isoquants horizontal lines in the Edgeworth box, and the contract curve is $O_X L O_M$. Obviously the corresponding ppc is a rectangle; it is possible to produce up to X_{max} of X (whose isoquant is $L O_M$) and up to M_{max} of M (whose isoquant is $O_X L$) with no cost in terms of lost output of the other good.

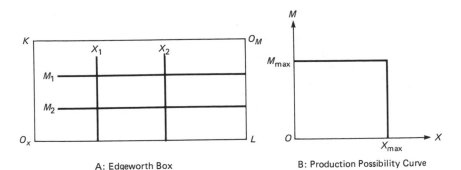

FIGURE 3–5
One-factor Production Functions

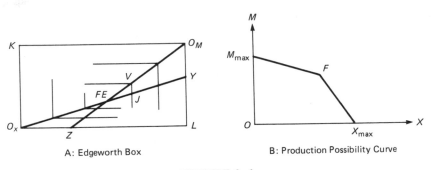

FIGURE 3–6
Fixed Coefficients Production Functions

The second interesting case is that of two Leontief-type fixed coefficients production functions. With X having the more labor-intensive fixed coefficients, the Edgeworth box appears as in figure 3–6A. The X isoquants are the L-shaped constructions along the ray $O_x Y$, and the M isoquants are the inverted L's along the ray from O_M to Z. Those two rays represent the technologically determined combinations of L and K in the production of X and M, respectively. Since input coefficients are fixed, there need not be full employment of both factors of production. For example, if production of X is at point J, there will only be enough labor left over to permit production of M at V, and VJ of capital will remain unutilized. This means that there is no well-defined contract curve in this model. In fact, the only point where both factors will be fully employed and the contract curve well defined is where the two production rays intersect, marked FE. However, the ppc is still perfectly definitely specified. It has two linear segments, one from X_{max} (equivalent to point Y in the Edgeworth box) to F where X

production is being contracted along *Y.FE* while *M* production expands along $O_M FE$, and the other from *F* to M_{max} where *X* production contracts along *FE.O_X* while *M* production expands along *FE.Z*. The reason that the opportunity cost of *X* is higher in the second segment is that the scarce factor of production switches from being *K* to being *L* after the point of full employment (*FE* in the Edgeworth box and the kink *F* in the ppc diagram) is passed, and *X* is, of course, the good intensive in *L*.

Finally, general equilibrium in the closed economy is determined by the interaction between the supply side, which is represented by the production possibility curve, and the demand side, which is represented by a set of community indifference curves (as introduced in chapter 2). This is shown by the point of tangency *E* in figure 3–7. The competitive relative price of *X* (that is, p_x/p_m), which will induce consumers to demand those same quantities X_E and M_E of the two goods that it will persuade producers to supply, is shown by the (negative of the) slope of the tangent (to *both* curves). A higher relative price of *X* is shown by a steeper set of price lines and would result in producers wishing to produce more *X* than X_E and consumers wishing to purchase less *X* than X_E, with resulting excess supply of *X* (and excess demand for *M*). Only at point *E* is there equilibrium.

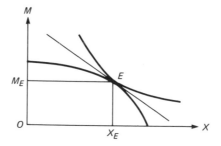

FIGURE 3–7
General Equilibrium in the Closed Economy

3.2 Heckscher-Ohlin Model

The Heckscher-Ohlin model is concerned with balanced trade between two neoclassical economies. The basic idea is that the country in which labor, for example, is relatively abundant will find itself able to produce the labor-intensive good relatively cheaply; thus, it will have a comparative advantage in production of that good. As in chapter 2, we assume that our country, U, has a comparative advantage in production of the L-intensive good X. This means that the relative price of good X would be higher in country W than in country U in the absence of trade. The assumption is that country U is a small economy able to trade at will at the prices set in the large country W. It is therefore merely necessary to introduce a line— or rather, a set of parallel lines—representing the exogenous terms of trade into figure 3–7. The result is shown in figure 3–8, with CP being the terms of trade line along which trade occurs.

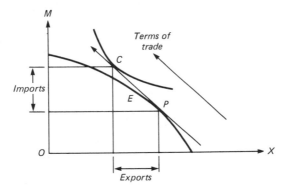

FIGURE 3–8
Small Economy in Equilibrium with Free Trade

The international price of X is higher than the autarky price shown in figure 3–7. As a consequence, producers adjust their output from E to P, the production point where the new price line is tangential to the ppc. Output of X increases, at the expense of the production of M. Real income is now sufficient to permit consumers to reach any point on PC, so in accordance with their preferences as represented by the social indifference curves, they pick the point of tangency C. Trade equilibrium (P, C) has the following properties in comparison with autarky equilibrium (E, E):[1]

1. X is more expensive and M is cheaper (in terms of each other).
2. Production of X increases and that of M decreases.
3. Real income is higher at P than at E, measured at free trade prices.
4. Consumption of M increases because of both a positive income effect and a positive substitution effect (M is now cheaper to consumers), while that of X may either increase (if the positive income effect is strong

1. The first term in parentheses indicates the point of production, and the second that of consumption.

enough) or decrease (if the negative substitution effect is strong enough).

5. The excess of the production over the consumption of X consists of exports, while the excess of the consumption over the production of M consists of imports (both shown on figure 3–8).

6. Since the slope of the line CP represents the terms of trade, that is, the price of exports in terms of imports, the value of exports is equal to that of imports.

7. Consumers are on a higher indifference curve at C than they were at E. In fact, free trade—trade along the terms of trade line CP—enables consumers to reach the highest position consistent with the technological limits on production represented by the ppc and the exogenous terms of trade represented by the slope of PC.

Underlying this important set of conclusions are three sets of assumptions. First, there are the assumptions about *technology* that were outlined in the previous section:

- that the production function is homogenous of the first degree (linear homogenous); that is, production processes exhibit constant returns to scale
- that the factors K and L are substitutes in production; that is, the production function is well behaved
- that there are no factor-intensity reversals
- that adjustment is instantaneous so that the economy is always in equilibrium.

Second, there is a set of assumptions which jointly guarantee that after trade the same price will prevail in our country as rules in the rest of the world:

- no transport costs
- free trade
- perfect competition in all markets (including factor markets).

Finally there are assumptions made for the sake of reducing the size of the problem to something manageable:

- that there are two goods, two factors of production, and two countries, one of which is small
- that the factors of production are available in fixed quantities (referred to as "endowments") and fully used
- that consumer preferences can be represented by a set of conventionally shaped (that is, convex to the origin) social indifference curves.

It is important not to fall into the trap of dismissing a conclusion that runs against some personal predilection just because the proof used to establish that conclusion adopted some unrealistic assumption. For example, the seventh proposition above concluded that free trade is a good thing. There *are* grounds on which that conclusion can be challenged (discussed in chapter 5). But it *cannot* be dismissed by pointing out that the assumption of no transport costs is unrealistic. Positive transport costs would simply mean that the internal price line would not be quite as steep as the external price line (by an amount representing the costs of transport), but welfare would still be maximized by letting producers maximize profits and consumers maximize utility and reconciling the differences between production and consumption through free trade.

Of course, it is not always as obvious as this whether a conclusion will remain valid when one of the supporting assumptions is relaxed. For example, if preferences cannot be represented by a set of social indifference curves, because income distribution varies and tastes differ, then there is not much that one can conclude with any rigor. However, many economists are willing to take the position that, in the absence of any specific evidence to the contrary, it is reasonable to draw conclusions as though a set of social indifference curves existed. This amounts to adopting the view of the agnostic—if one does not know who will benefit or how to weigh their gains against the losers' losses, just count an extra peso of income as the same to everyone.[2]

While often difficult to do, it is important to develop a sense of the extent to which the conclusions depend on the assumptions being strictly satisfied. An assumption critical to a particular conclusion will often be indicated in the text, but it is simply not possible to do this in a comprehensive way, at least without making the book unreadable. In addition, it would still not be adequate, for new contexts will constantly arise. There is absolutely no substitute for individual, independent consideration of the implications of assumptions by the reader. For example, consider whether the laissez faire proposition is dependent upon the assumption of substitution in production (see figs. 3–5 and 3–6). How about constant returns to scale (see chap. 4.1)? How about many goods and factors?

---

2. Where economists do differ quite sharply is in their willingness to modify the agnostic position. On one side are those who argue that, since any departure from this position requires the application of subjective weights, there should be no such departures. On the other side are those who argue that the agnostic position itself implies a particular (and morally questionable) set of distributional weights, in which the marginal social utility of income is treated as the same no matter to whom the income accrues. Those who take this position are relatively willing to attach subjective distributional weights to gains and losses and to use slender evidence as to who is gaining and who is losing in order to justify and guide government intervention.

3.3 Heckscher-Ohlin Theorem

The Heckscher-Ohlin theorem is a famous proposition about the pattern of trade between two economies each of which has the characteristics described in the previous section. It may be stated as follows: each country will export the good that is intensive in its abundant factor. In our example, the abundant factor of production in country U is labor, L. The theorem therefore predicts that the country will export X, the labor-intensive good.

Most of the assumptions needed to prove the theorem have already been made in the previous section. What remains is merely to ensure that the two countries are equal in various respects: (1) that country W also has all the characteristics previously attributed to U (this is not necessary when we are merely characterizing the impact on U of its interaction with a parametric rest of the world, but it is necessary when, as now, we wish to compare the situation in U with that in W); (2) that both countries have identical technology; and (3) that tastes are identical and homothetic in the two countries.[3] These assumptions mean that the two countries differ in only two respects: with regard to their size and with respect to the ratio K/L in which they are endowed with capital and labor. In other words, the two countries differ only with regard to the dimensions of the Edgeworth boxes.

The proof of the theorem starts by noting that with equal tastes in both countries and with prices of goods equalized through free, competitive, and costless trade, the pattern of consumption must be identical in the two countries. Suppose that both countries also produced the two goods in the same ratio in which they were consumed, so that there was no trade. This situation is shown by points C and D in figure 3–9, which displays the Edgeworth box of our small labor-abundant country U at the bottom left-hand corner of the box for the large and relatively capital-abundant

---

3. The treatment in the text defines relative factor abundance in physical terms, so that L is the abundant factor in U when $L/K > L^*/K^*$. When this definition is used, it is necessary to add the assumption of identical (and homothetic) preferences in order to prove the theorem. There is, however, an alternative approach, which is to define L as being the abundant factor in U when $p_l/p_k < p_l^*/p_k^*$ in the absence of trade. That is, the abundant factor is defined as the one that would be relatively cheap if the economies were closed. This definition has the advantage of avoiding the need to make an additional assumption about consumer tastes, since if a greater physical abundance of labor were to be outweighed by a greater consumer preference for the labor-intensive good, this would already be reflected in a higher relative price of labor in autarky. The drawback with this alternative definition is that, since we do not observe countries in autarky, we cannot even in principle know which factor is the abundant one. In my view this criticism is decisive, which is why the alternative approach has been relegated to a footnote.

country W, whose variables are denoted by asterisks.[4] It is clear that, when C and D represent the same ratio of X/M production in the two countries, the slope of the ray from O_x to C must be greater than the slope of the ray from O_x to D. But this implies that the K/L ratio in the production of X in W (shown by the slope of the ray from O_x to C) must be greater than that in U. It is also true that the K/L ratio will be greater in W than in U in the production of M (to see this geometrically, redraw the two Edgeworth boxes with U's box now sharing the top right-hand origin O_M with $O_M{}^*$). In other words, with equal production ratios the capital intensity of production would be greater in both industries in the capital-abundant country (which is reassuringly unsurprising).

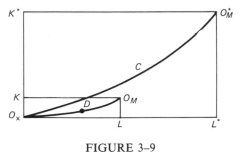

FIGURE 3–9
Two Edgeworth Boxes

But greater capital intensity implies that the capital-intensive good will have a lower opportunity cost—it will be necessary to give up less of the labor-intensive good in order to secure a marginal increase in the output of the capital-intensive good. Conversely, the labor-intensive good will have a higher opportunity cost where capital intensity K/L is greater. So the opportunity cost of M must be lower in W, and that of X must be lower in U, when production ratios are similar, that is, along any ray in the production possibility curve diagram (see fig. 3–10). A lower opportunity cost of M is shown by a steeper ppc (along any ray such as OR), since that represents a situation in which a given sacrifice of X allows a greater increase in M. Thus W's ppc is steeper along every ray than is U's, as shown. In particular, if OR is the ray that represents equilibrium in the

4. Note that, while U's Edgeworth box has been drawn smaller than W's to remind us of the small economy assumption, its scale is nevertheless much enlarged as compared to that of W. (The small economy assumption implies that U is negligibly small relative to W, but there would be no point in drawing a negligibly small Edgeworth box for U since then we could not see what was happening there.)

43

large country W, where the social indifference curve is tangential to the ppc, then U's production point P must lie to the right of OR. However, U's consumption point must lie on OR (as already established by virtue of equal tastes and prices), so U must be producing more of the L-intensive good X than it consumes, and exporting the excess. Correspondingly, W must be producing more of the K-intensive good M than it consumes (although the diagram does not show this difference by virtue of the assumption that W is so much larger relative to U as to make the displacement from OR along W's ppc insignificant), and exporting the excess.

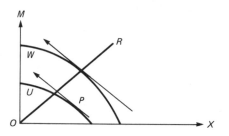

FIGURE 3–10
Two Production Possibility Curves

3.4   Leontief Paradox

In 1953 the Russian-born economist Wassily Leontief (b. 1906) published an article in which he described an attempt to verify empirically the Heckscher-Ohlin theorem. His earlier work, for which he was awarded the Nobel Prize in 1973, had involved the development of input-output theory. In response to his work, statistical efforts to construct input-output tables began. The first table to be published was for the United States in 1947. Leontief recognized that this provided the opportunity to make empirical estimates of the total factor content of United States trade and thus to see whether its exports were capital intensive and its imports labor intensive as the Heckscher-Ohlin theorem predicts. (In 1947 the United States unquestionably had far more capital per head than virtually all of its trading partners, so there seemed no question which was the abundant factor.)

Leontief encountered no difficulty in using the input-output tables plus data on the commodity composition of exports in order to construct an estimate of the quantities of capital and labor embodied in a representative $1 million of exports. However, he could not do the same for *imports,* because he had an input-output table only for the United States and not for the countries from which the United States was buying its imports. Instead he calculated from United States data the factor intensity of the *import substitutes* that would have been bought from United States sources had a representative $1 million of imports not been available.

The results of this exercise showed that exports were more *labor intensive* than were import substitutes, contrary to the prediction of the Heckscher-Ohlin model. Paradoxically, the world's most capital-abundant country appeared to be exporting goods more labor intensive than it was importing. There are several ways to explain, or explain away, this paradox:

Statistical Error. One possible explanation might be that Leontief's sums were wrong, or he happened to pick data that were in some way unrepresentative. There is, however, no evidence to support this conjecture. On the contrary, many subsequent investigations have repeated the type of test pioneered by Leontief and his results have often, though by no means always, been replicated. There is not much reason to doubt that capital-abundant countries do sometimes export more labor-intensive goods than they import.

Factor Intensity Reversal. Ronald Jones (b. 1931) argued that the Leontief Paradox might be due to a factor-intensity reversal as shown in figure 3–3B. In fact, it was the attempt to resolve the Leontief Paradox that prompted the search for empirical instances of factor-intensity reversal, which yielded the example cited earlier of rice-growing being labor intensive in Thailand and capital intensive in Texas. This explanation implies that, while United States import substitutes would be more capital intensive than United States exports, United States *imports* would be more labor intensive, as predicted by the Heckscher-Ohlin model. While theoretically interesting, there does not seem to be evidence that factor-intensity reversals are so commonplace as to be the sole explanation of the general tendency of the United States to export more labor-intensive goods than its import substitutes

Demand Conditions. Another theoretical possibility is that the paradox could be due to Americans having such strong preferences for capital-intensive goods as to outweigh the greater abundance of capital in the United States. There is not the slightest doubt that in reality tastes do vary from one country to another, rather than being identical as we have been assuming. There also seems to be a pretty systematic tendency for people to have an exceptionally pronounced taste for the goods that their own country is good at producing: Brazilians drink vast quantities of coffee and the French large quantities of wine. But the evidence also suggests that these differences on the demand side are dwarfed by those on the supply side.

There is, therefore, not much basis for using differences in tastes to explain the Leontief Paradox.

Protection. Our model assumes free trade, whereas in fact the United States (like all other countries) had very high levels of protection in 1947. Suppose United States tariffs were directed principally at excluding labor-intensive goods from their home market (as they were, for reasons that will become apparent in the next section). Then possibly, the only goods other countries had the chance of exporting to the United States *were* rather capital intensive. A problem with this explanation is that it is not clear why other countries would have wanted to trade with the United States if they could only export goods they were bad at making in exchange for goods in which they had a comparative advantage. However, if the model is extended to include natural resources as suggested below then this difficulty is overcome, and it may well be that in reality the structure of United States tariffs did partly explain the Leontief Paradox.

Better United States Workers. Leontief's own explanation was that United States workers were so much more efficient than their foreign counterparts that the country was really a labor-abundant and not a capital-abundant country. He was *not* saying that each worker produced three times (that was his figure) as much because he had much more capital to aid him, but that with a *given* capital stock a United States worker would produce three times as much because he worked that much better. Some economists (no doubt mainly those without close ties to the United States) have a certain emotional resistance to this explanation, but that does not constitute a scientific ground for rejecting it. Rejected it nevertheless should be, on the eminently scientific ground that empirical testing of theories would be a complete farce if any finding at odds with a priori expectations could be explained away by changing the unit of measurement by three without rigorous demonstration that such a change was empirically justified on the basis of evidence other than the finding to be explained away.

More Factors of Production. To be more charitable to Leontief's original explanation, one might interpret him as groping for what is probably accepted as the leading explanation at the present time: the contention that human capital is important. The charge is that putting only the two factors labor and capital in the Heckscher-Ohlin model has oversimplified to the point of obscuring what is central. Specifically, it is argued that an understanding of the determination of comparative advantage and the pattern of trade demands a model with at least four factors of production—capital, unskilled labor, professionally trained labor, and land. The latter represents all natural resources, and it is in fact again a gross simplification to aggregate all of these into a single factor—land suitable for growing coffee is not

46

the same as that suitable for growing tea, let alone for growing rice or mining iron ore or copper. For some purposes it would obviously be essential to recognize the heterogeneity of natural resources: indeed, it is exactly the possession of some scarce natural resource that provides the basis for the bulk of the exports of many developing countries. For present purposes we can note that many United States exports were (and are) intensive in some of the many natural resources with which the United States is abundantly endowed and it may well be that production of resource-intensive goods is more labor intensive than capital intensive. Research of the past twenty years has also amply confirmed the economic importance of the human capital embodied in technically trained and professional labor. The argument is that the most abundant factor in the United States was *not* the physical capital captured by Leontief's measure but the human capital whose reward was included by Leontief among labor costs. Discrimination between human capital, which is relatively abundant in the United States, and unskilled labor, which is the scarce factor (relative to other countries), has shown that it is indeed the former and not the latter that is embodied in United States exports.

Heckscher-Ohlin Is Wrong. An obvious possible explanation that has received rather little attention in the literature (perhaps reflecting the low regard in which empirical evidence is held by too many economists) is that the Heckscher-Ohlin theorem is wrong. Not logically wrong, of course, but wrong in the sense that it directs attention to something—factor endowment—that is in practice not very important in determining the pattern of trade. This heretical thought will be discussed in the next chapter.

3.5 Stolper-Samuelson Theorem

As already shown, free trade permits a country to increase its real income. Until the classic article "Protection and Real Wages" by Wolfgang Stolper (b. 1912) and Paul Samuelson in 1941, it had been taken for granted that this implied that free trade would normally—at least after transitional problems of adjustment were sorted out—be advantageous to everyone. Stolper and Samuelson proved that in the Heckscher-Ohlin model this is not true. Those who supply the scarce factor of production can gain real income in absolute terms through protection that restricts imports, even though society as a whole loses. Hence unskilled labor has an incentive in the United States to seek protective tariffs on (unskilled) labor-intensive goods.

The theorem may be stated formally as follows: a tariff will increase the income of the factor used intensively in the good that receives protection. In our example, this means that a tariff on M[5] would increase the income of capital, K.

The assumptions needed to establish this theorem are a subset of those that were introduced as underlying the Heckscher-Ohlin model: that technology can be represented by constant-returns-to-scale production functions with substitution between factors; that there are two goods and two factors available in fixed quantities; that perfect competition prevails in goods and factor markets; and that adjustment is instantaneous. An implication of the latter assumption is that labor and capital always receive the same return (equal to their respective marginal products) in both industries.[6]

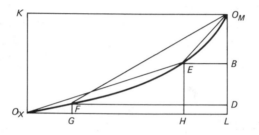

FIGURE 3–11
Effect of a Tariff on Production

Because of the assumptions on technology, this economy can be portrayed by the Edgeworth box shown in figure 3–11. Suppose that free trade equilibrium occurs at point E. The effect of a tariff on M will be to raise the internal relative price of M and thus to provide an incentive to produce more M and less X (this is a model with constant full employment). Production will therefore shift to some lower point on the contract curve, like F. At F the K/L ratio is lower than it was at E in *both* goods:

$$\frac{FG}{O_X G} < \frac{EH}{O_X H} \text{ and } \frac{O_M D}{FD} < \frac{O_M B}{EB}.$$

5. Obviously the imposition of a tariff on X would not affect anything, since the country does not import X anyway.

6. Incidentally, the return to capital in this type of model should be conceived of as a weekly rental paid by the entrepreneur who hires capital (as well as labor) in the (always unrealized) hope of making a profit, to the capitalists who own a stock of homogeneous machines that they rent out each week to the entrepreneur who makes the highest bid.

Now the higher is *K/L*, the lower is the marginal product of capital (which is represented by the slope of the total product curve, see fig. 3–12). As illustrated for the case of *X* in figure 3–12, this implies that the marginal product of capital *(MPK)* is higher at *F* than at *E*. But with constant returns to scale a higher *MPK* implies a lower *MPL* (marginal product of labor) and therefore, given perfect competition, a lower real wage (in terms of *X*). The argument can be repeated to show that the real wage also falls in terms of *M*. The abundant factor thus loses real income as a result of the tariff (or, for that matter, any other exogenous change that increases the price of imports). Conversely, as asserted by the Stolper-Samuelson theorem, the scarce factor gains. The intuitive reason is that the increase in the price of the goods that is intensive in that factor increases the demand for it and therefore its price.

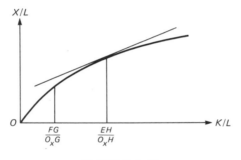

FIGURE 3–12
Total Product (Per Capita) Curve

The theorem implies that in the typical developing country, where unskilled labor is certainly an abundant factor of production, a policy of protection will reduce real wages. This may seem surprising—will not the urban working class gain from the increased demand for their services to increase output of the protected industrial goods? That depends on whether, or how nearly, the critical assumption of perfect factor mobility is satisfied. Where it is satisfied completely, the reduced demand for labor in the labor-intensive export sector, usually agriculture, will outweigh the increased demand for labor in the capital-intensive industrial sector. With complete immobility of labor, the commonsense reasoning is correct. In the real world, labor is typically partially mobile, and it is an empirical question as to which effect will dominate.

An interesting diagrammatic analysis of a different form of imperfect factor mobility has recently been developed by the Irish economist Peter

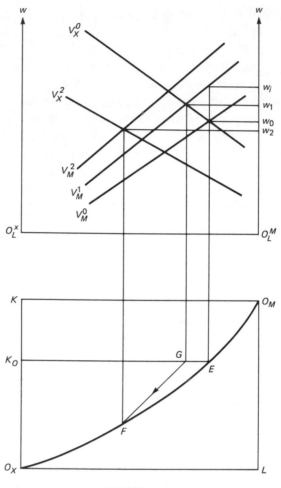

FIGURE 3–13

Slow Adjustment with Imperfect Capital Mobility

Neary (b. 1950). The bottom segment of figure 3–13 reproduces the Edge-worth box of figure 3–11, with E representing the initial free trade equilibrium and F the new equilibrium after factors have been redeployed in the optimal way following the new higher price of M. Above the Edgeworth box is drawn a diagram showing how the value marginal product of labor (V), equal to the wage w, varies. The value marginal product of labor in the X industry, V_X, is:

$$V_X = p_x \cdot \partial X / \partial L$$

where p_x is the price of X and $\partial X / \partial L$ is the marginal product of labor, which is, of course, an increasing function of the quantity of capital employed in the X industry. For any given price of X, p_x, and quantity of capital in the X industry, we can therefore draw a curve in the top segment of the diagram showing how the marginal value product of labor in the X industry declines as the quantity of labor employed in that industry increases. For example, the curve V_X^o shows how the value marginal product of labor declines in the X industry as employment in that industry increases (right from $O_L{}^x$, the point of zero employment of L in X), *given* the free trade price p_x and the free trade allocation of capital to X, $O_x K_o$. Similarly, the curve V_M^o shows how the value marginal product of labor in the M industry declines as employment in that industry increases (which is measured *leftward* from the point O_L^M of zero employment of L in M, since the M industry employs what the X industry does not, and the total equals the length of the Edgeworth box), given the free trade price p_m and the free trade allocation of capital to M, which is $K_o K$. Long-run labor market equilibrium under free trade is therefore represented by the intersection of V_X^o and V_M^o with the resulting wage rate of w_o.

Now consider what happens when a tariff is imposed and the price of M rises in consequence. That rise in the price of M will serve to shift V_M up, say to V_M^1, in proportion to the rise in p_m. In the Stolper-Samuelson story, there would be an immediate reallocation of K from X to M, thus shifting V_M up further (say to V_M^2) and shifting V_X down (to V_X^2). The Stolper-Samuelson theorem tells us that the new equilibrium wage w_2 would be less than w_o in terms of both goods, and since the price of X is unchanged that implies that w_2 must fall in money terms, as shown. But suppose there were not this instantaneous mobility of both factors. Suppose as a first alternative that there was no mobility of either factor. Then the money wage in the X industry would remain at w_o, which would mean that the real wage to workers in that industry would fall, given the rise in the price of M. In contrast the money wage in the M industry would rise in line with p_m to w_i, implying that the real wage in the M industry would rise in terms of X and stay constant in terms of M, and thus increase overall, as already noted.

Suppose, as a second alternative, that in the short run labor is mobile between industries but capital is not. This means that the two curves determining short-run labor market equilibrium are V_X^o and V_M^1, giving a short-run money wage of w_1 and a short-run allocation of the factors represented by point G in the Edgeworth box. In this short run the real wage is higher in terms of X but lower in terms of M, so one cannot say whether the overall real wage will increase or decrease without knowing the pattern of consumption of labor. Conversely, in this short run the real return to capital will be higher in the M industry than the X industry—this must be true because the point G is above the contract curve, and the wage is the same in both industries. Accordingly, there is an incentive to reallocate capital from the X industry to the M industry, and as this gradually occurs—for example, as depreciation occurs and capital can therefore be reinvested at will—the economy moves down GF and in the long run arrives at the Stolper-Samuelson solution at point F. The only problem with this story is that, over the same time that capital can be reallocated between industries, the size of the total capital stock cannot legitimately be taken to be fixed.

Thus it becomes obvious that the effect of a tariff (or other price change) on income distribution is not a trivial matter to be settled by appeal to some handed-down formula as an eternal truth. Economists can hope to say useful things but only after facts have been examined *and* theories understood.

3.6 Rybczynski Theorem

Another of the great theorems is due to T. Rybczynski (b. 1923), a Pole by birth and a British banker since the graduate student days when, in 1955, he published the paper introducing the theorem that bears his name. This theorem may be stated as follows: an increase in the endowment of one factor will reduce the production of the goods intensive in the *other* factor. In our example, this says that an increase in the quantity of labor (for example) would reduce output of M. At first this may seem surprising, inasmuch as an increase in the supplies of the factors of production is the basis of economic growth, and one associates growth with increases rather than decreases in the output of goods.

The assumptions on which this theorem is based are once more the 2 $\times$ 2 neoclassical technology, perfect factor mobility, and, in this case, that the country accepts parametrically the commodity prices determined on the world market (the small country assumption). The relative commodity price given by the world market dictates that a particular point, for example, E in figure 3–14, should be the equilibrium point on the contract curve (not shown) that runs from O_x to O_M^o when the labor supply is $O_x L_o$. Suppose, however, that the labor supply expands to $O_x L_1$, because of an influx of migrant workers forced to return home when recession strikes the former host country. What can be said about the new optimum point on the new contract curve (again not shown) that runs from O_x to O_M^j? Since commodity prices (and technology) are by assumption unchanged, factor prices must also remain unchanged. But in that case, given that the production functions are linear homogeneous, production of X and M must still take place with the same factor proportions as before. This means that production of X must take place on the ray O_xE extended, while that of M must lie on a ray O_M^1F from O_M^1 parallel to O_M^oE, that is, the new production point must be F in figure 3–14. (Point F must lie on the new contract curve because the slopes of both X and M isoquants are—by virtue of the linear homogeneity of the production functions—the same at F as at E and are therefore equal to one another at F as they were by assumption at E.) But at F the output of M is lower than at E, as the theorem says.

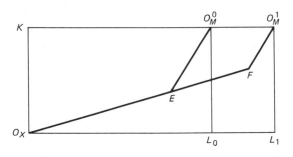

FIGURE 3–14
Effect of a Population Influx

Economic growth typically involves relative growth in the stock of capital, rather than the isolated growth of the labor force considered in the above example. The Rybczynski theorem tells us that countries enjoying such growth should expect to see the size of their labor-intensive industries contract. Unfortunately for both countries trying to industrialize and consumers in developed countries, most members of the parliaments of the industrialized countries are not acquainted with the Rybczynski theorem, and consequently many of them attempt to sustain their labor-intensive industries though protection. Those who have grasped the implications of the Rybczynski theorem realize that comparative advantage is not something given once and for all, to be clung to obstinately as factor supplies change, any more than it is to be spurned as something that condemns a country to the role of hewer of wood and drawer of water; rather it should be exploited at any moment while striving to expand supplies of capital and qualified manpower. To the extent that those endeavors succeed, the comparative advantage of the country will move up to more sophisticated products, while economic pressures make for a withdrawal from yesterday's more basic and labor-intensive goods, in the process making way for newcomers to develop manufactured exports and take their first steps up the ladder of economic progress. Such is, at least, the optimistic story of how an export-oriented strategy can harness dynamic comparative advantage in the cause of development (see chap. 11).

3.7 Summary

Orthodox trade theory has for the past fifty years been based on the idea that the fundamental determinant of the pattern of trade is the relative endowment of the factors of production that a country has at a given time. A country with an abundant supply of labor relative to capital will export labor-intensive goods, and vice versa—a proposition known as the Heckscher-Ohlin theorem. Two other important theorems about the implications of the Heckscher-Ohlin model were established: the Stolper-Samuelson theorem, which says that a tariff will increase the real income of the scarce factor of production (through diminishing the real income of the abundant factor by more), and the Rybczynski theorem, which says that an increase in the supply of one factor of production will decrease the output of the good intensive in the other factor (though increasing the output of the good intensive in the factor with the increased supply by more).

Leontief's empirical study, intended to confirm the Heckscher-Ohlin theorem, yielded instead the paradoxical result that the United States tended to import capital-intensive goods and export labor-intensive goods. While there are a number of possible explanations of the paradox, one that appears to be empirically important and consistent with the spirit of the Heckscher-Ohlin model involves recognizing the existence of more factors of production than homogeneous capital and homogeneous labor. Specifically, trade patterns appear to be importantly influenced by supplies of skilled labor and of natural resources. The United States exports labor-intensive goods because the high salaries that accrue to her abundant supply of skilled labor, which should, from an analytic point of view, be considered a return to human capital, are from a statistical viewpoint counted as labor income. Similarly, the exports of many countries reflect their exploitation of particular natural resource endowments.

Although the Heckscher-Ohlin model has been presented in this chapter as the embodiment of neoclassical trade theory, it is worth noting two variants found in the literature. The first was actually termed the neoclassical theory—as opposed to the modern theory stemming from Heckscher and

Ohlin—in the famous 1965–66 survey of trade theory by John Chipman (b. 1926). This analysis was also introduced during the interwar period by Gottfried Haberler. It involved utilization of the production possibility curve as a direct representation of supply conditions, reflecting increasing opportunity costs without analysis of the underlying production structure. The fact that Haberler could show the optimality of free trade on the basis of that analysis demonstrates that the conclusion is not dependent on the strict Heckscher-Ohlin assumptions, such as identical technology and non-reversal of factor intensities. The second variant is known as the sector-specific capital model. This is in fact the short-run model (see chap. 3.5) where capital was immobile between sectors, that is, specific to a particular sector.

3.8 Addendum: The Large Economy

The Heckscher-Ohlin theorem remains valid in the large economy, though it is more difficult to prove. The same is true of the conclusion regarding the benefits of free trade. The Stolper-Samuelson theorem normally remains valid as well, although there arises the possibility (known as the Metzler Paradox, after Lloyd B. Metzler, b. 1913) that a tariff might actually improve the country's terms of trade to such a degree that the internal relative price of the imported goods *falls.* In that case the tariff would have the opposite effect to that asserted in the Stolper-Samuelson theorem and *increase* the price of the abundant factor. The Rybczynski theorem depends on the assumption that commodity prices remain unchanged when factor supplies increase, which is normally true only for the small country. Hence this theorem does not generalize to the case of the large country.

A fourth important theorem is usually included in discussion of the Heckscher-Ohlin model: the factor price equalization theorem first enunciated by Paul Samuelson in 1948. Heckscher and Ohlin had argued that trade would produce a *tendency* toward the equalization of factor prices, on the intuitive argument that, since a country would export goods intensive in its abundant factor of production and import goods intensive in its scarce factor, the effect of the trade would be to increase the derived demand for the abundant factor and relieve the derived scarcity of the scarce factor and so reduce international differences in factor prices. What Samuelson proved was that the logic of the technological assumptions embodied in the

Heckscher-Ohlin model, in conjunction with those of perfect competition, laissez faire, and zero transport costs so as to guarantee equal commodity prices, permitted a much stronger result: that factor prices would be *completely* equalized by trade in goods alone, without any factor movements.

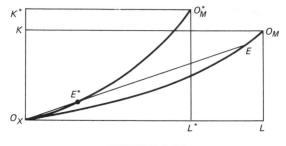

FIGURE 3–15
Factor Price Equalization

The logic of the argument has in fact already been used in the proof of the Rybczynski theorem. Trade equalizes commodity prices between the two countries. With a given neoclassical technology, factor prices determine commodity prices uniquely, since the factor prices determine the cost-minimizing point on the isoquant and with perfect competition and constant returns to scale price is equal to cost $w \cdot L + p_K \cdot K$. Hence both countries produce along the same ray from O_X and parallel rays from O_M and O_M^* as shown in figure 3–15, which is only a minor modification of figure 3–14.

The interest lies in establishing the set of assumptions that are necessary for this argument to hold. First, there are the technological assumptions of constant returns to scale, substitutability in production, an absence of factor intensity reversals, and identical technology in both countries. The last two of these assumptions are of particular interest, inasmuch as it can be shown that factor intensity reversals can actually cause trade to widen factor price differentials, and the assumption that two countries have identical technology is much stronger than the assumption that each individual country has a neoclassical technology. Second, there are the relatively innocuous assumptions of no transport costs, free trade, and perfect competition needed to guarantee commodity price equalization. Relaxing these would simply mean that trade could not completely equalize factor prices, but the tendency would remain. Third, there are the simplifying assumptions of two goods and two factors in fixed supply. These can be generalized to some extent, by allowing factor supplies to vary and by increasing the number of goods and factors, provided that the number of goods remain equal to or greater than the number of factors. But this is a big proviso: we do not even have a satisfactory way of deciding how goods or factors should be defined, given that they are not in reality homogeneous. Finally, there is an assumption specific to the factor price equalization theorem: that the factor endowments not be so different as to drive one or other of the countries to specialization. This last requisite for the factor price equalization theorem dictates that it be treated in this addendum. Figure 3–16 shows that the small economy would indeed specialize, unless total world demand for the good X intensive in its abundant factor were negligible.

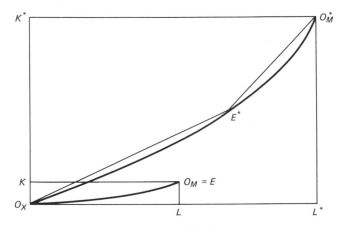

FIGURE 3–16
Specialization and Nonequalization of Factor Prices in the Small Economy

We know from reading newspapers, looking at statistics, or keeping our eyes open when we travel that in reality factor prices are not equal between countries or, for that matter, within countries. It is also abundantly clear that some factor prices are a lot more equal than others: specifically, that the returns to internationally mobile factors like capital or skilled labor are far less unequal than those to the factors with minimal mobility, like land and unskilled labor. In other words, the empirical evidence suggests that commodity trade alone does not equalize factor prices, contrary to the conclusion suggested by the factor price equalization theorem. The questions that arise are why that is so and whether this dictates a rejection of the Heckscher-Ohlin model *in toto*.

There is no question but that the factor price equalization theorem does involve some very strong assumptions: in particular, those on identical technologies, the number of goods and factors, and an economy sufficiently large to avoid specialization. Presumably the technologies actually available to countries do differ drastically, given the vast differences in the supply of technically trained manpower. As noted above, we have no idea whether the condition on the relative number of goods and factors is satisfied. Similarly, do countries specialize? Obviously none of them produces only one good, but there are lots of small countries which produce only a small part of the total range of goods that they consume. So perhaps it is not surprising to find so little evidence of factor price equalization in the real world. However, this discussion leaves intact the commonsense argument with which we started: that trade can be expected to raise the derived demand for abundant factors and relieve the shortage of scarce factors, and in that way to have a (partial) equalizing impact on factor prices. Recent empirical studies in countries like Brazil have provided reinforcement to the belief that a greater opening of the economy to foreign trade would have this effect.

Can one set aside the factor price equalization theorem without simultaneously rejecting the rest of the Heckscher-Ohlin approach? The answer is yes. One does not need all of the above assumptions to support the other main conclusions drawn from the Heckscher-Ohlin model: namely, the Heckscher-Ohlin, Stolper-Samuelson and Rybczynski theorems and the conclusion regarding the benefits of free trade. For example, the Heckscher-Ohlin theorem does not require nonspecialization, and it would presumably survive if technologies were similar though not identical. The Stolper-Samuelson and Rybczynski theorems do not involve comparisons between countries, so they certainly do not rely on the identical technology assumption. And the free-trade conclusion relies on none of the three questionable assumptions. In other words, it is a mistake to suppose that the Heckscher-Ohlin model is something that either has to be accepted as an all-embracing explanation of trade or else totally rejected as reactionary orthodoxy. Like all models, it is a way of representing reality that picks out certain features as crucial and enables us to understand their implications. In those contexts where the features modeled are in fact the crucial ones, the model can be useful. Application of the model in other contexts can be misleading and mischievous. The job of an applied economist involves deciding what model is appropriate to the particular problem under analysis. The Heckscher-Ohlin model should always be considered when the question concerns trade and will often be found useful.

3.9 Bibliography

The classic work introducing the Heckscher-Ohlin model is B. Ohlin, *International and Interregional Trade* (Cambridge, Mass.: Harvard University Press, 1933). The main work of formalizing the model was undertaken in a series of papers by Paul Samuelson, now conveniently available in J. E. Stiglitz, ed., *The Collected Scientific Works of Paul A. Samuelson* vol. 2 (Cambridge, Mass.: MIT Press, 1966), part. 9; chap. 66 is the Stolper-Samuelson theorem and chaps. 67–71 deal with factor price equalization. The Rybczynski theorem appeared in T. M. Rybczynski, "Factor Endowment and Relative Commodity Prices," *Economica,* Nov. 1955, reprinted in R. E. Caves and H. G. Johnson, eds., *Readings in International Economics* (Homewood, Ill.: Irwin, 1968).

The outstanding contemporary exponent of the Heckscher-Ohlin model is Ronald Jones. A collection of his most important papers is in R. W. Jones, *Essays in Trade Theory* (Amsterdam: North-Holland, 1979). The last chapter of that book, also available as *In Defense of "Twoness,"* Princeton Special Paper in International Economics No. 12 (1977), deals with the important and still not completely resolved question of the extent to which the conclusions of the orthodox Heckscher-Ohlin model depend upon the $2 \times 2 \times 2$ simplification. Famous (relatively advanced) surveys of trade theory which place major emphasis on Heckscher-Ohlin are J. N. Bhagwati, "A Survey of the Theory of International Trade," *Economic Journal,* March 1964 [reprinted in his *Trade, Tariffs and Growth* (Amsterdam: North-Holland, 1971)], and J. S. Chipman, "A Survey of the Theory of International Trade," *Econometrica,* July and Oct. 1965 and Jan. 1966.

The analysis of dynamic adjustment following a tariff change is in J. P. Neary, "Short-run Capital Specificity and the Pure Theory of International Trade," *Economic Journal,* Sept. 1978.

Leontief first published the results that became known as the Leontief Paradox in 1953; the paper is reprinted as "Domestic Production and Foreign Trade," in Caves and Johnson, *Readings.* Surveys of the subsequent literature are provided by R. E. Baldwin, "Determinants of the Commodity Structure of United States Trade," *American Economic Review,* May 1971, reprinted in R. E. Baldwin and J. D. Richardson, eds., *International Trade and Finance: Readings,* 2nd ed. (Boston: Little, Brown, 1981), and by R. Stern, "Testing Trade Theories," in P. B. Kenen, ed., *International Trade and Finance* (Cambridge: Cambridge University Press, 1975).

Empirical studies of the impact of a greater opening to foreign trade in Brazil have been undertaken by FUNCEX, the Fundação Centro do Estudos de Comércio Exterior, Rio de Janeiro. A summary of some of the results, in English, is provided by B. Balassa, "Incentive Policies in Brazil," *World Development,* Nov. 1979.

A new and difficult area of trade theory not treated in the text concerns the introduction of uncertainty into trade models. The authoritative work on this topic is E. Helpman and A. Razin, *A Theory of International Trade under Uncertainty* (New York: Academic Press, 1978).

4

Trade in Manufactures

ONE possible explanation of the Leontief Paradox mentioned in the previous chapter was that the Heckscher-Ohlin model is wrong in identifying differences in resource endowment as the basis of all trade. This possibility has won increasing support in recent years. Paul Krugman (b. 1953), among others, has made important strides in formalizing an alternative approach to trade theory. He has argued that there are three stylized facts about world trade which appear paradoxical from the standpoint of the Heckscher-Ohlin model, as did the Leontief Paradox itself.

1. The existence of intense and rapidly expanding trade between countries with similar resource endowments, such as the members of the European Economic Community (EEC). The Heckscher-Ohlin theory suggests that there would be little such trade and that the most intense trade would instead occur between countries in very different supply situations, such as industrialized and primary producing countries.

2. The exchange of large quantities of very similar products; for example, Italian exports of cars to Germany, occurring simultaneously with German exports of cars to Italy. The Heckscher-Ohlin model implies that one country will sell one range of goods and import a different range of goods embodying a different factor content.

3. The minimal social conflict that accompanied the enormous liberalization of trade among the industrial countries during the post-war period. The

Stolper-Samuelson theorem leads one to expect that trade liberalization will reduce the real income of one factor of production, which would therefore be expected to resist such liberalization bitterly.

The theory that has been emerging to explain these paradoxes contains two basic strands: the idea that consumer demand for diversity leads to the production of differentiated products, and the idea that the typical product line is not produced on a sufficient scale to exhaust all available economies of scale. Both are ideas that seem relevant to trade in manufactures rather than to all trade.[1] Various attempts have been made to formalize these ideas so that they can be incorporated in models similar to, or comparable to, the Heckscher-Ohlin model. As yet there is no single model that would be accepted as embodying the essential ideas in a general way, like the Heckscher-Ohlin model, and there probably never will be. However, there are three approaches which jointly give a reasonable grasp of the implications of the assumptions that trade in manufactures is driven by product differentiation and scale economies rather than by factor endowment.

4.1 Economies of Scale

In the one case that can be analyzed using the same techniques as those developed in the previous two chapters there are two distinct (as opposed to differentiated) products both subject to increasing returns to scale. Consider first the implications of economies of scale (*alias* increasing return to scale or a production function homogeneous of degree greater than one) for the production possibility curve of a single country. In a world with only one factor of production, it is clear that increasing returns would imply a production possibility frontier *convex* to the origin, as shown in figure 4–1A. (To emphasize that we believe these models to be relevant to trade in manufactures rather than to all trade, we call the two goods M_1 and M_2.) With all the single factor devoted to the production of M_1 it would be possible to produce M_1^{max}, and with it all devoted to the production of M_2 it would be possible to produce M_2^{max}, but with half devoted to the production of each it would not be possible to produce as much as $(\frac{1}{2}M_1^{max}, \frac{1}{2}M_2^{max})$, but only $(\bar{M}_1, \bar{M}_2)$. Because a doubling of input permits more than a doubling of output, from $\bar{M}_1$ to M_1^{max}, and from $\bar{M}_2$ to M_2^{max}, the centerpoint of the ppc must lie *inside* the straight line from M_1^{max} to M_2^{max}. That is, the ppc is convex to the origin as shown.

1. Trade of this type is sometimes referred to as "intraindustry trade" or as "trade in differentiated products" rather than the title used here, "trade in manufactures."

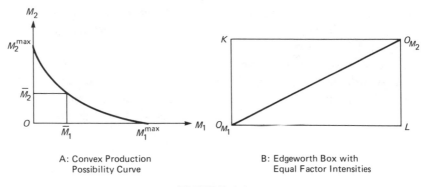

A: Convex Production
Possibility Curve

B: Edgeworth Box with
Equal Factor Intensities

FIGURE 4–1

Production Possibilities under Increasing Return to Scale

Consider next the situation with two factors of production, but where the factor intensities of the two goods happen to be equal. Then the Edgeworth box has the diagonal as contract curve, as shown in figure 4–1B. The midpoint of that contract curve corresponds to the isoquants of $(\bar{M}_1, \bar{M}_2)$ in figure 4–1A, while the corners correspond to $M_1^{\max}$ (at O_{M_2}) and $M_2^{\max}$ (at O_{M_1}). Because of increasing returns, $M_1^{\max}$ would be more than $2\bar{M}_1$ and $M_2^{\max}$ would be more than $2\bar{M}_2$. Once again, therefore, we would get a convex ppc as in figure 4–1A.

In general, of course, factor intensities are not equal. Changes in the scale of production of the two goods therefore require changes in the factor intensity in each industry in order to maintain full utilization of both factors, and so the contract curve lies below (or above) the diagonal. With constant returns to scale these differing factor intensities imply a concave ppc (see chap. 3). With increasing returns to scale and different factor intensities we therefore have two effects at work and operating in opposite directions: increasing returns making for convexity of the ppc, differing factor intensities making for concavity. Where the second factor dominates, we have the same analysis as in the previous chapter.[2] Where the two factors just counterbalance one another, we would be back to the straightline ppc of chapter 2. And where increasing returns outweigh differing factor intensities, we get a convex ppc. This case is more probable the greater are increasing returns and the less are the differences in factor intensities.

Consider next what would happen in a world with two countries each

2. There is an important qualification to this statement. Even though the ppc is concave, the existence of increasing returns makes the perpetuation of perfect competition impossible. Thus the analysis should really be modified to incorporate imperfect rather than perfect competition.

possessing a convex ppc. To clarify the central point, let us suppose that these two countries are identical in every respect: not only with respect to technology and tastes as assumed in the previous chapter but also with respect to size and relative factor endowments. It follows that their ppc's, as well as their social indifference curves, would be identical. Suppose that they both have the form shown in figure 4–2A, in which increasing returns to scale outweigh the effect of differing factor intensities. This would give rise to a *world* ppc with the form shown by the heavy curve in figure 4–2B. The reason for this strange shape can be seen as follows. If they both specialized in the production of M_1, it would be possible to achieve a world output of $2M_1^{max}$ (and zero M_2). Similarly, if both produced only M_2, total world production of M_2 would be $2M_2^{max}$. It would also be possible to achieve the point E, with production at M_1^{max} and M_2^{max}, by having one (either one) country specialize in the production of M_1 and the other specialize in the production of M_2. If each country divided its factors between the two industries rather than specializing world production would reach only $2\bar{M}_1$, $2\bar{M}_2$, because neither of them would be exploiting the available economies of scale. Between E and $2M_1^{max}$, the world ppc would follow the form of the national ppc in figure 4–2A, since one country would specialize on M_1 while the other would divide its factors between M_1 and M_2. The world ppc would follow an identical form between E and $2M_2^{max}$, with one country specializing (producing M_2) and the other producing both goods.

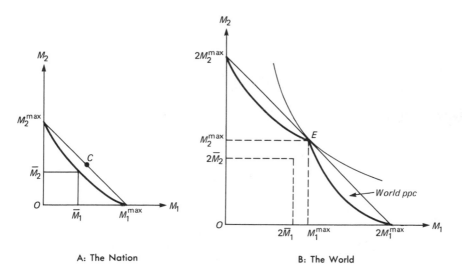

FIGURE 4–2

National and World Production Possibilities with Increasing Returns

Suppose that world conditions of demand happened to be as portrayed by the social indifference curve in figure 4–2B, which not only touches the world ppc at E but also is tangential to the straight line from $2M_1^{max}$ to $2M_2^{max}$ through E. In this case both countries can gain by agreeing to specialize—it does not matter on which product—and then trading along the world price line to consume at C in figure 4–2A, which lies outside the national ppc. The point is that increasing returns to scale provide an *additional* source of gain from trade: countries that are identical with respect to factor endowments and tastes can *still* gain from mutual exchange.

However, there is no reason to suppose that world demand would be such as to lead to the symmetrical outcome portrayed in figure 4–2. It is easy to imagine a situation where demand is much stronger for M_2, for example, than for M_1, as shown in figure 4–3.[3] It can be seen from figure 4–3B that the world can still reach the highest possible indifference curve by both countries specializing, but, as seen in figure 4–3A, the country that specializes in the product M_1 in lesser demand will end up at point C with much lower real income than the one that specializes in M_2 and can trade down to point D. The country producing M_1 might well rue the historical accident that had resulted in its specializing in M_1 rather than M_2 but nevertheless conclude that the cost of trying to displace an established foreign monopoly in the production of M_2 would be prohibitive. The economists of the so-called dependency school, led by the Egyptian Samir Amin (b. 1931), tend to view the world division of labor between Northern producers of manufactures and Southern producers of primary products in somewhat these terms.

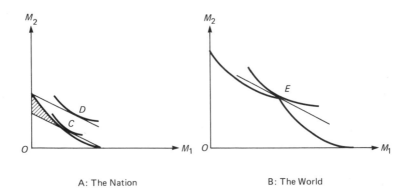

A: The Nation   B: The World

FIGURE 4–3

Problems of World Equilibrium with Increasing Returns

3. The argument developed below would be even stronger if the point of tangency between the world indifference curve and the world ppc occurred at a point other than E.

There is another problem with the equilibrium portrayed in figure 4–3: it is not clear that it *is* an equilibrium. The equilibria encountered in the previous chapter had all points preferred by consumers to the equilibrium point *above* the price line (which is still true here) and the whole of the production set below the price line (which is not true of the shaded area in figure 4–3A). This means that at the prevailing prices producers could make more money if they were to switch their resources from the production of M_1 to M_2. If they did this they would not *in fact* make more money, since the price of M_2 would decline; but no individual *competitive* producer would recognize this. In other words, perfect competition could not sustain the equilibrium shown in figure 4–3. This should not occasion surprise, since increasing returns is one of the classic causes of the breakdown of perfect competition. But it is useful to have this reminder that trade in manufactures is generally not conducted under market conditions approximating perfect competition. The norm, especially for consumer goods, is for the firm to list a price and sell all that is demanded at that price. The British economist Sir John Hicks (b. 1904), winner of the Nobel Prize in 1972, called markets where this occurs *fixprice* markets. (With capital goods, prices are often individually negotiated.) Among manufactures, it is only intermediate goods where market conditions at all often approach the *flexprice* markets[4] which provide the basis for the competitive abstraction beloved of economic theory.

Thus increasing returns to scale provide an *additional* factor motivating trade, which may lead to both countries benefiting from trade even when they are *identical* with respect to technology and tastes. However, such trade cannot be carried on in conditions of perfect competition, and equilibrium will require that the firms involved have some degree of market power. Moreover, it is by no means guaranteed that the benefits of trade will be distributed symmetrically, and it is entirely possible that those who gain relatively less will regard such an asymmetrical distribution of the benefits as inequitable, even though they too are better off with trade than without.

4.2 The Central Role of Demand

The first systematic attempt to explain the pattern of trade in manufactures was made in 1961 by the Swedish economist and politician Staffan

---

4. An alternative terminology is "customer markets" for fixprice markets and "auction markets" for flexprice markets.

Linder (b. 1931). In *An Essay on Trade and Transformation* he drew a sharp distinction between trade in primary products, which he argued would be determined on the basis of factor endowments, especially of natural resources, as in the traditional Heckscher-Ohlin model and trade in manufactures. In the case of the latter, he argued that factor intensities were much the same and that the principal determinant of the pattern of trade was to be found in the structure of demand.

Linder regarded the structure of demand as the *qualities* of differentiated products demanded in a country. He argued that the principal determinant of the demand structure would be the level of per capita income: countries with high average real income would not just tend to consume *more* cars, for example, but also *better quality* cars. The idea is illustrated in figure 4–4. We have to suppose that it is possible to array the quality of the various makes of a product—cars provide a good example—in an unambiguous way from the worst below Q_1 to the best above Q_6. On Linder's supposition that the quality of product a consumer wants is rigidly linked to his income level, a consumer with income Y_A would demand a product of quality Q_4. However, because in any country incomes are unequal, a country with *average* income level Y_A will demand a *range* of product qualities between Q_2 and Q_6. Similarly, a country with average per capita income Y_B, whose representative consumer would demand a product of quality Q_3, would have demands for a range of products spread from Q_1 to Q_5. Obviously this general picture of a range of demands spread around a mean determined by mean (or perhaps median or modal) per capita income would not be essentially affected if we admitted, as surely we must, that the world contains many people who choose not to consume the particular product quality that is typical at their income level. Recognition of this simply provides an additional reason for expecting a demand for a range of product qualities of any good.

Linder argued that each country would confine its production to goods within the range of product qualities *consumed* domestically. In the example in the figure, a country with average income Y_A would produce products within the quality range from Q_2 to Q_6, and a country with average income Y_B would produce products within the range between Q_1 and Q_5. He cited three reasons for believing that countries would not initiate production outside those ranges, that is, for the export market. First, the limited information of entrepreneurs would prevent their discerning the existence of demand for a good that was not being consumed locally. Second, even if the need for a good with certain qualities in potential demand abroad were to be correctly perceived, lack of familiarity would impede invention of a product with the right characteristics. Third, even if a basically appropriate

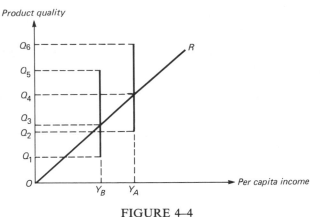

FIGURE 4–4

Per Capita Income, Product Quality and Trade

product were to be conceived, the distance from the market would make it difficult and expensive to make those continuous adaptations to the quality of the product that are necessary for commercial success. For these reasons, production is *initiated* to serve the domestic market, and only *afterward* do some of those products start being exported. This account also helps to show why trade in primary products is so different: there is normally no question of inventing or even adapting the quality of the product but just the need to perceive the external market. Linder argued that situations where the necessary natural resources exist but are not being exploited by local entrepreneurs because of the failure to perceive the external market are exactly those where multinationals are attracted into extractive industry.

The last question to consider is which of the various products a country will tend to export. Linder's answer is that, again in terms of figure 4–4, the countries will exchange products in the quality range from Q_2 to Q_5, where their consumption patterns overlap. From this he derives one of his basic conclusions: that the potential for trade in manufactures is greatest as between countries at *similar* income levels. This is, of course, the reverse of the conclusion suggested by the Heckscher-Ohlin model, where differences in per capita income signify different capital-labor ratios and therefore a *greater* potential for intratrade. Linder also suggested that countries will tend to produce products designed to satisfy the representative demands in their own countries, like Q_4 in the country with mean income Y_A and Q_3 in the country with mean income Y_B, and export these goods that satisfy typical demands at home in order to satisfy minority tastes in other countries. Although he did not provide a completely satisfactory rationale as to why this would be likely to happen, it is not difficult to fill the gap. If there are economies of scale and transport costs, firms will have a competitive advantage in producing those products with greatest sales levels at home and exploiting the scale economies realized by high production volumes in order to export to satisfy unusual tastes abroad. The converse strategy, producing to satisfy minority tastes and exporting the bulk of output, could still realize the scale economies but would involve a larger bill for transportation and therefore be uneconomic without some differences in factor endowment or technology that more than compensated.

In the twenty-odd years since Linder wrote his paper, there has been an explosive growth in international travel and communication. It stands to reason that this has reduced the barriers to perceiving foreign markets, to understanding the type of product needed to cater to them, and to modifying product characteristics in the light of market reactions. These factors nonetheless remain important.

4.3 Monopolistic Competition

In recent years there have been several attempts to use the theory of monopolistic competition to understand trade in manufactures. Unfortunately even the simplest models, based on highly restrictive assumptions about demand and technology, involve a level of complexity beyond the range of this book. Fortunately, however, it is possible to gain some intuitive grasp of what this type of model implies without presenting formal models and proofs by studying the central ideas of Paul Krugman's 1981 paper entitled "Intraindustry Specialization and the Gains from Trade."

Krugman first sets up a model of monopolistic competition in a closed economy. He makes some very strong simplifying assumptions in order to have a model that he can solve explicitly:

1. There are only two goods, each of which is produced in a variety of products.
2. Each firm produces one product according to a cost function
$$C = wl = w(\alpha + \beta x)$$
where C = total cost, w = the wage rate of the relevant type of labor, l = the quantity employed of the relevant type of labor, α = the quantity of labor required to maintain a production line (so αw is fixed cost), β = the input of labor required to produce an extra unit of output, and x = output of the product (so βwx is total variable cost and βw is marginal cost, see fig. 4–5).

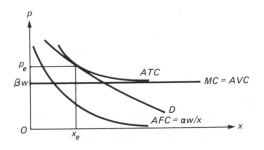

FIGURE 4–5

Equilibrium under Monopolistic Competition

3. The only factors of production are the two types of labor, which are available in fixed quantities, with each type being used exclusively by one of the two industries.
4. All consumers have identical utility functions of a specific and symmetric functional form, which involve a unit elasticity of substitution between the two goods and a higher elasticity of substitution between the different types of product within an industry.

Solution of this model for a closed economy reveals the following properties. First, each consumer always spends a half of his income on each good, so that the revenues of the two industries are always equal. This is a consequence of the assumptions of symmetry and unit elasticity of substitution imposed on the utility functions. Second, again as a result of the strong symmetry of the utility function, each consumer buys the same quantity of each product (within an industry) that is being produced. Third, the number of products produced by each industry is determined by the zero-profit condition, which guarantees Chamberlin's condition of tangency between the demand curve and the average cost curve. As long as positive (negative) profits exist, more firms enter (leave) and this pushes the demand curve of each firm to the left (right), so that in equilibrium the tangency condition must hold (see fig. 4–5). Fourth, the higher the elasticity of substitution between products, the fewer will be the number of different products produced, with each of them being produced on a larger scale and hence with fewer unrealized economies of scale. The scale economies originate from the fixed cost of production of each firm, which imply that average cost is always greater than marginal cost (see fig. 4–5). Finally, relative wages of the two types of labor depend *inversely* on their endowments. Actually, because of the assumed symmetry and unit elasticity of substitution, which guarantee equal revenues of the two industries, the relative wage in industry 1 is equal to

$$w_1/w_2 = \psi/(l - \psi)$$

where ψ is the fraction of the labor force in industry 2. Thus if $\psi > \frac{1}{2}$, so that there are more workers available to the second industry than to the first, the wage in the first industry will be higher than that in the second.

So much for the closed economy. Consider now what would happen if two such economies, identical in every respect except with regard to their factor proportions ψ, were to open up free (and, as usual, costless) trade between each other. Krugman actually analyzes a very special case, where the two countries' factor proportions ψ are the exact obverse of one another, so that the second country has the fraction ψ of its labor force in industry 1 and $(1-\psi)$ in industry 2. This enables him to take the difference of ψ from one-half as an unambiguous index of the difference in factor proportions between the two countries. If $\psi = \frac{1}{2}$, endowments will be identical; with ψ close to 0 or 1, they would be radically different.

Opening up trade has no effect on the level of output nor on the number of firms producing each product in either country in this model. The changes occur not in the pattern of production but in that of consumption. Consumers now have twice the number of products available, and given their taste for diversity (embodied in their utility functions) they consume some of all of them in equal quantities. The fact that in this model consumers benefit only through increased product diversity rather than also through the economies of scale realized by higher output levels of industrial products is a consequence of the special form of the utility function adopted in the interests of simplicity. In general one would expect trade in differentiated products produced subject to increasing returns to benefit consumers through both channels.

Given that consumers distribute their expenditures equally over both goods and all products, it follows that a half of all expenditure is on imports. This is in contrast to the Linder model, where the presumption was that staples would be produced at home and imports would be confined to goods in less intense demand. Note in particular that the level of trade in this model is *independent* of the similarity of factor endowments. This is in contrast to both the Heckscher-Ohlin model, where trade arises from differences in factor proportions, and the Linder analysis, where it was argued that trade was potentially greatest between countries with similar factor proportions. Krugman offered this result as a resolution of the first of the three empirical paradoxes about trade noted at the beginning of this chapter, the intense and growing trade between countries with similar factor supplies. But that paradox is also resolved by both the other models studied earlier in this chapter.

The reason that the level of trade is independent of relative factor supplies in Krugman's model is that there are two different *types* of trade involved and the increase in one type of trade as factor endowments become more different just happens to counterbalance the decrease in the other type of trade. With equal factor proportions, all trade is *intraindustrial:* a country exports as much of each good as it imports, so that there is no net exchange of the two goods. If, at the other extreme, each country had just one type of labor, then each country would obviously be able to produce only one type of good and trade would consist entirely of an exchange of the (differentiated) products of one industry for those of another. This second type of trade may be called *Heckscher-Ohlin trade* because it is motivated by differences in factor proportions. With less special assumptions, one would not expect these two effects to imply exactly the same total of trade whatever the factor endowments. But one can still see that, as factor proportions become more equal, so the proportion of intraindustrial trade would be expected to grow. This provides a reconciliation of the second paradox, the exchange of large quantities of very similar goods. (This paradox is again resolved by the Linder analysis.)

It is easy to believe that Krugman's model implies the equalization of factor prices: wages in each industry depend only on the value of world expenditure on each type of good (always 50 percent of total expenditure) divided by the number of workers in the industry in the world as a whole (always 50 percent of the labor force). In fact, wages are equalized not merely across countries but also between industries. This leveling of wages will react to the detriment of workers in the industry with the smaller labor force prior to the initiation of trade, just as implied by the Stolper-Samuelson theorem. On the other hand, all workers will gain in their capacity as consumers from the greater product diversity resulting from the opening of trade links. Where factor proportions are very similar, this second effect will dominate the first (Stolper-Samuelson) effect and everyone will gain from trade liberalization. This is Krugman's explanation of the third paradox, the observation that the great liberalization of trade among the industrial countries did not lead to bitter resistance on the part of a factor that had its real income threatened. But trade liberalization vis-à-vis the new industrial countries (NICs), like Brazil, Mexico, Korea, and Taiwan, may be much less easy for the old industrial countries to accept, since the NICs are likely to have exports based on different factor proportions—cheap labor, to be specific—that threatens the position of whole industries and of a large segment of the labor force in the importing countries.

The Krugman model utilizes a set of very restrictive assumptions in order to generate its clear-cut results, but this is not the main criticism that has been leveled against it. A more serious shortcoming lies in its specification of consumer demand, which has each consumer maximizing utility by consuming a little bit of everything on the market. That is surely not typical of the markets for differentiated products: typically a consumer picks one (or at most two) type of car, rather than some equal combination of Fiat, Ford, Leyland, Renault, Toyota, etc. Reformulating the model to take appropriate account of this indivisibility phenomenon complicates model-building many times over. The main result to have emerged to date is that there is some presumption that after the opening of trade the total range of products produced will decline (especially at the cheap end of the market), and hence part of the benefits of trade will take the form of increased realization of economies of scale.

4.4   Product Cycle

Another theory of trade in sophisticated manufactured products, developed principally by Raymond Vernon (b. 1913), is known as the *product cycle model.* The basic idea is that new products are developed and first produced in the most advanced economies, above all the United States, for two reinforcing types of reasons: demand first appears where incomes are high and tastes are sophisticated, and the high level of technical skill of the labor force gives a comparative advantage in development and initial production, before it has been reduced to routine. Subsequently demand spreads abroad and is first satisfied by exports from the United States. However, as foreign demand grows and the production process becomes increasingly standardized, it becomes progressively more attractive to initiate foreign production. As the product goes through its natural cycle, from being intensive in research and development and skilled labor, to being intensive in capital and/or unskilled labor, so its main production location migrates to less advanced countries, with a reversal in the direction of trade. The product cycle model is closely allied to the theory of direct investment (see chap. 6.5), a topic deliberately being left on one side in this book because of the very different range of issues that are raised by what is best considered international industrial economics.

4.5   Summary

The differences in factor proportions that provide the basis for trade in the traditional Heckscher-Ohlin model are not the only possible such basis.

Indeed, there are rather strong reasons for believing that a large part of the trade among the industrial countries—and probably also of trade among semiindustrial countries at a similar stage of development—is explained by quite other factors, notably scale economies and product differentiation. The models that have been presented to analyze the trade stemming from these sources are by no means as well articulated and explored as the orthodox model analyzed previously, but they do go quite a long way toward providing an analytical framework capable of illuminating this other type of trade. Accepting the usefulness of these models does not require one to reject the Heckscher-Ohlin model as wrong or redundant; on the contrary, both Linder and Krugman showed how the models were complementary. These new models are providing the applied economist with a wider range from which to select a tool relevant to whatever issue he may be facing.

4.6 Bibliography

Linder's analysis was presented in S. B. Linder, *An Essay on Trade and Transformation,* (New York: John Wiley, 1961); an extract is reprinted as chap. 3 in R. E. Baldwin and J. D. Richardson, cds., *International Trade and Finance: Readings,* 2nd ed. (Boston: Little, Brown, 1981). Paul Krugman showed that Linder's conclusion that countries will export the goods for which their domestic demand is relatively great can be generated by a model of monopolistic competition with increasing returns to scale and transportation costs; "Scale Economies, Product Differentiation, and the Pattern of Trade," *American Economic Review,* Dec. 1981. A rare attempt to test an elaboration of the Linder analysis empirically was presented by R. Hocking, "Trade in Motor Cars Between the Major European Producers," *Economic Journal,* Sept. 1980; the conclusion is generally favorable to the approach.

Of Paul Krugman's several papers on the subject, the one that forms the basis of the treatment in the chapter is "Intraindustry Specialization and the Gains from Trade," *Journal of Political Economy,* Oct. 1981. The criticism of the Krugman model in the text is met by the alternative treatment of K. Lancaster, "Intraindustry Trade under Perfect Monopolistic Competition" *Journal of International Economics,* May 1980.

Monopolistic competition in general equilibrium is treated by A. K. Dixit and V. Norman, *Theory of International Trade: A Dual General Equilibrium Approach* (Cambridge: Cambridge University Press, 1980). This provides an excellent advanced text in pure trade theory for those with adequate mathematical background, including a command of duality theory. The most comprehensive work on intraindustry trade to date is H. G. Grubel and P. J. Lloyd, *Intra-Industry Trade* (London: Macmillan, 1975).

The product cycle model was presented in R. Vernon, "International Investment and International Trade in the Product Cycle," *Quarterly Journal of Economics,* May 1966, reproduced in Baldwin and Richardson, *International Trade.*

5

Protection

EVERY one of the models studied in the last three chapters has shown how countries can benefit through engaging in trade. Adam Smith showed the gain possible when each country had an absolute advantage. Ricardo showed that this required only the existence of comparative advantage, which (unlike an absolute advantage) is almost certain to be present. Heckscher and Ohlin showed how comparative advantage is based on differences in factor endowments and how a country could benefit by exporting goods intensive in its abundant factor of production. The models of trade in manufactures studied in the last chapter showed how trade based on the exploitation of scale economies and product differentiation could satisfy tastes for diversity, raise real income, and benefit both parties even if factor proportions and tastes were identical. Not only do these models all suggest that some trade is a good thing, but that *free* trade is a good thing. Yet protection did not die out with the mercantilists; governments continue to protect their domestic industries to a greater or lesser extent in most countries, and popular opinion takes it as virtually axiomatic that it is irrational to import something that could be made at home. Is this simple ignorance, or are there qualifications to the case for free trade suggested by our models? The present chapter aims to answer that question.

5.1 Forms of Protection

Protection normally refers to an advantage afforded to domestic producers in competing against imports in the home markets, although a wide interpretation of the concept might also embrace export promotion. The typical method of protection involves levying a tariff (that is, a tax) on imports as they enter a country. It is most commonly levied as a specified *ad valorem* percentage of the value of imports, but may alternatively take the form of a specific duty (for example, so many pesos per kilogram).

There are, however, many other forms of protection. The principal alternatives are outlined below.

Quotas. A quota is a quantitative restriction, limiting imports of a particular good to a specified number of units, or to a certain total value, per period of time. Only those holding a license to import are allowed to bring goods into the country, and the sum of the licenses issued is set equal to the quota.

State Trading. Governments, especially, though not exclusively, those of a socialist or communist persuasion, sometimes grant monopoly importing rights in certain goods to state enterprises. The government can then reduce imports by administrative fiat—at least in principle. In reality, state enterprises can be distinctly truculent, and buy what they believe is in their interest rather than what the government believes to be in the national interest.

Exchange Controls. An exchange control is an administrative restriction on transactions involving foreign exchange. If exchange control is imposed on import payments, this means that only those with permission from the central bank to buy foreign exchange to pay for imports have the ability to import. Imports can be restricted by reducing the permits granted.

Import Prohibition. The strongest form of import control is a prohibition on the import of certain categories of goods—typically luxuries.

Buy-local Laws. Countries sometimes enact laws requiring that certain local goods be bought in preference to foreign ones whenever a comparable local product is available. This most commonly occurs with capital goods.

Nontariff Barriers. Although all the preceding forms of restriction involve methods other than tariffs, the phrase "nontariff barriers" has come to mean restrictions imposed by the bureaucracy as part of its normal functioning rather than through rules specifically promulgated against imports. In some cases there may be an explicit intention to discriminate against imports, as when a government imposes a "shadow tariff" on public sector purchases, that is, decides that it will buy imported goods only if they are more than x percent cheaper than the alternative. In other cases, protection may be an incidental result of the normal operations of the bureaucracy. For example, there may be some perfectly sensible tests of the safety standards of cars that must be passed before a model may be sold on the domestic market: it may just happen that it is more difficult and expensive for foreign cars to pass the tests, whether because the cars have to be shipped halfway around the world, the exporter's technicians don't speak the bureaucrats' language very well, or the foreigners aren't sure who has to be bribed or how much before anyone will bother to do the tests. And then there are intermediate cases where no one really knows whether the protective effect is intended or not: who can say whether a bureaucrat's willingness to buy a more expensive local product is due to his belief that its superior quality makes it the best buy, rather than to a surge of patriotism when he is spending someone else's money? Negotiators in the Tokyo Round of trade negotiations (see chapter 13.1) spent years just trying to define the nature of nontariff barriers as a necessary precondition to the establishment of any international control.

Each different form of protection has some distinctive economic effects. However, it would be tedious to develop a taxonomy of these. The relevant principles can be grasped by considering, first, the classic case of the tariff, and, second, the important alternative of the quota. The consequences of other protective instruments can then be deduced as an exercise in applied economics.

5.2 Tariffs

Consider a tariff at rate τ levied on the import of M. This will raise the price of the import good, p_m, in proportion above the world price, p_m^*, on the assumptions that the domestic M market is competitive and that imports of M continue:

$$p_m = (1 + \tau)p_m^*$$

Figure 5–1A shows the effect of such a rise in the price of goods M in country U in terms of the elementary demand and supply diagram. Without a tariff, the domestic price is equal to the world price p_m^* and hence domestic production is q_1 (determined by the domestic supply curve) and domestic consumption (determined by the demand curve) is q_4. The tariff raises the price to $(1 + \tau)p_m^*$, which stimulates production to q_2 and cuts consumption to q_3. The level of imports falls from $(q_4 - q_1)$ to $(q_3 - q_2)$.

There are many purposes for which the simple partial equilibrium analysis shown in figure 5–1A is perfectly adequate. This is the appropriate technique to use whenever one is considering a change in the tariff on an individual good. But there are also circumstances where the *ceteris paribus* assumptions that underlie partial equilibrium analysis are seriously vi-

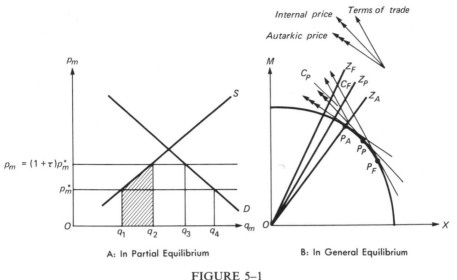

FIGURE 5–1
Displacement of Equilibrium by a Tariff

olated. This is the case, for example, when one is comparing a general policy of import substitution based on protection with a policy of free trade or export promotion. In such a case one needs to employ a general equilibrium analysis. In practice we resort to the simple two-good general equilibrium analysis developed in chapter 3.

Figure 5–1B shows the effect of a tariff in general equilibrium terms. P_A is the point of production and consumption under autarky; we know that this occurs where there is a social indifference curve tangential to the production possibility curve. From now on, however, it will be simpler to represent tastes by an income-consumption curve, rather than by the indifference curves themselves. An income-consumption curve consists of the locus of points of tangency between budget line and indifference curve as income is expanded with a fixed relative price; the assumption of identical homothetic tastes implies that each income-consumption curve is a straight line from the origin (that is, a ray). Thus the ray Z_A in figure 5–1B shows the consumption of X and M at various income levels when p_m/p_x is the autarkic price, such as to be tangential to the ppc at P_A. In particular, with the income generated by production at P_A, consumers will choose to buy the combination of goods represented by P_A, so that the autarkic economy would indeed be in equilibrium with the price that generates Z_A.

The world relative price of M is lower than the autarkic price (since our

77

country imports M). This lower price of M is represented in figure 5–1B by the terms of trade lines, which are steeper than the autarkic-price lines, since more M exchanges for a given quantity of X. At the lower price of M, consumers substitute M for X, so the income-consumption curve is steeper than the autarkic one, as shown by Z_F. Equilibrium under free trade is shown by production at P_F and consumption at C_F, both of which lie on the same budget line when the relative price is equal to the terms of trade. This is identical to the equilibrium in figure 3–8, except that preferences have been represented by income-consumption lines instead of by social-indifference curves. It involves country U producing more (less) X (M) than it consumes and exporting (importing) the difference, while trade remains balanced in value.

Next we have to consider the effect of the imposition of a nonprohibitive tariff, that is, a tariff that does not choke off imports completely. This has an effect on internal relative prices which is parallel to that in partial equilibrium analysis:

$$p_m/p_x = (1 + \tau) (p_m^*/p_x^*) = (1 + \tau) [1/(terms\ of\ trade)].$$

This means that the internal relative prices in U are represented by a set of price lines that are flatter than the terms of trade but steeper than the autarkic price, as shown by the set of price lines with double arrows in figure 5–1B. This price gives rise to an income-consumption line with intermediate slope, as shown by Z_p (P for *protection,* to match F for *free trade* and A for *autarky*). Equilibrium consumption must lie on the line Z_p with the tariff τ. And, of course, equilibrium production must occur at the point P_P where the with-tariff price line is tangential to the ppc. But the country trades along the terms of trade line P_PC_P, not along the internal price line from P_P.[1] The point is that consumers and producers are motivated by the internal with-tariff prices, but traders are nonetheless able to trade with foreigners at world prices. The country exports the excess of its X-production at P_P over its X-consumption at C_P, in exchange for the excess of its M-consumption at C_P over its M-production at P_P.

---

1. There is an implicit assumption here that the government redistributes the tariff revenue to consumers, and in a way that does not influence their perception of the relative price they are confronting in the market. If the government did not redistribute the revenue yielded by the tariff, or spend it itself, then society would not be able to trade up the terms-of-trade line P_pC_p. And if the government redistributed tariff proceeds according to how much each household had paid (which is a simple rule for preserving distributional neutrality) and households recognized the rule, they would realise that the true relative price confronting them was p_m^*/p_x^* instead of p_m/p_x.

5.3 Effects of a Tariff

In his famous textbook, *International Economics*, Charles Kindelberger (b. 1910) distinguished eight effects of a tariff. Seven of these are found in the small economy and will be analyzed here; the eighth is restricted to the large economy and therefore noted in the addendum to the chapter.

PRODUCTION EFFECT

As can be seen from both parts of figure 5–1, a tariff increases the output of the good M that receives protection. Figure 5–1B also shows explicitly that this increase in output of the protected good comes at the cost of a cut in the output of the nonprotected good X. This must be true so long as we are comparing full-employment efficient-factor-combination equilibria, which is exactly what are compared along the production possibility curve. In fact the same thing can be inferred from figure 5–1A, since the area under the supply curve represents the opportunity cost of the factors of production absorbed in M production. The shaded area represents the value of the factors withdrawn from the X industry (or, in general, from the rest of the economy), whose output must therefore fall on the full-employment assumption.

Other things being equal, the production effect reduces economic welfare. This can be seen most clearly in figure 5–1B; the set of consumption possibilities that are feasible with production at P_P is less extensive than the set that are attainable with production at P_F, given the terms of trade that are tangential to the ppc at that point. Hence it is proper to regard the change in production as a distortion—as something that prevents the marginal conditions for an optimum from being satisfied.[2] The distorting nature of the production change can also be seen in figure 5–1A, from the fact that the value of the resources absorbed in additional M production, represented by the shaded area, exceeds the value at world prices—and therefore at the social opportunity cost—of the additional output, which is the rectangular part of the shaded area, $p_m^* (q_2 - q_1)$. The triangular part of the shaded area, which with a linear supply curve is equal to $\frac{1}{2}\tau p_m^* (q_2 - q_1)$, represents the inefficiency induced by a tariff.

---

2. The relevant marginal condition is the requirement that the marginal rate of transformation (the slope of the ppc) be equal to the opportunity cost of one good in terms of the other in trade (the slope of the terms of trade line).

Since the above argument holds for any positive tariff, we have just shown that, other things being equal, free trade is desirable inasmuch as it avoids production inefficiencies. The next step is to consider what is hidden in the qualifying phrase "other things being equal." In principle, this requires that all the other conditions for a Pareto optimum hold, since the theory of the second best says that satisfaction of one marginal condition does not necessarily improve welfare unless all other marginal conditions are already satisfied. Since they never are—there are always distortions elsewhere in the economy—some purist-minded theorists have in effect drawn the conclusion that one can never legitimately say anything about the desirability of policy changes, such as liberalizing trade. Applied economists perforce have to be more pragmatic: they take the attitude that one disregards such second-best considerations *unless there are specific reasons for believing that there are divergences between social and private costs or benefits,* in which case one does one's best to quantify the deviations and evaluate their policy implications. That is the attitude that will be taken here.

Historically, support for protective tariffs has been based on two arguments (infant industry and strategic), which have asserted that in specific circumstances the social benefits of a high level of domestic production of a good exceed the private benefits.

The *infant-industry argument* faults the standard analysis for treating the production possibility curve as exogenous. The argument is that it is difficult for industry to establish itself in an underdeveloped country—such as England was when the argument was used in the reign of Elizabeth I or Germany was when the argument was popularized by its most famous exponent, Friedrich List (1789–1846)—if it has to face the blast of free competition from established industries elsewhere. Even though domestic production may be relatively inefficient in the short run, it is argued that there is a long-run national advantage in establishing or extending the industrial base as a necessary condition for economic development. Hence it may be desirable to nurture an infant industry that has the potential of becoming viable in time. Most economists accept that this may make sense, although a handful of the most dedicated disciples of free markets are prepared to argue that any industry that is potentially profitable to a country would also be potentially profitable to capitalist investors and should therefore not need pampering by protection. There are various counterarguments, such as the assertion that society can rationally accept a degree of risk that appears prohibitive to an individual entrepreneur because society is in a position to pool a number of such risks, and the argument that a part of the costs of being a pioneer is the cost of training a suitable labor force which cannot be guaranteed to stay with the firm that provides the training (at least in a nonslave society). But even those who accept these counterarguments are usually anxious to qualify the infant-industry argument by emphasizing (1) that it is not worth succoring an infant unless one expects it to develop into a healthy adult that will no longer need the prop of protection, and (2) that one should always ask whether tariffs are a better way of providing support than, say, a subsidy to internal production (this point will be discussed further in section 5.4).

The *strategic argument* is that certain industries are needed for national security and therefore confer a social benefit greater than the private benefits. Armaments industries are an obvious example (at least according to the concept of social benefits customarily taken for granted by national governments). Agriculture was another traditional European example, not just to feed the populace in time of war but also because peasants were supposed to make more dependable cannon fodder than proletarians. There obviously exist (rather common) value judgments that legitimize this argument, but economists may still be able to perform the social function of pointing out the frightening price tags sometimes attached to programs justified in the name of national security or of investigating the cost effectiveness of stockpiling rather than producing a strategic commodity.

CONSUMPTION EFFECT

Figure 5–1A (or 5–2A) shows that the tariff will reduce consumption of the protected good, from q_4 to q_3. Figure 5–1B also shows that consumption of M must decline, due to two reinforcing effects; the income effect[3] (real income declines from the level represented by $P_F C_F$ to that represented by $P_P C_P$), and the substitution effect of M becoming more expensive relative to X. Conversely, what happens to consumption of X is ambiguous: the income effect tending to reduce consumption will work in the opposite direction to the substitution effect, since X will be cheaper. In an n-good model the income effect would be rather unimportant, but ambiguity about the sign of the effect on the consumption of products other than that on which the tariff was imposed would remain, the effect depending on whether goods were substitutes or complements to the good with the tariff.

Figure 5–2B provides an enlarged view of the critical part of figure 5–1B, showing the consumption possibility line $P_P C_P$ (with slope determined by the terms of trade) from the production point P_P as before. We showed that consumers would select the point C_P on that line, on the income-consump-

3. Assuming that M is not an inferior good.

tion curve Z_P which holds when consumers confront the internal prices represented by the double-arrowed lines. But suppose that consumers confronted the world prices that represent social opportunity costs rather than internal prices; they would then choose a consumption point on the income-consumption curve Z_F (which holds with free trade prices). They would therefore choose the point C_J. It is easy to see that C_J lies on a higher indifference curve than C_P, since the indifference curve at C_J is tangential to $P_P C_J$, while that at C_P cuts $P_P C_J$ (and is tangential to the internal price line). The difference between the indifference curves at C_J and C_P represents the cost of the consumption distortion. Once again, it can also be measured in the partial equilibrium diagram (see fig. 5–2A). The utility value of consumption is represented by the area under the demand curve, so the reduction in that value is represented by the area of the quadrilateral JHq_4q_3. Of this, the square GHq_4q_3 represents the social value of the resources released by this reduction in consumption, while the triangle JGH represents the social waste stemming from the consumption distortion.

It is difficult to think of a reason why a government would welcome a consumption distortion. If it believes that consumption of a good is too high because of social costs in excess of private costs (the costs of publicly provided medical care for cancer caused by cigarette smoking, for example), the appropriate remedy is a tax on *all* consumption, not just on consumption of imports. It is true that governments sometimes act in a way which looks as though they think consumption of imports deserves to be discouraged: wine-growing countries tend to tax whisky more heavily than wine, for example. But what they are probably seeking is the production effect on wine, to placate their wine lobby, rather than the consumption effect on whisky.

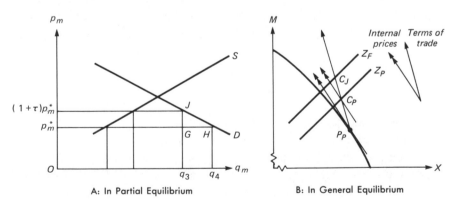

A: In Partial Equilibrium

B: In General Equilibrium

FIGURE 5–2
Consumption Distortion

Protection

Many economists have argued that, in order to avoid the consumption distortion, it would be better to protect a deserving infant industry by giving it a production subsidy rather than a tariff. In fact this provides one example of a general principle known as the theory of optimal intervention in the presence of distortions: one taxes or subsidizes the specific thing that one wishes to discourage or encourage. If one wishes to establish an infant industry, one subsidizes its output and thus avoids the social loss involved in having consumers cut back their consumption of a good to a point where its marginal utility exceeds its social opportunity cost. The same principle provides one of the arguments in favor of a tax on cigarette consumption rather than a tariff as a means of discouraging consumption: a tariff would stimulate domestic production at costs in excess of the social opportunity cost of imports and thus create an unnecessary production distortion.

REVENUE EFFECT

Imposition of a nonprohibitive tariff yields revenue to the government. The quantity of this revenue can be seen very easily in the partial equilibrium diagram, as the value of the tariff multiplied by the volume of imports, $(\tau p_m^*) \, (q_3 - q_2)$ in figure 5–1A. (In the general equilibrium diagram of figure 5–1B, the effect of the tariff revenue would be to restrict consumers to a budget line equal to the internal price line tangential to the ppc at P_P, but the question then arises as to what the government does with the tariff revenues. As stated in note 1 above, the theory makes the rather artificial assumption that the government gives it all back to consumers in a nondistortionary way so that their budget line is $P_P C_P$. Thus the general equilibrium analysis abstracts from the revenue effect.)

Governments need to raise revenue somehow, and any method of doing so involves collection costs. These include the costs of tax administration to the government and also the costs imposed on the taxpayers in complying with the tax law while minimizing their tax burdens. In addition, virtually any tax imposes distortions. Taxes on particular products create a consumption distortion exactly like that analyzed in the previous section. Even income taxes distort the choice between income and leisure. There is still an unfortunate tradition in international economics of glibly supposing that governments have unlimited powers to raise lump-sum taxes and give lump-sum subsidies at zero cost, which suppresses these considerations. The correct procedure is to compare the collection costs and distortions involved in raising revenue through a tariff with those involved in raising revenue in alternative possible ways.

In some countries this can provide a respectable case for tariffs, or even more for export taxes, since these happen to be among the easiest of all taxes to administer—they need only a handful of bureaucrats stationed at a limited number of ports (or points) of entry and exit, administering relatively straightforward rules on well-documented and easily inspected consignments. Countries at an early stage of development with limited trained manpower to devote to tax raising and few import-competing industries have traditionally relied on tariffs as a major instrument for revenue raising, and this is perfectly rational, since the production distortion is absent and the consumption distortion is created by *any* indirect tax. As development proceeds the case against tariffs grows stronger, since the establishment of import-competing industries means that, once the infant-industry stage is passed, tariffs involve a production distortion, while the growing ability to administer alternative taxes implies that there is less need to rely on tariff revenue. But even in semi-industrial countries the fact that a tariff raises revenue while a subsidy makes a call on the government budget tends to count against the use of a production subsidy in preference to a tariff as an instrument in support of infant-industries. It can, however, be shown that in principle it is better to protect with subsidies and then to finance those with tariffs and export taxes specifically chosen to minimize distortions, rather than relying on one set of tariffs to both protect and raise revenue.

INCOME DISTRIBUTION EFFECT

The Stolper-Samuelson theorem revealed that a tariff influences the distribution of income. Specifically, the theorem states that, with perfect factor mobility in the Heckscher-Ohlin model, a tariff would benefit the country's scarce factor of production and penalize its abundant factor of production. The intuitive reason is that exports augment the derived demand for the abundant factor and imports relieve the scarcity of the scarce factor, and that a tariff impedes trade and therefore reverses those two influences. However, subsequent discussion in chapter 3 also established that this conclusion was quite sensitive to the assumption of perfect factor mobility. If there were zero mobility between industries, then all the factors in the industry gaining protection would gain real income, and all those in the other industry would lose. We also found that with one factor mobile in the short run and the other not, it was possible for the mobile factor to gain real income in the short run even though it would lose in the long run. In chapter 4 it was concluded that the presence or absence of tariffs between countries with similar factor endowments does not have any strong effects on income distribution. One may conclude that it would be necessary to have a considerable amount of empirical knowledge of an economy—of factor intensities, factor endowments, and factor mobility—before it would be possible to predict the effect of a tariff on the distribution of income.

The fact that tariffs influence the distribution of income does not mean that their impact is a desirable one, still less that they provide an efficient instrument for influencing income distribution. On the contrary, it can be shown that they are in general not the best way of redistributing income. The theory of optimal intervention again indicates that the best policy to redistribute income is to employ taxes and subsidies on income, and for the net revenue loss to be financed in the minimum-distortion way (allowing for collection costs).

COMPETITIVE EFFECT

It was possible to demonstrate all the preceding four effects in terms of the Heckscher-Ohlin model (although none of them is specific to that model). This is not possible in the present case, since the Heckscher-Ohlin model assumes perfect competition with or without a tariff. But in reality perfect competition is pretty much confined to agriculture and the financial markets, while the markets for most industrial products and most services are oligopolistic or monopolistically competitive. In such markets the degree of competition can be drastically reduced by the effective exclusion of imports from the domestic market through high protection. This effect is most important in small economies, where the domestic market is large enough to support only one or two producers at an efficient scale of operations. If competition from imports is effectively excluded by very high tariffs (or in other ways), the domestic producers face little incentive to keep down prices or to pursue efficiency in production.

It is rather difficult to think of reasons why society as a whole might be expected to benefit by shielding domestic producers against foreign competition. But the producers themselves can be expected to favor such shielding and to wield their political influence (and in some cases other instruments, varying from personal friendships to bribery) to establish, enhance, or perpetuate it.

INCOME EFFECT AND BALANCE OF PAYMENTS EFFECT

We come finally to two effects that arise when we relax the assumption on which the preceding model-building has been based, and which can

85

conveniently be treated together. The first is the effect on the level of *income* and employment. This has been excluded from the analysis up to now by the assumption that the economy is always on the production possibility curve, but of course this is not always true: unemployment occurs in the real world and is represented in the model by production at a point inside the ppc. A tariff is one of a number of ways in which income and output can be stimulated (as will be discussed in the balance of payments theory in chapter 8). The second is the effect on the *balance of payments*. This has been excluded from the analysis up to now by the assumption that trade is always balanced (which is represented in the general equilibrium diagram by the fact that the country always exchanges exports for imports along its terms-of-trade line). The macroeconomic analysis of chapter 8 will demonstrate that relaxation of this assumption leads to the expectation that imposition of a tariff will improve the balance of payments on current account, at least in the short run.

Since restoring income to full employment and improving the balance of payments are generally regarded as good, it might seem that these macroeconomic considerations provide a powerful case for protection. This view is not widely held by economists.[4] The reason is that there are other policies that can be used to restore a satisfactory macroeconomic equilibrium, notably fiscal policy, monetary policy, and exchange-rate policy. These alternative policies involve the use of macroeconomic instruments, which are superior to the microeconomic instruments (like protection) for attaining macroeconomic ends in three respects. First, they do not involve the creation of microeconomic distortions in production and consumption (the first two effects analyzed). Devaluation, which is an alternative to increased tariffs from the macroeconomic point of view, stimulates exports and reduces imports evenly, while tariffs act only on the import side (and may even reduce exports because of increased tariffs on inputs). Second, macroeconomic instruments generally involve much smaller shifts in the structure of production when policy must be adjusted in order to offset shocks. (Just imagine the adjustment costs that would be involved if every cyclical downturn was met by increased protection, which was then reversed a year or two later when the economy picked up!) Third, they are less likely to involve policy conflicts between countries—a policy of increased protection to counter a recession would worsen other countries' recessions, which would be a sure recipe for international tension, given the stylised fact that the business cycle is internationally synchronized (see chap. 17).

4. It is, however, a point of view argued by the Cambridge Economic Policy Group.

Protection

5.4 Evaluation of the Case for Tariffs

Most economists, since the time of Adam Smith, have been hostile to protection. The basic argument is that there are other and superior methods of obtaining the *macroeconomic* objectives that can be furthered by tariff protection, while the latter involves accepting *microeconomic* distortions in production and consumption and limitations on competition, all of which involve a reduction in welfare.

Several possible reasons for overriding the general presumption against tariffs have attracted the support of economists, notably the infant-industry argument, the strategic argument, and the revenue effect. The circumstances under which tariffs are the first-best policy for furthering those objectives are, however, quite limited. For example, there may be a good reason for establishing an infant industry, but this could not occur without intervention because the costs of labor training would be high and the pioneering firm would be unable to prevent competition bidding away labor once it had been trained. Then the best policy would be to subsidize the cost of labor training. This first-best policy would eliminate the divergence between social and private cost without creating further distortions. The second-best policy would be to subsidize production: the disadvantage of this is that firms would not have the right incentive to provide labor training. Tariffs, which bring a consumption distortion as well, would be only third best. Without taking account of collection costs, at least, it is very difficult to find circumstances in which tariffs seem to be a first-best policy. And even when collection costs are taken into account, it requires something of a coincidence for tariffs to provide a desirable method of *protection* (though they may form a part of an efficient *tax structure*).

5.5 Effective Protection

Suppose our country has a 20 percent import tariff on footwear, while the tariff on clothes is only 10 percent. At first glance it might appear that the producers of footwear are being more heavily protected than the clothing manufacturers. In fact, this is by no means necessarily true. The tariff on the final good that competes with the industry's output tells only part of the story about how much protection the industry is receiving.

The other element is the tariff the industry must pay on the *inputs* that it buys.

To see why this is important, let us assume that 50 percent of the costs of both industries consisted of imported materials and that the tariff on leather was 40 percent while that on textiles was zero. The footwear industry would then find that its 20 percent tariff on shoes was all used to pay for the 40 percent addition to the cost of the leather it has to buy, leaving it with zero effective protection. In contrast, the clothing industry does not have to pay tariffs on its inputs, so its apparently modest protection of 10 percent survives to give real—or effective—protection to the value added in the clothes-making industry. The industry with the lower nominal tariff therefore receives the higher effective protection.

The concept of effective protection was developed primarily by the Australian economist Max Corden (b. 1927) and the Canadian Harry Johnson (1923–77). The rate of effective protection is defined as the proportionate increase in value added in an industry that is possible as a result of the whole structure of protection, on both the output and the input of the industry. The basic formula for measuring the rate of effective protection, τ_e, is

$$\tau_e = (\tau_1 - \omega\tau_2)/(1 - \omega)$$

where τ_1 = tariff rate on output,

τ_2 = tariff rate on input,

ω = proportion of total price accounted for by inputs.

While the formula looks simple enough, the problems of actually measuring effective protection are formidable. A first problem is that any given industry will usually face a variety of tariff rates on its output and certainly on the several inputs that it buys, so that both τ_1 and τ_2 must be measured as weighted averages rather than simply looked up in the tariff regulations. A second difficulty is that where an input is also supplied locally, its price need not rise by the full amount of the tariff if domestic supply increases to the point where imports are eliminated. But it would be wrong to then reduce ω to reflect the fall in the import component, since domestic input supplies are also more expensive as a result of the tariff. What is needed is an estimate of the extent to which the cost of input rises as a result of the tariff. A third difficulty is that the calculations should also include implicit protection given by quotas and the effects of taxes and subsidies.

Despite the difficulties, a lot of serious work has gone into the measurement of effective protection. Three important general conclusions have emerged. The first is that the differences between nominal and effective rates of protection are substantial: use of the former to measure the protection given to an industry is likely to be highly misleading. The second is that effective rates of protection are generally highly uneven. The impact of protection on resource allocation is determined largely by *relative* effective rates of protection, which lends importance to the third finding: that there is a rather general tendency for the industrial countries (at least) to give more protection to the final stages of production. In other words, the tariff on leather is typically less than that on shoes, implying that the domestic footwear industry receives more effective protection than the nominal tariff would suggest. Since the final stages of production tend to be those involving the more advanced technology, this is a factor making it more difficult for the NICs to diversify their exports into technologically more sophisticated products.

5.6   Export Subsidies and Taxes

Before turning to the analysis of quota protection, it is worth noting the similarities and differences between import tariffs and export subsidies. An export subsidy is a payment made to exporters: it typically takes the form of a payment of a certain proportion (say μ) of the value of the goods exported (where the proportion μ may be based on the taxes on average incurred in the production of the good involved). Payment of such a subsidy increases the internal price of X to $(1 + \mu)p_x^*$, where p_x^* is the world price (the price in the large country W). The impact of this on the internal market for X is shown in partial equilibrium terms in figure 5–3A. To find the effect in general equilibrium terms, note that the ratio of internal relative prices is

$$(p_x/p_m) = (1 + \mu)\,p_x^*/p_m^* = (1 + \mu)\,(terms\ of\ trade)$$

so that the internal price line is steeper than the terms-of-trade line, as shown in figure 5–3B. Note that an equal tariff τ on the import good and export subsidy μ on the export good would cancel out, leaving no net effect on relative prices or therefore on equilibrium.[5]

The production effect of an export subsidy is exactly symmetrical to that of an import tariff: it increases the output of the export good, from q_3 to q_4 in figure 5–3A and from the point represented by P_F to that represented

5. This conclusion relates to equilibrium: there would be macroeconomic effects out of equilibrium, since both changes would tend to stimulate income and create a payments surplus.

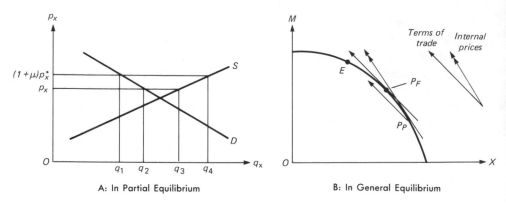

FIGURE 5–3

Effect of an Export Subsidy

by P_P in figure 5–3B, and in the process cuts output of M. One can use exactly the same argument as before to show that this production effect must in general be considered a distortion: in particular, the set of consumption possibilities attainable along the terms of trade line from P_P is dominated by the set attainable along the terms of trade line tangential to the ppc at P_F. Once again, also, one might wish to argue that it makes sense to give an export subsidy to help establish a particular industry with export potential in foreign markets—an infant-export-industry argument. There might also be circumstances in which strategic considerations would point to the desirability of maintaining excess capacity, which might conceivably be most economically achieved by subsidizing exports.

The consumption effect is also symmetrical: it involves an unambiguous fall in the consumption of X, from q_2 to q_1 in figure 5–3A, and by an amount that could be, but is not, shown in figure 5–3B. The effect is unambiguous because both the income and the substitution effect contribute to depressing the consumption of X. The effect on the consumption of M is, however, ambiguous, since the income effect is negative while the substitution effect is positive. The same argument as before can be used to show that the change in consumption, from the point that would result if consumers were allowed to trade at the terms of trade to the point that they would choose if they confronted internal prices, results in a lower level of welfare. That is, the consumption effect again produces a distortion.

While a tariff brings in revenue to the government, an export subsidy increases government expenditure. This is no doubt one reason why export subsidies are less popular policy instruments than tariffs.

The effects on the distribution of income are again symmetrical. That is,

90

with perfect factor mobility the abundant factor would benefit and the scarce factor would lose, while with industry-specific factors those employed in the X industry would gain and those in the M industry would lose.

A major difference between import tariffs and export subsidies stems from the effect on competition. A tariff, especially in a small country, serves to shield local producers from foreign competition and to induce production of a range of products each produced on an inefficiently small scale. An export subsidy serves to give local producers an advantage on the world market, but it still pays them to produce a limited range of products on an efficient scale.

The macroeconomic effects of tariffs and of export subsidies are identical. Both serve to stimulate income and to improve the balance of payments, subject to *ceteris paribus* assumptions that will become explicit in the course of part III.

The analysis of an export tax is now easy. The domestic price of a particular good whose export is taxed would fall: in terms of the partial equilibrium diagram, the internal price line would lie below the external price line by a distance representing the export tax. If all exports were taxed (equally), so that an analysis in terms of general equilibrium were appropriate, the effect would be to make the internal price line flatter than the terms of trade line, exactly as in the case of a tariff on M. There is indeed a famous theorem, called the Lerner Symmetry theorem, after the English-born economist Abba Lerner (b. 1903), which asserts that a uniform export tax is equivalent to a uniform import tariff exactly on those grounds. It is important to understand that this is a microeconomic theorem, relating to the comparison between two positions of equilibrium; the macroeconomic effects on income or the balance of payments are of course exactly opposite. It is also worth bearing in mind that uniform tariffs and subsidies are analytical abstractions rather than realistic policy options: it is particularly difficult to tax all invisibles, and not even clear whether it is always conceptually appropriate (for example, on interest or dividend payments or on emigrants' remittances).

It may sound paradoxical, but there are many economists who would nowadays argue that the best method of providing infant-industry protection in a developing country is often to tax traditional exports. The symmetry theorem says that that is equivalent to granting an import tariff: to understand why let us anticipate the macroeconomic analysis to come and say that the export tax will depreciate the currency and so protect import-competing industries. The export tax raises revenue and encourages the promotion of nontraditional exports equally with import substitution (see chap. 11).

5.7 Quotas

A second way of providing protection to an import-competing industry is through the imposition of an import quota. An import quota is a *quantitative* restriction of the amount that can be imported: so many thousand tons of butter or so many cars or whatever. (Sometimes the quota is expressed in value terms, so many millions of pesos worth of trucks. This is most common where the product is sufficiently heterogeneous that a significant amplification of the value of imports through an upgrading of the quality of the products imported would be possible if the quota were expressed in physical terms.)

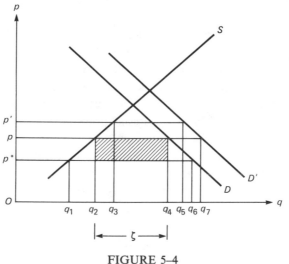

FIGURE 5–4
Effects of an Import Quota

In figure 5–4 the demand and supply curves for some product are illustrated by D and S and an import quota equal to ξ is imposed. Assuming that ξ is less than the quantity that would be imported under free trade, so that the quota does indeed provide protection, the result will be an equilibrium where the horizontal distance between the demand and supply curves is equal to ξ. The price will therefore rise above the free trade level p^* to a point p where the joint effect of the increased supply and reduced demand is to cut back imports to ξ (or $q_4 - q_2$), in contrast to the free trade level of imports of $(q_6 - q_1)$.

These effects are exactly the same as those that would have resulted from the imposition of a tariff τ equal to $(p/p^* - 1)$, that is, a tariff whose value

τp^* would be represented by the distance $(p - p^*)$ in figure 5-4. Both would result in a rise in domestic production from q_1 to q_2, a fall in domestic consumption from q_6 to q_4, a rise in the internal price from p^* to p, and the same volume and value of imports. For this reason the tariff τ is said to be *equivalent* to the quota ξ: *ceteris paribus* they have the same effects on prices and quantities, given the assumption of perfect competition. Because of this equivalence, it is unnecessary to examine the general equilibrium effects of a quota. At this level of abstraction they are identical to those of the equivalent tariff.

However, the equivalence of a quota and a tariff is a result that needs to be used with care; a lot hangs on the *ceteris paribus* and perfect competition qualifications noted above. Once one relaxes those restrictions, three major differences between the effects of a tariff and those of a quota emerge.

1. A first difference concerns their implications for *government revenue*. We saw earlier that with a tariff the shaded area in figure 5–4 accrues to the government as revenue. But with a quota this is not, in general, the case. If the government distributes import licenses (the sum of which is of course equal to the quota) to importers free, which is the normal practice, then it is the lucky importers who will get the shaded area—for they will be able to buy on the world market at price p^* and sell on the domestic market at price p, pocketing the difference. It is only if the government *sells* import licenses for what the market will bear, which under competitive conditions means for the equivalent tariff, that the profits generated by an import quota could be recouped by the government and this difference would be eliminated. Countries have occasionally done just this, by auctioning off import licenses: Brazil and Iran in the 1950s are the two leading examples.

2. A second difference concerns the reaction to a *shift in demand or supply*; in technical jargon, the comparative statics implications. Consider the case of a shift in demand from D to D' as shown in figure 5–4. With a tariff, consumption would expand to q_7 by virtue of an increase in imports of $(q_7 - q_4)$. In contrast, a quota prevents the increase in imports, and hence the price rises instead to p' in order to ration the available supply (which can increase only through a rise in domestic output) in the face of the increase in demand. Thus shifts in demand (or for that matter in supply) provoke changes in the *quantity* of imports with a tariff and changes in the internal *price* with a quota. (After such a shift there is still, of course, a tariff that is equivalent to the quota, but it is a different tariff.) Governments with a strong inclination toward central planning tend to regard this difference as an advantage for a system of quotas, since their use ensures that the volume of imports does not depart from the planned level 'just' because demand or supply were forecast incorrectly. Mainstream economists regard

this as superficial: they argue that higher or lower levels of demand or supply signify that the good has a higher or lower social value than had been supposed, and thus that the quantity *should* be allowed to adjust, as permitted by the tariff.

3. A third difference concerns secondary distortions introduced through the need to allocate import licenses. This is a point whose importance has only come to be recognized in recent years, following an important research project comparing the trade and payments policies of a number of developing countries that was carried out under the joint direction of the Indian economist Jagdish Bhagwati (b. 1934) and Anne Krueger (b. 1934). Unless import licenses are auctioned, some bureaucrat has to decide *who* is to receive them. Since import licenses are valuable—each one is worth $(p - p^*)$—it is probable that some importers will seek ways of bribing the bureaucrat into allocating more to them. But suppose that the country has a civil service full of scrupulously honest persons dedicated to the pursuit of social good rather than of private gain, as in the best Fabian fables. They still have to decide how maximizing the social good translates into dividing the import quota between rival claimants. They may be relied on to avoid the obvious error of giving all the licenses to one or two firms, who could then collude to import less than permitted and drive the price up to monopolistic levels. Much more likely is that they will seek to make judgments about which industries are socially meritorious or which types of end use (investment or exports rather than consumption) deserve support or which regions or which types of firms (state rather than private enterprises) are most deserving. Even accepting that such judgments can be made, allocating import licenses is not an efficient way of putting them into effect. The reason is that the value of a particular good varies: what may be a crucial input to a consumption goods industry may be a marginal frill to some investment project. As noted in the earlier discussion of optimal intervention, the most efficient way to promote something is generally to subsidize it directly rather than to give it special privileges that may be of greater value to others. Or else the bureaucrat may seek some objective basis for distributing the licenses, such as in relation to capacity or to use in some base period (for imports of intermediate goods). The former gives an incentive to expand capacity, not where more capacity is socially needed but in order to qualify for more import licenses. This could help explain why India (a country that has relied heavily on quota protection) has such a high ICOR[6] for a country at its stage of development. The latter leads to a freezing of industrial structure; progressive firms cannot get the input they need to expand more rapidly than others.

6. Incremental capital output ratio.

Protection

In short, no matter how conscientious the bureaucrat, it is virtually impossible for him to distribute the licenses without creating secondary distortions. And the evidence is that the cost of these distortions is typically much more than marginal.

There are probably few areas of economics where the conclusions are as clear-cut as here: if one is going to protect, careful thought should be given to whether subsidies would be better than tariffs, but certainly a tariff would be better than a quota; and if one insists on using a quota, then the licenses should be auctioned off.

5.8 Customs Unions and Free Trade Areas

A customs union is a group of countries among whom there is free trade and who have a common tariff barrier against the rest of the world. A free trade area shares the feature of internal free trade, but does not involve the members standardizing their tariffs against the rest of the world. The leading historical examples of customs unions are the Zollverein, first formed in 1834 and which led up to German unification, and in our day the European Economic Community (EEC). Free trade areas have included the European Free Trade Area (EFTA) and the Andean Group. Free trade areas have had a tendency to be partial rather than complete, in regard to both the coverage of products and the extent to which tariffs have been cut.

The theory of customs unions and of free trade areas is almost identical; but the analysis of a free trade area is slightly simpler. To analyze a free trade area one needs to consider at least *three* countries—the two who form the free trade area and the one that is excluded. (Without the first two there is no free trade area, and without the third we would be back to the case of free trade, already studied.) Consider, therefore, the formation of a free trade area between our country U and a neighboring country V, and let the excluded country be the large country called W.

The central concepts of customs union theory, introduced by the Canadian economist Jacob Viner (1892–1970), are trade creation and trade diversion. *Trade creation* occurs when a country starts to import a good that it previously produced at home, while *trade diversion* occurs when a country starts to import from a partner country a good that it previously imported from the outside world. The concepts can be illustrated in the simplest Ricardian model with constant opportunity costs. Consider U's trade in a particular good with production cost equal to c_u in U, c_v in V, and c_w in W. Prior to formation of the free trade area, country

U's supply would come from whichever area had the minimum cost to the consumer:

$$c_u; (1 + \tau)c_v; (1 + \tau)c_w$$

where τ is the tariff rate. On the formation of the free trade area, the tariff on imports from V is withdrawn, so that imports would come from the minimum of

$$c_u; c_v; (1 + \tau)c_w.$$

Since the cost of buying from the partner country falls while the costs of buying from the other two areas remain constant,[7] imports from V may be stimulated. Specifically, if

$$(1 + \tau)c_v > c_u > c_v$$

and the country previously produced the good itself rather than imported from W, then in the new situation it will cease domestic production and import instead from its partner V. This is trade creation. If, on the other hand,

$$(1 + \tau)c_w > c_v > c_w$$

and the country previously imported from W rather than producing the good itself, then in the new situation it will buy from V instead of W. This is trade diversion. The concepts are, however, in no way restricted to the Ricardian constant-cost model. Trade expansion with the partner country will still be trade creation so long as it involves an expansion in the total level of trade, and it will still be trade diversion when it involves the redirection of trade from third countries, even if the industries involved face increasing costs due to factor substitution or decreasing costs due to increasing returns to scale, or if they are imperfectly competitive.

Trade creation implies that the country has replaced expensive (domestic) supply by cheaper (partner-country) imports. *Ceteris paribus,* that produces a welfare gain. The magnitude of that gain can be shown in the partial equilibrium tariff diagram (see fig. 5–5), which is drawn for simplicity on the assumption that V as well as W is large relative to U. Prior

7. This is where the analysis of a customs union differs from that of a free trade area. Establishment of a common external tariff implies that in general the tariff on imports from outside the area will change. If it falls, there is the possibility that the country will start importing from W a good that was previously produced at home: this is called "external trade creation." If it rises, the country may start to produce what it previously imported from W: this may be termed "external trade destruction."

to formation of the free trade area, U was producing q_2 at the supply price $c_u = (1 + \tau)c_v$, and consuming q_3. Following trade liberalization, price (equals cost) falls to c_v, production falls to q_1, consumption rises to q_4, and imports rise to $(q_4 - q_1)$. Welfare is given by the area under the demand curve: it rises by $q_3 q_4 ZX$, which consists of the cost of extra imports of $q_3 q_4 ZY$ and a net benefit (consumer's surplus) of the triangle XYZ. The cost of domestic production falls by the reduction of the area under the supply curve, which consists of $q_1 q_2 KH$; of this, $q_1 q_2 JH$ represents the cost of the additional imports, while the triangle HJK is a net social saving. Consumer expenditure also falls by $c_u c_v HK$ and $KJYX$, but these represent transfers rather than pure social benefits; the former are profits foregone by producers of the good in question, while the latter is the tariff revenue lost by the government. Thus the net social gain is the two small triangles. On the assumption of linear demand and supply curves, this is equal to half the tariff suppressed multiplied by the volume of trade created—a number that can be sensibly estimated with relative ease.

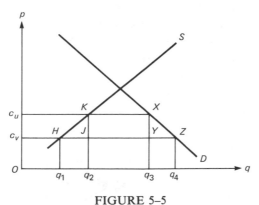

FIGURE 5–5
Welfare Gain from Trade Creation

Trade diversion implies that the country has replaced cheap imports from the outside world by expensive imports from its new partner. This is clearly disadvantageous. The loss in welfare can again be estimated as half the tariff whose removal stimulated the redirection of trade, multiplied by the volume of trade diversion.

Empirical studies of common markets and free trade areas have suggested that trade creation has predominated (by as much as 4 to 1 in the case of the EEC) in integration among developed countries. Even where trade creation was overwhelming, however, many economists (especially Harry Johnson) have argued that integration is of minimal quantitative importance. Trade is typically 20 percent of GNP; the intratrade being liberalized is perhaps a half of total trade; it may be expected to expand by 50 percent odd;[8] and the tariff removed is at most 10 percent on average. Therefore, applying the formula for the benefit of trade creation and ignoring the losses for trade diversion, we have a potential gain of the order of 0.25 percent of GNP. Double any of the estimates and the gain is still derisory. And for integration movements between developing countries the theory indicates losses rather than gains of any size, inasmuch as the empirical estimates have typically suggested a predominance of trade diversion rather than creation.

This theory is, however, seriously incomplete. First, the above calculations ignore the favorable effect on the terms of trade of increased exports. There is no contradiction between the assumptions that the country is small and can sell all it wants to at the world price, and the assumption that it would get better prices if it had tariff-free access to foreign markets. A study by the Canadians Paul and Ronald Wonnacott (b. 1933, b. 1930) suggested that as much as two-thirds of the benefits to Canada of free trade with the United States would come from this source. Second, figure 5–5 shows the welfare gain realized from additional trade in increasing-cost Heckscher-Ohlin goods, not in decreasing-cost differentiated products. Some fairly major extensions of the theory are needed to take account of this type of case. It is necessary, for example, to recognize that a country which is able to capture its partners' market will benefit from a *cost-reduction effect* enabling it to supply its domestic market more cheaply. Because of this, the welfare gain can quite easily exceed the increase in trade multiplied by the size of the tariff removed. Empirical evidence shows that it is mainly this type of trade that has expanded as a result of trade liberalization among industrial countries. This is not to claim that common markets are a magic key to instant wealth, but it is to suggest that their benefits can amount to a useful several percent of GNP rather than a derisory fraction of 1 percent.

It is commonly held that attempts at trade integration among developing countries have failed (see chap. 13.2). Not only does the statistical evidence suggest that trade diversion may have exceeded trade creation, but members have often squabbled bitterly about the distribution of new industry attracted by the enlarged market. The conclusion that these facts show the attempt at integration to have been misguided can, however, be challenged. Countries on the road to industrialization generally want to establish infant industries: their aim in forming a common market or free trade area is to

8. That was the estimate officially accepted in the British White Paper of 1971 on the effect of British entry to the EEC (*The United Kingdom and the European Communities,* Cmnd 4715, July 1971).

provide a bigger market to permit them to establish and expand infant industries more rapidly, and/or more cheaply, than would otherwise be possible. Another name for the establishment of your own infant industry would be *trade destruction*—the opposite of trade creation. And establishment of an infant industry in your partner's country, from which you then buy, involves trade diversion. In other words, the fact that trade diversion exceeds trade creation is not necessarily a sign of failure at all; if the aim of the union is the promotion of import-substituting industrialization, it is in fact consistent with success! But that success does not guarantee that the members will all be happy with the result of integration. Even when it is collectively desired, trade diversion still involves a cost to the importer, who has to pay more. Members gain (assuming infant-industry collective import substitution to be rational) when new industries are established in their country and lose when they are established in their partner's. No wonder they squabble about the location of new industry! But that does not prove that the task they attempted was foolish, it just shows that it is inherently more difficult to maintain a balance from which all members gain than it is when integration occurs between countries each of which already has a full industrial structure so that mutual gain can flow from increased intraindustry trade in differentiated products.

5.9 Summary

In general, there is a presumption that free trade maximizes economic efficiency and therefore economic welfare: what has been called the central theorem of trade and welfare states that laissez faire is Pareto-efficient for a perfectly competitive economy with no monopoly power in trade. There are, however, circumstances under which most economists accept that a measure of protection may be rational; notably to support infant industries or strategic industries or to raise revenue. There are strong reasons for believing that tariffs are a more efficient way of providing protection than are quotas. The theory of optimal intervention suggests that a production subsidy would often be even better—especially when revenue considerations can be ignored.

A customs union or free trade area could in principle diminish economic welfare, as a result of trade diversion outweighing trade creation. Evidence suggests that this has not happened in unions between developed countries. It may well have occurred in trading arrangements involving developing countries, but, while that explains the tensions such arrangements have encountered, it does not imply they failed, inasmuch as the main purpose was that of promoting infant industries through providing them with a joint market.

5.10 Addendum: The Large Economy

The most common concept of a large economy in international economics is one that is large enough to be able to influence its terms of trade, rather than acting as a perfect competitor in that it can sell and buy all it wants to at the going price. For such an economy a tariff has an eighth effect in addition to the seven treated in the chapter; it will improve the country's terms of trade. We have already seen that the effect of a tariff is to reduce the quantity of exports that the country places on the world market and the quantity of imports that it seeks to buy on the world market. These reductions will tend to increase the price of exports (since world *supply* falls by a nonnegligible quantity) and to reduce the price of imports (whose *demand* decreases). Since the terms of trade is defined as the ratio of the price of exports to the price of imports, both changes will tend to increase the terms of trade. An increase in the terms of trade is referred to as an improvement, since it means that a given quantity of exports can buy more imports, which is *ceteris paribus* a good thing for the country.

The effect of endogenous terms of trade on the general equilibrium analysis of the chapter is illustrated in figure 5–6. The point of production under free trade is P_F, and the point of consumption is C_F, reached by trading along the free-trade terms of trade here shown by a single arrow. With a tariff the internal relative price of M must increase, say to the value represented by the lines with double arrows. The equilibrium point of production is thus P_P. So much is unchanged. The novelty is that the country no longer has to trade up from the point P_P at the original free-trade terms of trade. Instead, the terms of trade improve; that is, the relative price of X rises on the world market. This means that the with-tariff terms-of-trade line is *steeper* than the free-trade terms-of-trade line, as shown by the line with the triple arrow in figure 5–6. It is evident that this terms-of-trade line $P_P C_P$ may cut the free trade terms-of-trade line $P_F C_F$ and then rise above it. It is evident also that the consumption equilibrium C_P (the point on $P_P C_P$ where an indifference curve is tangential to an *internal price line*) may lie on a higher social indifference curve than does the free-trade equilibrium

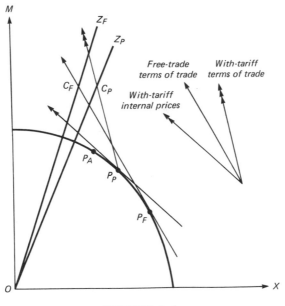

FIGURE 5–6
Terms of Trade Effect of a Tariff

C_F. That is, the country may be able to improve its level of welfare by imposing a tariff.

In fact, it can be shown (though we shall not prove it)[9] that a small tariff must always improve the welfare of the country that imposes it, *ceteris paribus,* if that country can influence its terms of trade. On the other hand, a prohibitive tariff eliminates trade altogether and drives the country back to the point of autarky P_A where consumption is equal to production. So as the tariff is increased from zero to the point at which trade ceases, welfare first rises and then falls. The point where it reaches a maximum is known as the *optimum tariff,* and the desire to increase welfare by improving the terms of trade is known as the *optimum tariff argument for protection.* It has to be added to the list of the infant-industry argument, the strategic argument, and the fiscal revenue argument, as a potential rationale for protection.

We saw in chapter 5.6 that in the long run a uniform tax on exports has the same effect as a uniform tariff on imports. This suggests that the benefits of an optimum tariff can be secured equally well by imposing a tax on exports, and this is correct. Indeed, since in an n-good world one wishes

9. The intuitive argument is that the first δ of tariff causes a terms of trade improvement that acts on the whole free-trade value of trade, whereas the cost in terms of induced distortions impinges initially on only marginal shifts in production and consumption.

to restrict the supply of (or demand for) the particular export goods (import goods) with inelastic supply (demand), it is generally optimal to impose export taxes rather than import tariffs.

How significant a factor is the optimum tariff argument? Quite a lot of countries have some influence over their terms of trade: even countries that would certainly be counted as small in all other respects have some influence over the world price of one or two principal export products, for example, Zambia and Zaire over the price of cobalt and copper. (Very few countries have any market power on the import side.) Furthermore, the optimum tariff argument might be important for a group of countries if they could act jointly even though each individual country acting alone had negligible influence over its export prices (this will be discussed again in chapter 16). On the other hand, elasticities of supply of many primary products are much higher in the long run than in the short run, when output may not be able to vary much because new trees take years to grow or new mines take years to develop. This means that a country trying to exploit the optimum tariff argument by restricting the supply of exports might succeed in the short run but find its market position seriously eroded by the emergence of alternative suppliers in the long run—which is what happened to Brazil when it restricted exports of coffee in the 1930s.

Finally, it is important to note that the optimum tariff is an optimum strictly from a national point of view. However, better terms of trade for one country necessarily imply worse terms for its trading partners. Moreover, since the process of achieving the gain in the terms of trade involves introducing distortions in production and consumption that are a deadweight loss for the world as a whole, the losses of the partners exceed the gains of the country imposing protection. Naturally those countries may resent what they regard as an attempt to exploit them, and they may seek to retaliate by imposing protection, too. That is the path to commercial warfare as occurred in the 1930s. Chapter 13 considers how international mechanisms have been created to try to prevent a repetition of that sad chapter in economic history.

5.11 Bibliography

The literature on protection is vast. A classic statement of the sense in which free trade is optimal is provided by P. A. Samuelson, "The Gains from International Trade Once Again," *Economic Journal,* Dec. 1962, reprinted as chap. 10 in J. Bhagwati, ed., *International Trade: Selected Readings* (Cambridge, Mass.: MIT Press, 1981) and as chap. 62 in J. E. Stiglitz, ed., *The Collected Scientific Works of Paul A. Samuelson,* vol. 2 (Cambridge, Mass.: MIT Press,

1966). For the theory of optimal intervention, see the classic article of H. G. Johnson, "Optimal Trade Intervention in the Presence of Domestic Distortions," in R. E. Baldwin, et al., *Trade, Growth, and the Balance of Payments* (Chicago: Rand McNally, 1965), reprinted in J. N. Bhagwati, ed., *International Trade*. See also J. N. Bhagwati, "The Generalized Theory of Distortions and Welfare," in J. N. Bhagwati, R. W. Jones, R. A. Mundell, J. Vanek, eds., *Trade, Balance of Payments, and Growth* (Amsterdam: North-Holland, 1972) and reprinted in Bhagwati, ed. *International Trade*. For effective protection, see W. M. Corden, "The Structure of a Tariff System and the Effective Protection Rate," *Journal of Political Economy,* June 1966, reprinted in Bhagwati, ed., *International Trade*. The Bhagwati-Krueger studies referred to in chapter 5.7 are the National Bureau of Economic Research series on "Foreign Trade Regimes and Economic Development," which consisted of ten country studies and two summary volumes published in the mid-1970s (New York: Columbia University Press). An admirable review article which summarizes and surveys the principal themes and conclusions is provided by R. I. McKinnon, "Foreign Trade Regimes and Economic Development: A Review Article," *Journal of International Economics,* August 1979.

The most authoritative treatment of the theory of protection is to be found in two volumes of W. M. Corden, *The Theory of Protection* (1971) and *Trade Policy and Economic Welfare* (1974), both published by Oxford University Press. An earlier classic on the subject was J. E. Meade, *The Theory of International Economic Policy: vol. 2, Trade and Welfare* (London: Oxford University Press, 1955).

Customs union theory was initiated by J. Viner, *The Customs Union Issue* (New York: Carnegie Endowment for International Peace, 1950). The next major milestone was J. E. Meade, *The Theory of Customs Unions* (Amsterdam: North-Holland, 1955). A useful collection of readings on the topic can be found in M. B. Krauss, ed., *The Economics of Integration* (London: Allen and Unwin, 1973). The study of the Wonnacotts referred to in the text is R. J. and P. Wonnacott, *Free Trade Between the United States and Canada: The Potential Economic Effects* (Cambridge, Mass.: Harvard University Press, 1967).

6

International
Investment

THE analysis has up to this point been conducted on the assumptions that trade is always balanced and that the economy is always operating at full capacity. In the present chapter we modify the first of these assumptions while retaining the second. Specifically, we inquire into the rationale of international capital movements which finance deficits or surpluses on current account. This means that we continue to rule out balance of payment problems, in the sense of reserve losses (which occur when there is a current account deficit not matched by a capital inflow), as well as inflation and unemployment: these are the macroeconomic problems that provide the focus of the next part of the book.

International capital movements permit countries to change the time profile of the stream of income and absorption. Although capital movements typically involve both elements, it is analytically useful to distinguish two motivations: (1) borrowing or lending to enhance income over time; and (2) borrowing or lending to change the time pattern of absorption.

6.1 The Transfer Process

The standard diagram used to illustrate general equilibrium with trade in previous chapters is modified to show the case of a trade deficit in figure

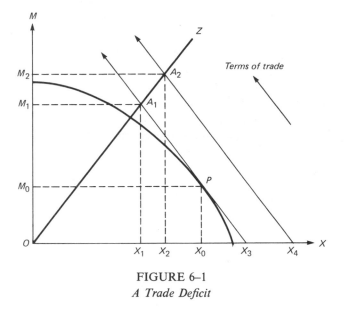

FIGURE 6–1
A Trade Deficit

6–1. In the case studied in previous chapters, production occurs at point P, and consumption at point A_1. Now that the analysis is being extended to recognize the existence of expenditures on investment as well as on consumption, it is no longer appropriate to use the term consumption or its symbol C. That is why the point is labeled A_1, the A standing for absorption—a term that has been used in macroeconomic analysis for some years to signify the total quantity of real resources absorbed in the economy.[1]

The case of a trade deficit is illustrated by absorption at A_2 rather than at A_1. Since prices remain constant—the terms-of-trade line from X_4 is parallel to that from X_3—there is no reason for production to change in this model. However, suppose that there is a capital inflow equal to $(X_4 - X_3)$, when its value is measured in terms of the exportable. That enables the country to expand absorption from A_1 to A_2—with the absorption of X rising from X_1 to X_2 and that of M rising from M_1 to M_2. Hence exports fall from $(X_0 - X_1)$ to $(X_0 - X_2)$, while imports rise from $(M_1 - M_0)$ to $(M_2 - M_0)$, giving a trade deficit measured by the distance between the two budget lines in place of the previous balance. The country is thus a net importer of real resources, which is consistent with the maintenance of overall balance of payments equilibrium because the trade deficit is being financed by the capital inflow. When a capital flow lends to an offsetting

1. See chap. 8.4 for the historical origin of the term.

adjustment in the current account, it is said to be transferred—which is why this section is titled the "Transfer Process."

The conclusion that a capital inflow will not change relative prices or, therefore, the production point is specific to the particular model presented above. It would not, for example, remain valid in the case of a large country whose terms of trade changed when it developed a trade deficit. Neither does it remain valid in a small country with exogenous terms of trade but in which some of the goods do not enter into international trade. This can be shown by examining the so-called dependent economy model that was initially developed by Australian economists, notably W. E. G. Salter (1929–63).

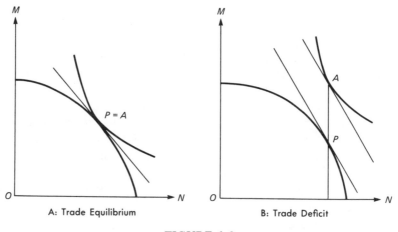

FIGURE 6–2
Dependent Economy Model

Figure 6–2 shows the dependent economy. On the horizontal axis is plotted the nontraded good, N: one thinks of nontraded goods as being mainly services and construction, although some services are also traded and some agricultural or manufactured goods are sufficiently bulky (or sufficiently heavily protected) to qualify as nontraded. On the vertical axis is the composite traded good, for which we retain the nomenclature M; it is legitimate to lump imports and exports together in this way just as long as their relative price (the terms of trade) remains constant. The fact that the terms of trade are exogenous to the small (or dependent) economy provides the justification for treating traded goods as a Hicksian composite. But it must be remembered that exogeneity is *not* the same thing as constancy and, accordingly, that an exogenous shift in the terms of trade changes the basis on which the figure is constructed.

Figure 6–2A shows the case of balanced trade, while figure 6–2B shows the case of a trade deficit. In both cases production is equal to absorption of the nontraded good, for one cannot import haircuts (for example). Balanced trade implies that in aggregate production is also equal to absorption of the traded good (although that is perfectly consistent with the simultaneous export and import of different commodities whose relative price remains constant), as is shown in figure 6–2A by the fact that the consumption point lies on the production possibility curve. Conversely, a trade deficit implies that absorption of M exceeds production, so that A lies vertically above P, the difference being equal to the trade deficit. In order to move from the situation of equilibrium in figure 6–2A to deficit in figure 6–2B it is necessary for the relative price of N to rise (the budget line to become steeper), so as to induce producers to shift their production toward N and consumers to shift their purchases toward M, the sum of the two effects being sufficient to absorb the additional supply of M that is imported from the outside world.

From now on the dependent economy model rather than the exportable-importable model will be used as the standard frame of reference. In the real world, of course, there are exportables, importables, and nontraded goods (not to mention many different kinds of each, as well as marginal cases that might be allocated to two or three of the categories or shift between them depending on relative prices); the point is that even three-good models are too complex to be readily used to gain understanding of particular analytical points, so that it is more fruitful to use a two-good model which is easy to understand. But this procedure requires that the two goods be selected with a view to highlighting whatever happens to be the focus of interest. Up to now the subject matter involved the exchange of goods, and the center of interest therefore lay in the characteristics of the goods being exported as opposed to those of the goods being imported. But capital flows, and subsequently payments imbalances, involve primarily adjustments between traded goods on the one hand and the domestic economy on the other, so that the traded versus nontraded goods distinction is generally more revealing.

It is often useful to check that both models give the same answer. When they do, one can be fairly certain that the solution is robust, in the sense that it would continue to hold in a more complex model—or in the real world. When they give different answers, one needs to ask which model is more applicable to the particular problem in hand. In the case of the question as to whether the emergence of a trade deficit will generate changes in relative prices and resource allocation, the answer is clear: the existence of nontradables is a sufficient condition to ensure that the relative price of nontradables must rise to generate a trade deficit, and the relative price of tradables must rise to generate a trade surplus. But in both models a trade deficit involves an excess of absorption over income while a trade surplus involves an excess of income over absorption; this is a robust property that is independent of the details of the transfer process.

6.2 Borrowing or Lending to Enhance Income

When a country borrows, therefore, it gains the ability to finance a trade deficit which permits absorption to rise above output. When it ceases borrowing and has to service its debt, either by paying interest or by repaying the principal (or amortizing its debt, as repayment by stages is called), the contrary occurs: it has to restrict absorption to a level lower than income in order to generate a trade surplus. Borrowing therefore involves an early period when absorption exceeds income followed by a later period when income exceeds absorption. Conversely, lending involves an initial period when income exceeds absorption, followed by a later period when the lender can enjoy the fruits of his earlier abstinence by absorbing more than his income.

The first motivation for borrowing (or lending) that we shall study is that of enhancing the stream of income over time. Consider the standard type of Keynesian investment function shown in figure 6–3, in which the marginal efficiency of investment is a declining function of the rate of investment. Suppose also that savings were interest-inelastic as in standard Keynesian models, so that the savings schedule is vertical as shown. Then the interest rate consistent with macroeconomic equilibrium in a closed economy would be i_0. If the government tried to use monetary policy to push the interest rate down below i_0 and so stimulate investment to raise growth, it could succeed only to the extent that the monetary expansion created inflation and so generated forced savings. The wisdom of such a policy raises a range of issues that we shall not go into here, where we shall assume that the country selects its monetary policy to generate the equilibrium interest rate i_0 and hence the level of investment I_0.

Now suppose that our country discovers that it has the option of borrow-

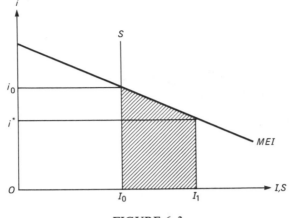

FIGURE 6–3
Investment-Savings Equilibrium

ing unlimited sums on the world capital market at the going world interest rate $i*$. (This assumes that creditors would not start to worry about the debtor's creditworthiness as its indebtedness mounted, as well as that the country is small in the world capital market.) Clearly it will be advantageous for it to borrow (I_1-I_0) and expand investment up to the point I_1 where the marginal efficiency of investment is equal to the world interest rate. This increases future income by a sum equal to the shaded area. Of that, the rectangular part has to be paid as interest to the foreign lenders, while the triangle remains as a net benefit to us. As and when debt-service payments come to exceed capital inflows, our country will need to generate a trade surplus, and absorption will in consequence fall short of income. But as long as our country never overborrows, in the sense of contracting loans with a higher interest cost than the return on the additional investment they are used to undertake, then the country will necessarily be better off for having borrowed and invested the proceeds.

The impact of such productive loans on the time path of income and absorption is shown in figure 6–4. The lower curve shows the path that income (equals absorption) would take under capital-account autarky. However, when the marginal efficiency of the investment financed by domestic savings exceeds the world rate of interest, it pays to borrow, which enables A to exceed Y by the amount of the capital inflow. Because of the additional investment, Y grows faster than it otherwise would,[2] as shown

2. The relevant concept of income here is GDP (gross domestic product) rather than GNP. For the difference, see chap. 7.4.

109

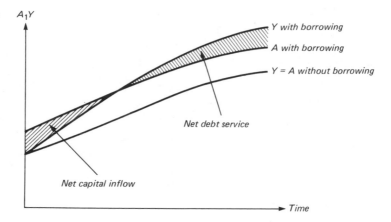

FIGURE 6–4

Impact of Productive Loans on Income and Absorption

by the curve *Y with borrowing.* Absorption starts off above *Y* and remains above so long as capital inflows exceed debt service (that is, so long as the net capital inflow is positive), but eventually net debt service turns positive and in consequence *A* falls below *Y with borrowing* (though remaining above the *Y = A* curve), as shown by *A with borrowing.*

In the case just discussed, the forces of thrift and productivity led the country to borrow. But it is evident that, had the saving curve of figure 6–3 lain to the right of the point I_1 (where the *MEI* falls to *i**) instead of to the left, the whole argument would have had to go into reverse. Our country would then have found it advantageous to lend the excess of its saving over and above the domestic investment that was expected to generate a return as high as the world interest rate. So long as this net lending was in progress, absorption would have fallen below income. But as and when interest earnings and amortization came to exceed new lending, absorption would rise above income. Later *A* would also rise above the *Y = A* curve of capital autarky, assuming that the country did not overlend. Lenders, as well as borrowers, can hope to gain through this process of international investment, which increases world output by relocating investment from areas where returns would be low to those where they are high. That is why one is not surprised to find that capital generally flows from the capital-rich industrial countries or the oil-producing surplus states with small populations to the capital-poor developing countries and the resource-rich primary producers, neither of which generate enough domestic savings to exhaust the investment opportunities that are profitable at the world interest rate.

International Investment

6.3 Borrowing or Lending to Modify the Time Path of Absorption

The second general motivation for international capital flows is that of modifying the time path of absorption. To permit a sharp distinction between this case and the previous one, we must suppose that the time path of domestic investment is given, which implies that the path of income (GDP) is independent of capital flows. Given that assumption, figure 6–5 shows the three cases that may arise.

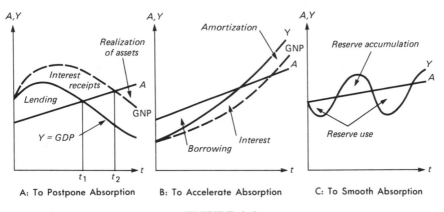

FIGURE 6–5

International Capital Flows to Modify the Time Path of Absorption

Figure 6–5A shows the use of the international capital market to postpone consumption. (Given that investment is being held constant, postponing absorption is the same thing as postponing consumption.) This describes the situation of one of the low-absorbing oil exporters. They are currently enjoying a high level of gross[3] domestic income, which may even increase in the near future but must be expected to fall off in the medium term. Instead of splurging all this income on consumption, and then facing the

3. Conceptually correct (though not currently conventional) accounting would treat the depletion of oil reserves in the ground on a par with the depletion of produced capital goods. This would mean that the overwhelming part of oil revenue would not qualify as a part of net domestic product, although it does of course contribute to GDP. The point is important in assessing the income level of the oil producers relative to that of the industrial countries, which is grossly exaggerated by current accounting practices.

next generation with the need to accept a fall in its standard of living, it is natural and rational for such a country to run a current account surplus in the short run and invest the proceeds abroad. This will permit the maintenance of constant or rising consumption even after domestically generated income starts to decline. There will come a time (t_1 in the diagram) when absorption will overtake income and the country will start to live off its investment income. For a time the country will in fact continue to make additional loans of a value less than the interest income (shown as the excess of the dotted curve over the Y-curve), but eventually (beyond t_2) it will start to realize its assets. Note that the equation describing the sources and uses of income is

$$Y + iF = A + \dot{F} \qquad (6.1)$$

where F is the country's stock of foreign assets and a dot over a variable denotes its time derivative ($\dot{F} = dF/dt$). From (6.1) it follows that $\dot{F} = iF$ at time t_1 and $A = Y + iF$ at time t_2.

The converse case is shown in figure 6–5B, a country that borrows in order to raise present consumption at the expense of future consumption. Such consumption loans are sometimes attacked as irresponsible because they mortgage future generations. That can, of course, occur. But where there is a country with strong growth prospects, as pictured in figure 6–5B, it is not at all evident that the present generation is to be condemned for taking some of the benefit of that future growth for itself instead of leaving all the benefits for the next generation (which is in any event going to live better than itself) while bearing all the costs that make that future growth possible. Such consumption loans will take place to the extent that savings are interest-elastic, as figure 6–6 shows. Taking advantage of the world capital market raises investment from I_0 to I_1, and also cuts savings from I_0 to I_2, so that the proportion $(I_1 - I_0)/(I_1 - I_2)$ of the capital inflow is a production loan and the proportion $(I_0 - I_2)/(I_1 - I_2)$ is a consumption loan.

Figure 6–5C shows a third possibility, using the international capital market to smooth out absorption in the face of variations in income. Traditionally, this has been regarded as a principal reason for holding reserves, so the diagram is labeled on the assumption that reserves are used for this purpose, but there is no reason why a country need use reserves rather than borrow, or accumulate reserves rather than lend in other ways. (Interest payments are omitted from the diagram for reasons of simplicity.) The most important variations in income are those stemming from changes in the terms of trade and crop failures. The oil price increases of 1973 and 1979 caused important adverse movements in the terms of trade of oil-importing countries, which they largely accepted as increased current account deficits

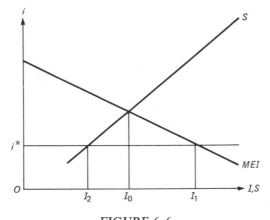

FIGURE 6–6

Savings-investment Equilibrium with Interest-elastic Savings

in the short run, and financed by borrowing or reserve decreases. Exporters of primary products often face equally dramatic changes in their terms of trade as a result of a rise or fall in the price of a principal export product. Or else countries may experience a crop failure that deprives them of a principal export product or creates the need to import to substitute for lost domestic production. These events may easily be linked: the loss of a large part of the Brazilian coffee crop from frost in 1976 caused a rise in the price of coffee which benefited the terms of trade of other coffee exporters like Colombia. There will sometimes be a problem in being confident that swings in the terms of trade are temporary. But, to the extent that a government believes that it is able to diagnose temporary swings, there is a strong case for financing them rather than forcing absorption to follow the fluctuations in income.

6.4 Neoclassical Growth Model

Let us now turn to an examination of the impact that the possibility of international borrowing and lending would have in the neoclassical growth model developed by Robert Solow (b. 1924). In its simplest form, the model postulates that output is always at the full employment level determined by a Cobb-Douglas production function

$$Y = \beta K^{\alpha} L^{1-\alpha} \qquad \text{or} \qquad y = \beta k^{\alpha} \qquad (6.2)$$

113

where $y = Y/L$, $k = K/L$, are income and capital stock per capita respectively. Saving is assumed to be proportional to income, $S = sY$, and the labor force is assumed to grow at the constant proportional rate λ, so that[4]

$$\hat{k} = \dot{K}/K - \dot{L}/L = sY/K - \lambda = sy/k - \lambda. \tag{6.3}$$

Substituting this in the logarithmic time derivative of (6.2) yields

$$\hat{y} = \alpha\hat{k} = \alpha\,(sy/k - \lambda). \tag{6.4}$$

Certain extensions of the model, to include such factors as exogenous technical progress and radioactive depreciation, are straightforward, but the above version suffices for our purposes.

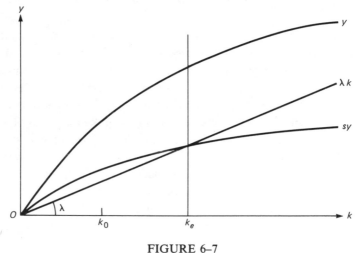

FIGURE 6–7
Neoclassical Growth Model

The model of (6.2) to (6.4) is illustrated in figure 6–7. Capital per head is shown on the horizontal axis, and output per head on the vertical axis. The production function in its per capita form is shown by the curve y and exhibits positive but decreasing returns throughout. Savings per head sy are a constant fraction of output per head, as also shown. The third line, labeled λk, is a ray from the origin with slope λ which shows the investment (per head) needed to equip each new member of the labor force with the quantity of capital equipment (k) that the existing workers have. To the left of k_e,

4. A circumflex is used to denote a proportionate rate of change: $\hat{k} \equiv (1/k)\,(\dot{k}) \equiv d(\ln k)/dt \equiv (L/K)\,(d(K/L)/dt) \equiv \dot{K}/K - \dot{L}/L \equiv \hat{K} - \hat{L}$.

savings exceed the investment needed to maintain the existing level of capital per head, and so capital per head (k) is increasing. To the right, it would decrease. It is clear that k_e is a stable long-run equilibrium, though simulation calculations have shown that it is to be interpreted as a position that would only be approximated in the *very* long run (after a century rather than a decade). It is of course the point where $\hat{k} = \hat{y} = 0$, by (6.3) and (6.4).

As capital accumulation proceeds from some initial point, for example, k_0, toward the equilibrium k_e, the marginal product of capital—shown by the slope of the y-curve—falls, and that of labor rises. Due to the unit elasticity of substitution between capital and labor that characterizes the Cobb-Douglas production function, this effect is exactly offset in the simple model by the accumulation of capital relative to labor, and so the profit-wage distribution of income remains stable over time. (In reality the elasticity of substitution appears to be less than unity, so that the accumulation of capital tends to be associated with a shift in the distribution of income in favor of labor.)

That completes the description of the neoclassical growth model in a closed economy. What happens if we allow this economy to borrow and lend unlimited sums on the world capital market at a constant world interest rate i^*? That depends on the relationship between i^* and the marginal product of capital at k_e. Suppose they happen to be equal: what would happen if the country integrated its capital market when its capital stock were $k_0 < k_e$? The answer is clear: the return to capital is higher in U than in the rest of the world, so our citizens would be anxious to borrow and W would be willing to lend. Capital would flood in, investment would shoot up—with the country importing the capital goods needed to raise its capital stock quickly to the steady-state level k_e. Development would occur in the short term.

Let us push to one side for a moment any misgivings as to whether the development process can be short-circuited quite so easily and consider the situation that would arise according to the model. Figure 6–8 shows that our per capita income would rise only from y_0 to y_1: the remainder of the rise in output, $(y_e - y_1)$, would accrue as profit income to foreigners, who are lending $(k_e - k_0)$ at a rate of return represented by the slope of the tangent to the production function at k_e. Nevertheless, national income (GNP) does rise—albeit not as much as national output (GDP)—in the short run. Since savings did not fall, all the borrowing was productive rather than for consumption purposes, and (except for the marginal unit) its product exceeds the rate of return it is paid.

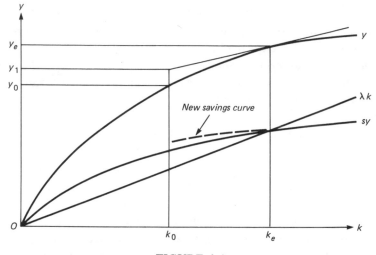

FIGURE 6–8
Neoclassical Growth Equilibrium with Foreign Borrowing

The immediate rise in national income is split between consumption and savings, as before. The sy-curve therefore shifts up, as shown by the dotted curve. The new savings now go, not into new domestic capital formation but into redeeming foreign debt. Since this has a lower opportunity cost than capital would have had at levels of the capital stock intermediate between k_0 and k_e, the subsequent rate of growth of domestic income would actually be slower than it would have been without foreign borrowing. Nevertheless, the initial jump in income is sufficient to outweigh any subsequent slower growth and ensures that the approach to long-run equilibrium income, though not immediate as was the jump in output, is faster than it would have been without foreign borrowing. The equilibrium itself is unaffected: as cumulated domestic savings approach the value of the equilibrium capital stock, the opportunities afforded by foreign borrowing and lending become irrelevant. In the long run the country would return to self-sufficiency and be neither a lender nor a borrower.

The last conclusion is critically dependent upon the assumption that the country had a marginal product of capital at its autarky equilibrium k_e just equal to the world interest rate. If that interest rate were higher, the country would initially borrow less, and its output level would jump to and subsequently remain at the point where the production function has a slope equal to i^*. Savings would continue even after the point where the country had repaid its foreign borrowing, as it became a creditor. In fact, there is no steady state in this case: the stock of foreign assets would grow ever larger. Starting from the equilibrium shown in figure 6–8, this case could be pro-

116

duced by an upward shift in s (or a downward shift in λ), as well as by a rise in i^*.

Second, consider the implications of a world interest rate lower than the marginal product of capital at k_e. In that case output would jump to and remain at a level higher than the closed economy equilibrium y_e, but the country would never repay all its foreign borrowing and it would remain a net debtor when it reached its steady state.

There is, of course, one grossly implausible result in the preceding analysis: the notion that the capital stock would suddenly jump to its steady-state level once capital mobility was permitted. No one imagines that a decision by, say, Rwanda to allow capital inflows would result in the overnight emergence of a modern industrial state. The reason is that the process of capital formation requires time, especially where human capital—an essential complement to physical capital if the latter is to be used efficiently in its more sophisticated forms—is concerned. In other words, figure 6–3, which shows diminishing returns to the rate of investment, shows a factor at least as important as does figure 6–7, which shows diminishing returns to the *stock of capital.* This should not come as too much of a surprise: Joan Robinson and her Cambridge disciples have been warning us for years that we are asking for trouble if we take seriously stories about a homogeneous jelly called capital that we can recombine with raw labor at will. But most economists still believe that we can extract useful insights from these simple models. The basic ideas about the gains to both borrowers and lenders that are potentially available from allowing capital movements in accordance with the dictates of thrift and productivity—movements that may be reversed only after many years, after higher incomes have allowed savings to catch up with investment opportunities, or, indeed, that may never be reversed at all—provide examples of such insights. When one observes a world with such gross disparities in capital per head as exist at the moment, it is difficult to believe that all the potential opportunities for advantageous capital movements are being exhausted. It is a point of view to remember when you reach the analysis of the world capital market in chapter 14.

6.5 Direct Investment

The bulk of international capital flows take the form of portfolio investment: that is to say, a lender makes a loan to, or buys a financial obligation from, a borrower in another country. However, there is a second form of international investment that has a significance much greater than its proportion in total capital flows would imply. This is direct investment by a multinational enterprise in a subsidiary.

The reason for the disproportionate importance of direct investment is that the actual flow of capital is incidental. Someone who is simply seeking a higher rate of return (or a different mix of risks) in one country than is available in their home country has the option of buying a security, which does not bring the troubles of management with it. Similarly, a firm does not invest abroad unless it believes that it can obtain rewards that exceed those available at home by a margin large enough to compensate for its additional risks and difficulties of operating in an unfamiliar environment.

These observations suggest that there must be some special incentives underlying direct investment. A consensus has gradually emerged that the primary source of these incentives is to be found in the *intangible property* commanded by an oligopolistic firm. Intangible property means patents, know-how, trademarks, recipes, copyrights—anything that enables a firm to sell something that its competitors cannot. It is their command of such intangible capital that gives oligopolists the ability to sell a distinctive product, with the expectation of supernormal profits that that brings.

When a firm has such a product (or, in practice, range of products) to sell, it naturally does not wish to restrict itself to the home market—not, at least, unless there are good substitutes already available in foreign markets. In deciding how to exploit foreign markets, it has a threeway choice: between exporting, licensing a foreign firm to produce and sell its product, and investing to create a local subsidiary. The choice between these three strategies depends on a series of factors: the scale of the foreign market (small scale points toward exporting), protection (which discourages serving the foreign market by exports), the danger of losing control of trade secrets (which argues against licensing), the desire for an easy life or constraints on the ability to expand the size of one's firm (which point toward licensing), etc. Firms generally create foreign subsidiaries when the arguments point toward local production. Licensing is usually regarded as a second best, except when it involves a process too small to justify the establishment of a subsidiary, to be resorted to only if the firm is constrained by managerial or financial limits from expanding as it would wish.

The above description is based on the typical form of contemporary direct investment, which is an oligopolized manufacturing industry to supply the local market. In former periods, direct investment designed to exploit local natural resources and serve an international market was also important. This has declined with the diffusion of technical knowledge and the desire of most countries to control their natural resources. A relatively new variant that has now achieved importance, especially in East Asia, is the multinational that establishes assembly plants (or other production processes) in countries with cheap labor supplies and sells the resulting products on the international market.

Multinationals have been welcomed as the great instrument for spreading technology around the world and cursed for perpetuating neocolonial control. They have been criticized for exporting jobs from the developed countries and for exploiting cheap labor in developing countries and praised for doing for factor price equalization what trade has not. Their supporters have seen them as spreading enlightened management techniques and introducing competition, and their critics as perpetrating corruption and seeking monopoly positions. Most people get much more excited about these issues than I do, so it seems better to recommend readers to the literature at this point.

6.6 Summary

International investment permits a transfer of real resources from countries where savings are abundant relative to investment opportunities to those in an opposite situation. Both parties can increase their welfare through such international, intertemporal resource reallocation, either by enhancing their level of income or by modifying the time path of absorption relative to that of income, or both.

Direct investment has the incidental effect of permitting a transfer of real resources, but it is typically motivated by the desire of an oligopolistic firm to exploit the intangible property that gives it a distinctive range of products.

6.7 Addendum: The Large Economy

The preceding analysis is based on the assumption that the country is unable to influence the world interest rate i^* at which it borrows and lends. This is, of course, a small economy assumption. A large economy will tend to push i^* up the more it borrows and push it down the more it lends.

Ability to influence the world rate of interest introduces considerations into welfare analysis analogous to those in the optimal tariff literature. A large country concerned with maximizing its national welfare (and able to count on an absence of foreign retaliation) will seek to restrict its export of capital, if it is a creditor, or its import of capital, if it is a debtor, so as to move the capital terms of trade in its favor.

Even small debtor countries may have an incentive to act in this way to the extent that they face a national borrowing rate that increases with the level of their indebtedness, because of fears as to their continued creditworthiness.

The standard analysis would suggest that the United States, as a large creditor country, could be expected to restrict its capital exports. While the United States did in fact try to restrict the outflow of capital in the 1960s, the motivation for this was concern over the balance of payments: the United States was keen to liberalize those restrictions, while many of the capital-importing countries (at least the developed ones) were urging they be maintained or strengthened. These facts appear paradoxical from the standpoint of the theory that countries try to manipulate their capital terms of trade in pursuit of national advantage. They can, however, be neatly explained by the Marxist hypothesis that governments are the creatures of their capitalist ruling classes rather than dedicated to pursuit of the general social good as interpreted by economists, since United States capitalists stood to gain by free export of capital from the United States.

6.8   Bibliography

The dependent economy model was introduced by W. E. G. Salter, "Internal and External Balance: The Role of Price and Expenditure Effects," *Economic Record,* Aug. 1959. Figures 6–4 and 6–5 are adapted from D. R. Lessard, "Financial Mechanisms for International Risk Sharing: Issues and Prospects" (paper presented to the Second International Conference on Latin American and Caribbean Financial Developments, Caraballeda, Venezuela, Apr. 1981). The neoclassical growth model was introduced by R. M. Solow, "A Contribution to the Theory of Economic Growth," *Quarterly Journal of Economics,* Feb. 1956.

While the literature about the basic logic of international investment is rather thin, that on multinationals is vast. The "industrial organization" viewpoint of direct foreign investment was pioneered by Stephen Hymer, one of the very few Marxists to have influenced the development of "conventional" economic thought in recent years, in his doctoral thesis, subsequently (and posthumously) published as *The International Operations of National Firms: A Study of Direct Foreign Investment* (Cambridge, Mass.: MIT Press, 1976). A convenient, conventional summary is R. E. Caves, "International Corporations: The Industrial Economics of Foreign Investment," *Economica,* Feb. 1971. The most recent drawing together of the work of one of the leading researchers in this area is R. Vernon, *Storm over the Multinationals,* (Cambridge, Mass.: Harvard University Press, 1977). For a lively denunciation, see R. J. Barnet and R. E. Miller, *Global Reach* (New York: Simon and Schuster, 1974).

A pioneering discussion of the welfare effects of foreign investment is G. D. A. Mac-Dougall's "The Benefits and Costs of Private Investment from Abroad," *Economic Record,* Mar. 1960, reprinted in J. N. Bhagwati, ed., *International Trade* (London: Penguin, 1969). A recent review of the literature in this area is J. N. Bhagwati, "International Factor Movements and National Advantage," *Indian Economic Review,* Oct. 1979.

III

MACROECONOMICS

THIS part of the book is devoted to the study of what has usually been termed international monetary theory or balance of payments theory. The more general expression open economy macroeconomics has recently gained ground at the expense of those traditional terms, as a result of growing recognition that the balance of payments is determined simultaneously with all other aspects of macroeconomic equilibrium.

7

Accounting Framework

IN the last five chapters we studied the impact of the openness of an economy on the microeconomic issues of resource allocation and income distribution. As is customary in microeconomic analysis, it was assumed throughout that the economy was in macroeconomic equilibrium: that is, with resources fully employed and payments always in balance. These assumptions were adopted not because of any belief that they are descriptively accurate but to help analysis by permitting the study of one set of issues at a time. In this part of the book the focus of attention is changed: we abstract from the microeconomic issues by aggregation, taking it for granted that the government is adopting whatever commercial policies it deems desirable on microeconomic grounds, and study the macroeconomic problems of unemployment, inflation, and payments deficits and surpluses.

The appropriate tools for this purpose are the macroeconomic models of Keynes and monetary theory. The logical place to start this analysis is with an examination of the accounting relationships that provide the framework of concepts, definitions, classifications, and identities into which behavioral hypotheses are fitted in the subsequent chapters in order to provide theories. A preliminary section is devoted to clarifying the relationship between the preceding micro analysis and the macro analysis that follows, by showing how and to what extent macroeconomic disequilibrium can be illustrated in the micro diagrams of part II.

123

7.1 Micro- and Macroeconomics

Consider the production possibility curve shown in figure 7–1A, which was used in the bulk of part II. Up to now we have always assumed that production possibilities are fully exploited, so that production always occurs at some point—like P_0, with the prices shown—on the ppc. This position is conventionally described as one of full employment, although it is important to understand that, in most developing countries, production possibilities are constrained by the stock of capital and/or skilled labor and/or land rather than by that of labor in general, so that full employment can be consistent with much disguised or even open unemployment of unskilled labor. A better description would be that of full capacity, but we shall continue to use the conventional terms.

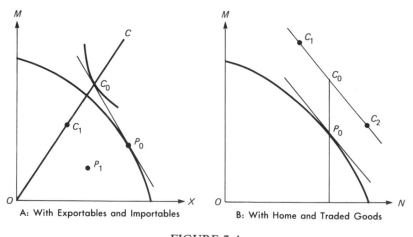

A: With Exportables and Importables   B: With Home and Traded Goods

FIGURE 7–1
Macroeconomic Disequilibrium in a Microeconomic Diagram

Unemployment, as that term is used in macroeconomics, refers to a point like P_1 *inside* the production possibility curve. Unfortunately, the idea of excess demand, or overfull employment or excessive demand pressure, cannot be illustrated equally well in the model with exportables and importables shown in figure 7–1A. We would have to represent it as a point outside the ppc and argue that the latter shows the maximum level of production that can be sustained in the medium term, while higher output is possible

124

in the short run by inducing workers to undertake abnormal overtime work, postponing maintenance, pushing unemployment below the natural rate, or whatever.

Reverting to the supposition that output is equal to the full employment level P_0 in figure 7–1A, the assumption of payments equilibrium implies that consumption must be at the point C_0 where a social indifference curve is tangential to the terms-of-trade line through P_0. At that point income is equal to expenditure (measured at world prices). Suppose, however, that expenditure were less than income for some reason; assuming homothetic preferences, the consumption point would lie on the ray OC inside C_0, at a point like C_1. The value of exports would exceed the value of imports (make sure you can see why), and so the country would have a surplus on the current account of the balance of payments. Conversely, if the value of consumption exceeded the value of income, consumption would lie on OC beyond C_0 and the country would have a current account deficit (this is in fact the case already considered in chapter 6.1).

Consider also the alternative two-good model introduced in chapter 6, with a composite traded good M and a nontraded or home good N as shown in figure 7–1B. The price of M is determined on the world market and its domestic price is simply its world price multiplied by the exchange rate. For the price of N, we may entertain two hypotheses; the first that it is flexible in the short run, the second that it is sticky. When it is flexible, the production and consumption points must always lie on the same vertical line, like P_0 and C_0, where the demand for home goods is equal to the supply—the case of chapter 6.1. The vertical excess of C_0 over P_0 represents the payments deficit—the excess demand for traded goods. If C_0 lay below P_0, income would exceed expenditure and there would be a corresponding payments surplus. But consumption could not be at a point like C_2 because the excess demand for home goods could not be satisfied through a trade deficit but would instead drive up the price of N, thus steepening the price line and so driving the production mix down the ppc to the right and shifting the consumption mix away from N toward M until demand for N were equal to supply. With sticky prices, on the other hand, it would be possible for demand to remain at C_2 in the short run. This would still be a situation of excess demand for N and thus of inflationary pressure. Similarly, if consumption were at C_1, there would be excess supply of home goods, and therefore (under sticky prices) unemployment.

However, while it is possible to *illustrate* macroeconomic problems in microeconomic diagrams, it is not possible to get far in *analyzing* them. For that one needs macroeconomic analysis.

7.2 Balance of Payments Accounts

The balance of payments accounts attempt to record all transactions between the residents of one country and the residents of other countries during a certain period of time (typically a year, though quarterly accounts are also fairly common). The criterion for inclusion is that a transaction be between the residents of different countries, not that it involve a sale or purchase of a foreign currency. The two are, of course, often associated: an importer usually has to buy foreign exchange to pay his foreign supplier. But the import enters the balance of payments even if he happens to draw down a foreign-currency bank account to make payments. When you travel or study abroad, your expenditures conceptually enter the balance of payments when you pay your restaurant bills, not when you buy foreign exchange.

Table 7–1 shows the balance of payments for our country *U* for the year 1981. Our currency is the peso, so all figures are expressed in millions of pesos. (Countries with particularly rapid inflation sometimes choose to present their payments accounts in dollars rather than national currency.) There is a certain amount of choice as to how the balance of payments accounts are presented: for example, it is possible to show all the receipts in one column and all the payments in another rather than in the form

TABLE 7–1

Balance of Payments of Country U, 1981
(in millions of pesos)

Row				
	Current Account			
1	Exports	1203		
2	Imports	1304		
3	Trade balance		− 101	
4	Balance on nonfactor services		− 87	
5	Interest, profits, and dividends		−203	
6	Unilateral transfers		+153	
7	Balance on current account			−236
	Capital Account			
8	Direct investment		+ 96	
9	Medium and long-term loans		+141	
10	Short-term loans		+ 11	
11	Balance on capital account			+221
12	Errors and omissions			− 22
13	Change in reserves			− 37

SOURCE: Central Statistical Office of Country *U.*

shown. Some observers have found profound significance in the fact that the sum of the two columns must in principle be equal (*in principle,* because in practice this is achieved by putting in an "errors and omissions" item to *make* them equal). Why? Because any payment to a resident that is not matched by a payment by a resident (including that resident deciding to hold his foreign exchange in that form rather than convert it into pesos, which counts as making a foreign investment) is matched instead by the central bank buying the foreign exchange, which shows up in the last line.

The format shown in table 7–1 is more common than the double column form. Only exports and imports of goods—visible trade—are shown gross. The trade balance is the excess of the value of exports over that of imports; in the example shown, imports exceed exports, so there is a deficit, shown by a minus sign. The minus signifies that residents are paying more than they are receiving. All subsequent entries in the table are shown net, that is, in a form equivalent to the trade balance rather than to the gross flows that underlie it. Exports are usually shown f.o.b., free on board, that is, excluding the cost of transportation beyond the port of export, while imports are usually presented c.i.f., that is, with the cost of international insurance and freight included.

The next two items in the table, rows 4 and 5, consist of services, or invisible trade—purchases or sales of anything that cannot be seen and touched. *U* has a deficit on services of 290; since trade in services is typically about 30 percent of that in goods, it probably has gross service exports of the order of 250. (It is important to understand why.)

There is an important analytical distinction between nonfactor services, like holidays, ocean freights, insurance, or engineering contracting, and factor services, which consist principally of interest, profits, and dividends —payments for factors of production employed in a country other than where their owner resides. Nonfactor services are in economic respects similar to goods: they are *outputs* whose demand is subject to similar influences, notably income and prices. Factor services, in contrast, are *inputs* (or, in the case of loans, give the power to buy inputs), and the payments made for these are heavily influenced by the stock of factors that has come into, or left, the country in question.

Unilateral transfers refer to unrequited payments across national frontiers. There are two principal elements covered here. First, there are remittances sent by migrant workers to their families back home. This element has become important for quite a large number of countries in recent years —as a debit item for the United States, Northern Europe, and the Arab Gulf states, and as a corresponding credit item in the Caribbean, Mediterranean,

127

and Muslim nonoil countries respectively. Second, there are grants—pure aid—made by one government to another.

The sum of the above items constitutes the *current account* of the balance of payments.[1] The distinguishing characteristic of current transactions is that they do not involve the participant acquiring or surrendering claims vis-à-vis the residents of another country. Such transactions are presented in the *capital account*.

The most basic distinction within the capital account is between *direct* investment and *portfolio* investment. Direct investment occurs when the investor acquires an ownership claim that involves his control of the asset. In its typical form a multinational corporation transfers funds in order to finance the expansion of a foreign subsidiary. But an individual transferring funds in order to buy a holiday home also satisfies the definition.

Portfolio investment can be broken down in a number of ways. The most important are into equity investment and loans, by maturity, and by direction of investment. Equity investment involves the acquisition of shares, which are ownership claims on a firm—but without giving effective control, so that they are effectively financial claims which involve the investor participating in the residual risk of the enterprise. Loans, by contrast, involve the investor having a preferred claim, but a claim limited to a specified rate of interest. The distinction by maturity relates only to loans (since ownership claims are by definition of indefinite maturity). The normal distinctions are short-term (under one year); medium-term (one to five or ten years); and long-term (over five or ten years). These definitions may relate either to the *original life* of the asset, or to the *term to maturity* as from the date the asset is bought (which is economically more meaningful but administratively more complex to record). The direction of investment refers to whether the investor is acquiring an asset in a foreign country, or whether he is surrendering one—for example, because the borrowing country is making amortization payments. In the example presented in table 7–1, U has an inflow of both direct investment and loans; equity investment is negligible and is therefore not recorded separately. The figures are presented broken down by maturity, but amortization is not shown separately.

Line 12 in table 7–1 is a measure of the statisticians' incompetence and bad luck. In principle, any receipts on lines 1 through 11 that are not matched by payments should generate a receipt of reserves by the central bank, that is, a surplus in line 13. In practice the central bank knows perfectly well whether or not it has been buying reserves, but the statisticians fail to record all the transactions that account for those reserve

1. Aid is sometimes put below the line in the capital account, but this violates the principle of the next sentence in the text.

changes. The "errors and omissions" item is inserted to make the accounts balance. It typically reflects mainly errors in the estimation of capital flows, although current account errors are also important for some countries, especially those with large illegal exports, of which the most important cases involve narcotics.

The last line records whether the central bank has been buying or selling reserves and is equal to the sum of the preceding rows. In the example shown, U had a deficit of 37 million pesos because it bought goods and services on current account worth that much more than the capital inflow. (The difference between the recorded current deficit and the recorded capital account surplus is only 15, but the errors and omissions item tells us that the current deficit must have been 22 larger or the capital inflow 22 smaller or some combination of the two.) The central bank of U must therefore have drawn on its international reserves to an extent equivalent to 37 million pesos. Typically, it would have sold United States dollars. It might also have sold some SDRs (see chap. 15), borrowed from the IMF, or sold some other currency that it was holding. In principle it might have sold some gold, though this is not very likely nowadays.

7.3 External Wealth Accounts

Another important, though less familiar and less available, set of accounts shows a country's wealth position vis-à-vis the rest of the world. Such accounts have the nature of a balance sheet: they show the *stock* of a country's assets and liabilities with respect to other countries as of a particular date. U's accounts are shown, again in millions of pesos, in table 7–2.

The main distinction is once again that between *financial* claims and *real* claims. Financial claims are shown in the table disaggregated between equities, loans (themselves disaggregated), trade credit, and international reserves. The net total of these financial claims constitutes the balance of indebtedness: it can be seen that U has a net debt of 1,115 million pesos, made up of a gross debt of 1,766 million pesos partly offset by assets totaling 651 million pesos. The statistical estimates of debt are typically somewhat worse than those of capital flows, insofar as they are compiled by cumulating the flow figures and include an early period when data collection was less adequate.

In addition to these debts, countries incur assets and liabilities abroad in

TABLE 7–2
External Wealth Accounts of U, *December 31, 1981*
(in millions of pesos)

Assets		Liabilities		
Equity holdings	53	Equity	42	
Loans: by banks	130	Loans to public sector	947	
by others	36	to private sector	604	
International reserves	432	Trade credit received (net)	173	
Balance of international				
indebtedness				−1115
Direct investment	79	Direct investment	864	
Total assets	730	Total liabilities	2630	
Net wealth position				−1900

SOURCE: Central Statistical Office of Country *U*.

the form of direct investments. *U* is shown as a typical capital-importing country in that its own firms have made only modest overseas investments, but the value of direct investments within the country by foreign multinationals is substantial. It should be noted that these statistics of the value of direct investments are usually quite unreliable, if indeed they exist at all. The reason is that the current value of a subsidiary is a pretty subjective notion. Even if there is a statistical requirement to report such a figure, which there usually isn't, accountants can within quite wide limits report whatever figure is most to their client's liking: there is no market test of their choice. In principle the increase in the value of an enterprise should be equal to the sum of new investment and retained earnings, but this would occur in practice only if the reported figure for profits reflected correctly changes in the value of existing assets.

The *changes* in the balance sheet positions of table 7–2 are of course related to the balance of payments of table 7–1. In particular, since there was a current account deficit of 236 during 1981, it must be true that the net wealth position vis-à-vis the rest of the world was − 1664 at the end of 1980. Furthermore, since 96 of the current deficit of 236 was financed by an inflow of direct investment, which does not result in an increase in debt, the balance of international indebtedness at the end of 1980 must have been − 975 (1115 minus (236 − 96)). If the balance of payments accounts are to track the evolution of the value of direct investments correctly, not only must retained earnings be calculated correctly but they must be included in the profits figures shown in the current account *and* in direct investment in the capital account. Since the two entries have opposite signs, this makes no difference to the overall balance of payments, but it is very important in relation to the evolution of wealth.

7.4 National Income Accounts

A third set of accounts, which are of fundamental importance in macro-economic model building, are the national income accounts that form the basis for Keynesian analysis. Like the balance of payments accounts, the national income accounts show *flows* during a certain period of time (again typically a year, though some countries publish quarterly figures as well) rather than stocks at a moment of time. The accounts for U in 1981 are shown in table 7–3.

Total domestic expenditures, or absorption of goods and services, which we shall denote by A, is shown as made up of three components: consumption (C), investment (I), and government expenditure on goods and services (G). In short-term analysis and forecasting it is usual and useful to disaggregate investment into *fixed investment* and *stockbuilding* (or inventory accumulation), since the latter tends to be particularly volatile and its variations play a large role in determining the state of the business cycle. Gross domestic product (GDP) is the total value of all the goods produced within the economy: in a closed economy it would be equal to the value of total domestic expenditure, since everything produced is either sold or added to inventories (in which case it is counted as stock accumulation in the national income figures even if that accumulation was involuntary, due to a lack of demand). In an open economy, however, there is an additional source of demand in the form of exports (X) and an alternative source of supply in the form of imports (M), so it is necessary to add X to A and subtract M to arrive at GDP. Gross national product (GNP) is the value

TABLE 7–3

National Income Accounts for U, *1981*

(in millions of pesos)

1. Private consumption *(C)*	5428
2. Gross investment *(I)*	1587
3. Government purchases of goods and services *(G)*	1336
4. Total domestic expenditure *(A)*	8351
5. Exports *(X)*	1431
6. *minus* Imports *(M)*	1627
7. Gross domestic product (GDP, Y)	8155
8. *minus* Net factor payments abroad	203
9. Gross national product (GNP, Y)	7952

SOURCE: Central Statistical Office of Country *U.*

of the income accruing to the factors of production resident in U: in a closed economy it would be equal to GDP, since income would have no one to accrue to *but* domestic residents. In an open economy, however, there are payments of income on foreign capital (corresponding to row 5 in table 7–1, the balance of payments accounts) to be deducted from GDP to arrive at GNP. (In the case of a creditor country the receipts of income on capital invested abroad are of course added to GDP to give GNP.)

The national income accounts of table 7–3 are related to the balance of payments accounts of table 7–1. However, exports and imports are never identical in the two sets of accounts, for two reasons. First, rows 5 and 6 in table 7–3 show exports and imports of goods and *nonfactor services,* so that they include the gross value of line 4 in table 7–1, as well as lines 1 and 2. Second, there are timing discrepancies between the concepts underlying the two tables. Exports and imports are included in the balance of payments when they cross the frontier (that is, are recorded by customs), whereas in the national income accounts they enter at the moment of production or consumption. But for those timing discrepancies, the difference between GDP and A would be equal to the balance on goods and nonfactor services (rows 3 plus 4 of table 7–1). Row 8 of table 7–3, net factor payments abroad, corresponds to row 5 in table 7–1. The difference between GNP and A therefore corresponds to the deficit on current account, row 7 of table 7–1, plus unilateral transfers, row 6.

In the analysis of the following chapters we shall simplify by ignoring timing discrepancies and assuming that the only current account receipts or payments are those for exports and imports of goods. We thus eliminate rows 4, 5, and 6 of table 7–1 and row 8 of table 7–3, which makes the trade balance equal to the current account balance, GNP equal to GDP (hence both can be represented by Y), and the difference between the two equal to the current balance. The complications noted in the preceding paragraph are thus suppressed, and the national income accounts can be expressed by the familiar identity

$$Y = C + I + G + X - M \qquad (7.1)$$
$$= A + TB.$$

Income Y is equal to domestic expenditure, or absorption, plus the trade balance (TB).

There is another way of arranging equation (7.1) that can be revealing: to put it in a form equivalent to the "saving equals investment" condition of elementary Keynesian theory. Deduct taxation, which will be denoted by

T, from both sides of (7.1), note that private sector saving $S = Y - C - T$, and rearrange, to get

$$(S - I) \quad + \quad (T - G) \quad = \quad (X - M) \qquad (7.2)$$

or   Net saving of   +   Government   =   Net investment in
      private sector   saving   rest of world.

Or we can turn it around, to say

$$(M - X) \quad = \quad (I - S) \quad + \quad (G - T)$$

Import surplus   =   Excess of investment   +   Government
                     over saving by private   deficit.
                     sector

7.5 Monetary Accounts

The final set of accounts that are of fundamental importance in representing the open economy are the monetary accounts. Like the foreign wealth accounts of table 7–2, these represent a *stock* at a moment of time rather than a flow through time. Table 7–4 presents simplified versions of the balance sheets of the central bank and the commercial banking system of country *U*.

The central bank is shown as holding two types of asset, international reserves (R) and treasury bills (D_1), and as issuing one type of liability, base

TABLE 7–4

Balance Sheets of the Banking System of U, *December 31, 1981*
(in millions of pesos)

Assets	A: Central Bank Liabilities		Assets	B: Commercial Banks Liabilities	
Reserves	(R)432	Base money	(B) 639	Base money	(B)639	Bank deposits (H)4,210
Treasury bills	(D_1)207			Treasury bills Loans to private sector	(D_2)3571	

SOURCE: Central Bank of Country *U*.

money (B). In fact central banks always have other items in their balance sheets as well, but these are either other forms of government debt or else items of no theoretical significance for present purposes (though they may include loans to banks). The essentials are that a central bank holds *both* international reserves *and* assets issued domestically (hence the notation D, for domestic credit), and that it issues a liability which provides the monetary base (sometimes called "high-powered money").

With the central bank component of domestic credit (D_1) constant, a decline in reserves (line 13 in table 7–1) provokes a fall in base money. Why? Because an excess of imports over exports not matched by a capital inflow involves a net drawing by importers on their bank accounts to make payments to foreigners; this payment is made to the foreigners by the central bank out of its reserves, and the accounts of the importers' banks at the central bank are debited accordingly. The quantity of base money would therefore fall. If the central bank did not want this to happen, it could *sterilize* the payments deficit by expanding the central bank component of domestic credit, which in our simplified example necessarily means buying treasury bills. The concept of sterilization—of neutralizing the monetary impact of payments imbalances—is a very important one.

The simplifications of table 7–4B are more significant than those of table 7–4A. In particular, it is assumed that the whole of the base money issued by the central bank is held by the commercial banks as reserves, and that the money supply (denoted by H^2) consists entirely of bank deposits. In reality a part of base money provides notes and coin, which circulate as the other component of the money supply. This makes the formula for the money multiplier significantly more complex, but it does not alter the essential point, which is that an addition to base money permits the commercial banks to acquire more domestic assets D_2 and thus to expand the volume of bank deposits and the money supply by more than the addition to the monetary base. In the simple case shown, the money multiplier κ is the inverse of the reserve ratio φ maintained by the commercial banks. Of course, in order to treat κ as a constant and write

$$\Delta H = \kappa \Delta B,$$

it is necessary that the banks actually do maintain a constant reserve ratio.

---

2. The traditional symbols for money, M and L, have already been preempted by imports and labor. H is an alternative increasingly used, motivated initially by the mnemonic "high-powered money;" alternatively, one may prefer to remember that in monetary fables the money supply is traditionally increased by $h$elicopter distribution!

In fact this is not an overly strong assumption: while banks do have a stronger incentive to lend as much as they legally and prudently can when the interest rate is high, so that the money multiplier κ may increase to some extent when interest rates increase, the fact is that the banks *always* have an incentive to lend as much as they can.

The commercial bank component of domestic credit, D_2, is made up of liabilities issued by the government, here represented by treasury bills, and liabilities of the private sector, represented in the table by bank loans. The fact that these assets may take other forms (government bonds, commercial bills, etc.) is an institutional detail of no great significance. Likewise, commercial banks may issue liabilities (like savings deposits) that are not counted as a part of the money supply, at least on a narrow definition, but this too can be neglected without much harm. For our purposes, the important point is that an unsterilized reserve loss reduces the monetary base and that this sets in train a *multiple* contraction in the money supply. Each individual bank will seek to reduce its bills and loans (D_2) by $(1 - \varphi)$ times its loss in deposits, so as to restore its reserve ratio. However, each time a bank does this and reestablishes its own reserve ratio, it reduces the balances of another bank at the central bank and creates a pressure on that bank to reduce the credit that it is extending. The system as a whole is restored to equilibrium only when domestic credit has contracted by $(\kappa - 1)\Delta B$:

$$B + D_2 = H = \kappa B \text{ implies } \Delta D_2 = (\kappa - 1)\ \Delta B.$$

7.6 Summary

Macroeconomic analysis is carried out within a systematic accounting framework. The national income accounts show all income-generating transactions of the residents of our country over a period of time, while the balance of payments accounts show all transactions between the residents of our country and those of the rest of the world over a given period of time. Two other essential sets of accounts are the monetary accounts, which reveal the proximate determinants of the money supply, and the external wealth accounts, which record our country's assets and liabilities with respect to the rest of the world: both of these show stocks at a specific time rather than flows over time. Changes in certain of those stocks are derived from the flow accounts, for income or the balance of payments.

7.7 Bibliography

Reading at length about accounting practices is not most people's idea of fun; browsing through statistical publications to absorb some notion of the factual situation of your country should be much more worthwhile. Memorize how the stylized facts for your country differ from those for our mythical country U in such respects as:

- the average propensity to import, M/Y
- whether there is normally a surplus on visible trade
- the importance of service transactions
- whether there is a surplus or deficit on unilateral transfers
- whether there is normally a surplus or deficit on current account
- how the current imbalance is financed
- how large are errors and omissions
- how much variability there is in payments flows from one year to the next, and which are the volatile items
- whether the country is a net creditor or a net debtor (if you can't find any external wealth accounts, try drawing an inference from the balance of payments or national income statistics)
- whether the current imbalance is offset mainly by the private sector ($I \neq S$) or the public sector ($G \neq T$)
- the ratio between B and D_1, and the commercial bank reserve ratio φ.

You are unlikely to find all these accounts presented together (and may not be able to find any comprehensive external wealth accounts at all) and may have to search through various government publications, central bank reports, and commentaries of the conjunctural institute(s). Statistics on the various topics covered by the chapter are published on an internationally comparable basis by various international organisations. For example:

Balance of payments data: International Monetary Fund, *International Financial Statistics;* United Nations, *Monthly Bulletin of Statistics;* Organization for Economic Cooperation and Development, *Economic Outlook*.

External wealth accounts are difficult. The Bank for International Settlements *Annual Report* gives data on bank assets and liabilities. The World Bank's *World Debt Tables* report government and government-guaranteed medium- and long-term debts.

National accounts data: sources are the same as for balance of payments data, plus enormous detail, much in arrears, in the United Nation's *Yearbook of National Income Statistics.*

Monetary statistics: International Monetary Fund, *International Financial Statistics.*

8

Current Account

THIS ANALYSIS of balance of pay-
ments theory begins by making two simplifying assumptions: that there are
no capital movements, and that the exchange rate is fixed by the action of
the central bank. Both of these assumptions are relaxed later: capital mobility is introduced in the next chapter and flexible exchange rates in chapter
10.

The chapter is organized around a series of different models, or approaches, that have been developed over the years. These are introduced in
the order in which they emerged historically, with a sketch of the circumstances that prompted their evolution. Several of these approaches were
presented by their creators as representing a conflict with the preceding
approaches, which have indeed been derided by some as erroneous orthodoxy. My view is that such exclusiveness is unmerited: that any adequate
understanding of the macroeconomics of an open economy demands an
integration of all the various approaches within the context of a general
equilibrium model. Accordingly, the final section of the chapter shows how
the various approaches can all be incorporated within the simplest general
equilibrium model available, namely the *IS/LM* model.

8.1   Hume's Price-Specie-Flow Mechanism

Chapter 2 described how the mercantilist preoccupation with achieving
a surplus on the balance of payments was faulted by Adam Smith for

neglecting the basic source of the gains from trade: the increase in consumption in both countries that is possible by exploitation of their absolute or, more generally, comparative advantage on the basis of balanced trade. But even before Adam Smith's writing, his fellow Scot David Hume (1711–76) had discredited the *macroeconomic* basis of the mercantilist position. In 1752 he showed that a permanent payments surplus was not feasible and therefore made no sense as a policy objective, while a deficit would cure itself, so that it was not necessary to worry about a country losing all its money supply and having to cease production in consequence. The basic claim was that the gold standard contained an *automatic* adjustment mechanism, the so-called price-specie-flow mechanism.

In order to understand this mechanism it is necessary to know what a gold standard is. The essential features are that the countries on the gold standard fix the values of their currencies in terms of gold, that they settle their balance of payments surpluses and deficits by transferring gold, and that they do not sterilize the effects of those gold flows on their money supplies. These conditions were satisfied in mideighteenth-century Europe for those countries, like Britain, that had a monetary unit equal to a defined weight of gold. Clearly each such currency had a value fixed in terms of gold (and therefore their values were also fixed in terms of one another). Gold could be, and was, shipped from one country to another to settle payments deficits; if British importers could not get enough francs from British exporters to France, they sent some gold sovereigns which were melted down and turned into francs. Finally, except occasionally in times of war, governments did not seek to maintain the money supply by printing paper money when gold flowed out, that is, they did not sterilize a payments deficit.

The basic idea of the gold standard adjustment mechanism was that a payments deficit caused a loss of reserves, which reduced the money supply, which lowered the price level, which made the home country's goods more competitive, which stimulated exports and reduced imports, which improved the balance of payments. This process continued until the deficit was eliminated. The converse process operated when a country had a surplus: gold flowed in, the money supply and prices rose, competitiveness declined and in consequence exports fell and imports expanded so that the payments surplus tended to be eliminated. In either case, therefore, a payments imbalance was self-eliminating so long as the automatic mechanisms inherent in the gold standard were allowed to play themselves out. To look at the matter in a slightly different way, a country had a "natural" quantity of money corresponding to its productive capacity: it could not sustain more than this quantity (any excess would generate a deficit and leak out), and any shortfall would be made up anyway, so the mercantilist preoccupation with the balance of payments was silly.

The steps in the chain of reasoning described verbally above may be summarized schematically:

Payments → Gold → Fall in money → Price
deficit   outflow   supply   decline
→ Greater → More exports, → Reduction in
competitiveness   less imports   payments deficit.

It is important to understand exactly what assumptions are necessary to justify each step in this causal chain.

1. An incipient payments deficit can be realized and lead to a loss of reserves (like gold) only if the country has a *fixed exchange rate.* With a flexible exchange rate, the monetary authority is not willing to supply internationally acceptable assets to absorb an excess supply of the currency it issues, so the consequence of such excess supply is a depreciation of the currency rather than a loss of reserves.

2. A reserve loss will lead to a fall in the money supply if the country follows a policy of nonsterilization, that is, does not compensate for the decline in reserves by increasing domestic credit. This became known as following the "rules of the game". It seems that central banks did not in fact follow this rule literally even at the apogee of the gold standard in the late nineteenth century. What they typically did was to sterilize partially. With a fractional reserve banking system (which was not a factor in Hume's day, but became important during the nineteenth century), it is possible for a central bank to partially sterilize a reserve loss but for the money supply to fall by more than the loss in reserves.[1] The essential condition for the second step to operate is therefore the *avoidance of complete sterilization.*

3. The assumption that a fall in the money supply would lead to a price decline was based on the *quantity theory of money,* which held that in the "equation of exchange"

$$MV = PT$$

V (velocity) and T (volume of transactions) are essentially constants, with

---

1. Recall from chap. 7.5 that the monetary base $B=R+D_1$ and $H=(1/\phi)B$. Define the "sterilization coefficient" α as that proportion of a change in reserves that is offset by a change in (central bank) domestic credit D_1, so that $\Delta D_1 = -\alpha\Delta R$. A value of α equal to unity signifies total sterilization, while a value of zero signifies zero sterilization. Differencing the first two equations, and substituting, shows that

$$\Delta H = (1/\phi) (\Delta R+\Delta D_1) = (1/\phi) (1-\alpha)\Delta R$$

from which it follows that the money supply will fall as long as sterilization is less than complete ($\alpha < 1$), and will fall by more than R when $(1-\alpha)/\phi > 1$.

the former determined by the technology of exchange and the latter by the condition that full employment prevail, while M is the independent variable, and P is the dependent variable. (This traditional nomenclature is not used in the rest of the book.) The validity of this interpretation of the equation of exchange has always been the chief issue underlying disputes between Keynesians and monetarists (though many on both sides of the disputes have been reluctant to acknowledge this). Hume was in this sense a monetarist: he wrote:

> Suppose that four-fifths of all the money in Great Britain [were] to be annihilated in one night, and the nation reduced to the same condition, with regard to specie, as in the reigns of the Harrys and Edwards, what would be the consequence? Must not the price of all labour and commodities sink in proportion, and everything be sold as cheap as they were in those ages? (Hume, 1752, in Cooper, 1969, p. 25)

4. A fall in domestic prices will increase international competitiveness provided that it increases the "real exchange rate," which is defined as $ep*/p$. This is, of course, simply the nominal exchange rate corrected for changes in the general level of prices abroad and at home. Since we have already assumed e to be constant, a fall in p will certainly increase competitiveness provided that *foreign prices remain constant or rise.* When a small country has a deficit one expects foreign prices to remain constant, while when a large country has a deficit its loss of gold will be sufficient to have a perceptible impact in raising money supplies and hence prices elsewhere.

5. The balance of trade will respond positively to variations in competitiveness provided there is sufficient elasticity in the demand and supply schedules. In the subsequent discussion of the elasticities approach, we shall derive something called the Marshall-Lerner condition, which is a condition on the elasticities that has to be satisfied if an improvement in competitiveness is to improve the balance of trade. Hume assumed (without knowing it) that the *Marshall-Lerner condition is satisfied.*

6. An improvement in the balance of trade must improve the overall balance of payments if trade is the only component of the balance of payments, as we are assuming. In particular, there must be *no capital mobility* to assure this result.

The italicized phrases in the six preceding paragraphs are the assumptions that are needed to ensure that the price-specie-flow mechanism works as described by Hume. There are in fact strong reasons for believing that the gold standard did *not* work like that. One reason is that capital mobility was very important by the late nineteenth century; assumption 6 was not satisfied. A loss of reserves led a central bank to raise its interest rates to attract a capital inflow and stem the fall in the money supply. In a Keynesian version of what happened next, the high interest rates led to a decline in aggregate demand, recession, and a fall in imports: the balance of payments on current account indeed improved, but at the cost of a loss of output, since assumption 3 was not satisfied. The Belgian economist Robert Triffin (b. 1916) argued that a rise in the British interest rate forced stock liquidation by the capital-importing peripheral countries which improved the British terms of trade and thus balance of trade: assumptions 4 and 5 failed. There is also a monetarist alternative interpretation in which prices are determined in each country by arbitrage from the world market (contrary to assumption 3), income is determined at the full employment level by the natural equilibrating forces of the market, and the balance of payments is determined by the condition that the demand for money be equal to the supply. (This will be taken up in chapters 8.6 and 9.4.)

While the reasons that the gold standard worked differ from one interpretation to another, all of them suggest that there *is* an inherent monetary equilibrating mechanism, albeit one that worked at the cost of output deflation (in the case of the Keynesian interpretation) or crises in the peripheral countries (in Triffin's interpretation). And it is a historical fact that the gold standard did work for the period prior to the First World War, especially the preceding forty-odd years—although interspersed with crises, often sharp but usually fairly short. Then came the war, which brought widespread abandonment of the gold standard and fixed exchange rates.

An attempt was made to restore the gold standard after the war, but in the 1920s there was no evidence of that automatic equilibration that had previously been the essence of the system. Two reasons were advanced to explain this. First, it was said that central banks no longer played by the rules of the game: the newly established Federal Reserve System in the United States, in particular, sterilized the gold inflow so as to avoid fanning inflation. Second, prices did not fall in the deficit countries (notably Britain) in response to tight monetary policies; instead, these suffered deflation and unemployment even amidst the brief spell of world prosperity in the late 1920s. When that prosperity gave way to the Great Depression, the tensions mounted. Britain left the gold standard in the midst of a financial panic in September 1931. From then on it was not sensible to treat Hume's analysis as the centerpiece of payments theory. It was necessary to develop models whose basic hypotheses were in greater accord with the realities of the time.

8.2 Multiplier Analysis in an Open Economy

The major professional response to the Great Depression was, of course, by the very famous British economist John Maynard Keynes (1883–1946), in his *General Theory of Employment, Interest, and Money,* published in 1936. In this work, he developed a macroeconomic theory of how the levels of income and employment were determined when prices do *not* adjust to clear markets as had traditionally been posited by economists. Although the *General Theory* assumed a closed economy virtually throughout, the basic ideas of Keynesian multiplier analysis were soon applied to balance of payments theory by the British economist Roy Harrod (later Sir Roy Harrod, 1900–78) and the Austrian-born economist Fritz Machlup (1902–83).[2]

The basic assumptions of multiplier analysis are that prices (including the exchange rate) are fixed, that the economy is operating below full employment so that output can respond to variations in demand, and that the money supply adjusts passively to variations in the demand for money (due, for example, to the central bank maintaining the interest rate constant). The starting point of the analysis is the income identity

$$Y = C + I + G + X - M. \tag{8.1}$$

Consumption can be taken as determined by a conventional consumption function $C = C(Y)$, or, in linear form

$$C = c_0 + cY \tag{8.2}$$

where c is the marginal propensity to consume. Investment and government expenditure are taken as exogenous.

Exports may also be treated as exogenous.[3] Two alternative justifications for this assumption exist. The first is that the country is a small supplier of homogeneous primary products whose price is determined on world

2. It is an often-remarked irony of the intellectual history of the period that Keynes had previously (in a debate in the *Economic Journal* in 1929) combated the efforts of Ohlin to apply what later became regarded as the Keynesian analysis of income effects to analysis of the transfer problem posed by German reparations (see chap. 9.1 for the nature of the transfer problem).

3. It is sometimes argued that exports are diverted to the home market by a high level of demand, so that $X=X(Y)$, $\partial X/\partial Y < 0$, and there is empirical evidence supporting this hypothesis from some countries. The student should check that, if such an effect exists, it will reinforce the conclusions of the analysis of this section.

markets. It could sell more exports at the going price, but export sales are limited from the *supply* side to the level that is profitable at current prices. The second justification is that the country is selling manufactured goods produced at constant cost; it would like to sell more at current prices, but sales are limited from the *demand* side (given whatever fixprice the suppliers choose to quote).

Imports, on the other hand, are endogenous: more domestic income brings in more imports, which the country can buy at a fixed price, given that it is small in the markets for its import goods. An obvious specification for the import function is $M = M(Y)$ or, in linear form

$$M = m_0 + mY \tag{8.3}$$

where m is the marginal propensity to import. While it seems rather obvious, this specification in fact implies a quite strong assumption about the nature of the goods being imported. Since prices are constant, Y (income) represents output: hence equation (8.3) implies that more *production* requires more imports, as is indeed appropriate when imports consist of intermediate goods. But if imports consist of final goods, then one would expect them to be related to expenditure A rather than to income Y. For example, a fall in autonomous consumption exactly matched by a rise in exports would leave output, and therefore imports, unchanged if imports consisted of intermediate goods (petroleum, for example), while imports would fall (and therefore income would rise) if they consisted of consumer goods. In the real world, of course, imports consist of both intermediate and final goods. It is very important to recognize this when constructing econometric models for forecasting or planning purposes, since the import component of different types of expenditure is in fact very different: typically inventory accumulation has the highest import component, followed by fixed investment, followed by consumption or exports, with government expenditure normally least import intensive. However, alternative specifications of the import function make no difference to the qualitative theorems we shall derive below,[4] and so we shall use the simple form (8.3). Note that m_0 might be negative—domestic production of petroleum, say—without violating accounting conventions so long as $Y > |m_0/m|$.

---

4. It is worth checking this out by working through with the alternative import function $M = m_1 + m_2A$.

The basic multiplier formula is derived by substituting (8.2) and (8.3) into (8.1) and manipulating:

$$Y = (c_0 + cY) + I + G + X - (m_0 + mY)$$

$$(1 - c + m)Y = c_0 + I + G + X - m_0 \qquad (8.4)$$

$$Y = \frac{1}{s + m}(c_0 + I + G + X - m_0)$$

where $s = 1 - c$ is the marginal propensity to save. The term in front of the parenthesis is the multiplier, while that in the parentheses is the multiplicand. As compared to a closed economy, the effect of introducing foreign trade is to *reduce* the value of the multiplier (since m increases the *denominator* of the multiplier formula), and to *increase* the value of the multiplicand by exports less autonomous imports. The intuitive reason that the multiplier declines is that imports, like saving, constitute a leakage from the income stream, which means that a given level of income generates less (domestic) expenditure than it would in a closed economy. This does not imply that the level of equilibrium income is lower in an open economy, because the stimulating effect of exports in increasing the multiplicand also needs to be taken into account. In fact it is easy to see that the foreign sector has a net stimulating effect whenever there is a trade surplus ($X > M$), and leads to a net reduction in the level of income whenever there is a trade deficit.

The formula for the trade balance, TB, is

$$TB = X - M = X - m_0 - \frac{m}{s+m}(c_0 + I + G + X - m_0). \qquad (8.5)$$

We are now in a position to derive the basic multiplier theorems for an open economy. These relate to the effects of changes in the exogenous variables I, G, and X on the level of income Y and on the trade balance TB. Since I and G (not to mention the autonomous component of consumption, c_0) enter both (8.4) and (8.5) in an identical form, it suffices to treat one of them, say G. The comparative statics effects of changes in government spending are deduced by differentiating (8.4) and (8.5) with respect to G:

$$dY/dG = 1/(s+m) > 0 \qquad (8.7)$$
$$d(TB)/dG = -m/(s+m) < 0.$$

Thus an increase in government spending, or any other form of exogenous domestic spending, increases income by a multiplier effect, while it reduces the trade balance by a fraction of the exogenous increase in spending.

It is clear by inspection of (8.4) that an increase in exports would have exactly the same multiplier effect on *income* as an increase in domestic expenditures, but its effect on the balance of trade would differ:

$$d(TB)/dX = 1 - m/(s+m) = s/(s+m) > 0. \qquad (8.8)$$

The effect of the initial increase in exports in improving the trade balance is partially but not wholly offset by the increase in imports induced by the rise in income resulting from the higher exports.[5]

It is possible to develop the preceding analysis in diagrammatic form, using a modified version of the elementary Keynesian savings-investment diagram. Figure 8–1A shows the savings and investment schedules. One may either suppose that one is treating a simple model where there is no government, or else interpret the I-schedule to include G and the S-schedule to include T. Figure 8–1B shows the export and import schedules. Figure 8–1C shows the $(S-I)$ schedule, which is derived from figure 8–1A, and the $(X-M)$ schedule, which is derived from figure 8–1B. Recalling equation (7.2), we know that a condition for equilibrium income is that total domestic saving must be equal to the balance of trade: this condition is satisfied *ex ante* in figure 8–1C at the income level Y_0 where the two schedules intersect. It happens that the trade balance is negative at that point.

The comparative statics results already established algebraically can now be confirmed in terms of figure 8–1. The case shown is that of an exogenous increase in exports, which establishes a schedule $(X'-M)$. It can be seen that income rises (to Y_1) and that the trade balance increases (a deficit is replaced by a surplus), as indicated by equations (8.6) and (8.8). However, the increase in the trade balance is less than the increase in exports (which is measured by the vertical upward shift in $X-M$), because the $(S-I)$ schedule is positively sloped.

There are two major implications of the foreign trade multiplier analysis. The first is that Keynesian income effects are one of the key elements that have to be incorporated into any model seeking to explain the current account of the balance of payments as a part of the macroeconomic equilibrium of an open economy. The second is that it is possible to explain the

---

5. Another worthwhile exercise is to analyse the effects on Y and TB of an increase in the domestic production of petroleum.

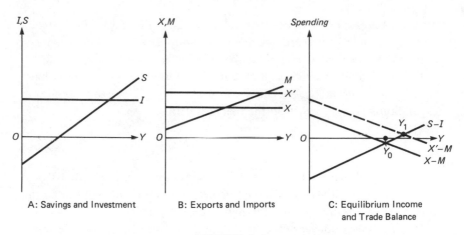

FIGURE 8–1

Savings, Investment, and the Trade Balance

international transmission of those economic disturbances known as the business cycle. Exports are exogenous to our country, but they are endogenous with respect to the level of income in our trading partners. Thus a boom there raises their imports and hence our exports, which produces an expansion here as well. In consequence the business cycle is effectively a world rather than a national phenomenon. (The implications of this fact will be explored in chapter 17.)

8.3 The Elasticities Approach

The economists who developed the foreign trade multiplier analysis were not under the impression that income effects were the only determinants of trade flows. In fact, one of them, Fritz Machlup, also played a leading role in developing the elasticities approach, which sought to analyze the impact on the trade accounts of the changes in relative prices induced by a devaluation. Analysis of this type was first developed by the great English economist Alfred Marshall (1842–1924), in the heyday of the gold standard, but it became an important part of payments theory only after the Keynesian revolution with the work of Abba Lerner, Joan Robinson, Fritz Machlup, and Gottfried Haberler.

The foreign trade multiplier asks what happens when income changes, with prices constant; the elasticities approach asks what happens when prices change, with income constant. It is simplest to start the analysis if we retain the Keynesian assumption that the general level of internal prices (in both countries) is constant and that changes in relative prices are the result of changes in the nominal exchange rate e. This makes it natural to construct an analysis showing how the demand for and supply of foreign exchange vary with the exchange rate. (However, the exchange rate is still assumed to be determined by an administrative decision rather than by market forces.)

The demand and supply curves are shown, with orthodox shapes, in figure 8–2. The horizontal axis shows the quantity of country W's currency, the dollar, that is demanded or offered in exchange for country U's currency, the peso. The dollar here represents foreign exchange in general— as it actually does in the foreign exchange markets of most countries, which are almost all conducted overwhelmingly or exclusively in terms of the United States dollar. If an importer in U wishes to pay a British exporter, his bank sells pesos to buy dollars and then sells the dollars on the sterling-dollar market to buy the pounds that the British exporter wishes to receive. Thus there is little abstraction from reality in assuming that all of U's external payments involve exchanges of pesos for dollars. The vertical axis shows the exchange rate, that is, the price of the dollar in terms of the peso. A higher value of e represents more pesos per dollar, that is, a devaluation of the peso.

The demand for dollars is determined by the need of U's importers to make payments to foreigners, who naturally wish to receive dollars rather than pesos. In reality the demand is supplemented by other sources as well

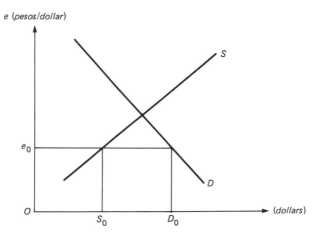

FIGURE 8–2
Demand and Supply in the Foreign Exchange Market

as payment for imports: payments for service imports, making loans to other countries, amortizing loans received from abroad, or any other debit item in the balance of payments. The present treatment is limited to visible trade, for simplicity of presentation, so that we shall analyze what lies behind the demand curve for dollars purely in terms of imports. The volume of imports is, it is supposed, determined by demand and supply. The demand curve for imports shows how the volume of imports will increase as the *peso* price p_m of imports falls, as in figure 8–3A. The supply curve of imports shows that country U can buy as many imports as it wants at the fixed world *dollar* price, $p_m{}^*$ (the small country assumption), as shown in figure 8–3B.

In order to find the demand for dollars, it is necessary to translate the demand at a given *peso* price shown in figure 8–3A into the demand at a given *dollar* price. Since $p_m = ep_m{}^*$, this can be done for any given exchange rate. The curve $D(e_0)$ in figure 8–3C represents the curve D of figure 8–3A at some exchange rate e_0. The demand for dollars at e_0 is the dollar price of imports $\bar{p}_m{}^*$ multiplied by the quantity of imports M_0, say D_0 (which is, of course, the area of the rectangle below the supply curve up to the point M_0 in figure 8–3C). The values e_0 and D_0 represent one point on the demand curve for dollars in figure 8–2.

Now consider the effect of a devaluation of the peso to some higher exchange rate e_1. This leaves the demand and supply curves of figures 8–3A and 8–3B unaffected, since they are both specified in terms of the currency

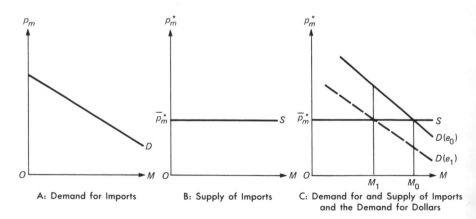

A: Demand for Imports   B: Supply of Imports   C: Demand for and Supply of Imports and the Demand for Dollars

FIGURE 8–3
Imports and the Demand for Dollars

that is relevant to those involved (the peso for buyers, the dollar for sellers). The supply curve in figure 8–3C is similarly unaffected. However, the translation of the peso demand curve of figure 8–3A into the dollar demand curve of figure 8–3C was done at the exchange rate e_0 and has to be revised now that the exchange rate has increased to e_1. The quantity M_0, for example, will now only be bought at a lower dollar price, such that $ep_m{}^*$, the peso price, is the same as it was before. At the price $p_m = e_1\bar{p}_m{}^*$, less than M_0 will be bought, say M_1. In other words, the demand curve in figure 8–3C moves down to $D(e_1)$. The new demand for dollars is $\bar{p}_m{}^*.M_1$, less than before. Hence at the higher exchange rate e_1 the demand for dollars is less: the demand curve of figure 8–2 slopes down, as drawn. Incidentally, the elasticity of the demand curve for dollars in figure 8–2 depends on the elasticity of the demand for imports in figure 8–3A: you can confirm this by considering a very inelastic demand for imports, which implies a very inelastic demand for dollars.

The analagous procedure for determining the supply of dollars is shown in figure 8–4. The small country is assumed to be able to sell all it wants on the world market at the fixed dollar price $\bar{p}_x{}^*$ (fig. 8–4A, carried over directly to fig. 8–4C). There is an upward-sloping supply curve of exports as a function of the peso price (see fig. 8–4B), which can be translated into a supply curve as a function of the dollar price for any defined exchange rate (see fig. 8–4C). The intersection of the demand and supply curves (given e_0) determines the quantity of exports X_0 and the supply S_0 of dollars

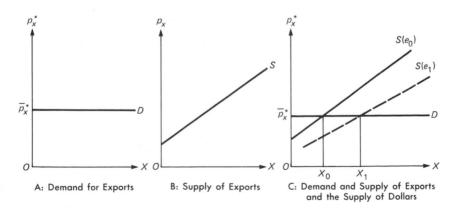

FIGURE 8–4

Exports and the Supply of Dollars

$\bar{p}_x{}^*X_0$, which can be associated with e_0 to determine a point on the supply curve of dollars in figure 8–2. The effect of increasing the exchange rate to e_1 is to increase the peso price $p_x = ep_x{}^*$ corresponding to any dollar price $p_x{}^*$, and thus to increase the supply of exports for any $p_x{}^*$; in other words, the supply curve in figure 8–4C shifts to the right as shown. The effect is to increase the quantity of exports to X_1 and the value of exports, or supply of dollars, to $\bar{p}_x{}^*{\cdot}X_1$. The supply curve in figure 8–2 is therefore upward sloping.

We have now shown that, for a small country which neutralizes any impact of an exchange rate change on the level of income, the demand curve for foreign exchange slopes down and the supply curve up. It follows that there is an equilibrium exchange rate e at which demand equals supply. At a lower exchange rate there is an excess demand for dollars, and at a higher exchange rate there is an excess supply. If the country adopts a policy of devaluing when there is excess demand for dollars and revaluing[6] when there is excess supply, it will approach the equilibrium e. In reality, however, implementing this advice is far from being as simple as it may look in figure 8–2, partly because no real world equilibrium remains constant over time and even more because trade flows respond to exchange rate changes with extended lags rather than instantaneously. We shall return to this point subsequently, but it is important to understand that the analysis of demand and supply applies to a specific time period, sufficiently long to allow volumes to respond to price changes.

The conclusion that a devaluation will always improve the trade balance is, as it happens, critically dependent upon the assumption that the country can sell as many exports as it chooses at the going world price. This is, however, a particularly strong assumption. Many countries that would certainly be described as small by any other economic criterion supply a sufficiently large part of the world market with one or two major export products so as not to face an infinitely elastic demand curve: Tanzania is not a small supplier to the world sisal market, nor is Thailand to the world rice or tapioca market. It is therefore important to examine how the analysis needs to be modified when a country faces a downward-sloping demand curve for its exports. Figure 8–4C is transformed to the form shown in figure 8–5A. Now it is no longer true that the rightward shift of the supply curve resulting from a devaluation will necessarily increase the country's dollar receipts from exports. In fact, the behavior of the dollar value of export

6. The term "revalue" is being used, according to current usage, as the opposite of "devalue," rather than in the old-fashioned (though less ambiguous) way to signify any change in the exchange rate, whether devaluation or "upvaluation."

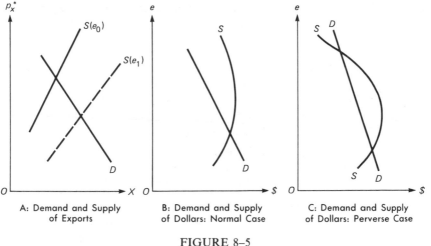

FIGURE 8–5

Inelastic Demand for Exports

receipts as e increases depends upon a very simple condition: whether or not the demand curve for exports is elastic. If demand is elastic (that is, if the elasticity of demand exceeds one), export receipts will necessarily increase, and the supply curve of dollars will slope upwards as in figure 8–2. But if demand is inelastic, the value of export receipts will fall when the exchange rate increases, and hence the supply curve of dollars will bend back as in figures 8–5B and 8–5C. This may not change the conclusion that devaluation will reduce the excess demand for dollars, as in figure 8–2B, where the decline in the demand for dollars induced by devaluation exceeds the decline in supply. But if the demand for imports happens to be very inelastic, it is possible that the demand for dollars declines less than the supply, as in figure 8–3C. Devaluation then worsens the trade balance, because the elasticities are perverse—that is, low.

Whether the perverse case shown in figure 8–5C occurs or not depends on the (price) elasticities of demand and supply for both exports and imports. There is a famous algebraic condition, known as the *Marshall-Lerner condition* (named for the two economists who first derived it), which must be satisfied if a devaluation is to improve the trade balance (under the assumptions listed earlier). On the assumption that trade is initially balanced,[7] the necessary and sufficient condition for devaluation to improve the balance of trade is that[8]

$$\frac{\epsilon_x \, (\eta_x - 1)}{\epsilon_x + \eta_x} + \frac{\eta_m \, (1 + \epsilon_m)}{\epsilon_m + \eta_m} > 0 \tag{8.9}$$

where ϵ_x = elasticity of supply of exports = $\hat{X}/\hat{p}_x$
   η_x = elasticity of demand for exports = $-\hat{X}/\hat{p}_x{}^*$
   ϵ_m = elasticity of supply of imports = $\hat{M}/\hat{p}_m{}^*$
   η_m = elasticity of demand for imports = $-\hat{M}/\hat{p}_m$.

Since the elasticities of demand (as well as of supply) have been defined to be positive, it is immediately evident from (8.9) that the perverse case where the Marshall-Lerner condition is not satisfied and devaluation worsens the trade balance can arise only if the demand for exports is inelastic.

There are two special cases of the Marshall-Lerner condition. The first is that of the small country which faces infinitely elastic foreign demand for its exports as well as supply of imports, $\eta_x = \epsilon_m = \infty$. Our previous finding in this case can be confirmed by taking the limit of (8.9) as those two elasticities go to infinity:

$$\operatorname*{Lim.}_{\eta_x, \epsilon_m \to \infty} \quad \frac{\epsilon_x(\eta_x - 1)}{\cancel{\epsilon}_x + \eta_x} + \frac{\eta_m(1 + \epsilon_m)}{\epsilon_m + \cancel{\eta}_m} = \epsilon_x + \eta_m > 0.$$

(The parameters with a line through them become negligibly small compared to η_x and ϵ_m, which can then be cancelled.) Thus the balance of payments necessarily improves in the small country case.

The second special case is the one that has traditionally received a lot of

---

7. This assumption is easily generalized: the first part of the expression in (8.9) must be weighted by the proportion of exports in total trade, and the second part by the proportion that imports constitute. See n.8.

8. Proof. From the definitions of ϵ_x and η_x and the identity $\hat{p}_x = \hat{e} + \hat{p}_x{}^*$, derive $\hat{p}_x{}^* = - \hat{X}/\eta_x = -\epsilon_x\hat{p}_x/\eta_x = - (\epsilon_x/\eta_x) \, (\hat{e} + \hat{p}_x{}^*)$, which solves to yield $\hat{p}_x{}^* = - [\epsilon_x/(\epsilon_x + \eta_x)]\hat{e}$ and $\hat{p}_x = [\eta_x/(\epsilon_x + \eta_x)]\hat{e}$. Similarly, the expressions for ϵ_m and η_m and the equivalent identity can be solved to give $\hat{p}_m{}^* = - [\eta_m/(\epsilon_m + \eta_m)] \, \hat{e}$ and $\hat{p}_m = (\epsilon_m/(\epsilon_m + \eta_m)]\hat{e}$. Since the trade balance in dollars is defined as $TB = p_x{}^*X - p_m{}^*M$, one can take the total differential and substitute:

$$
\begin{aligned}
d(TB) \quad &= Xdp_x{}^* + p_x{}^*dX - Mdp_m{}^* - p_m{}^*dM \\
&= Xp_x{}^*\hat{p}_x{}^* + p_x{}^*\epsilon_xX\hat{p}_x - Mp_m{}^*\hat{p}_m{}^* + p_m{}^*\eta_mM\hat{p}_m \\
&= Xp_x{}^* \frac{[-\epsilon_x + \epsilon_x\eta_x]}{\epsilon_x + \eta_x} \hat{e} + Mp_m{}^* \frac{[\eta_m + \eta_m\epsilon_m]}{\epsilon_m + \eta_m} \hat{e} \\
&= Xp_x{}^* \frac{\epsilon_x \, (\eta_x - 1)}{\epsilon^x + \eta_x} \hat{e} + Mp_m{}^* \frac{\eta_m(1 + \epsilon_m)}{\epsilon_m + \eta_m} \hat{e}.
\end{aligned}
$$

When $Xp_x{}^* = Mp_m{}^*$, it can be seen that devaluation ($\hat{e} > o$) will improve the trade balance TB if and only if the condition (8.9) regarding the elasticities is satisfied.

attention, and is indeed sometimes referred to as *the* Marshall-Lerner condition. It is a case that is supposed to be relevant for an industrialized country whose exports consist of manufactures, but most of whose manufactured output is placed on the home market. An addition to export demand will in this case call forth increased output at a constant price: the supply of exports, as well as the supply of imports, is infinitely elastic. Then

$$\lim_{\epsilon_x, \epsilon_m \to \infty} \left\{ \frac{\epsilon_x(\eta_x - 1)}{\epsilon_x + \eta_x} + \frac{\eta_m(1 + \epsilon_m)}{\epsilon_m + \eta_m} \right\} = \eta_x + \eta_m - 1 > 0$$
$$\text{or } \eta_x + \eta_m > 1. (8.10)$$

Thus devaluation will improve the balance of payments if and only if the sum of the demand elasticities exceeds one.

In fact, with one slight change (8.10) *is* the condition that is relevant for a small country exporting manufactures, but the model justifying it needs modification. Instead of imagining that cars and television sets are auctioned off in international markets like coffee and tea, and that Ford and Toyota have supply curves with determinate elasticities saying how much they will supply at each price in the London car market, it is more sensible to recognize that the typical manufactured good is sold in a fixprice market. The manufacturer sets the price and is pleased to sell everything that is demanded at that price. This price is typically fixed on a cost-plus basis, with the markup coefficient being selected not so much in the light of the level of sales as with a view to the prices being charged by competitors. When competitors' prices rise relative to the firm's own costs, the firm takes the chance of widening its profit margin; when its costs rise relative to competitors' prices, it accepts a squeeze on its profits in order to limit its loss of market share. Devaluation is exactly the sort of shock that increases foreign competitors' prices relative to own costs. Firms typically react by passing through some proportion θ of the exchange rate change—by adjusting their quoted foreign prices down (up) less than proportionately in response to a devaluation (revaluation). When U devalues, its exporters cut their quoted dollar prices (while allowing their peso profit margins to increase). W's exporters to U raise their quoted peso prices proportionately, given that U is a small country. U's trade balance improves provided that $\theta (\eta_x - 1) + \eta_m > 0$.[9]

---

9. Proof: The pass-through coefficient θ is defined as $-\hat{p}_x^*/\hat{e}$, which implies that $\hat{p}_x = (1 - \theta)\hat{e}$ given that $\hat{p}_x = \hat{e} + \hat{p}_x^*$. One again uses the formulae for the definition of η_x and η_m. Substitution in the total differential of the formula for *TB* gives

$$\begin{aligned} d(TB) &= Xdp_x^* + p_x^*dX - Mdp_m^* - p_m^*dM \\ &= Xp_x^*(-\theta\hat{e}) + p_x^*X\eta_x\theta\hat{e} + p_mM\eta_m\hat{e} \\ &= Xp_x^*(\eta_x - 1)\eta\hat{e} + Mp_m^*\eta_m\hat{e}. \end{aligned}$$

When in the 1940s econometricians began estimating elasticities, the estimates of η_x and η_m proved distinctly low. Serious doubt was cast on whether (8.10) was in fact satisfied. Those who held that the condition was likely to fail were dubbed "elasticity pessimists"—although it is not clear why, since if the condition really failed it would be extremely lucky for the country in question, which would be able to improve its trade balance *and* its terms of trade (not to mention cutting inflation) by *revaluing* its currency. The fact that countries that have allowed their real exchange rates to become overvalued have repeatedly encountered payments crises rather than ever-increasing surpluses is one of the factors that has since eroded the popularity of elasticity pessimism. Another is the realization that the "small-country assumption" implies that the trade balance *cannot* deteriorate as a result of devaluation. The third and perhaps dominant factor is a revision of what the econometric evidence seems to be saying: the typical estimates edged up to perhaps 1.5 for η_x and 0.5 to 1 for η_m.[10] In part this may be because the world changed: the early estimates were based on data for the 1930s and 1940s, when widespread controls did tend to make it difficult for trade flows to respond to price changes, while later estimates have been based on data for the more liberal period of the 1950s and beyond. In part it is also attributable to the development of econometric technique. In particular, while early estimates regressed *current* trade on current income and prices (or, at best, allowed a single year's lag), it is now routine to allow for the possibility of lengthy lags in response. The evidence is that, while trade responds quickly (within months) to changes in income, responses to price changes are distinctly slow: reasonably complete adjustment may take three or four years. Presumably this is because much trade is conducted with a customary supplier, and changing the source of supply is something that is done only after due consideration and when the benefits promise to continue long enough to make the switch worthwhile.

The slow adjustment of trade volumes to the price changes induced by devaluation gives rise to the phenomenon known as the "J-curve" (see fig. 8–6). Suppose that devaluation occurs at some date t_0. Because trade contracts are signed some time before delivery occurs and the transaction enters the trade statistics, there is no immediate effect on the *volume* of trade. But if, as is typically true among industrial countries, exports are predominantly invoiced in the country's own currency while imports are mainly invoiced in the trading partner's currency, the initial effect is to *worsen* the trade balance: the dollar value of exports falls, while the dollar value of imports

10. Note that there is no contradiction involved in every country facing a higher elasticity of demand for its exports than its own elasticity of demand for imports, since exports can substitute for the exports of other countries as well as for import substitutes.

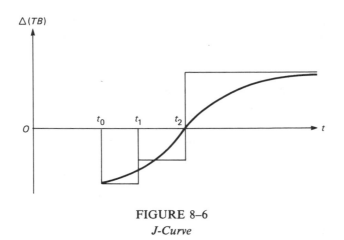

FIGURE 8-6

J-Curve

remains unchanged. If all trade contracts lasted the same time until delivery, this worsening would persist until some date t_1. From that point on, the contracts entering the trade figures would be those signed after t_0, and would thus reflect the higher *peso* prices charged by exporters to take advantage of the devaluation. The trade deficit would thus shrink, though not back to its predevaluation level until trade *volumes* adjusted in response to the price changes. If we suppose that happens simultaneously in all industries, at time t_2, we would get a path for the trade balance shown by the histograms: the final portion is positive provided the Marshall-Lerner condition is satisfied. But since not all trade contracts have the same time profile, in reality these three phases get muddled up, and the path of the trade balance is shown instead by something like the thick smooth curve. With a good dose of imagination it is possible to turn that into a J shape, hence the name J-curve. (Nonindustrial countries denominate their exports in dollars and are less prone to quote prices in their domestic currency, so their J-curves are weaker, if they exist at all.)

The analysis has up to now been conducted on the assumption that the price level in both countries is constant. However, we live in an inflationary world, and no analysis that cannot be generalized to recognize this fact is much use. In the present instance, we need to generalize in two directions. First, we need to recognize that what determines the degree of competitiveness of U's products on W's market (and vice versa) is not the nominal exchange rate e, but the real exchange rate ep^*/p.[11] One expects a devaluation to stimulate exports and promote import substitutes at the expense of

---

11. Note that recognition of the possibility of foreign inflation would require a reinterpretation of the horizontal axis of fig. 8-2 to refer to "real dollars" ($\$/p^*$), as well as of the vertical axis to refer to the real exchange rate ep^*/p.

imports only if $ep*/p$ is increased: a devaluation that leaves that ratio unchanged, because p has increased relative to $p*$, will simply prevent the trade balance worsening. Such a devaluation may be said to have the effect of neutralizing excess domestic inflation.

The second generalization that is needed is to recognize that devaluation is liable to increase the domestic price level. There are a variety of channels through which this can occur. Most directly, import prices rise: this pushes up prices of imported final goods and increases the costs of production and thus the prices of domestic goods that use imported materials and intermediates. The prices of exports and import substitutes are likely to rise, either because they are homogeneous goods with prices determined on world markets or because the devaluation lessens competitive pressure and permits the markup to be increased. Because workers face increased prices, trade unions are likely to demand higher wages; and because competitive pressures have been eased, employers are likely to concede them. Thus there are ample theoretical reasons for expecting devaluation to produce a spurt of inflation, and there is ample evidence that this does happen in practice. The fear that most or all of a devaluation will be neutralized by induced inflation is in fact the main current reason for questioning the efficacy of devaluation.

8.4. The Absorption Approach

In 1952 Sidney Alexander (b. 1916), then employed by the IMF, argued that the elasticities approach tended to give an overfacile view of the ease of correcting a deficit by devaluation—not because the elasticities were low nor because any devaluation would be neutralized by inflation but because devaluation cannot be relied on to increase the excess of income over expenditure. From the national income identity, we know that

$$TB = Y - A, \qquad \text{or} \qquad \Delta(TB) = \Delta Y - \Delta A.$$

It follows that, for devaluation to improve the trade balance, it must either increase real income Y or cut real expenditure (absorption) A. The question is why it should be expected to do either of those things.

The change in expenditure can be broken down into two components: that part which comes about as a result of any change in Y, through customary Keynesian "induced expenditure" effects, and that part which occurs for any other reason. The former component may be written $c\Delta Y$, where c is the marginal propensity to consume, or, more generally, the marginal propensity to absorb. Alexander argued that, since increases in investment, as well as consumption, might be induced by higher output, c could exceed unity, but few economists have subsequently taken this possibility seriously. The second component we shall denote by A_d: Alexander called it the "direct effect" on absorption, where it is "direct" in the sense that it includes all effects that are *not* the result of changes in income. Since $\Delta A = c\Delta Y + A_d$

$$\Delta(TB) = (1-c)\Delta Y - A_d. \tag{8.11}$$

Equation (8.11) says that in order to examine the effect of devaluation on the trade balance it is necessary to examine both its effect on income and its *direct* effect on absorption.

The obvious effect on income arises if the increased demand for exports and import substitutes (whose magnitude is determined by the elasticities) brings forth an increased supply. However, one of Alexander's central points was that this "idle resources effect" can operate only if the economy has idle capacity that can be brought into operation by an increase in demand. At the time when Alexander was writing, the world economy was in a virtually continuous boom and there was a general presumption that a country in deficit would not have a margin of spare capacity.

A second effect on income to which Alexander drew attention arises from a change in the terms of trade. It is generally assumed that a devaluation tends to worsen the terms of trade, except in the strict small-country case where they are independent of domestic policy. This is not necessarily true: it is possible for a devaluation to improve the terms of trade. There is in fact a very simple algebraic condition that determines whether the terms of trade worsen in the elasticities model of the previous section,[12] namely

$$\epsilon_x\epsilon_m > \eta_x\eta_m,$$

12. Proof. Substitute the expressions for $\hat{p}_x$ and $\hat{p}_m$ in n.8 into the formula for the change in the terms of trade:

$$\begin{aligned}
\hat{p}_x - \hat{p}_m &= \frac{\eta_x}{\epsilon_x + \eta_x}\hat{e} - \frac{\epsilon_m}{\epsilon_m + \eta_m}\hat{e} \\
&= \frac{\eta_x\epsilon_m + \eta_x\eta_m - \epsilon_m\epsilon_x - \epsilon_m\eta_x}{(\epsilon_x + \eta_x)(\epsilon_m + \eta_m)}\hat{e}. \\
&= \frac{(\eta_x\eta_m - \epsilon_m\epsilon_x)}{(\epsilon_x + \eta_x)(\epsilon_m + \eta_m)}\hat{e},
\end{aligned}$$

which is negative so long as $\epsilon_m\epsilon_x > \eta_x\eta_m$.

that is, that the product of the supply elasticities exceed the product of the demand elasticities. This condition is satisfied for the simple industrial country case. More relevant, the fixprice model also discussed in the previous section implies that the terms of trade will deteriorate if exporters cut their dollar prices by more than foreign suppliers cut the dollar prices at which they supply imports; given that the cut in domestic costs is important to exporters while U's market is a drop in the ocean to W's exporters, there is an overwhelming presumption that this condition is satisfied. Thus the general presumption—shared by Alexander—that devaluation would worsen the terms of trade (if it has any effect at all) is well grounded. This means that devaluation tends to *reduce* real income, which for constant real absorption implies a *bigger* trade deficit.[13]

In subsequent debate, Fritz Machlup added a third channel through which devaluation might influence real income, the resource allocation effect. He argued that a devaluation permitted a relaxation of controls and restrictions, which typically produce microeconomic distortions as analyzed in chapter 5. A program of simultaneously abolishing such restrictions and devaluing to maintain the same average incentive to export (or produce import substitutes) could be expected to improve allocative efficiency and thus increase real income. Packages of this character have frequently figured in IMF lending programs—an example of supply-side economics in action long before the term became faddish.

It is next necessary to examine why and how devaluation might be expected to affect absorption directly, that is, other than as a result of changes induced by changes in real income. The basic argument is that this can be expected, at least in certain circumstances and to some degree, as a result of the inflation that is induced by devaluation. For reasons that were discussed at the end of the previous section, prices rise after a devaluation. This *reduces* the competitive gains that persist, but on the other hand it tends to cut absorption. There are two broad channels through which this can occur, monetary and distributional. Assuming that the devaluation-induced inflation is not accompanied by an equivalent rise in the money supply (as may easily happen in countries with "passive" monetary policies dedicated to maintaining interest rates constant), the real value of the money supply H/P falls. In consequence interest rates rise and choke off

13. Almost every time a country devalues, its newspapers make an analytical error which grossly exaggerates the loss to real income from the terms-of-trade deterioration. They claim that the price for which exports are sold falls, while the price the country has to pay for its imports rises. Of course, there is a sense in which both statements are true; the *dollar* price of exports falls, while the *peso* price of imports rises. But to *compare* those two movements is erroneous: the terms of trade must be measured in a common currency. In dollars, the price of *both* exports and imports fall (if the latter changes at all), while in terms of pesos, they *both* rise.

investment (according to the traditional Keynesian analysis), while the negative real balance effect also causes consumers to seek to rebuild their liquid assets and thus curtail consumption (according to the wider perspective popularized by the Israeli economist Don Patinkin [b. 1922] and the leading monetarist and 1976 Nobel laureate Milton Friedman [b. 1912]).

The distributional channels involve government versus public and profits versus wages. A country with a progressive tax system tends to reap an increase in tax revenue more than proportional to the increase in the price level when inflation occurs, as a result of taxpayers moving into higher tax brackets. If expenditure remains constant in real terms, and thus increases proportionately in nominal terms, it follows that the real budget surplus increases as a result of inflation (a phenomenon known as "fiscal drag"). In other words, income is redistributed from the private sector to the public sector; since the latter is normally assumed to determine its spending independently of its short-run revenue, it has a marginal propensity to save of unity, and the income redistribution cuts absorption. Finally, since many prices (especially of traded goods) are pulled up rather directly by devaluation while any impact on wages is indirect and lagged, income may be redistributed from wages to profits. The Marxist savings function, which says that capitalists save a higher proportion of their income than do workers, implies that this redistribution will also cut absorption.

Looking back at equation (8.11), we can now see why Alexander was skeptical as to the potency of devaluation to affect the balance of payments. Even if we rule out the possibility $c > 1$, there is no guarantee that $\Delta(TB$ will be positive, especially if the country is initially at full employment so that Y cannot increase in response to higher external demand. What remains are the negative terms-of-trade effect and the positive resource-allocation effect on income, whose net effect is ambiguous, and the direct effects on absorption. Alexander argued that these would normally be rather weak. This certainly seems to be true of the redistributive effect toward the government. In fact, there is evidence that in many countries fiscal drag is negative: inflation speeds up government expenditures more than proportionately (for example, as a result of subsidized credits to favored sectors being made available at fixed *nominal* interest rates), while tax revenues lag. In consequence income is redistributed away from the government and demand is stimulated rather than constrained. Even if the other effects are more dependable, the net result may be rather small.

The policy conclusion implied is simple. When undertaken from an initial situation of full employment, devaluation must be accompanied by discretionary policy to reduce demand in order to make room for an improvement in the balance of payments. IMF stabilization programs designed to deal with a payments deficit typically involve deflationary fiscal and monetary measures, as well as devaluation, with this end in view.

8.5 Meade's Synthesis: Internal and External Balance

A similar conclusion can be drawn from the important work of the 1972 Nobel Prize-winning English economist James Meade (b. 1907), whose synthesis of the income and price effects studied in previous sections provides the most authoritative statement of what has been called orthodox balance of payments theory. The central focus of Meade's analysis was on the conditions that had to be satisfied if a country was to succeed in achieving simultaneously internal balance and external balance. The major conclusion was that this requires the use of *two* policy instruments, with differentiated effects on income and the balance of payments. The general idea that achievement of *n* targets requires the use of *n* independent instruments was developed simultaneously by one of the first (1969) winners of the Nobel Prize, the Dutch economist Jan Tinbergen (b. 1903), and is known as "the theory of economic policy."

The concept of *internal balance* refers to the achievement of as high a level of demand and employment as is consistent with avoidance of the stimulation of unacceptable inflationary pressure. Once upon a time it was customary to refer to this as the achievement of noninflationary full employment. Then in 1958 came the idea of the Phillips curve, named after the New Zealand economist W. A. Phillips (1912–67), which suggested that there was a continuous trade-off between unemployment and inflation rather than a sharp cutoff; this led to a reformulation of the concept of internal balance to refer to the optimal point on the Phillips curve, where society found the marginal benefit of any further diminution in unemployment would be outweighed by the marginal cost of the resulting increase in inflation. A decade later came the natural rate hypothesis of Edmund Phelps (b. 1933) and Milton Friedman, which held that there was only one rate of unemployment (the natural rate) that could be sustained in the long run, because any lower rate would stimulate more inflation than people were initially expecting, which would shift the Phillips curve up as everyone wrote contracts designed to safeguard their real income against the expected inflation. Similarly, unemployment higher than the natural rate was conceived to initiate a cumulative deceleration of inflation. The implication was that one had to learn to live with the facts of life, however much one might dislike them, and accept an unemployment target high enough to avoid accelerating inflation or even to reduce inflation, where inherited inflationary expectations are high. Internal balance thus becomes more or less synonymous with the natural rate of unemployment. But whatever one's theory of inflation, internal balance may be defined as the highest level of demand consistent with a prudent control of inflation.

The concept of external balance gives no difficulties in the present context, where there is no capital mobility. It clearly refers to a situation where the balance of payments is in equilibrium, and there is no need to choose whether this refers to equilibrium overall or on current account, since the two amount to the same thing. (The more difficult conceptual issues will be discussed in chapter 9.2.)

In order to study how policies need to be chosen to permit a country to achieve internal and external balance simultaneously, we shall utilize a diagram (see fig. 8–7) developed independently by the Australian economists W. E. G. Salter and Trevor Swan (b. 1918). On the horizontal axis is shown the level of domestic spending, or absorption. On the vertical axis is shown the international competitiveness of our goods, which can *ceteris paribus* be identified with the real exchange rate, ep^*/p.

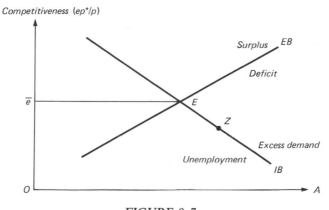

FIGURE 8–7
Internal and External Balance

The main property of the internal balance schedule can be established by the following argument. Suppose we have some combination of A and ep^*/p which produces just that pressure of demand that corresponds to our concept of internal balance. Consider the effect of adopting a policy (for example, cutting taxes) that stimulates absorption. This would tend to push the economy into a state of excess demand. To counter that and preserve internal balance one could appreciate the currency, so as to divert a part of demand away from domestic producers. Thus the locus of points of internal balance (*IB*) slopes down, as shown, with points of excess demand to the right and of wastefully high unemployment to the left.

A similar argument can be used to establish the slope of the external balance schedule. Suppose absorption increases because of a policy change. We know from the multiplier analysis that that will push the balance of payments into deficit. To preserve external balance, that must be compensated by changing the composition of spending in favor of domestically produced goods, by a real devaluation, as analyzed in the elasticities approach. Thus the external balance (*EB*) schedule slopes up, with a deficit to the right and a surplus to the left.

The basic theme of Meade's analysis was that in order to achieve internal and external balance simultaneously it is necessary to have one policy to influence the level of expenditure and one to influence its composition. This is clear from figure 8–7: for example, a country that controlled policy instruments able to influence only *A* could reach the point *E* of simultaneous internal and external balance only if competitiveness happened to be $\bar{e}$. If competitiveness were less, the currency would be overvalued and in consequence the country would have to choose between unemployment and a payments deficit (or some of each). Harry Johnson later called policies that influenced the level of expenditure "expenditure-reducing policies," and those that influenced its composition "expenditure-switching policies."

Expenditure-reducing policies—expenditure-changing would be a better term, since sometimes the need is to increase rather than reduce absorption —are simple to identify. They consist mainly of the demand management policies identified by Keynesian theory, namely, fiscal policy and monetary policy.

Expenditure-switching policies are those able to influence international competitiveness. Exchange rate changes are the leading example—though they will succeed in switching expenditure only to the extent that they lead to changes in the *real* exchange rate rather than being neutralized by induced inflation. However, there are many other policies that may be able to switch expenditure as well: for example, tariffs, export subsidies, quantitative import restrictions, other forms of protection, measures to improve the quality of domestically produced goods, export credit facilities . . . the list is virtually endless. These are the policies held constant in the *ceteris paribus* qualification that was inserted when the concept of competitiveness was equated to the real exchange rate. The argument for assigning pride of place to the real exchange rate is not that these other policies are necessarily unimportant, but that microeconomic efficiency rather than the needs of macroeconomic management should be the criterion that determines what is done in those respects. Macroeconomic management should be prosecuted with a *general* policy, so as to avoid producing microeconomic distortions.

Suppose that the economy were initially at a point such as Z in figure 8–7, in internal balance but with a payments deficit. It can be seen that reestablishment of payments balance might be accomplished simply by reducing A—by deflating—until one hit the EB-schedule. However, the cost would be unemployment. To avoid that cost one must switch expenditure toward domestic goods, for example, by devaluing. But to devalue without deflating would push the economy to a point vertically above Z where the competitive gain from devaluation would soon be eroded by the inflation resulting from excess demand. In other words, a successful devaluation from a point of full employment must be accompanied by a policy of expenditure reduction—the same policy conclusion as emerged from the absorption approach.

This conclusion, and especially the IMF policies based upon it, has been challenged in recent years by economists such as Richard Cooper (b. 1934), Paul Krugman, and Lance Taylor (b. 1940). They have recalled that devaluation does not just have expenditure-switching effects but also direct effects on absorption, that is, expenditure-reducing effects. A rise in e will reduce A as well as increase ep^*/p, with the relative importance of each dependent on the extent to which devaluation provokes inflation. Hence devaluation will push the economy diagonally upward and to the left from Z, not vertically up. It is possible that the economy will be pushed to a point *below IB* even without the reinforcing deflationary measures called for by IMF orthodoxy, in which case application of those orthodox measures will create wasteful unemployment.

One can make some conjectures as to the type of economy in which this is likely to happen. First, if devaluation provokes an offsetting rise in domestic prices, for example, because of the presence of real wage resistance, then devaluation will not have much effect in improving competitiveness to counter its absorption-reducing effect. Second, where there are few opportunities for substitution between domestically produced and foreign-produced goods, the IB curve will be very steep. The second factor suggests that countries like the Persian Gulf oil exporters or plantation-dominated economies are likely to fit the unorthodox case, while any economy suffering a high degree of real wage resistance may do so as well because of the first factor. Countries with low elasticities will experience an additional deflationary impact if they initially have a trade deficit, since the domestic-currency value of the trade deficit (which constitutes a leakage from the income stream) will increase.

The reason *why* an economy fits the unorthodox case is important in drawing policy implications. For countries with little elasticity in the production structure, the main alternative to a reduction in absorption has to be foreign borrowing, until such time as new investment can come on stream in the export or import-substituting industries. For countries suffering from real wage resistance, the opportunities may be somewhat broader. When orthodox fiscal-monetary-exchange rate policies are inadequate to restore simultaneous internal and external balance, the reason is that real income claims constrain the economy to points on or to the right of the curve *WR* (wage resistance) in figure 8–8. This curve *WR* might be vertical, or it might have a positive slope insofar as workers can be intimidated into accepting lower real wages (requiring lower absorption) by an uncompetitive exchange rate with its threat of bankruptcies. Devaluation from a point like *Z* would produce a neutralizing inflation that would at best leave ep^*/p unchanged while tending to reduce *A* through the direct effects. The only ways to restore simultaneous internal and external balance are to operate on the supply side, to the extent that may be feasible, or to develop an incomes policy capable of reconciling the labor force to the harsh facts of life, and thus push the curve *WR* left. Failure to do either guarantees repeated economic crises.

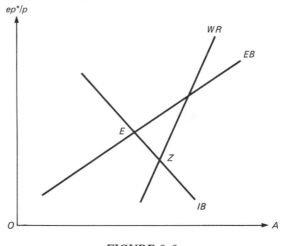

FIGURE 8–8
Implications of Real Wage Resistance

The model underlying the elasticities approach, which together with the multiplier analysis formed the basis for figure 8–7, is essentially a three-good model with exportables, importables, and a large nontraded goods sector. It is worth checking that the conclusions of Meade's synthesis are robust, which can be done by examining the dependent economy model introduced in chapter 6. Consider figure 8–9. Suppose that the price of the nontraded good N is fixed in domestic currency (or at least sticky), while that of the traded good M is determined by arbitrage from the world market at the level $p_m = ep_m{}^*$. Suppose that the resulting relative price is represented by budget curves with slope equal to that of A_0. If expenditure is initially in excess of income, at the level represented by the budget line A_0, then consumption will occur at the point C and production at the point P. There is internal balance because the production of home goods is equal to consumption, but an external deficit because the consumption of traded goods M exceeds their production. To achieve external balance by deflation alone would require cutting the value of absorption to A_1, but this would create an excess supply of home goods and thus unemployment. To achieve internal and external balance simultaneously requires a devaluation to raise the relative price of traded goods and thus induce substitution by consumers away from traded goods and by producers toward traded goods, combined with an expenditure-reducing policy to cut absorption to A_2. The combination can achieve the point of internal and external balance at Z.

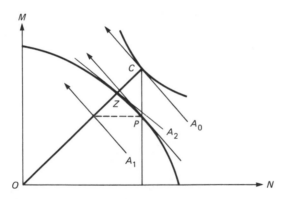

FIGURE 8–9
Internal and External Balance in the Dependent Economy Model

8.6 The Monetary Approach

The "orthodox" theory that developed from Keynesian ideas and that was presented in the preceding four sections does not preclude the operation of monetary factors. The money supply is recognized as one of the determinants of aggregate demand. By treating the money supply as a policy variable, it is implicitly assumed that the monetary consequences of payments imbalances are sterilized. It is recognized that a rise in the price level induced by devaluation will reduce real money balances and thus real demand. Money is therefore a part of the picture, but it is not placed at the center of the stage as it was in Hume's analysis of the gold standard. The monetary approach to the balance of payments has been developed by those who believe that giving money anything other than pride of place is misleading.

The monetary approach was developed by two distinct schools. The first was based at the IMF and initiated by the work of the Dutch economist J. J. Polak (b. 1914), the former research director of the Fund. This school was rather undogmatic, the main justification offered for the new approach being to develop models that would be usable to monitor macroeconomic management when only the most rudimentary statistical information—which typically centers on monetary statistics—was available. The second school developed at the University of Chicago in the 1960s under the intellectual leadership of the Canadians Robert Mundell (b. 1932) and Harry Johnson. Many of the writings of this school have had a polemical edge, involving some perceived clash with Keynesian orthodoxy.

The consolidated balance sheet of a simplified banking system like that presented in chapter 7 reveals the identity:

$$\text{Reserves} + \text{Domestic credit} = \text{Money supply, or } R + D = H. \quad (8.12)$$

Since a deficit on the balance of payments implies a loss of reserves, it follows from equation (8.12) that there must be a counterpart to a deficit in the form of either credit creation (sterilization) or dishoarding (a fall in H). Since dishoarding is a temporary or disequilibrium phenomenon, a payments deficit can persist only if it is accompanied by credit creation. To put the matter another way, any additional credit creation will ultimately leak out abroad. This is the central theorem of the monetary approach to the balance of payments.

The monetary approach claims to offer a theory of the balance of payments rather than of the current account. Consequently, our main consideration of it is postponed to the next chapter, after introduction of the capital account into the analysis. For the present we restrict our attention to those topics where the monetary approach has offered contributions specifically relevant to analysis of the current account. The first is a model of payments adjustment with a fixed exchange rate that was developed by Polak and that became the basis for the stabilization programs sponsored by the IMF. The second concerns the hypothesis that prices are determined by arbitrage, which was used by the German-born economist Rudiger Dornbusch (b. 1942) to analyze devaluation.

166

POLAK MODEL

The Polak model adopts a number of simplifying assumptions in order to highlight the essence of the monetary adjustment mechanism. In addition to assuming capital immobility and a fixed exchange rate, Polak took exports to be exogenous and domestic credit expansion to be a policy variable and therefore also exogenous. There are two substantive assumptions. The first is that the velocity of circulation is constant, as assumed in the old-fashioned quantity theory. That enables one to normalize velocity to unity, with no loss of generality, and to write

$$Y_t = H_t. \tag{8.13}$$

The second substantive assumption is that imports are always some fixed proportion m of the value of the previous period's nominal income:

$$M_t = mY_{t-1}. \tag{8.14}$$

This implies that the propensity to import is independent of whether a given nominal income is the result of a high price level and low output, or *vice versa*. There is no reason why this should be true, but the approximation simplifies model building enormously. The model is completed by the money supply and balance of payments identities:

$$\Delta H_t = \Delta R_t + \Delta D_t, \tag{8.15}$$
$$\Delta R_t = X_t - M_t. \tag{8.16}$$

Substitution of (8.14) and (8.15) into (8.13) yields

$$Y_t = H_t = H_{t-1} + \Delta H_t = Y_{t-1} + \Delta R_t + \Delta D_t. \tag{8.17}$$

This gives us the basic monetary theorem already deduced from (8.12). Since $Y_t = Y_{t-1}$ in equilibrium (by definition), a payments deficit ($\Delta R < 0$) can persist only when domestic credit creation (ΔD) is positive.

It is also possible to use the model to tell a story about the time path of imports and income following an exogenous shock, for example, an increase in domestic credit expansion. Suppose that initially, at $t = 0$, the economy is in equilibrium so $\Delta D = 0$ and $M = M_0$, and that this equilibrium is disturbed at $t = 1$ by an expansion of domestic credit of 1, which is maintained each period thereafter. Table 8–1 traces the expansion of imports and income that this would produce. Column (2) calculates (8.14), while column (3) cumulates the difference between current imports and initial imports from column (2). The final column calculates the equation

167

for ΔY derived by substituting (8.16) into (8.17) and recognizing that $X_t = X_0 = M_0$:

$$\Delta Y_t = \Delta D_t + \Delta R_t = \Delta D_t + X_t - M_t = \Delta D_t - (M_t - M_0).$$

TABLE 8–1

Dynamic Adjustment in the Polak Model

Time (1)	$\Delta M_t = m\Delta Y_{t-1}$ (2)	$M_t - M_0$ (3)	$\Delta Y_t = \Delta D_t - (M_t - M_0)$ (4)
0	0	0	0
1	0	0	1
2	m	m	$1-m$
3	$m(1-m)$	$m[1+(1-m)]$	$1-m(1+1-m) = (1-m)^2$
4	$m(1-m)^2$	$m[1+(1-m)+(1-m)^2]$	$(1-m)^3$
∞	0	1	0

The final row shows the limit as $t \to \infty$. Imports and income approach new stationary levels with $\Delta M = \Delta Y = 0$, where imports have increased to match the increase in credit creation, while income has increased by $1 + (1-m) + (1-m)^2 \ldots = 1/[1-(1-m)] = 1/m$, a multiple of the credit expansion determined by the import propensity. In this new "equilibrium" reserves are falling by the amount of credit creation—the whole of the additional credit is leaking out through the balance of payments. Insofar as that cannot persist indefinitely, because ultimately reserves would be exhausted, one cannot consider that to be a long-run equilibrium.

It is also possible to study the impact of a change in exports. The reader should confirm that the long-run impact of a rise in exports will be to increase Y, H and R by $\Delta X/m$ according to the multiplier formula, while imports will gradually rise to match the increase in exports.

The model is a simple one, but its conclusions are quite robust. It suffices to explain the prominent place that the IMF has traditionally given to limiting domestic credit expansion as an element of programs of balance of payments adjustment. Critics of the Fund claim that it has sometimes paid too little attention to the costs of the decline in income that the model shows will result from credit contraction, tending to assume too readily that falls in nominal income largely reflect lower prices rather than lower output.

ARBITRAGE

The second topic of this section is the role of arbitrage in determining national price levels. The orthodox theory tended to regard price levels as largely fixed by forces internal to each country, whether as constant, being

168

pushed up exogenously by costs, as determined by a Phillips curve, or, in orthodox monetarism, as determined by the quantity of money. In contrast, the global monetarism of the monetary approach argues that price levels are determined by arbitrage from the world market, according to the familiar formula

$$p = ep^*. \tag{8.18}$$

This assumption permits some elegant model building. An interesting example is Dornbusch's analysis of devaluation. Consider a small country whose price level is determined by (8.18)—Dornbusch actually assumed a one-good two-money model, to emphasize that devaluation need not necessarily involve relative price changes. Assume away capital flows and credit markets. Suppose that the public has an orthodox demand for money function expressed in real terms, so that $H_d = \alpha p$, but that it seeks to adjust any discrepancy between actual and desired money holdings only gradually, at the rate β. Then the rate of hoarding ΔH will be given by

$$\Delta H = \beta(\alpha p - H), \tag{8.19}$$

which implies that hoarding can be shown as a function of the real value of the money supply as in figure 8–10. Add the assumption of no credit creation, and the vertical axis also shows the payments surplus or deficit.

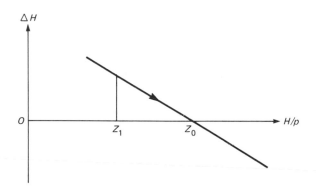

FIGURE 8–10
Dornbusch Model of Devaluation

Suppose that the economy is in equilibrium at point Z_0, and that the exchange rate is then increased by a sudden devaluation. By (8.18), the price level rises proportionately, which implies that H/p falls, for example, to Z_1. The public now finds itself short of real money balances, so it cuts back on buying goods, which leads to a trade surplus. Real balances climb back slowly toward their equilibrium at Z_0, as shown by the arrow. When they reach Z_0, the payments surplus disappears and the only variables that differ from the initial situation are the price level and the level of reserves. A conclusion much stressed by monetarists is that, while devaluation does indeed cause a surplus, that surplus is temporary.

The mechanism involved here is merely an extreme version of the one responsible for the direct effects on absorption in the absorption approach. From a Meadean perspective, the Dornbusch model implies that devaluation has only expenditure-changing and no expenditure-switching effects. There is very strong empirical evidence that this extreme assumption is not warranted: even traded goods are typically differentiated products, whose prices can differ as between different sources for similar goods, and prices of nontraded goods are even less subject to the influence of arbitrage. The dependent economy model is quite an illuminating way of analyzing the implications of the fact that while arbitrage does have a powerful influence on the prices of traded goods, it nevertheless does not equalize price levels between countries. But one should always remember that in the real world even the assumptions of that model, that the prices of traded goods are equalized by arbitrage, is satisfied only for homogeneous commodities, which do not constitute the bulk of trade.

8.7   General Equilibrium: IS/LM/BP

The balance of payments is determined simultaneously with all other macroeconomic variables. The way that economists recognize such interdependence is by constructing general equilibrium models. The simplest general equilibrium model that is reasonably adequate for integrating the analyses presented in preceding sections is the IS/LM model, extended by the addition of a curve representing balance of payments equilibrium. But even this model suffers from three important limitations, which will be noted subsequently.

The analysis is shown in figure 8–11. The horizontal axis shows real income, and the vertical axis shows the nominal (and real, since we assume away inflationary expectations) interest rate. The *IS* curve represents the locus of points of (flow) equilibrium in the goods market, which are charac-

170

terized by the condition that $I = S$ *ex ante*. [14] It slopes down because a lower interest rate stimulates investment, which requires a higher income level to generate a corresponding increase in saving. The *LM* curve represents the locus of points of (stock) equilibrium in the asset markets: with a model with only two assets, money and bonds, it matters not whether one describes that as equilibrium in the money market or the bond market. It slopes up because an increase in income raises the transactions demand for money and thus requires an increase in the interest rate to induce a corresponding reduction in speculative demand (to use the Keynesian terminology). In the short run (though a short run sufficiently long for the multiplier process to work itself out), the economy goes to an equilibrium at the intersection of the *IS* and *LM* curves.

The balance of payments can be introduced into this familiar diagram by recalling that the current account balance is lower the higher the level of income (from the multiplier analysis) is. The rate of interest, however, has no direct effect on the balance of payments: it is true that a higher interest rate might improve the current account, but it would do so by cutting income (that is, by inducing a movement along the *IS* curve) rather than directly. Hence the curve representing balance of payments equilibrium is a vertical line, labeled *BP,* at some value Y_1. There is a payments deficit to the right of *BP* and a surplus to the left. In the case shown in figure 8–11, with income at Y_e, the balance of payments would be in deficit.

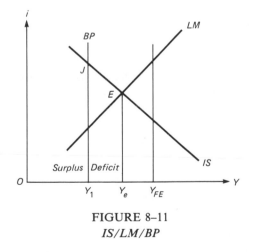

FIGURE 8–11
IS/LM/BP

14. In the extended model of an open economy with fiscal policy, the condition is of course $(I-S) + (G-T) + (X-M) = 0$.

171

The essential ideas of the various approaches analyzed in the preceding sections of this chapter are reflected in this model. First, there is the monetary mechanism of automatic adjustment of Hume and Polak. At the short-run equilibrium shown in figure 8–11, there is a current account deficit and hence, with no capital mobility, the country is losing reserves. As it does so, with no sterilization, the money supply falls and hence the *LM* curve shifts leftward. The process continues until the *LM* curve intersects the point *J* where *IS* crosses *BP*. At that point the balance of payments is also in equilibrium and so, with downward price rigidity, the economy is in long-run equilibrium. However, the postulated adjustment mechanism involves neither the exclusive price decline of Hume nor the possibility of a decline in prices as part of the fall in nominal income of Polak, but rather a reduction in real income as in Ohlin's analysis.

Second, consider the multiplier analysis. It has already been pointed out that the position of the *BP* curve reflects this factor. In addition, one needs to consider how the various comparative statics theorems are reflected in this model. An increase in investment pushes *IS* to the right and leaves *BP* unaffected. Since the multiplier analysis presupposes a constant interest rate, the central bank is assumed to accommodate the increase in the demand for money by expansionary open-market operations that push *LM* to the right just far enough to match the shift of *IS*. As the gap between Y_e and Y_1 increases, the balance of payment deteriorates. An increase in exports has the same effect on *IS* and *LM* but also pushes *BP* to the right (by more, though this is not obvious from the diagram), so that income still increases but the balance of payments improves.

Third, consider the elasticities approach. Since prices are not shown in figure 8–10, the effects of price changes have to be represented by shifts in the curves. A real devaluation definitely pushes *IS* to the right, though the assumption of the algebra is that this effect is neutralized by a contractionary fiscal policy (or by a contractionary monetary policy that pushes *LM* up by enough to maintain *Y* constant). It also pushes *BP* to the right provided the Marshall-Lerner condition is satisfied. However, a nominal devaluation has these effects only to the extent that it leads to a real devaluation rather than being neutralized by price changes. These effects may take several years to work themselves out, and in the interim the balance of payments may deteriorate even if income is held constant rather than being allowed to expand.

Fourth, recall that the absorption approach taught us that a rightward shift of *BP* may not be sufficient to improve the balance of payments. We need to recognize that figure 8–11 has another important curve, the full employment benchmark represented by the vertical line above Y_{FE}. If Y_e

initially coincides with Y_{FE}, output cannot expand to match an increase in demand, and hence any improvement in the balance of payments is conditional on a cut in absorption. This may come about automatically either because income redistribution has a leftward impact on *IS*, or because the inflation induced by devaluation reduces the real money supply and so pushes *LM* leftward. To the extent that these forces are insufficient to eliminate the inflationary gap, the government needs to take restrictive fiscal-monetary measures to push either *IS* or *LM* (or both) to the left.

Fifth, Meade's analysis is about the combination of policies needed to secure an intersection of all four curves (*IS*, *LM*, *BP* and Y_{FE}) at the same point. Internal balance is represented by *E* being on Y_{FE}, and external balance by *E* being on *BP*. To make *E* lie on both simultaneously we need to be able to shift *BP* and at least one of the two curves *IS* and *LM*. Shifting *BP* requires an expenditure-switching policy, while shifting *IS* or *LM* requires an expenditure-changing policy. If devaluation is used as the expenditure-switching policy, it will also shift *IS* right and *LM* left. Remember that it has been argued that in some economies with limited substitution possibilities the leftward shift of *LM* may exceed the rightward shift of *IS* so that it may be appropriate to accompany devaluation by expansionary fiscal or monetary policy even if the economy is initially at full capacity.

Finally, the monetary approach has stressed the impact of devaluation on *LM*, and even argued that this may be its *only* effect, as well as reviving the idea of the automatic monetary adjustment mechanism. Monetarists tend not to be overconcerned with the possibility that this will provide insufficient instruments to achieve internal and external balance simultaneously, because they assume that price flexibility can be relied on to secure internal balance without any help from government.

The IS/LM/BP model thus provides a simple general equilibrium framework that suffices to show that the various approaches to payments theory are complementary rather than competitive. The main difference in policy conclusions between monetarists and mainstream economists, which is whether or not one needs to worry about internal balance, does not stem from any inability of orthodox theory to incorporate the behavioral relations stressed in the monetary approach, but from their differing degree of faith in the ability of price flexibility to clear markets.

Useful as the IS/LM/BP model is, however, it must be recognized that it suffers from three important limitations. First, it assumes a given price level and does not incorporate a theory of inflation. Second, it assumes static expectations—of a constant future price level, for example, so that it is possible to equate the nominal and real rate of interest. Third, it assumes given stocks of the various assets—money, bonds, and physical capital.

These assumptions can, of course, be relaxed. Indeed, we have already noted the effects of varying the stock of money in shifting *LM*. It is particularly interesting to consider extending the model to include a theory of inflation. Suppose, therefore, that the wage level, instead of being constant, were determined by a Phillips curve (with or without adaptive expectations). It is easy to see that, with this addition, the IS/LM/BP model will generate all the monetarist conclusions as between two positions of long-run equilibrium (with $\hat{w} = 0$). For example, the monetary mechanism of adjustment no longer implies that income would remain at the less than full employment level Y_1 produced by *LM*'s migration to intersect *BP* and *IS* at *J*. The reason is that at *J* the unemployment would imply declining wages, which would improve competitiveness and so push both *IS* and *BP* right: equilibrium could occur only with full employment (specifically, with unemployment equal to the natural rate). Or, suppose one were to devalue from a position of long-run equilibrium. Unless the direct effects on absorption outweighed the substitution effects induced by the gain in competitiveness, income would increase and unemployment would fall below the natural rate, generating inflation, which would erode the competitive gain from devaluation. Thus the IS/LM/BP model extended by addition of a Phillips curve has long-run comparative statics properties that are essentially monetarist, while its short-run behavior is eminently Keynesian. This suggests that the relationship between monetarism and Keynesianism is one of the time span judged relevant for policy formation, with monetarists tending to dismiss the short-run and Keynesians to disregard the long-run consequences of policy.

8.8 Summary

The orthodox theory of the current account, incorporating the income effects of the multiplier analysis and the price effects of the elasticities approach as synthesised by Meade, can be summarized in the equation

$$TB = TB(\overset{-}{Y}, \overset{+}{ep*/p}). \qquad (8.20)$$

The signs over the arguments of the function TB (. . .) represent the direction of the effects of those variables on the trade balance (that is, the signs of the partial derivatives). The negative sign over Y comes from chapter 8.2, while the positive impact of competitiveness assumes that the

Marshall-Lerner condition is satisfied. Thus (8.20) should be interpreted in a medium-run rather than short-run sense. This equation is robust to the choice of model and will be used in subsequent chapters to summarize the results of the present chapter.

Even though they do not imply any modification to the current account equation (8.20), the absorption approach and the monetary approach also contribute important perspectives. The absorption approach shows that it will normally be necessary to accompany an expenditure-switching policy like devaluation by an expenditure-reducing policy if devaluation is to improve the balance of payments and the economy is initially at full employment. With capital immobility, the monetary approach shows how monetary factors would dominate the adjustment process in the long run even though the behavioral relations and therefore the short-run properties are impeccably Keynesian.

8.9 Addendum: The Large Economy

The implication for the price-specie-flow mechanism of assuming the domestic economy to be large was noted in the text. With a large economy, the gold outflow will have a nonnegligible effect in expanding foreign reserves, and thus the foreign money supply and price level. This *reinforces* the change in competitiveness and spreads the burden of adjustment.

The changes in domestic income analyzed in the multiplier approach will produce a *foreign repercussion* if the economy is large. For example, an increase in domestic investment raises income and increases imports, which are other countries' exports. Foreign income therefore rises by a nonnegligible amount, which raises their imports and, thus, our exports and income. The multiplier is therefore larger.

The large country need not face an infinitely elastic foreign supply of imports, just as it will almost certainly not face an infinitely elastic demand for exports. The implications of assuming a finite elasticity of demand for exports were already explored in the text, where it was found that this raised the possibility that a devaluation might worsen the balance of payments, if the Marshall-Lerner condition were not satisfied. A finite elasticity of supply of imports has no such significance, as can be seen by inserting an upward-sloping supply curve in figure 8–3C or looking at the second term in equation (8.9). Another implication is the possibility that a devaluation by one country might provoke devaluation by some others.

The remaining approaches do not require any modifications other than those consequential on the points noted above (for example, a leftward rather than rightward shift of *BP* being induced by devaluation if the Marshall-Lerner condition were to fail), except for the Dornbusch model of devaluation. This was originally presented in a two-country model where prices were continuously equated by arbitrage (but might alter during the adjustment process), while money supplies were slowly redistributed between countries until full equilibrium was achieved.

8.10 Bibliography

Hume's 1752 essay "Of the Balance of Trade" was reprinted in R. N. Cooper, ed., *International Finance* (London: Penguin, 1969). The most systematic development of the foreign trade multiplier analysis, F. Machlup, *International Trade and the National Income Multiplier* (Philadelphia: Blakiston, 1943), is now mainly of historical interest. The same might be said of the original writings on the elasticities approach: F. Machlup, "The Theory of Foreign Exchanges," *Economica,* Nov. 1939; and J. Robinson, "The Foreign Exchanges," in her *Essays in the Theory of Employment* (Oxford: Blackwell, 1937), both reprinted in H. S. Ellis and L. A. Metzler, eds., *Readings in the Theory of International Trade* (Philadelphia: Blakiston, 1949), and G. Haberler, "The Market for Foreign Exchange and the Stability of the Balance of Payments: A Theoretical Analysis," *Kyklos,* 1949, reprinted in Cooper, ed., *International Finance.* The absorption approach was introduced in S. S. Alexander, "Effects of a Devaluation on a Trade Balance," International Monetary Fund *Staff Papers,* Apr. 1952, reprinted in R. E. Caves and H. G. Johnson, eds., *Readings in International Economics* (Homewood, Ill.: Irwin 1968); the two most famous contributions to the ensuing controversy were F. Machlup, "Relative Prices and Aggregate Spending in the Analysis of Devaluation," *American Economic Review,* June 1955, and S. C. Tsiang, "The Role of Money in Trade-Balance Stability: Synthesis of the Elasticity and Absorption Approaches," *American Economic Review,* Dec. 1961, reprinted in Caves and Johnson, eds., *Readings,* and in Cooper, ed., *International Finance.* A useful guide to the empirical evidence on elasticities is R. M. Stern, J. Francis and B. Schumaker, *Price Elasticities in International Trade* (Toronto: Macmillan, 1976).

Meade's synthesis was developed in his careful taxonomic masterpiece, *The Theory of International Economic Policy, vol. 1: The Balance of Payments* (London: Oxford University Press, 1951). Its popularization in diagrams like fig. 8–7 was due to T. Swan, "Economic Control in a Dependent Economy," *Economic Record,* Mar. 1960 (first written in 1955); W. E. G. Salter, "Internal and External Balance: The Role of Price and Expenditure Effects," *Economic Record,* Aug. 1959; and W. M. Corden, "The Geometric Representation of Policies to Attain Internal and External Balance," *Review of Economic Studies,* Oct. 1960, reprinted in Cooper, ed., *International Finance.* The generalization to expenditure-reducing versus expenditure-switching effects was due to H. G. Johnson, "Towards a General Theory of the Balance of Payments," in his *International Trade and Economic Growth* (Cambridge, Mass.: Harvard University Press, 1961) and reprinted in Caves and Johnson, *Readings,* and Cooper, ed., *International Finance.* For the argument that the expenditure-reducing effects of devaluation on income may exceed the effects of expenditure switching, see R. N. Cooper, *Currency Devaluation in Developing Countries,* Princeton Essays in International Finance No. 86 (1971); and P. Krugman and L. Taylor, "Contractionary Effects of Devaluation," *Journal of International Economics,* Aug. 1978.

Current Account

The Polak model was presented in J. J. Polak, "Monetary Analysis of Income Formation," *International Monetary Fund Staff Papers,* Nov. 1957, reprinted in H. R. Heller and R. R. Rhomberg, eds., *The Monetary Approach to the Balance of Payments* (Washington, D.C.: International Monetary Fund, 1977), which also contains the other basic papers from the IMF's version of the monetary approach. A discussion of the IMF's approach to stabilization can be found in J. Williamson, *The Lending Policies of the International Monetary Fund* (Washington, D.C.: Institute for International Economics, 1982). The Dornbusch model of devaluation can be found in R. Dornbusch, "Devaluation, Money, and Non-traded Goods," *American Economic Review,* Dec. 1973; the gist of this paper, together with an elegant exploration of current account payments theory (in more mathematical terms than those used here), can be found in his *Open Economy Macroeconomics* (New York: Basic Books, 1980), chaps. 3–9. Most of the principal papers of the Chicago version of the monetary approach are to be found in J. A. Frenkel and H. G. Johnson, eds., *The Monetary Approach to the Balance of Payments* (London: Allen and Unwin, 1976).

The balance of payments was first incorporated into the IS/LM analysis by D. Wrighton, "IS, LM, and External Equilibrium: A Graphical Analysis," *American Economic Review,* Mar. 1970.

For further reading on the gold standard, see the bibliography to chap. 15.

9

Capital Mobility

THIS CHAPTER extends balance of payments analysis to include the capital account. This is a vital step under present-day conditions: it seems that more than two-thirds of the value of international transactions are nowadays on capital rather than current account. Many are speculative transactions that are essential to enable a system of floating rates to function at all (see chap. 10), but that still leaves vast flows of funds on longer maturities, which is the concern of this chapter.

The first section examines the way in which a capital flow induces an adjustment in the current account, so as to transfer real capital—that is, real resources. This is followed by two sections about alternative theories of the determinants of flows of portfolio capital: the flow theory of the late 1950s and early 1960s, and the stock theory that largely supplanted it in the late 1960s. The final section turns to the monetary approach, which is directed at explaining the balance of payments as a whole rather than either the current or capital accounts individually. It is argued that the monetary approach should be treated as a complement to rather than a competitor to the other approaches.

9.1 The Transfer Problem

Suppose that our country has a capital inflow—perhaps because its banks start to raise a stream of loans on the Eurodollar market[1] to expand their

1. See chap. 14.1 for a discussion of the Eurocurrency markets.

domestic lending. It is possible that the country already had a current account deficit that needed financing—indeed, that might well be why the government ordered a tightening of monetary policy that pushed the banks into borrowing abroad. But, in order to see how the transfer process is brought about, let us suppose that there was previously a balance on current account. Then the banks start selling the dollars that they have borrowed in order to acquire pesos to expand their loans. That means the central bank starts gaining reserves. The question at issue is: how would a constant stream of capital inflows induce an adjustment to restore payments equilibrium and achieve the transfer process that was illustrated in chapter 6.1, with a current account deficit equal to the capital account surplus?

The short answer is "it all depends," but an understanding of chapter 8 takes one further than this rather unhelpful answer to identify *on what* it depends. For example, if the central bank sterilizes the monetary consequences of the reserve accumulation resulting from the capital inflow, then there will be no further adjustments. The firms that are able to expand their spending by using the resources borrowed abroad will be counterbalanced by those that have to reduce their spending in consequence of the reduction in domestic credit involved in sterilization. When a country is initially in internal balance and the government seeks to perpetuate that by sterilizing the capital inflow, the consequence is to frustrate the transfer. There is a limit to the extent to which sterilization is feasible; it is set by the stock of domestic assets that the central bank can sell and the willingness of the private market to buy such assets at interest rates the authorities are prepared to tolerate. Within that limit, however, which is quite wide in countries with well-developed capital markets, adjustment can be prevented.

Suppose, instead, that the central bank does not sterilize. Then autonomous expenditure will rise, presumably by the amount of the capital inflow. Imports rise, thus transferring at least a part of the capital inflow. Will the whole of the inflow be transferred? Initially no, if there is unemployment. (Why?) Quickly yes, if there is full employment, as inflation reduces competitiveness and brings expenditure switching toward foreign goods. Eventually yes in any event, as the monetary mechanism of adjustment comes into play.

Or suppose that the authorities want to preserve internal balance, including the prevention of inflation, but they wish to secure the inward transfer. What policies would be necessary? The answer is given by the Meade analysis in chapter 8.5. The inflow on capital account means that payments balance now occurs in the part of figure 8–7 where the current balance is in deficit; that is, the external balance curve moves to the right. Preservation of internal and external balance therefore requires a combination of an expenditure-increasing policy (such as allowing the capital inflow to increase the money supply) and an expenditure-switching policy (revaluation or tariff reduction) to prevent the reflation creating excess demand for home-produced goods.

It is also worth referring back to figure 6–2 to see the changes that occur in the dependent economy model between the position of balanced trade in figure 6–2A and that of a trade deficit in figure 6–2B. With full employment both before and after the transfer is effected, the two changes needed to secure transfer are an expansion in absorption and an increase in the relative price of nontraded goods. These are precisely the changes that the analysis of the previous paragraph showed to be necessary, when we recognize that expenditure-switching policies are those that change the relative price of nontraded goods. (There will also be a terms-of-trade change in the case of the country with less than infinitely elastic demand for its exports.) And the previous paragraph argued that such expenditure switching would occur automatically as a result of inflation if it were not pursued deliberately by revaluation or equivalent policies.

Ensuring that transfer occurs therefore requires no more than an application of the analysis of chapter 8. Why then should it have been conceived as a problem? For two general reasons. First, because governments have sometimes willed the ends without willing the means; they have wished to change the trade balance while preserving internal balance and fixed exchange rates. That is just not possible, except by luck (which is, admittedly, the politician's favorite policy weapon). Second, because we have considered the easy case of securing an inward transfer to match a capital inflow, rather than the difficult case of creating a surplus to match a capital outflow (or reparations payments). That requires a cut in absorption and a fall in real wages, which is, not surprisingly, usually conceived to be a problem by the country involved.

9.2 The Flow Theory

As noted in chapter 7.2, capital flows take various forms—direct investment, export credits, amortization, and portfolio movements. It is the last of these that are responsive to short-run macroeconomic conditions and which have therefore formed the focus of theoretical interest in attempts to explain the capital account. The transfer of capital resulting from direct investment is incidental to a decision to exploit an investment opportunity; given the

long-run time perspective that a firm needs to employ when reaching investment decisions, these are unlikely to be strongly dependent on the current
conjunctural situation. Export credits extended and received depend principally on trade volumes, especially of capital goods. Amortization is largely
determined by the pattern of past capital movements. Moreover, to the
extent that any of those elements are variable in response to current economic conditions, the variations will tend to move with the flow of portfolio
capital. Thus we can restrict our theoretical analysis to the latter case.

In explaining movements of private portfolio capital, economists have
typically given pride of place to interest rates. This was already true when
economists first began to analyze capital flows seriously in the closing years
of the gold standard. They observed that interest rates were normally higher
in the peripheral or developing countries of that time (notably the countries
of recent settlement) than in the European capital-exporting countries, thus
inducing a flow of long-term capital from the center to the periphery to
exploit international differences in thrift and productivity. They also observed that the rules of the game involved countries in deficit raising their
interest rates, which quickly drew in funds from abroad and stemmed the
gold loss by adjusting the capital account long before the monetary contraction involved in raising interest rates could have had any impact on the
current account. That is not to argue that the current account adjustment
was an unimportant part of the mechanism: if the high interest rates were
maintained for long they would reduce real income and possibly prices, thus
ensuring that the current account would adjust for the reasons studied in
chapter 8. The existence of this backstop presumably helped sustain the
general confidence that exchange rates could and would remain constant
which gave high interest rates their power to attract capital inflows and thus
to obviate the need for costly current account adjustment.

Although the gold standard suffered from occasional financial panics, it
functioned blissfully in comparison to the period following the collapse of
1931. Any semblance of an international capital market disappeared, and
such international capital flows as occurred took the form of flows of "hot
money" seeking to avoid an impending devaluation or political persecution.
When there is no confidence that the exchange rate will be maintained,
interest rate increases are powerless to stem a capital flight. (A 10 percent
devaluation one week hence would require an interest rate at an annual rate
of about 14,000 percent for that week[2] to compensate a holder for not
selling!) The collapse of a rational international capital market was so
complete that when the wartime allies were planning how to reconstruct the

2. $(1.1)^{52} = 142$, or over 14,000 percent per annum.

postwar world economy they decided to create the World Bank—to provide an official substitute for the private market whose disappearance was taken to be permanent.

There was therefore not much capital mobility to merit great attention or explanation when James Meade was writing his opus *The Balance of Payments* in the late 1940s, which is presumably why he gave his book that title even though its subject matter was largely restricted to an analysis of the current account. In such treatment as capital flows did receive, one can find three ideas: (1) the notion that some capital flows can be treated as exogenous, which, it was argued above, still holds good; (2) the idea that variations in the capital account have a tendency to reinforce those in the current account, as a deterioration in the latter ignites the fear of devaluation and provokes a speculative run (to the extent that this is true, capital flows do not finance swings in the current account and open up the possibilities of welfare gain illustrated in chapter 6, but rather serve to amplify the payments variations that have to be financed through the reserves in order to stabilize absorption as shown in figure 6–5C); (3) the old idea dating back to the gold standard literature that capital would flow in response to differential interest rates.

When the private international capital market confounded expectations by reviving in the 1950s, that last idea was the natural one (or the only one around) for explaining endogenous, noncrisis capital movements. Without really thinking too much about what they were doing, economists began writing capital flow equations of the form

$$\dot{F} = f(\overset{+}{i}, \overset{-}{i}*),\qquad(9.1)$$

where F is the stock of net foreign liabilities of the private sector, and $\dot{F}$ is therefore the net inflow of capital.[3] Equation (9.1) says that the inflow of capital depends positively on the domestic interest rate and negatively on the foreign interest rate.[4] This is called the flow theory because it postulates a relationship between the flow of capital and the level of interest rates. One can, of course, add a term representing direct investment and subtract a term representing amortization payments without altering anything fundamental, provided that both are exogenous with respect to the level of short-run endogenous variables like interest and income (as it was previously argued they are).

---

3. Note that the nomenclature of chap. 7 has been reversed: F is now being used to signify foreign *liabilities* rather than *assets*.

4. This specification is crucially dependent on the assumption that the exchange rate is fixed and expected to remain so. With a flexible exchange rate the relevant comparison is between i and $i* + E\hat{e}$, where $E\hat{e}$ is the expected rate of depreciation (see chap. 10.4).

Capital Mobility

Consider next what happens when we insert (9.1) into an equation for the balance of payments, utilizing the model of the current account developed in the previous chapter:

$$\dot{R} = TB(Y,ep^*/p) + f(i,i^*).\qquad(9.2)$$

This has an important consequence in terms of the IS/LM/BP analysis. Instead of being vertical as before, the BP curve is now positively sloping as shown in figure 9–1, assuming that we interpret external balance as a zero change in reserves ($\dot{R} = 0$). The reason is that, while an increase in income will still worsen the current account, this can now be offset by an increase in the domestic interest rate, which will attract a capital inflow and thus preserve balance of payments equilibrium.

Virtually all the properties of the IS/LM/BP model with a positively sloping BP curve are the same as those of the model with a vertical BP curve studied in chapter 8.7. For example, figure 9–1 shows a deficit; this means that reserves would be falling, so unless the central bank is creating credit the LM curve will be shifting left, which will continue until it passes through the IS/BP intersection.

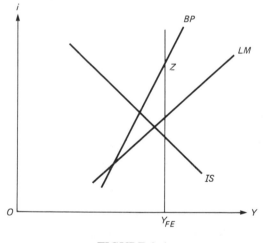

FIGURE 9–1
IS/LM/BP with Capital Mobility

When analyzing the IS/LM/BP model without capital mobility, we argued that in order to achieve simultaneous internal and external balance it was essential to have at the disposal of the authorities an instrument for securing expenditure switching. The reason was that both the internal balance curve (Y_{FE}) and the external balance curve (BP) were vertical, and

183

hence, unless they happened to coincide, an instrument to shift *BP* to make them coincide was indispensable to satisfactory policy management. However, with *BP* no longer vertical in the case with capital mobility, there is a point (*Z* in figure 9–1) where it intersects with Y_{FE}. Robert Mundell argued that this implied that it would be possible to attain internal and external balance simultaneously by an appropriate choice of fiscal and monetary policy, without any need for exchange rate changes or some other expenditure-switching policy. In the case shown in figure 9–1, one needs an expansionary fiscal policy to push *IS* up till it passes through the point *Z*, combined with a restrictive monetary policy to push *LM* up till it too passes through *Z*. That particular "mix" of fiscal and monetary policy (two instruments, which now have differential effects on the two objectives) can secure the two targets of internal and external balance.

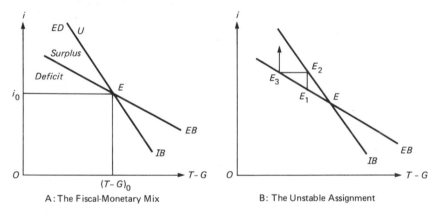

FIGURE 9–2
The Fiscal-Monetary Mix and the Assignment Problem

The same analysis can be presented in a diagram similar to the one that Mundell himself used. Figure 9–2 shows the fiscal surplus, representing fiscal policy, on the horizontal axis, and the interest rate, representing monetary policy, on the vertical axis. Suppose we have a point (like *E*) of internal balance. If the fiscal surplus were increased, this would have a contractionary effect on demand; to preserve internal balance, we would need to counteract this with a more expansionary monetary policy. The internal balance curve therefore slopes down, with points of unemployment (U) above it and excess demand (ED) below it. Now consider a point (again like *E*, by coincidence) of external balance. A tighter fiscal policy would

184

increase the current surplus,[5] hence to preserve external balance one would need to loosen monetary policy, which would decrease the current surplus *and* the capital surplus. The external balance curve therefore also slopes down, with a surplus above and a deficit below. Moreover, it is less steep than the internal balance curve. The reason is that income and therefore the current account remain constant along *IB*, while the change in the interest rate means that the capital account and therefore the overall balance of payments alter; specifically, as one goes down *IB* the capital inflow falls, which means that at some point one goes from surplus to deficit (as shown), which is possible only if *IB* is steeper than *EB*. Given that the two curves have different slopes, a point of intersection *E* exists. The policy mix $(T - G)_0, i_0$ corresponding to *E* is that which would shift *IS* and *LM* to intersect at *Z* in figure 9–1.

Mundell used his model to analyze what he called the *assignment problem:* whether one should direct, or assign, monetary policy to pursue the internal balance target and fiscal policy to the external balance target, or vice versa. If one assigned monetary policy to internal balance, one would tell the central bank to increase interest rates whenever there was excess demand and cut them whenever unemployment developed. Similarly, assigning fiscal policy to external balance would mean telling the Treasury (or Ministry of Finance, as the case may be) to increase the budget deficit whenever the balance of payments was in surplus and to decrease it when there was a payments deficit. Figure 9–2B shows what would happen with this assignment. Suppose the economy were initially at E_1. The Treasury would be happy, but the central bank would be duty bound to fight the inflation caused by excess demand, which it would do by raising the rate of interest till the excess demand was eliminated. That would leave the Treasury facing the embarrassment of a payments surplus, which it would fight by cutting taxes or increasing government spending till the economy reached E_3. Thereupon the central bank would embark on another round of raising interest rates . . . with the economy moving steadily away from the optimal mix at *E*. The moral is that one should assign each instrument to the objective over which it has relatively most influence: monetary policy to external balance and fiscal policy to internal balance. That guarantees that uncoordinated policy actions by the central bank and the Treasury will lead the economy to converge to the point *E*.

How much sense does this analysis make? Consider first the idea of

---

5. Or reduce the current deficit. This symmetry is henceforth taken for granted rather than constantly reiterated. I am deliberately avoiding the common but pernicious shorthand "improving the current account"—a larger surplus or smaller deficit is not necessarily to be desired.

assigning instruments to targets. If one is going to assign instruments to targets at all, then certainly Mundell's analysis shows how it should be done and the dangers of doing it wrongly. But the idea of assignment is suspect: achieving simultaneous internal and external balance is a general equilibrium problem which demands a general equilibrium solution, in the form of a simultaneous choice of policy instruments. With perfect information, this would enable the authorities to guide the economy straight to *E* and avoid the zig-zag approach involved in even the stable assignment. The notion that this cannot be done because the two instruments are controlled by different sets of bureaucrats is not very convincing: they can after all call each other. (Even the most undeveloped of countries have telephones between the Treasury and the central bank.) A more persuasive defense is that the authorities do not have perfect information and therefore cannot lead the economy straight to *E*. They have to feel their way in that direction, and in doing that they need a rule as to when each policy should be adjusted. But even with imperfect information, one can argue that the authorities should sit down together and seek a strategy that takes account of the moves the other is about to make, which means that an assignment is primarily of public relations rather than of operational significance.

Consider next the idea of determining the mix of fiscal and monetary policy by the desire to secure simultaneous internal and external balance. The fundamental problem with this proposal was long ago identified by Mundell (among others): that it leaves the *composition* of the balance of payments—its division between current and capital accounts—at the mercy of what are essentially arbitrary forces. Suppose that the equilibrium *E* shown in figure 9–2 were a position in which there was a capital inflow financing a current account deficit consistent with the forces of thrift and productivity analyzed in chapter 6, when suddenly the price of a major import good (like oil) increased (with no expectation that it would subsequently fall). The worsening of the terms of trade would push *EB* up and *IB* down, and *E* would in consequence move up and to the left, indicating that the appropriate policy mix would be tighter monetary and easier fiscal policy. The country would maintain its level of output and absorption constant, and would finance rather than seek to adjust away the increase in its current account deficit. It would borrow, to sustain consumption (for the higher interest rate would even be tending to reduce investment), and then borrow some more to pay the interest. That is the road to ruin, not the rational intertemporal reallocation of consumption that capital mobility offers in accordance with the analysis of chapter 6. The problem is that the 'mix' involves having the current account (at full employment and your present exchange rate) determine the capital account, whereas the classical analysis depends on exactly the reverse. The conclusion is inescapable: it is absolutely essential to have some mechanism to secure current account adjustment in the medium term, rather than to finance any old deficit or surplus that arises from chance events.

Can one, however, justify the mix as a short-term policy expedient, to finance the current account while longer-term adjustment measures are brought into play? In general, the answer is no. Figure 6–5C showed how the accumulation and decumulation of reserves over time could enable a country to smooth the path of absorption despite fluctuations in income. Reserves raised welfare by being used, not by being maintained constant. The whole point of holding reserves is to act as a buffer stock that can be allowed to fluctuate to help stabilize some other variables that have some real significance for economic welfare, like output or absorption. In short, the target of external balance should *not* be interpreted as a constant level of reserves, certainly not in a short-run sense.

There is just one case in which the "mix" analysis comes into its own, and that is when a country cannot afford to run down its reserves any more. In that case it is better to raise interest rates to attract a capital inflow than to allow the waste of unemployment to eliminate the current deficit. But that in no way undermines the need to ensure that there is a mechanism to secure adjustment in the current account over the medium run.

If we are denying ourselves the easy option of defining external balance as a zero change in reserves, how *should* it be defined? The natural criterion is to go back to the analysis of chapter 6 and define it as the current account surplus or deficit that is needed to transfer the capital outflow or inflow dictated by the real forces of thrift and productivity. That means that the payments target in the IS/LM/BP analysis is again vertical, as in figure 8–10, rather than sloping, as in figure 9–1, and so attaining payments objectives requires the use of an expenditure-switching policy. This should, however, be interpreted as a medium-run target, with short-run payments variations being accepted and financed through reserve changes.

There is one special (though famous) case that requires separate analysis before we leave the flow theory, since it leads to conclusions that are qualitatively different from those yielded by the case of no capital mobility. This is the case of perfect capital mobility, shown by a horizontal *BP* curve in figure 9–3. Perfect capital mobility requires that domestic and foreign bonds are considered perfect substitutes by wealth owners. Consequently,

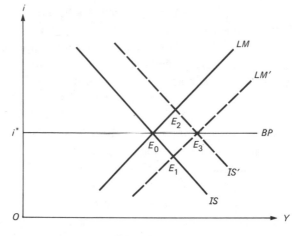

FIGURE 9–3
IS/LM/BP with Perfect Capital Mobility

any excess of the domestic interest rate over the foreign interest rate would attract a flood of capital inflows (or any deficiency would provoke a rush to sell domestic assets), implying that *BP* is horizontal.

Suppose that the central bank tried to expand income through an expansionary monetary policy, shifting the *LM* curve to *LM'*. Since *IS* is unchanged, the new equilibrium would be at E_1 with the new higher money supply. But E_1 involves a lower interest rate than i^*, which means that investors would rush to sell domestic bonds, and then domestic money, to buy foreign exchange to buy foreign bonds. This would continue till *LM'* returned to *LM* and i returned to i^*. The conclusion is simple: with perfect capital mobility (and a fixed exchange rate), monetary policy has no power to influence the level of income. But it is an admirable instrument to influence the level of reserves, since it can control them with zero cost in terms of forcing deviations from domestic objectives.

Suppose, on the other hand, that the government attempted to expand income by adopting an expansionary fiscal policy, pushing *IS* to the right to *IS'*. Without capital mobility, the new equilibrium would be at E_2. But E_2 involves an interest rate above i^*, which is not feasible: it would attract a vast capital inflow that would push *LM* to the right, until it reached the point E_3 where *IS'* cuts *BP*. Thus fiscal policy becomes more potent in influencing income: it attracts a capital inflow that increases the money supply and so avoids the rise in the interest rate that otherwise dampens the rise in income.

188

9.3 The Stock Theory

The flow theory that we have just studied implies that with a given constellation of interest rates a country can expect to experience a constant rate of inflow (or outflow) of capital period after period. In the second half of the 1960s, economists came to realize that this was inconsistent with the emergent approach of portfolio theory. The stock theory of the capital account incorporates the implications for international capital flows of portfolio theory.

The basic idea of *portfolio theory* is that investors[6] seek to distribute their wealth between the various assets available in such a way as to maximize their utility. Assets, of course, unlike consumer goods, do not yield utility directly but only because of the income that they bring. Why then is it not possible to say that investors buy the assets that will maximize their income? A moment's reflection will reveal why: the income yielded by an asset is rarely certain, and the assets offering to pay the most are usually the most risky. In deciding how to distribute his wealth, the rational investor needs to take into account both expected return and risk, and his preferences as regards the trade-off between them.

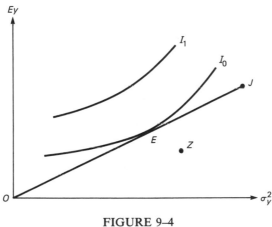

FIGURE 9–4
Simple Case of Portfolio Choice

Figure 9–4 illustrates the simplest case of the analysis. On the vertical axis we plot the average or expected return, denoted *Ey*, where *E* is the

6. One is speaking here of investors in financial assets, rather than of the concept of investment in real capital goods that is normal in macroeconomic analysis.

189

expectations operator and y represents income. On the horizontal axis is plotted the variance of income (the variance is the square of the standard deviation), denoted σ_y^2, which is the most common statistical measure of risk. Since risk is a "bad" to most investors (who are described on this account as being "risk averse") while a high level of expected return is a "good," the indifference curves of a typical investor will be upward sloping and convex from below, as shown by I_0 and I_1 in figure 9–4. The object of the investor is that of attaining the highest possible indifference curve subject to the wealth he has available to invest.

Different assets promise different combinations of expected return and risk. For example, there might be a perfectly safe asset ($\sigma_y^2 = 0$) that paid no return (money, in a country with no inflation and no danger of inflation, if you can imagine such). If his entire wealth were placed in that asset, the investor would be at the point *0*. Or imagine that there were also a risky asset, with Ey and σ_y^2 such that, if all wealth were placed in that form, the investor would achieve the combination of expected return and risk represented by the point *J*. A third asset might yield the point *Z*. Such an asset would, however, not be bought by our investor, who could instead choose a combination of the first two assets which would yield him the same expected return for less risk, or a greater expected return for the same risk, than the third asset. Combinations of the first two assets could in fact yield the investor any point on the straight line *OJ*. Given his preferences, it is clear that he will choose that combination of the first two assets that will take him to the point *E*.

Simple as this model is, we can draw from it a number of conclusions.

1. An investor will not necessarily buy some of every asset on the market, but in order to spread his risks he will normally diversify his holdings over a number of assets.

2. The demand for a particular asset will depend positively on the expected yield and negatively on its risk as perceived by investors.

3. The demand for all assets will go up as the total wealth available for investment rises.

Portfolio theory implies a fourth conclusion that is of particular significance for international investment, though unfortunately it cannot be illustrated directly from figure 9–4. This conclusion relates to the significance of the *relationship between the risks* on two different assets. If an asset *A* always tends to have a high yield at the same time as a second asset *B*, then one cannot do much to reduce one's risk by diversifying one's portfolio between the two. In technical terms, one says there is a positive covariance between the returns on *A* and *B*, $\sigma_{ab}^2 > 0$. But suppose instead that we had two assets *A* and *B*, each of which had the same expected return Ez and the same risk σ_z^2 as the asset shown by the point *Z* in figure 9–4, but with perfect negative covariance ($\sigma_{a,b2}^2 = -1$). In nontechnical terms, this means that the greater the return to the one, the less the return to the other, as shown in figure 9–5. Suppose now that one were to make up a compound asset (or mini portfolio) consisting half of A and half of B. Then one would be *guaranteed* a return equal to Ez. This compound asset would therefore fall in figure 9–4 at the same height as Z but on the vertical axis, thus driving the riskless asset out of the portfolio and raising the investor's utility. It is evident that the covariances between the yields on different assets are very important in portfolio selection: in technical terms, the optimal portfolio depends on the whole variance-covariance matrix and not just the risk of each asset considered in isolation. We may now (somewhat loosely) state the fourth conclusion.

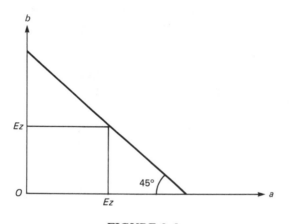

FIGURE 9–5
Perfect Negative Covariance

4. The demand for an asset will be greater the more negative is the covariance between its return and the return on alternative assets.

This conclusion is particularly significant for international capital movements because returns in different countries are in fact considerably less closely correlated than those within a single country. This means that investors in each country can hope to gain by diversifying their holdings over assets drawn from a number of other countries, without this necessarily involving any net flows of capital or therefore net transfers of real resources. Some estimates (Lessard, 1981) suggest that the potential welfare gains from this risk diversification are quite substantial, and flows of equity capital among the industrial countries—which are the form for which the analysis is most relevant—are becoming quite significant. The conclusion is also cheering news for developing countries, since it implies that investors may seek to put a proportion of their assets into the liabilities of developing countries even though they may regard these as relatively risky, provided that they believe that those risks are inversely correlated with the risks of investments in the developed countries. Whether or not what is bad for the rich is actually good for the poor, a belief to that effect will actually be good for the poor.

However, the main implication that has been drawn from the portfolio theory for international capital flows relates more to the second point than to the fourth. Let us assume that our country U is a capital-importing country which does not permit its citizens to make investments abroad, and also that the foreign liabilities F issued by its residents on the world capital market can be considered a homogeneous asset from the standpoint of the rest of the world's investors. Then the demand for F can be written:

$$F_d = f(\overset{+}{i}, \overset{-}{i}\ast, \overset{+}{creditworthiness}, \overset{+}{wealth}). \tag{9.3}$$

It is obviously necessary to include $i\ast$, the interest rate on the alternative asset available to investors, as well as i. When we come to apply the portfolio model to the context of international capital flows, the idea of risk can be translated into a country's creditworthiness—roughly speaking, the confidence investors feel that the country will remain able and willing to service its debt. Finally, the relevant wealth variable is the total value of the assets of the lenders and potential lenders.

Suppose for the moment that creditworthiness and wealth remain constant. Then equation (9.3) says that a given pair of interest rates, i and $i\ast$, will make investors wish to lend a certain sum F_d, and no more. Suppose they make those loans in period t, and that both interest rates remain constant in period $(t + 1)$. Then the *stock* of loans F_d will remain constant. But since the capital inflow is the difference between the stock of loans at $(t + 1)$ and the stock at t, the capital inflow will be zero. Contrast this with the flow theory, which assumed that a given pair of interest rates maintained through time would sustain a continuing constant capital flow. According to the stock theory, a rise in the domestic interest rate would provoke a one-time capital inflow as portfolios were rearranged to include a larger proportion of the now-more-attractive assets issued by domestic residents. After that, the capital flow would cease—unlike under the flow theory.[7]

7. A generalization of the stock theory, known as the stock adjustment model, postulates that the process of portfolio reallocation is spread out through time rather than occurring instantaneously. It is typically postulated that the capital flow can be described by an equation of the form $\dot{F} = \alpha(\overline{F} - F)$, where $\overline{F}$ is the equilibrium stock. Such a specification has often been found useful in econometric estimation. This alternative version does not, however, have significantly different theoretical implications from those of the pure stock theory discussed in the text. In particular, while a rise in the domestic interest rate will cause a capital inflow spread out over some period of time, the flow will gradually fall back to zero as F approaches $\overline{F}$.

Acceptance of the stock theory has important implications for the IS/LM/BP model and the Mundellian fiscal-monetary mix. It implies that one can no longer expect the *BP* curve of figure 9–1 or the *EB* curve of figure 9–2 to remain constant through time, since this period's capital inflow depends upon last period's inflow, as well as this period's interest rate. Financing a constant current account deficit through attracting a capital inflow would require a continuing *increase* in the domestic interest rate, rather than merely the maintenance of a constant interest rate *differential*. This provides yet another reason for rejecting the Mundellian mix as a component of rational economic management.

However, the flow analysis of the preceding section can be partially salvaged by taking account of the final term in equation (9.3). The stock of our liabilities that foreigners wish to hold depends not merely on relative interest rates and creditworthiness but also on the size of the total portfolios that foreigners have available to invest. Since those are normally growing as a result of savings (that reflect real growth) and inflation, a country which is already a net debtor can expect an increase in the quantity of its liabilities that foreigners are willing to hold even without an increase in its interest rate. If the wealth of investors increases by 10 percent, then one can expect that *ceteris paribus* there will be a capital inflow equal to 10 percent of one's existing liabilities. This is known as the *portfolio growth effect*.

Suppose therefore that the domestic interest rate were increased. This would induce a portfolio redistribution effect that would result in a one-time capital inflow as investors rearranged their portfolios to include a larger proportion of our liabilities. After that, things would settle down again, but with a permanently larger capital inflow than before to the extent that our liabilities now constitute a larger proportion of their portfolio, which is still growing at the same rate. The portfolio growth effect would be larger, because the same rate of growth would be applied to a bigger base. In consequence the *BP* curve of figure 9–1 would slope up, in addition to the sudden but temporary jump that it would undergo every time the interest rate changed.

It is also worth noting that there is one case in which the analysis is exactly the same under the stock theory as under the flow theory, and that is in the case of perfect capital mobility. The results that monetary policy is unable to influence income, although having a one-for-one impact on the level of reserves, while the potency of fiscal policy in influencing income is increased, are preserved unchanged.

A useful model for studying the macroeconomic implications of the stock theory has recently been suggested by the Argentine economist Roberto Frenkel (b. 1943), from whose work the following has been adapted. Instead of analyzing the money market, as has been traditional, the model focuses on the market for credit (or loans, if you prefer). It is assumed that the banks are the only source of loans, and also that they alone have access to the international capital market. (Nothing fundamental depends on these assumptions, which are made for expositional simplicity.) Credit is demanded by the government to finance the sum of its past deficits and by the private sector to finance investment, working capital, and even consumption loans. This demand for credit is responsive to the interest rate and may therefore be shown by a downward sloping demand curve, D_d in figure 9–6.

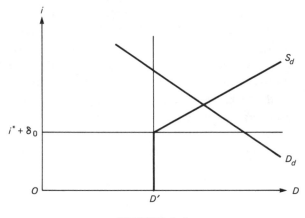

FIGURE 9–6
Market for Credit

The supply of credit is divided into two components. The first, labeled D' in figure 9–6, is the quantity of loans that the banking system would be able to make even without any resort to foreign borrowing. If the money multiplier is independent of the interest rate, the supply of loans from this source is a vertical line as shown.[8]

The second element of the supply of credit is that which results from foreign borrowing. The bank which contracts a loan abroad and switches it into pesos at the central bank gains additional funds which it can use in

8. The formula for D' is $(1/\phi)(D_1+R-F) - (R-F)$, treating D_1 (central bank domestic credit) as constant. This can be seen by setting out the T-accounts for the central bank and commercial banks, as below, and then asking what would be (D_1+D_2) on the assumptions that F was zero, that D_1 remained unchanged, and that $B = \phi H$.

Central Bank		Commercial Banks	
Assets	Liabilities	Assets	Liabilities
R	B	B	H
D_1		D_2	F

194

order to expand its domestic loans. Naturally banks will be prepared to do such borrowing only if the interest return they expect to receive exceeds the foreign interest rate $i*$ by a margin δ large enough to compensate them for their trouble, cost, and risk. Furthermore, one might expect that the margin above $i*$ needed to induce further borrowing will tend to rise with the size of that borrowing, for two reasons. The first is that as the country's international indebtedness rises, its creditworthiness may decline, and to compensate for that foreign lenders may be expected to charge an increasing premium. This does not appear to be a major factor in practice: although spreads may widen by 1 percent or 2 percent first, the main consequence of eroded creditworthiness is to make loans unavailable at any price beyond a certain point. The second reason is that the borrowers, in this case the banks, may become concerned about the risk involved in their foreign exchange exposure, in that they would suffer a capital loss if the peso were to be devalued.[9] They require a higher interest differential to compensate them for accepting an increasing amount of this risk.

The slope of the S_d curve to the right of D' therefore depends in part on how rapidly the interest differential required by the banks rises as their foreign exchange exposure increases. The more slowly it rises, the flatter is S_d. In the limit, if the differential needed did not rise, one would have a horizontal line: that is essentially the case of perfect capital mobility. At the other limit, if the banks were unwilling to borrow anything at any differential, the whole of S_d would be a vertical line at D'. In between is the zone of finite capital mobility. In this intermediate zone the slope of S_d depends on a second factor beside the degree of capital mobility, namely the value of the money multiplier, or the reserve ratio ϕ of the commercial banks. The reason is that when one bank switches in dollars and then makes peso loans, it provides additional base money to the banking system which can form the basis for a multiple expansion of the money supply. The banks whose deposits increase as a result of the customers of the first bank spending their loans are in turn able to expand their loans, and so on, until the banking system is again fully loaned up. Hence, the smaller is ϕ, and the larger is the money multiplier, the flatter will be S_d for any given level of capital mobility.

The model can be used to establish various comparative statics results. The most famous case is that of an expansionary monetary policy. An increase in the central bank component of domestic credit D_1 would increase D' (by $\Delta D_1/\phi$, see note 8). The diagram shows this would push

9. It may be possible for the banks to shift their exchange risk, if a forward market exists, but *someone* will still have to bear the risk and will charge a risk premium for so doing (see the app. to chap. 10 for a sketch of the forward market).

S_d to the right, lower the interest rate, increase total credit, and reduce foreign borrowing.

In an important paper, "International Capital Flows and Portfolio Equilibrium," the Finnish economist Pentti Kouri (b. 1949) and the Australian economist Michael Porter (b. 1943) focused on that last consequence. They asked: if the central bank increases domestic credit D_1 by a certain sum, how much of that will result in an increase in the monetary base (and thus in the money supply), and how much will be offset by an outflow of capital (a reduction in foreign borrowing in the present instance)? They christened the latter fraction the *offset coefficient*. It varies from zero when capital mobility is zero to unity when capital mobility is perfect and in fact provides the most satisfactory measure of the degree of capital mobility. Empirical estimates of offset coefficients have typically fallen in the range 0.4 to 0.8, substantially less than the unity that would signify perfect capital mobility.

An expansionary fiscal policy would in time increase the size of government debt to be financed, and so push D_d to the right. The interest rate would increase, foreign borrowing would be pulled in, and (the commercial bank component of) domestic credit would rise even without monetary expansion by the central bank, assuming only that it did not sterilize.

A current surplus would push D' to the right (see note 8, remembering that a current surplus increases R while leaving F constant). This would have consequences similar to those of a monetary expansion, though less powerful, peso for peso, since the country has to lend its reserve increase abroad. (That is what holding reserves means.)

All that is on the assumption that the premium required by the banks to switch in funds would remain constant for any given level of foreign borrowing. But that is not in all circumstances a very reasonable assumption. One expects the required premium to depend, not just on the level of foreign borrowing, but also on confidence that the exchange rate will be maintained, which in turn depends on such factors as the level of reserves and expectations as to the evolution of the current account. Clearly a reduction in confidence would mean that larger premiums would be needed to induce a given level of foreign borrowing: the S_d curve would rotate up in its nonvertical section. This provides an explanation of the making of a foreign exchange crisis. Suppose that the current account goes unexpectedly into deficit, thus both reducing D' and causing S_d to rotate up. If the authorities accept the resulting rise in interest rates, they may manage to preserve confidence and avert a crisis. But if they endeavor to limit the rise in interest rates, by credit creation, there is a real danger that their action will make it attractive for the banks to reduce foreign indebtedness still more, which will reduce the reserves, undermine confidence, and rotate S_d up yet again in a self-aggravating crisis. A deterioration in the current account sets off a chain of events which leads to an outflow of capital—exactly the pattern that was a part of the conventional wisdom in Meade's 1940s, but had been lost sight of in more recent modeling (although by no means absent from the real world as witness the experience of Frenkel's own country of Argentina).[10] A virtue of Frenkel's model is that it points one toward studying the forces that can lead to a speculative crisis, as well as helps one see the implications of policy changes under more normal circumstances.

9.4 The Monetary Approach

Advocates of a monetary approach, especially Michael Mussa (b. 1944), have emphasized that what analysis of the money market can hope to furnish is a theory of the *balance of payments* rather than of the balance of trade or the balance on current account. They have argued that it is a mistaken strategy to try and predict the balance of payments (ΔR) on the basis of an equation like (9.2), as the sum of separately determined current and capital accounts. The overall balance of payments is, they argue (and no one can deny it), an inflow or outflow of money; and if you want to explain that, the natural place to start is in the money market, to see if there is an excess demand or an excess supply there. A typical monetarist model of the balance of payments therefore has the following structure:

$$H_d \qquad = H(\overset{+}{p}, \overset{+}{Y}, \overset{-}{i}) \qquad\qquad (9.4)$$

$$H_s \qquad = (1/\phi)(R + D_1) \qquad\qquad (9.5)$$

$$\therefore \quad R + D_1 \quad = \phi H(p, Y, i) \qquad\qquad (9.6)$$

$$\therefore \quad dR \qquad = H d\phi + \phi H_1 dp + \phi H_2 dY + \phi H_3 di - dD_1. \quad (9.7)$$

Equation (9.4) is a demand for money function, with its conventional partial derivatives: higher prices or income increase the demand for money, while a higher interest rate reduces it. Equation (9.5) is the supply of money function: ϕ is the reserve ratio of the commercial banks, $1/\phi$ is therefore the money multiplier, and ($R + D_1$) is the monetary base. Equation (9.6) equates demand and supply. Equation (9.7) is written to imply that reserve

10. Perhaps one should remark that Frenkel's paper predated, if not by much, the great Argentine exchange crisis of 1981.

changes are the consequence of changes in the reserve ratio, prices, income, interest rates, and (central bank) credit expansion. This is a (or even the) typical monetary approach equation for the balance of payments.

At least some monetarists, most notably Harry Johnson, have interpreted equation (9.7) as representing a fundamental challenge to orthodox theories as summarized in equation (9.2). Why? Because equation (9.2) says that an increase in income will pull in imports and so worsen the balance of payments; that an increase in prices will erode competitiveness and so worsen the balance of payments (assuming the Marshall-Lerner condition to be satisfied); and that an increase in the domestic interest rate will improve the balance of payments because it will pull in capital. A look at equation (9.7) and the partial derivatives in (9.4) shows that it says exactly the opposite: an increase in income or prices will increase the demand for money and so pull in reserves, while an increase in the interest rate will decrease the demand for money and so cause a payments deficit. Thus, there is the setting for a great Keynesian-monetarist battle.

Or is there? We have already seen at the end of chapter 8 that without capital mobility there is no conflict at this level of theory between Keynesian and monetarist approaches when both are cast in a general equilibrium setting. There are certainly policy differences, but these stem from differing judgments on whether changes in income will principally take the form of price changes or output changes, not from theoretically inconsistent systems of equations.

The same is true with capital mobility. The question is whether Y, p, and i can be considered exogenous variables: if they can, then (9.2) and (9.7) cannot *both* determine the balance of payments and a choice must be made between them. But if they are not exogenous, then Y, p, and i must be determined within a general equilibrium system that may perfectly well accommodate both equations—there is, after all, no contradiction whatever between the underlying behavioral relations embodied in the two equations.

Some monetarists—essentially those that subscribe to the extreme version that has earned the label global monetarism—have indeed argued that Y, p, and i are exogeneous. Y is said to be determined at its full employment level by wage flexibility, while p and i are treated as determined from the world market by perfect arbitrage in goods and securities, respectively. Under those conditions the balance of payments would be determined by equation (9.7). In fact, under perfect capital mobility, equation (9.2) is useless for telling one the change in reserves, since the second term on the right-hand side tells one that i must equal i^*, and when it does the change in reserves can be anything at all.

Capital Mobility

Consider a country where Y, p, and i are determined as is assumed in the global monetarist literature:

$$Y = Y_{FE}$$
$$p = ep* \qquad (9.8)$$
$$i = i*.$$

Suppose we plug these assumptions into our standard version of orthodoxy, namely the IS/LM/BP model. As in figure 9.3, the *BP* curve is horizontal because of perfect capital mobility, and the *LM* curve will be shifted as much as is necessary to ensure that the economy is always on the *BP* curve. But now (see fig. 9–7) there is a new element introduced by the assumption of full employment: the economy must lie on Y_{FE} in short-run equilibrium. That means that equilibrium E is determined by the intersection of Y_{FE} and *BP*. But equilibrium also lies at the intersection of *IS* and *LM*. As noted above, *LM* shifts endogenously because of the inflow or outflow of money so that it will cut the point E. The assumption of perfect arbitrage does exactly the same thing for the *IS* curve: any deficiency in domestic demand caused by a higher interest rate can be compensated by selling more on the world market, so the *IS* curve will move endogenously to the point needed to ensure that equilibrium occurs at E.

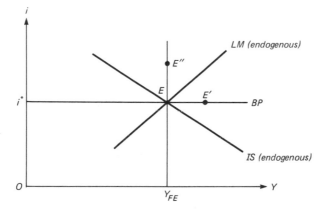

FIGURE 9–7
IS/LM/BP under Global Monetarism

Now ask what happens if p, Y, or i change in this model:

1. How does an increase in p come about? Only as a result of an increase in e or $p*$. Given that $ep*/p$ remains unchanged by perfect arbitrage, *IS*

will remain unchanged, as do *BP* and Y_{FE}. On the other hand, the price increase reduces *M/p* and pushes *LM* up. To preserve equilibrium at *E*, the money supply must be reestablished in real terms, which requires an *influx* of reserves. Thus the orthodox model with the global monetarist assumptions incorporated gives the monetarist result.

2. How does *Y* increase? Only by an increase in Y_{FE}. *E* therefore moves to the right, say to *E'*, which requires that *LM* shift down, which requires an *inflow* of reserves. Once again, therefore, the orthodox model gives the monetarist result after incorporating monetarist assumptions.

3. How does *i* increase? Only as a result of *i** increasing. That shifts *BP* up, to give a new equilibrium at, say, *E''*. To get *LM* to shift there, it is necessary to reduce *M/p*, which means to cut *M*, which requires a reserve *outflow*—once again, the monetarist result.

Hence in the special (global monetarist) case where *p*, *Y*, and *i* are exogenous, both models give the same (global monetarist) results. In the general case where *p*, *Y*, and *i* are endogenous, it makes no sense to ask questions such as: what is the effect of an increase in *i* on the balance of payments? The answer is: it all depends. Specifically, it all depends on what causes *i* to increase. If *i* increases because *i** increases, then the orthodox model will tell one that capital will flow out—indeed, that is the mechanism that causes *i* to increase. If, on the other hand, *i* increases because of a contractionary monetary policy (a fall in D_1), which is the reason for changes in interest rates that Keynesians normally had in mind, then the monetarist equation will also predict a reserve inflow, as the negative coefficient on dD_1 in equation (9.7) suggests. One can reason the same way as regards prices. What should determine whether an observer should predict that the balance of payments will move toward surplus or deficit when *p* increases is not his ideological position on the Keynesian-monetarist spectrum, but his judgment as to whether prices were pushed up by domestic forces (Keynesian case) or pulled up by foreign inflation (monetarist case). The argument is slightly more complex as regards a change in income. An increase in income that results from an increase in supply capacity may even increase the current balance (depending on how prices move and whether imports are essential inputs or substitutes to domestic output). On the other hand, an increase in income that results from an increase in demand will certainly tend to cause a current account deficit, but, depending on the degree of capital mobility and the interest and income elasticities of demand for money, this may be more than offset by an induced capital inflow (always assuming that the increased demand was not the result of lower interest rates produced by monetary expansion).

The conclusion is clear. It is quite wrong to conclude that orthodox and monetarist approaches to the balance of payments imply different conclusions. A general equilibrium model needs to contain both equations. When one recognizes that within such a context p, Y, and i cannot be considered exogenous, one cannot ask how changes in them will affect the balance of payments: one needs to go back and ask that question with regard to whatever was the exogenous change that started things off. And to the correct question, the two approaches give the same answers.

That still leaves two important questions. The first is: do the global-monetarist assumptions embodied in equation (9.8) represent a useful approximation to the truth?

There is a good deal of empirical evidence on the effectiveness of arbitrage in goods markets. Economists like Irving Kravis (b. 1916), Robert Lipsey (b. 1926), and Peter Isard (b. 1943) have done painstakingly detailed comparisons of changes in prices quoted by sellers from different countries at the most disaggregated levels possible. A whole issue of the *Journal of International Economics* (May, 1978) was devoted to reporting the proceedings of a conference that examined the evidence on this question. The results of this careful research support casual observation: it is only the prices of homogeneous primary commodities that are equated internationally by arbitrage, while the prices of manufactures deviate quite widely depending on the source of supply. Exchange rate changes influence relative prices, certainly in the short run and even persisting into the medium run. The hypothesis that arbitrage quickly equates goods prices internationally has probably been rejected more decisively by empirical evidence than any other hypothesis in the history of economics.

There is also evidence on the effectiveness of arbitrage in securities markets. The results of various econometric estimates of the elasticity of substitution between holdings of domestic and foreign bonds have been surprisingly low. Econometric estimates of the offset coefficient described in section 9.3 have also generally been well below one, again implying that capital mobility is far from perfect. It would seem that the reason for occasional vast capital flows is not that capital mobility is particularly high but that the *incentive* to shift capital is sometimes enormous. It is again not possible to adopt the monetarist hypothesis of perfect arbitrage equating yields without doing grave violence to the facts.

How about the exogeneity of real income? There is an influential school, known as the new classical macroeconomists, whose basic position is indeed that deviations of Y from full employment are essentially random and cannot be influenced by systematically expansionary or contractionary demand management policies. Only shocks to demand that take the public unaware can have that effect, for example, by deceiving workers into accepting a lower real wage than expected, or by confusing firms into thinking that the *relative* price of their output has risen. This theorem is proved on the basis of two assumptions, rational expectations[11] and ubiquitous flexprice markets. It is the first of these assumptions that is always emphasized in the new classical literature, whereas it is the second that critics believe to be a travesty of the facts. There is still a vigorous debate on what the empirical evidence shows. The new classical macroeconomists point to the substantial evidence that faster trend monetary expansion does not increase employment in order to support their position, while their critics reply that fixprice markets and adaptive expectations are also consistent with that finding. These critics point instead to the evidence that deviations from any concept of full employment are highly serially correlated, whereas the simple version of the new classical theory predicts they would be essentially random. The new classical macroeconomists reply that such serial correlation could be caused by delays in the transmission of the information that enables agents to distinguish between relative and absolute prices or by the costs of adjusting employment to fluctuations in desired output or by delayed effects of capital or inventory accumulation. Most critics, including the author, probably base their rejection of the new classical story less on formal evidence, important as it is, than on an inability to believe that the vast extent of unemployment (32 million in the OECD area in early 1983) can possibly be explained away as the result of people being confused into setting false prices, still less that any substantial part of the rise in unemployment since the early 1970s was voluntary.

The empirical evidence therefore indicates that one must reject the global monetarist assumptions of equation (9.8). However, the need to reject this extreme version of monetarism should not lead one to dismiss the whole monetarist contribution: that would be to impute guilt by association. There is in fact an important sense in which the monetary approach is correct and useful. And, as in the case of no capital mobility, it is bound up with the question of the time period of analysis. At the end of chapter 8, it was argued that the monetary approach gives the correct asymptotic solution to a comprehensive general equilibrium model with properties that are fully Keynesian in the short run—that is, that the monetary approach gets the answer right in the long run but not in the short run. The reason the monetary approach gets the answer right only in the long run is that, with capital immobility, establishment of monetary equilibrium between countries requires current account surpluses and deficits, which, having the dimension of a flow, necessarily require time for the flows to cumulate to

11. See chap. 10.4 for an explanation and discussion of rational expectations.

a change in the equilibrium stock. But with capital mobility on the stock theory,[12] the situation is reversed. The level of reserves can now change in the short run in such a way as to reestablish monetary equilibrium, even while an underlying portfolio disequilibrium persists and generates current account surpluses or deficits. That being so, the monetarist balance of payments equation becomes a useful tool for predicting the overall balance of payments (reserve change).

This synthesis of Keynesian and monetarist payments theory was first advanced by Kouri and Porter in 1974. What they did was to accept the monetarist payments equation (9.7) and use it, in conjunction with the current balance equation (8.20), in order to predict the capital account:

$$ d\dot{F} = dR(\overset{+}{d\phi}, \overset{+}{dp}, \overset{+}{dY}, \overset{+}{di}, \overset{-}{dD_1}) - TB(\overset{-}{Y}, \overset{+}{ep*/p}), \qquad (9.9) $$

where dR (. . .) is simply a restatement of (9.7). Equation (9.9) says that the capital inflow is that part of the shortfall of money supply below money demand that is not made good by a current account surplus, where the latter is determined by the usual Keynesian variables, which can be considered predetermined in the short-run period necessary for adjustment of the financial markets.

Just as we earlier argued that equations (9.2) and (9.7) were mutually consistent, so there is no reason to regard equations (9.3) and (9.9) as mutually exclusive. They are alternatives only in the sense that one may be better adapted than another as a tool for forecasting. And it is as a tool for short-term forecasting of payments flows in countries with a high degree of capital mobility that equation (9.9) and therefore the monetary approach comes into its own. To see why, note that in (9.9) most of the key variables —p, Y, e, $p*$ and presumbly ϕ—can be taken as predetermined in the short run. The same is true of D_1 for countries whose monetary policy is based on the control of domestic credit expansion (as opposed to control of the money supply or the pursuit of an interest rate target), that is, who do not sterilize.[13] That leaves only the interest rate i as endogenous in equation (9.9). But i also appears in equation (9.3). Indeed, whereas the interest elasticity of the demand for money is generally not so high as to make the capital flow forecast by (9.9) too sensitive to errors in forecasting i, the role of i is quite critical in (9.3), and a small error in the forecast can make all

12. With capital mobility on the flow theory, the situation is essentially the same as with capital immobility, since correction of monetary disequilibrium through payments flows again necessarily requires time (see Frenkel, Gylfason, and Helliwell, 1980).

13. Countries that sterilize in a reasonably systematic way can be analyzed by a slight extension of the analysis, involving introduction of the concept of the "sterilization coefficient" —the proportion of any reserve flow whose effect on the monetary base is neutralized through a change in domestic credit.

the difference between a large surplus and a large deficit. In other words, the monetary approach is quite indispensable to short-run payments forecasting under conditions of high capital mobility.

9.5 Summary

Capital mobility has become one of the dominant facts of international economic life over the past quarter-century. Initial attempts to explain capital flows centered on the flow theory, which postulated that a given interest differential would induce a permanent inflow or outflow. Portfolio theory showed that this was theoretically implausible; instead one should expect a change in interest rates to stimulate a *temporary* capital flow, although with a possibility of some more permanent effect on flows because of the portfolio growth effect. The resulting stock theory of the capital account is consistent with the monetary approach to the balance of payments, which is in general the best way of forecasting reserve changes for countries with a high degree of capital mobility and a monetary policy based on the control of domestic credit.

9.6 Bibliography

Classic articles on the transfer problem include J. M. Keynes, "The German Transfer Problem," *Economic Journal,* Mar. 1929; B. Ohlin, "The Reparation Problem: A Discussion," *Economic Journal,* June 1929; and L. A. Metzler, "The Transfer Problem Reconsidered," *Journal of Political Economy,* June 1942; all reprinted in H. S. Ellis and L. A. Metzler, eds., *Readings in the Theory of International Trade* (Homewood, Ill.: Irwin, 1950); P. A. Samuelson, "The Transfer Problem and Transport Costs: The Terms of Trade When Impediments Are Absent," *Economic Journal,* June 1952, reprinted in J. E. Stiglitz, ed., *The Collected Works of Paul A. Samuelson,* vol. 2 (Cambridge, Mass.: MIT Press, 1966); and H. G. Johnson, "The Transfer Problem and Exchange Stability," *Journal of Political Economy,* June 1956, reprinted in his *International Trade and Economic Growth* (Cambridge, Mass.: Harvard University Press, 1961), and in R. E. Caves and H. G. Johnson, eds., *Readings in International Economics* (Homewood, Ill.: Irwin, 1968).

The traditional classic on capital movements in general is C. Iversen, *Aspects of the Theory of International Capital Movements* (Copenhagen: Levin and Munksgaard, 1936), reprinted by Augustus M. Kelley Publishers (New York, 1967).

Mundell's analysis of the fiscal-monetary mix was published as R. A. Mundell, "The Appropriate Use of Monetary and Fiscal Policy under Fixed Exchange Rates," International Monetary Fund *Staff Papers,* March 1962, reprinted in his *International Economics* (London: Macmillan, 1968).

Capital Mobility

Portfolio theory was developed by H. Markowitz, "Portfolio Selection," *Journal of Finance,* Mar. 1952; and J. Tobin, "Liquidity Preference as Behavior Towards Risk," *Review of Economic Studies,* Feb. 1958. It was first applied extensively to the study of international capital movements by W. H. Branson, *Financial Capital Flows in the United States Balance of Payments* (Amsterdam: North-Holland, 1968). Lessard's estimates of the welfare gains from risk diversification are in D. R. Lessard, "Financial Mechanisms for International Risk Sharing; Issues and Prospects" (paper presented to the Second International Conference on Latin America and Caribbean Financial Development, Caraballeda, Venezuela, Apr. 1981). The model of Roberto Frenkel is included in his paper entitled "Financial Liberalization and Capital Flows; the Case of Argentina," to appear in R. Ffrench-Davis, ed., *External Financial Relations and Their Impact on the Latin American Economies* (London: Macmillan, forthcoming). Dornbusch's treatment of capital mobility with a fixed exchange rate is contained in chap. 10 of his *Open Economy Macroeconomics* (New York: Basic Books, 1980).

For the monetary approach one should again consult J. A. Frenkel and H. G. Johnson, eds., *The Monetary Approach to the Balance of Payments* (London: Allen and Unwin, 1976), especially the paper of Michael Mussa. A reconciliation of orthodox and monetary approaches, incorporating the flow theory into the orthodox equation and therefore reaching results qualitatively similar to those reached at the end of the last chapter, is to be found in J. A. Frenkel, T. Gylfason, and J. F. Helliwell, "A Synthesis of Monetary and Keynesian Approaches to Short-run Balance-of-Payments Theory," *Economic Journal,* Sept. 1980. The Kouri-Porter synthesis appeared in P. J. K. Kouri and M. G. Porter, "International Capital Flows and Portfolio Equilibrium," *Journal of Political Economy,* May 1974.

Both that paper and R. J. Herring and R. C. Marston, *National Monetary Policies and International Financial Markets* (Amsterdam: North-Holland, 1977), contain estimates of offset coefficients (and also of sterilization coefficients). Evidence against the perfect arbitrage hypothesis is to be found in the *Journal of International Economics,* May 1978 (see especially the paper of I. B. Kravis and R. E. Lipsey), and in P. Isard, "How Far Can We Push the Law of One Price?" *American Economic Review,* Dec. 1977. The main sources for the new classical macroeconomics are R. E. Lucas, "Expectations and the Neutrality of Money," *Journal of Economic Theory,* Apr. 1972; "Some International Evidence on Ouput-Inflation Trade-offs," *American Economic Review,* June 1973; and "An Equilibrium Model of the Business Cycle," *Journal of Political Economy,* Dec. 1975; T. Sargent and N. Wallace, "Rational Expectations, the Optimal Monetary Instrument, and the Optimal Money Supply Rule," *Journal of Political Economy,* Apr. 1975; and R. J. Barro, "Rational Expectations and the Role of Monetary Policy," *Journal of Monetary Economics,* Jan. 1976.

10

Flexible Exchange Rates

THE ANALYSIS in the preceding two chapters has been conducted on the assumption that the exchange rate is fixed by the central bank. It was not necessarily assumed that the rate of exchange is fixed in the sense of being unalterable: on the contrary, the implications of changes in the exchange rate were often analyzed. Such changes were, however, considered to be exogenous. The main point of the present chapter is to study how the rate of exchange is determined when it is not determined by governmental decision but by market forces. This sets the stage for a discussion of different forms of exchange-rate flexibility, and the factors that should govern a country's choice of exchange-rate policy, in the final section of the chapter.

An exchange rate whose value is not held within certain preannounced limits by official action—to act as the residual buyer or seller of foreign exchange whenever necessary—is said to float. The following sections consider four theories of how the value of a floating rate is determined: the current balance model, the purchasing power parity (PPP) model, the Mundell-Fleming model, and the asset market view. In addition to describing the theories themselves, some of their principal implications, as regards the impact of various policy measures, are studied and compared to the results under a regime of fixed exchange rates.

Flexible Exchange Rates

10.1   The Current Balance Model

If there were no capital mobility, and if the exchange rate were floating freely—meaning that the central bank does not intervene in the foreign exchange market at all—then the current account would have to be in equilibrium if the foreign exchange market were to clear, since there would be no other accounts to balance out any disequilibrium in the current account. What force would make it clear? Just as price theory shows how price flexibility can clear other competitive markets, so the traditional answer is that variations in the price of foreign exchange—that is, in the exchange rate—could ensure that the foreign exchange market clears. This answer provides the basis for one of the oldest theories of what determines the exchange rate under floating: that the rate will adjust to the point where the demand for foreign exchange to buy imports and make other current payments will equal the supply that is forthcoming from the sale of exports and other current receipts.

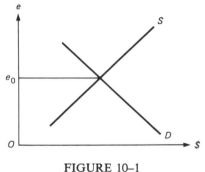

FIGURE 10–1
Current Balance Model

In terms of figure 10–1, the exchange rate would be determined at the value of e_0, where demand for dollars equals the supply. What lies behind the demand and supply curves of figure 10–1 was examined in the course of the elasticities analysis of chapter 8. (There is, however, one difference in interpretation. The demand and supply curves were there defined on the assumption that real income was being held constant by compensatory fiscal-monetary policy, but any such assumption would be out of place in the present context.)

There is another technical point that has to be mentioned before proceeding to the substantive analysis: whether one can reasonably assume that the demand and supply curves have the shapes shown in figure 10–1. The answer given in chapter 8 was that when one is considering the demand and supply curves that incorporate the adjustments taking place over several years, this is entirely reasonable: empirical evidence is pretty conclusive that the Marshall-Lerner condition is satisfied in the medium run. But the foreign exchange market has to clear day-by-day or even hour-by-hour, not lumping together all the demands and supplies over a couple of years. The discussion of the J-curve in chapter 8 showed why an increase in the exchange rate can normally be expected (at least for industrial countries) to result in a short-run *decrease* in the trade balance. (The impact effect of depreciation is to reduce the dollar value of exports, which are largely denominated in pesos, relative to that of imports, which are largely denominated in dollars. Even when existing contracts have been fulfilled, the greater reduction in the dollar price of exports relative to the reduction in the dollar price of imports—for countries with some market power at least on the export side—will leave the trade balance in greater deficit or smaller surplus than it would have been without depreciation until volumes have time to adjust.) That means that a depreciation would increase the excess demand for dollars and so increase the pressure toward depreciation. In sum, a freely floating exchange rate of a country with pricing practices typical for an industrial country would be dynamically unstable without capital mobility!

There are two ways around this problem. One is to suppose that the foreign exchange market is exclusively a forward market. That disposes of the denomination problem completely, since traders know the exchange rate they will receive at the time they sign their contracts, and it also opens the possibility of price movements going sufficiently far to kill or kindle the interest of buyers as necessary to ensure short-run stability. The second way around the problem is more realistic, although it does not enable one to tell a story in strict conformity with the assumption of capital immobility. This is to assume that there are well-informed speculators in the market, who are prepared to take short-term positions buying or selling one currency for the other to smooth out excess demands or supplies that may arise, but because they are well informed their interventions cancel out to zero over the course of each year or so, thus leaving the current account in balance over that time. It is, of course, worth remembering that it was necessary to make an assumption like this in order to be able to develop the model: where there are reasons to doubt the realism of the assumption, a floating exchange rate should be expected not to function very efficiently—it would tend to gyrate wildly before enough speculators were drawn in to dampen the natural instability of the current account.

Flexible Exchange Rates

One of the principal theorems to have been drawn from the current balance model is that a floating rate will *insulate* a country against foreign shocks to real income or to prices. The analysis of the foreign trade multiplier in chapter 8 showed how a foreign boom would raise foreign imports and thus our exports and, in turn, our imports. This mechanism cannot work under a floating rate that maintains the current balance in equilibrium, or $X - M = 0$:

$$Y = A(Y,i) + (X-M) = A(Y,i) \tag{10.1}$$

becomes independent of X. Intuitively, the rise in the demand for exports causes the peso to appreciate to whatever extent is necessary to prevent a trade surplus emerging, and thus the domestic economy is insulated from the foreign boom.[1] The theorem is symmetrical: the rest of the world no longer imports our expansions or depressions.

Since the foreign interest rate influences our economy only indirectly via its effect on foreign incomes and thus imports in the current balance model,

[1] It was in fact argued by Laursen and Metzler in 1950 that a foreign boom would tend to cause a *fall* in our income under a floating rate—the exact opposite of the result of the foreign trade multiplier under a fixed rate. The reason is that the foreign boom causes our currency to appreciate, which improves our terms of trade, which raises our real income in terms of a price index of final goods, which raises both consumption and saving in terms of *that* price index—but *reduces* consumption in terms of a price index of home goods alone, which means that it increases unemployment. To show this, postulate that consumption is the only element of home demand, and

$$C/p = \alpha + \beta(Y/p), \text{ or } C = \alpha p + \beta Y$$

where p is the price index of final goods

$$p = p_n{}^\gamma p_m{}^{(1-\gamma)}.$$

Current balance implies $X = M$ (in nominal terms), so

$$Y = C + X - M = C = \alpha p + \beta Y$$

implies

$$(1-\beta)Y = \alpha \, p_n{}^\gamma \, p_m{}^{(1-\gamma)}$$

or

$$Y/p_n = [\alpha/(1-\beta)]p_m{}^{(1-\gamma)}p_n{}^{(\gamma-1)},$$

so

$$\frac{\partial(Y/p_n)}{\partial p_m} = \frac{\alpha(1-\gamma)}{(1-\beta)} \cdot p_n{}^{(\gamma-1)} \cdot p_m{}^{-\gamma} > 0.$$

Thus a boom in the rest of the world, which cuts the domestic currency price of imports as a result of the induced appreciation, *reduces* income in terms of home goods. Although this Laursen-Metzler effect of an inverse cycle is famous, it is a second-order effect.

one may draw the corollary that a floating rate also insulates against changes in the foreign interest rate.

The analysis of the last two chapters has also emphasized that, under a fixed exchange rate, shocks to foreign prices will tend to spread to our economy via (imperfect) arbitrage. This mechanism is also ruptured by a floating exchange rate determined by the current balance model. A rise in foreign prices, for example, would tend to increase the real exchange rate and so generate a surplus unless it were offset by an equivalent fall in *e*, to maintain *ep** constant. Conclusion: *e* will vary to insulate the domestic economy from variations in *p**. Symmetrically, we can neutralize the external effects of an inflation greater than that in the rest of the world by depreciating at a rate equal to the inflation differential:

$$\hat{e} = \hat{p} - \hat{p}*. \tag{10.2}$$

A second important theorem states that fiscal and monetary policy will both have *more* effect (on the level of real income and thus employment) with a floating rate than with a fixed rate. The analysis assumes fixed prices in the Keynesian tradition. The theorem can be illustrated with a diagram introduced by Mundell (see fig. 10–2). Real income is on the horizontal axis and the exchange rate on the vertical axis. The curve *XX* shows the locus of points of equilibrium in the goods market. It slopes up because an increase in income implies an equal rise in output, while aggregate demand will rise by less (so long as the marginal propensity to consume is less than one); a depreciation of the currency is needed to stimulate exports and substitute imports and so close the output gap. There is excess demand for goods (EDG) above *XX* and excess supply below. The curve *FF* shows the

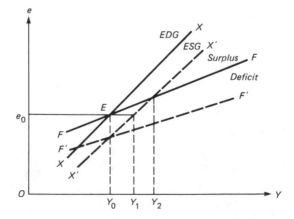

FIGURE 10–2
Policy Changes in the Current Balance Model

points of balance of payments equilibrium. It too slopes up because a rise in income pulls in imports which have to be paid for by stimulating more exports, which, in turn, requires a depreciation. *FF* is less steeply sloped than *XX* since a given increase in *Y* requires a larger depreciation to restore goods market equilibrium than to restore payments equilibrium, due to the fact that leakages from the spending stream take the forms of saving and taxes, as well as imports. The balance of payments is in surplus above *FF* and in deficit below. Given a floating exchange rate that guarantees current account balance, the economy goes to point *E.*

An expansionary fiscal or monetary policy pushes the *XX* curve right, to a position such as *X'X',* which was previously in the area of excess supply of goods. If the exchange rate were fixed, output would expand from Y_0 to Y_1. But given that the current balance must remain in equilibrium, the economy must remain on *FF* and so output must expand to Y_2, which is greater than Y_1. Therefore, expansionary fiscal-monetary policies are more potent under floating rates without capital mobility. Intuitively, the leakage from the expenditure stream represented by an increased current deficit is plugged by floating the exchange rate, thus increasing the multiplier.

The analysis of chapter 8 showed that another way of expanding income under a fixed exchange rate was by a restrictive commercial policy, such as increasing tariffs on imports. This again has the effect of shifting *XX* to the right, to *X'X'.* However, it also increases the balance of payments surplus corresponding to any combination of *Y* and *e;* that is, it shifts the *FF* curve down. In fact, it must shift *FF* down far enough to intersect *X'X'* at the initial income level Y_0. One can see this by referring back to equation (10.1) which shows that no policy that operates by influencing *M*—when there is a constraint that says $X - M = 0$ —can succeed in influencing *Y.* [2] Commercial policy is therefore completely impotent to influence income under floating rates.

The classic article "Flexible Exchange Rates and Employment Policy," in which Mundell first established the two preceding theorems, was written when his native Canada had a floating exchange rate and a governor of its central bank called James E. Coyne. Mr. Coyne wanted to fight inflation by a restrictive monetary policy (pushing *XX* to the left) and simultaneously to fight unemployment by increasing protection (pushing *XX* back to the right and *FF* down). Mundell's analysis showed once and for all (one hopes) why this was not a very bright idea: however much one may desire supplementary policies to reduce the unemployment cost of fighting inflation through a restrictive monetary policy, a restrictive commercial policy does not solve the problem.

2. When the Laursen-Metzler effect exists (see n. 1), *FF* actually shifts down *more* than *XX* and in consequence employment *falls* as a result of increased protection!

211

10.2   Purchasing Power Parity

Another old theory about what determines the exchange rate of a floating currency, first analyzed extensively by the Swedish economist Gustav Cassell (1866–1945) although it has been traced back to 1601, appeals to the concept of purchasing power parity (henceforth PPP). The basic idea is that the exchange rate will adjust to ensure that a dollar will buy as much in our country as it would at home. The strong version of PPP incorporating that idea may be expressed:

$$e = p/p^*, \tag{10.3}$$

the exchange rate is the ratio of our price level to the foreign price level. There is also a weak version of PPP, which argues that for various reasons (some of which will be discussed in due course) the exchange rate may differ from p/p^*, but that this divergence will depend on structural characteristics and thus be constant or at least exogenous. This version may be expressed:

$$e = \pi p/p^* \tag{10.4}$$

which, for the case of a constant (rather than merely exogenous) π implies equation (10.2):

$$\hat{e} = \hat{p} - \hat{p}^*.$$

The depreciation of the exchange rate will equal the excess of domestic inflation over world inflation.

There are at least three different views of the economic forces that are supposed to underlie equation (10.3) or (10.4). In one view there is something inherent in the nature of money and economic rationality that must lead to PPP and there is no need to specify an adjustment mechanism that ultimately leads to establishment of the PPP condition (I do not pretend to understand this view). A second interpretation appeals to goods arbitrage: if $p > ep^*$, our country would be inundated by foreign goods seeking to take advantage of the better prices available in our market. There are two difficulties with this view. The first is that it does not explain why e rather than p adjusts when $p > ep^*$. The second is that there is abundant empirical evidence[3] that arbitrage is not sufficiently perfect to guarantee that p always remains close to ep^*. But this does not, as has sometimes been assumed, dispose of the usefulness of the PPP concept in explaining exchange rates,

3. See the relevant references cited in the last paragraph of chap. 9.6.

for there is a third and much more persuasive interpretation of what lies behind PPP.

The third view is that PPP is a necessary condition for equilibrium. The equation for the current account is $TB(Y, ep*/p)$. If we require of equilibrium both that $TB(. . .) = 0$, as in the current balance model of the last section, and that $Y = Y_{FE}$, that is, full employment, then $ep*/p$ must have a well-defined value in equilibrium. Call that value π, and we have equation (10.4) as a necessary condition for equilibrium. This interpretation, it is true, works only for the weak version of equation (10.4) and not the strong version of (10.3).

There is in fact strong empirical evidence, not just that π is not necessarily equal to unity, but that it varies in a systematic way with the level of per capita real income or the stage of development of a country. The reason is that the rise in productivity that occurs in the course of development and that is the primary cause of rising per capita income is spread unevenly between sectors. Specifically, productivity tends to rise most rapidly in sectors like manufacturing and agriculture that largely produce traded goods and to grow much less in most services which are predominantly nontraded goods. Assuming that wages are equalized by competition between the two sectors,[4] this means that the relative price of nontraded goods (p_n/p_m) rises in the course of development. In a rich country, haircuts and restaurant meals become expensive relative to radios and cars because they present much less opportunity for raising labor productivity. But p and $p*$ are indices of the general price level, which consists of the prices of both traded and nontraded goods. Since p_m, the price of traded goods, is more or less equalized by arbitrage, it follows that the general price index (expressed in a common currency) will tend to be higher in the more developed country.[5]

This stylized fact about differential productivity growth explains what at first sight seemed to be a contradiction to PPP. During the 1960s, it was observed that the most rapidly growing countries, notably Japan, were

4. Empirically, this is an exaggeration. However, the wage shortfall in the service sector does not increase sufficiently rapidly to dominate the differential productivity growth.

5. Proof. Define n, $n*$ as the price-wage ratios in the N-industries in the two countries, and m, $m*$ as the price-wage ratios in the M-industries. Then W's higher productivity and the stylized fact of greater technical progress in the M-industry imply $n/m < n*/m*$. Assuming the price index to have the Cobb-Douglas form $p = p_n{}^\alpha p_m{}^{1-\alpha}$, substitution of $p_n = nw$, $p_m = mw$, yields $p = (n/m)^\alpha p_m$. Similar substitution in the formula for $p*$ yields $p* = (n*/m*)^\alpha p_m*$. Given the perfect arbitrage hypothesis $p_m = ep_m*$, it is clear that

$$p = (n/m)^\alpha p_m < ep* = (n*/m*)^\alpha ep_m* = (n*/m*)^\alpha p_m$$

so long as $(n/m) < (n*/m*)$ as postulated.

experiencing rates of inflation well above those in their more slowly growing trading partners, like the United States. A simple application of the elasticities analysis would have suggested that the current account of the balance of payments would develop a deficit. However, the price index that showed fast Japanese inflation was the consumer price index (CPI), and that fast inflation reflected the rapid rise in the relative price of nontraded goods that was a consequence of the rapid productivity growth in traded goods. If one looked at a price index confined to traded goods, like the unit value index for exports, one found that Japanese prices were *declining* relative to United States prices. Despite the relative behavior of the CPIs, Japan was in fact gaining competitiveness relative to the United States, a fact that finally resulted in an explosion of the Japanese current account surplus at the end of the decade. The example illustrates just how essential it is to take account of differences in trend productivity growth in making PPP comparisons.

There are two other implications of differential productivity growth that are sufficiently interesting and important to merit a brief discussion, even though they represent diversions from the theme of PPP as a determinant of the exchange rate. The first involves cross-section comparisons between real income levels in countries at different stages of development. The crude way to make such comparisons is to take figures for GNP per head in terms of the national currency and convert them into dollars at the going exchange rate. The result of this all-too-common procedure is to grossly exaggerate the differences in real income between rich and poor countries, since nontraded goods are counted in the rich country's income at a much higher price (reflecting the differences in productivity in the traded-goods industries) than they are in the poor country. That is not for a moment to deny that international differences in real income are large: in fact they are still staggering even when computed correctly, as has now been done for a large number of countries by the research team based at the University of Pennsylvania and headed by Irving Kravis. The correct basis of comparison involves establishing the cost of buying specified quantities of comparable goods in each of numerous expenditure categories for each of the countries to be compared to yield a PPP for each category of expenditure relative to a numeraire country. Those PPPs are then used to convert expenditure in each category to the numeraire currency unit. The ratio between a country's expenditures and those of the numeraire country then reflect the ratio of the quantities consumed in the two countries.

The second diversion relates to what is known as the Scandinavian model of inflation. The model considers a small country with a fixed exchange rate and a passive monetary policy in which the prices of traded goods are determined by arbitrage, from which it follows that the rate of inflation in traded goods is determined by, and equal to, the world rate of inflation in traded goods $(\hat{p}_m{}^*)$. Wages are assumed to be settled each year at the level that the market will bear but no more, which implies that wage inflation is $\hat{w} = \hat{p}_m{}^* + \rho$, where ρ is the rate of productivity growth in the traded goods industries. Suppose for simplicity (only) that productivity growth is zero in the nontraded goods industries. Then, assuming that the trade unions or competition in the labor market ensure that wages grow at the same rate in both sectors, inflation in nontraded goods will equal wage growth, $\hat{p}_n = \hat{w}$. If nontraded and traded goods have weights of α and $(1 - \alpha)$, respectively, in the price index, the overall rate of inflation is given by

$$\begin{aligned} \hat{p} &= \alpha(\hat{p}_m{}^* + \rho) + (1 - \alpha)\hat{p}_m{}^* \\ &= \hat{p}_m{}^* + \alpha\rho. \end{aligned} \tag{10.5}$$

Thus inflation is determined by international inflation plus a fraction of the rate of productivity growth. Two features are worth noting. First, faster productivity growth *raises* inflation—in direct contrast to models based on Phillips curves or real wage resistance, where higher productivity reduces price increases for any given level of wage inflation or helps to reconcile inconsistent real income claims. Second, a country that has a rate of productivity growth greater than that abroad can import more inflation than is present in the exporting country! That is, in fact, just what happened in countries like Germany, Japan, and Sweden in the 1960s.

However, the main purpose of this section is to consider the usefulness of the notion of PPP in explaining the level of a floating exchange rate. It has so far been suggested that the relative version of PPP is a necessary condition for equilibrium but that the value of π can be expected to change systematically over time depending on relative rates of productivity growth. In the simple case considered in the preceding paragraph, where productivity is constant in the nontraded goods industry, it is easy to confirm[6] that

$$\hat{\pi} = \alpha(\rho^* - \rho).$$

6. Proof. From the logarithmic time derivative of (10.4), PPP will be preserved at a fixed exchange rate if

$$\hat{\pi} = \hat{p}^* - \hat{p}.$$

Substituting from (10.5) and the equivalent result $\hat{p}^* = \hat{p}_m{}^* + \alpha\rho^*$,

$$\hat{\pi} = \hat{p}_m{}^* + \alpha\rho^* - (\hat{p}_m{}^* + \alpha\rho) = \alpha\,(\rho^* - \rho).$$

The equilibrium rate of depreciation therefore becomes

$$\hat{e} = \hat{p} - \hat{p}* - \alpha(\rho - \rho*). \tag{10.6}$$

Our depreciation can be slower if our productivity growth (in traded goods) is greater than that abroad.[7]

There are certain circumstances under which equation (10.6) will give an exact rule for the depreciation necessary to restore equilibrium: when equilibrium is disturbed by a monetary shock. The classic case is Milton Friedman's helicopter sprinkling fiat money around, which everyone then rushes out to spend, driving prices up. Everyone knows that any well-behaved economy is homogeneous of degree zero in all nominal variables. That means that H, p, and e must increase in the same proportion to re-establish equilibrium: equation (10.6) must be exactly satisfied when p rises because of a pure monetary shock.

In reality the money supply is not typically increased by helicopter distribution but rather by government spending programs that have powerful transitional real effects. Nevertheless, after the monetary expansion has ended the real effects will tend to die away and what remains is essentially a monetary change. It was in just these circumstances, when the monetary expansions undertaken to finance belligerents' efforts in the First World War had come to an end but had left a legacy of vastly different cumulative inflations since the prewar fixed exchange rates were abandoned, that Gustav Cassell applied his theory in order to calculate the parities at which rates ought once again to be fixed. Countries like Britain that ignored such calculations and returned to their prewar parities for the sake of nostalgia paid a hideous price in terms of unemployment and social strife as the government tried to force wages down. Another good example of the helpful role that a PPP calculation can fulfill in neutralizing an essentially monetary change is provided by the experience of a country like Brazil, which has followed monetary policies markedly more inflationary than those in its main trading partners but eliminated the damage this would otherwise cause to the balance of payments by depreciating the cruzeiro broadly in accordance with PPP.

There are other circumstances under which equation (10.6) will not give a correct figure for the exchange rate change necessary to restore equilibrium. These circumstances arise whenever the shock that disturbs equilibrium is essentially a real shock rather than a monetary shock. Suppose, for

7. This expression can be further amplified to take account of growth, which makes it necessary to introduce price and income elasticities of demand for exports and imports as developed in Johnson (1954).

example, that the price of oil rises, thus worsening the country's terms of trade, and that it is necessary to adjust this deficit as has been assumed so far in this chapter. That adjustment would require either a fall in real income or a real depreciation. Ruling out the former as involving an irrational waste of real resources, it becomes necessary in this case to depreciate more than is indicated by (10.6). How much more? That cannot be answered by PPP: it requires instead a knowledge of the elasticities. The moral is that PPP should not be applied blindly, but that consideration needs to be given as to whether there are real shocks that create a need for changes in π. The need to exercise such care does not constitute a reason for refusing to exploit such guidance as the theory can give.

10.3 The Mundell-Fleming Model

The model that now bears the name of Robert Mundell and the British economist J. Marcus Fleming (1911–76) was introduced more or less simultaneously and apparently independently by the two of them in the early 1960s, shortly after they ceased to be colleagues in the IMF's Research Department because of Mundell's move to Chicago. It advances on the work so far discussed in this chapter in introducing capital mobility, in the form of the flow theory examined in chapter 9.2.

The other assumptions are conventional enough. The basic framework is the IS/LM/BP model, with prices (or at least wages) assumed to be fixed. The balance on current account is determined by income and relative prices, ep^*/p. There are no lags: the economy moves to its new equilibrium immediately. The exchange rate floats freely, so that the current deficit is equal to the capital inflow (or vice versa) with no change in reserves. Finally, expectations are static: agents always expect the indefinite perpetuation of the present. The last assumption is crucial in enabling one to treat the interest rates in the two countries as representing the opportunity costs of holding assets in the one country rather than the other, and thus continuing to use a capital flow equation of the form $f(i, i^*)$ introduced in chapter 9.2. In general, of course, one would expect that investors will be interested in comparing their total expected yields from holding foreign rather than domestic assets, which points to the need for a specification $f(i, i^* + E\hat{e})$. This generalization is introduced in the following section. For the moment, one just has to imagine that investors never have any expectation that the exchange rate is more likely to rise than to fall.

A lot of attention is paid in the literature to the case of perfect capital mobility—perhaps more than it deserves. With a floating exchange rate, capital mobility could be perfect only if investors had complete confidence in the future maintenance of today's exchange rate, or else if they were completely risk neutral. The former assumption is totally implausible, given that actual floating rates are forever bobbing around. The latter assumption is usually regarded as a very strong one. Accordingly, the case of perfect capital mobility should be treated more as a point of intellectual reference —like the case of perfect immobility, the current balance model of chapter 10.1—than as a model to be seriously applied in understanding the real world or giving policy advice. The important case is the intermediate one of finite capital mobility.

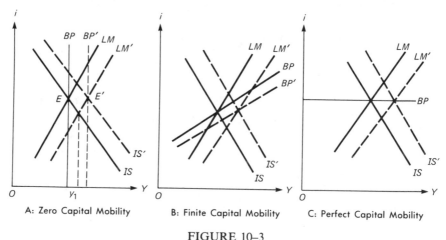

FIGURE 10–3

Monetary Policy in the Mundell-Fleming Model

The analysis of monetary policy in the Mundell-Fleming model is illustrated in figure 10–3 for the three cases of capital mobility. Consider first the case of zero capital mobility (shown in figure 10–3A), which is reflected in a vertical *BP* curve. Initial equilibrium is at *E*. The *BP* curve necessarily cuts the *IS/LM* intersection at *E* because of the assumption of a floating exchange rate, which guarantees that the balance of payments be in equilibrium. Now consider the effect of an expansionary monetary policy, that is, an increase in domestic credit. The effect of this is to push the *LM* curve to the right, to *LM'*. With a fixed exchange rate that would be the end of the story, at least in the short run:[8] income would expand by y_1 and the

8. In the long run, the payments deficit would lead to *LM* migrating leftward until it again intersected *IS* at *E*, assuming an absence of sterilization.

balance of payments would go into deficit. But with a floating exchange rate the story cannot end there, even in the short run, because the balance of payments cannot go into deficit. The incipient deficit instead causes the exchange rate to rise (that is, the domestic currency to depreciate), which pushes both IS and BP to the right as analyzed in the elasticities approach analysis of chapter 8.3. This continues until all three curves intersect at the same point, E'. (We can be sure that all three curves will intersect at the same point because we are requiring payments equilibrium, as well as equilibrium in the goods and money markets, and there is a third endogenous variable, e, to add to the pair Y, i of the fixed-rate case.) This necessarily occurs with a Y that has risen by more than Y_1, thus showing that monetary expansion is more effective in raising income with a floating exchange rate in the case of zero capital mobility.

TABLE 10–1

Short-run Comparative Static Effects in the Mundell-Fleming Model

	Fixed Exchange Rate			Floating Exchange Rate		
Degree of capital mobility	0	+	∞	0	+	∞
Monetary expansion, $\Delta D > 0$	$y_1 > 0$	y_1	0	$> y_1$	$> y_1$	$> y_1$
Fiscal expansion, $\Delta G > 0$	$y_2 > 0$	y_2	$> y_2$	$> y_2$	$+, \gtreqless y_2$	0
Commercial restriction, $\Delta \tau > 0$	$y_3 > 0$	y_3	$> y_3$	0^a	0^a	0^a

^{a}Or negative, if the Laursen-Metzler effect holds (see nn. 1 and 2)

Table 10–1 has been designed to combine the various results that will be established in this section. The results just established are entered in the first row, which shows the effects on Y of a monetary expansion ($\Delta D > 0$). The first column records that with a fixed rate and zero capital mobility the monetary expansion raises Y by an amount $y_1 > 0$ as illustrated in figure 10–3A. The fourth column records that with a floating rate the effect on Y is bigger than y_1, which is used as a standard of reference.

The analysis is little changed in the case of finite capital mobility shown by a positively sloping BP curve in figure 10–3B. Monetary expansion shifts the LM curve right exactly as before, and hence the short-run equilibrium is the same with finite capital mobility as with capital immobility. At the point where IS and LM' intersect there is again an incipient deficit, which implies that the exchange rate must increase. Equilibrium again occurs where the three curves intersect, with an income expansion larger than with fixed rates.

The case of perfect capital mobility differs in that, as already seen in chapter 9.2, a monetary expansion under fixed rates is immediately reversed through a capital outflow. Thus monetary policy is impotent to influence income with a fixed exchange rate, as reflected in the zero entry in table 10–1. With a floating rate, however, the monetary expansion causes a depreciation and an increase in income until such point as the demand for money has risen (because of the increased income) to match the rise in supply. At that point the country has developed a current account surplus matched by a capital outflow. It can be seen that income again expands by more than in the reference case.

Consider next the effects of a fiscal expansion (an increase in government spending or cut in taxes), illustrated in figure 10–4. The impact effect is to shift the *IS* curve right to *IS'*. With a fixed exchange rate and zero capital mobility short-run equilibrium would be at *E'*, with a payments deficit. The income expansion of y_2 thus provides our reference case. Since there is a deficit at *E'*, the currency must depreciate, pushing *IS* and *BP* to the right until their intersection falls on *LM* at *E"*. Thus income expands more than under fixed rates; the potency of fiscal as well as monetary policy is increased by floating, as we found in chapter 10.1.

This conclusion is critically dependent upon the assumption of zero capital mobility, as figure 10–4B shows. *E'* is now a position of payments *surplus,* not deficit; at least, that is, in the case illustrated, where *LM* is steeper than *BP*. In that case, the exchange rate must fall, pushing *IS* left and *BP* up till an equilibrium occurs somewhere on the segment of *LM* between *E* and *E'*. Income still expands as a result of the expansionary fiscal policy, but by *less* than under fixed rates. Had *BP* been steeper than *LM*, however (reflecting a lower degree of capital mobility), income would have

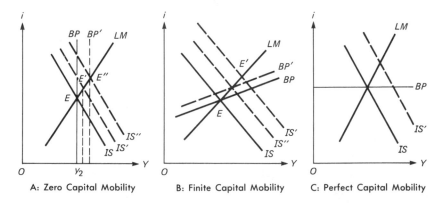

FIGURE 10–4
Fiscal Policy in the Mundell-Fleming Model

risen more than in the reference case. In either event income rises, but the rise may be greater than, equal to, or less than the rise in the reference case, as the entry in table 10–1 is intended to indicate.

With perfect capital mobility the situation is different again. With a fixed exchange rate the rightward move of the *IS* curve is matched by a rightward shift of the *LM* curve induced by a capital inflow, as seen in chapter 9.2: fiscal policy is thus very effective. With a floating rate, however, *LM* cannot move right—the money supply is fixed. Equilibrium therefore has to remain where it was, at the intersection of *LM* and *BP*, since neither move. The exchange rate makes this happen, by falling to the extent necessary to crowd out a volume of net export expenditures equal to the fiscal stimulus. Thus in this case fiscal policy is impotent to influence income. This provides the final element of a famous set of results: monetary policy is impotent under fixed rates but very effective under floating, while fiscal policy is the exact reverse—all, however, under the assumption of perfect capital mobility.

Consider now the effects of a restrictive commercial policy, for example, an increase in tariffs. The impact effect of this is to push both *IS* and *BP* to the right. The intersection of *IS'* and *LM* establishes our reference case, the rise in income that would be induced under a fixed rate, at *E'*. However, *BP* moves to the right by more than does *IS*: the *Y* that equilibrates the balance of payments increases by $(1/m)$ times the reduction in imports due to expenditure switching, while the *Y* that balances the goods market (for a given level of the interest rate) increases by only $1/(s + m)$ times the initial cut in imports. This means that *E'* is a point of payments surplus, and so the domestic currency must appreciate to restore equilibrium. In fact, since *BP'* lies to the right of *IS'* as long as *IS'* is to the right of *IS*, equilibrium must lie at point *E*. Commercial policy cannot increase income (as was already found in chapter 10.1) under a floating exchange rate with capital immobility.[9]

Figures 10–5B and 10–5C show that the analysis is essentially the same with finite or even perfect capital mobility. In both cases the exchange rate has to fall enough to crowd out completely the expenditure-switching induced by the rise in tariffs. Mr. Coyne's proposed policy mix cannot be saved by appealing to capital mobility.

Another question that is interesting to ask is whether the conclusion that a flexible exchange rate isolates a country from foreign shocks (to real income, the interest rate, or prices) remains valid under capital mobility. Unfortunately, this question cannot be answered by using the graphical analysis that has sufficed up to now, but requires slightly more advanced

9. Once again, with the Laursen-Metzler effect the new equilibrium would actually lie to the left of *E.*

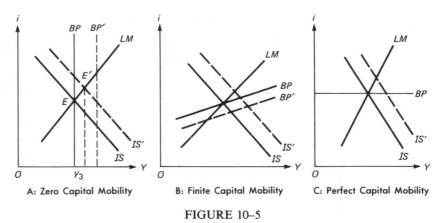

A: Zero Capital Mobility   B: Finite Capital Mobility   C: Perfect Capital Mobility

FIGURE 10–5
Commercial Policy in the Mundell-Fleming Model

mathematical techniques. (Those not familiar with elementary matrix algebra are advised to pass straight to the conclusions of the analysis.)

The model that has been analyzed graphically above may be represented algebraically by three equations: the first (*IS*) representing equilibrium in the market for goods, the second (*LM*) representing equilibrium in the market for money, and the third (*BP*) representing equilibrium in the market for foreign exchange. Letters have the same meanings as we have been giving them, except that all have been written in lower-case form and are to be interpreted as *logarithms* of the variables in question: this is because the specification supposes that the model is log linear. (An exception concerns the interest rate: *i* has to be interpreted as unity plus the rate of interest in fractional form—for example, a rate of interest of 5 percent is represented by $i = 1.05$ and not by log 5 or log 0.05.) Greek letters represent parameters, which are in fact elasticities in view of the log linear specification. Ignoring constant terms, that is, considering deviations from an initial equilibrium, the model is then:

$$y = \alpha(e + p^* - p) + \beta y^* - \gamma i \qquad (10.7)$$
$$h - p = \xi y - \eta i \qquad (10.8)$$

either $\quad i = i^* \qquad (10.9a)$

or $\quad \alpha(e + p^* - p) + \beta y^* - \theta y + \lambda(i - i^*) = 0. \qquad (10.9b)$

Equation (10.9a) represents the case of perfect capital mobility, while (10.9b) represents imperfect capital mobility (or complete immobility with $\lambda = 0$). Note that, while it is entirely natural to put the same coefficient

β in (10.7) and (10.9b), putting α in both involves assuming that the terms of trade are exogenous.

The simple case is that of perfect mobility. After substituting (10.9b) into (10.7) and (10.8), rearranging to put endogenous variables on the left-hand side and exogenous variables (which include h under floating rates) on the right, and putting in matrix form, one has

$$\begin{bmatrix} 1 & -\alpha \\ \xi & 0 \end{bmatrix} \begin{bmatrix} y \\ e \end{bmatrix} = \begin{bmatrix} \alpha\,(p^* - p) + \beta y^* - \gamma i^* \\ h - p + \eta i^* \end{bmatrix}.$$

Inverting the matrix to solve for the endogenous variables, one gets

$$\begin{bmatrix} y \\ e \end{bmatrix} = \frac{1}{\Delta} \begin{bmatrix} 0 & \alpha \\ -\xi & 1 \end{bmatrix} \begin{bmatrix} \alpha(p^* - p) + \beta y^* - \gamma i^* \\ h - p + \eta i^* \end{bmatrix} \quad (10.10)$$

where $\Delta = \alpha\,\xi > 0$.

The question of interest is how y and e adjust when the foreign variables y^*, i^* and p^* change. One extracts from (10.10):

$$dy/dy^* = 0, \qquad\qquad de/dy^* = -\beta/\alpha < 0.$$

With perfect capital mobility an increase in foreign income still causes an appreciation of the domestic currency sufficient to prevent any increase in domestic income: the business cycle would be desynchronized internationally. Second,

$$dy/di^* = \eta/\xi > 0, \qquad\qquad de/di^* = \gamma/\alpha + \eta/\alpha\xi > 0.$$

The increase in the foreign interest rate is transmitted to the domestic economy by incipient interest arbitrage, which causes the currency to depreciate and income to rise by as much as is needed to restore the demand for money (which fell because of the higher interest rate) to equal the unchanged supply. Finally,

$$dy/dp^* = 0, \qquad\qquad de/dp^* = -1.$$

The currency appreciates to neutralize the foreign inflation and leave income unchanged. Thus with perfect capital mobility the only foreign shock that influences the domestic economy is one to the interest rate, and this has an effect *opposite* to that under fixed rates: a higher foreign interest rate stimulates domestic income.

Before leaving the case of perfect capital mobility, it is worth checking that a neutral domestic inflation, that is, an equal proportionate rise in the money stock h and domestic prices p, can be neutralized through a proportionate depreciation:

$$dy/dp|_{dp=dh} = 0, \qquad de/dp|_{dp=dh} = 1.$$

The case of imperfect capital mobility incorporating (10.9b) instead of (10.9a) is somewhat more complex, since we now have three endogenous variables y, e, and i and three equations:

$$\begin{bmatrix} 1 & -\alpha & \gamma \\ \xi & 0 & -\eta \\ \theta & -\alpha & -\lambda \end{bmatrix} \begin{bmatrix} y \\ e \\ i \end{bmatrix} = \begin{bmatrix} \alpha(p^* - p) + \beta y^* \\ h - p \\ \alpha(p^* - p) + \beta y^* - \lambda i^* \end{bmatrix}.$$

Matrix inversion yields

$$\begin{bmatrix} y \\ e \\ i \end{bmatrix} = \frac{1}{\Delta} \begin{bmatrix} -\alpha\eta & -\alpha(\lambda + \gamma) & \alpha\eta \\ \lambda\xi - \theta\eta & -(\lambda + \gamma\theta) & \eta + \gamma\xi \\ -\alpha\xi & \alpha(1 - \theta) & \alpha\xi \end{bmatrix} \begin{bmatrix} \alpha(p^* - p) + \beta y^* \\ h - p \\ \alpha(p^* - p) + \beta y^* - \lambda i^* \end{bmatrix}$$

where $\Delta = -\alpha\eta (1 - \theta) - \alpha\xi(\gamma + \lambda) < 0$, since $\theta < 1$. (10.11)
One again extracts the relevant total derivatives, from (10.11):

$$dy/dy^* = 0, \qquad de/dy^* = -\beta/\alpha$$
$$dy/di^* = -\alpha\lambda\eta/\Delta > 0, \qquad de/di^* = -\lambda(\eta + \gamma\xi)/\Delta > 0$$
$$dy/dp^* = 0, \qquad de/dp^* = -1$$
$$dy/dp|_{dh=dp} = 0, \qquad de/dp|_{dh=dp} = 1.$$

With the exception of the more complicated (but still qualitatively similar) formulae for the effect of a change in the foreign interest rate, these results are identical to those in the case of perfect mobility. A floating exchange rate still insulates the domestic economy from everything except interest rate changes, where the direction of effect remains the opposite of that in the fixed exchange rate case, and it still neutralizes the external effects of a neutral domestic inflation. The intuitive explanations given for the case of perfect mobility remain valid.

Students who have the technical ability to deal with the preceding mathematics will find it an excellent exercise to use the algebraic model (extending it as necessary) to confirm the theorems about the effects of changes in monetary, fiscal, and commercial policy that were previously established diagramatically.

10.4 The Asset Market Approach

More or less coincidentally with the move of the main industrial countries to floating exchange rates in 1973, economists became gravely dissatisfied with the inadequacies of the Mundell-Fleming model. It embodies a number of assumptions, like the flow theory of the capital account and yield comparisons made purely in terms of interest rates with no consideration of expected changes in the exchange rate, that are clearly unrealistic but are vital to the conclusions that emerge. Furthermore, the conclusion that floating rates would break the international synchronization of the business cycle did not seem to be consistent with the facts, nor was it borne out by the simulation of macroeconometric models like the Canadian RDX–2.

The needed theoretical advance was launched in a series of papers at the Flexible Exchange Rates and Stabilization Policy Conference near Stockholm in 1975. The new generation of models were quickly dubbed the "asset market approach," because of their emphasis that monies are assets and that their relative price (the nominal exchange rate) is therefore determined by the willingness to hold the existing stocks of those monies. Ever since Keynes economists have recognized that the price of bonds (or, what amounts to the same thing, the rate of interest) is determined by the stocks of money and bonds in conjunction with the portfolio preferences of wealth owners: the asset market approach argues that international capital mobility is sufficiently high to make that same type of force dominant in the foreign exchange market. This is not to deny that over any period of time the flow demand for foreign exchange must equal the flow supply but to affirm that current account flows are so dwarfed by the flows on capital account that might potentially be generated by portfolio adjustments that one can treat the latter factor as the proximate determinant of the exchange rate. This is nothing other than an application of the stock theory of the capital account to the context where the exchange rate floats instead of being pegged by the central bank.

It is important at this point to distinguish between two aspects of the concept of perfect capital mobility. One relates to instantaneous adjustment, the other to perfect substitutability between assets. The Mundell-Fleming concept assumes both, but it is quite possible to conceive of either without the other. In fact, the asset market approach always assumes instantaneous adjustment: this is almost tautological, inasmuch as this approach represents the application of the stock theory of the capital account to a regime of floating rates. In contrast, perfect substitutability is sometimes assumed and sometimes not. Since the empirical evidence points strongly against the validity of the perfect substitutability assumption, it would be highly desirable to analyze the more general case. Unfortunately models that do this become very complicated, and so most of this section will assume perfect substitutability between assets (perfect interest arbitrage).

The simplest version of the asset market approach is the monetary approach, introduced at the Stockholm conference by the Israeli economist Jacob Frenkel (b. 1943). This postulates that national price levels are determined by the quantity theory, while the strong version of PPP then determines the exchange rate at the level that equates prices internationally. This sort of theory provides a useful first approximation in the circumstances of the German hyperinflation of the 1920s to which Frenkel applied it. But it is not adequate in more normal circumstances, where changes in real exchange rates and interest rates are not necessarily overwhelmed by changes in inflation rates.

More general versions of the asset market approach improve on the Mundell-Fleming model in recognizing that investors are not interested in the comparison between nominal interest rates on two different currencies but rather in the comparison between their yields, including the expected rate of appreciation of one in terms of the other. With perfect interest arbitrage, that implies

$$i = i^* + E\hat{e}. \tag{10.12}$$

The domestic interest rate must be equal to the foreign interest rate plus the expected rate of depreciation.

Equation (10.12) directs attention to another way in which the asset market approach breaks decisively with the models that have been examined up to now: the yields on different assets, and thus the prices that investors will be prepared to pay for them, depend not merely on objective interest rates but also on subjective *expectations*. Expectations can sometimes change rapidly, due to anything from climatic disasters to political assassinations to rumors about what the latest money supply figures signify. Such sudden changes in expectations, it is argued, are what lie behind the sudden price changes that are typical of all asset markets, including the exchange markets.

It is evident that any model that intends to include expectations as an element that determines yields, and thus asset prices, needs to embody a hypothesis about how expectations are formed. Traditionally economists have tended to minimize the role of such factors as those mentioned in the last paragraph and to concentrate on alternative possible ways in which the actual changes in some variable, say *x*, may influence expectations as to its own future value, x_{+1}. The four leading simple hypotheses are the following:

1. Static expectations, $Ex_{+1} = x$. Agents expect the present value of x to be maintained in the future. This is the simple hypothesis utilized in the Mundell-Fleming model and implicitly in many other places where expectations were not explicitly mentioned.

2. Adaptive expectations, $Ex_{+1} = E_{-1}x + a(x - E_{-1}x) = ax + (1-a)E_{-1}x$. Agents have some expectation before the present period starts of the value that x will take; this prior expectation is denoted $E_{-1}x$. When they observe the value that x actually takes on in this period, they adapt their expectation for the future a part (a) of the way toward what actually happened this period. This is equivalent to taking a weighted average of what actually happened and what was previously expected to happen as one's estimate of what is likely to happen in the next period, as is shown after the second equality sign. This hypothesis became famous in the analysis of inflation, where it formalized the argument that an inflation that exceeded the expected rate would serve to pull up that expected rate, which would in turn shift up the Phillips curve and so ensure that any given unemployment level below the so-called natural rate would result in permanently accelerating inflation. It also implies that any value that is maintained constant long enough will come to be the expected value.

3. Extrapolative expectations, $Ex_{+1} = x + a(x - x_{-1}) = (1 + a)x - ax_{-1}$. Agents extrapolate the change $(x - x_{-1})$ that they have just observed into the future, adding some fraction or multiple of the latest change on to the latest value observed. This is a description of the behavior that leads to bandwagon effects or speculative runs: the exchange rate starts moving (up or down), which provokes more sales or purchases in the hope of getting out or in before it is too late.

4. Regressive expectations, $Ex_{+1} = ax + (1 - a)\bar{x}$. Agents have some estimate $\bar{x}$ of the normal or equilibrium value of x, and when x deviates from $\bar{x}$ they expect that it will tend to return to $\bar{x}$, though not necessarily immediately.

Note that, with the exception of regressive expectations, which provide scope for any sort of information to make an impact on $\bar{x}$, all of these hypotheses amount to using some arbitrary rule of thumb based only on the past behavior of x in order to forecast future values of x. This, it is now argued, is in general a patently irrational way of forming expectations: if a popular and responsible president is assassinated, that fact is likely to suggest that x will be different from what it would otherwise have been, and one can decide that without waiting to see what starts to happen to x. The now-popular concept of *rational expectations* is based on the idea that agents seek to make the best possible use of the information available to them in forming their expectations. That may seem a pretty obvious idea —so much so that the student might wonder why anyone should ever have entertained any other hypothesis. The reason is that it still leaves the very big question: what is implied by making the best possible use of all available information? It was only after[10] John Muth (b. 1930) had suggested an answer that was both intuitively appealing and amenable to theoretical modeling that rational expectations emerged as the leading expectational hypothesis. Muth's answer was: the best available forecast is the forecast that comes out of using the available information in the analyst's own model. So the modeling strategy is: we assume that the agents know the model and assume it to be true, ask how that implies they make their forecast, and then add that forecasting procedure to the model. The result is to generate forecasts that have the important property of internal consistency: if everyone acts that way, events will tend to ratify the decisions made on the basis of the forecasts. In fact, when there are no stochastic shocks, this procedure generates exactly the perfect foresight path, along which events indeed unfold as they had been expected to unfold. Rational expectations are the stochastic analogue of perfect foresight.

It is worth noting that rational expectations are not necessarily inconsistent with all of the other hypotheses about expectations formation. In particular, where agents do not know what the economic structure is, but have to learn, adaptive expectations are rational. Or, where there is an equilibrium with some asymptotic adjustment mechanism pushing x toward it, regressive expectations are rational.

Many of the asset market models also break with the Mundell-Fleming model by abandoning the assumption that the domestic price level is fixed. The alternative assumptions incorporated in the models have varied, although they have all been simple: for example, determination by the quantity theory, or sticky prices whose rate of change depends on the level of excess demand (a Phillips-curve type of specification).

The most famous of the asset market models is due to Dornbusch. It assumes perfect interest arbitrage, so (10.12) provides one of the equations:

$$i = i^* + E\hat{e}. \tag{10.12}$$

Expectations of exchange rate changes are assumed to be determined in accordance with the regressive expectations formula: the exchange rate will adjust part way toward its equilibrium value $\bar{e}$. This is in fact in accord with rational expectations (for the appropriate value of θ), since the postulated theory of inflation is one where prices adjust depending on the extent of

10. Quite a long time after—the idea took about ten years to be noticed!

excess demand, which falls toward zero as prices and therefore the exchange rate approach equilibrium.

$$E\hat{e} = \theta(\bar{e} - e).^{11} \tag{10.13}$$

Asset market equilibrium requires that the supply of money be equal to the demand, as in (10.8) of the Mundell-Fleming model:

$$h = p + \xi y - \eta i.$$

In the simple version of the model, it is assumed that y can be treated as an exogenous variable, whose value is fixed at the full employment level. Furthermore, prices are assumed sticky, so that p is predetermined at any moment of time. The above three equations therefore determine the values of the three endogenous variables i, e and $E\hat{e}$ as functions of the exogenous variables i^*, $\bar{e}$, h, and y and the predetermined variable p. The equations represent the conditions that have to be satisfied if the asset markets are to be in equilibrium, that is, if investors are to be satisfied to hold the existing stocks of money, of domestic bonds with peso yield i, and of foreign bonds with peso yield $i^* + E\hat{e}$.

The above equations can be solved out by substitution to derive a relation between e and p that must be satisfied if the asset markets are to be in equilibrium:

$\eta i = p - h + \xi y$	rearranging (10.8)
$\eta[\theta(\bar{e} - e) + i^*] = p - h + \xi y$	substituting from (10.12) and (10.13)
$\theta\eta(e - \bar{e}) = -[p - h + \xi y - \eta i^*]$	multiplying by (-1)
$e = \bar{e} - (1/\theta\eta)[p - h + \xi y - \eta i^*].$	(10.14)

Equation (10.14) is represented by the curve AA in figure 10–6, the curve that gives the locus of points consistent with equilibrium in the asset markets. Given a price level p, it reflects what the exchange rate e must be in order to persuade investors to distribute their demands for the various assets in proportion to the available supply.[12] Equation (10.14) shows that it slopes down, since p has a negative coefficient $(-1/\theta\eta)$. The intuitive explanation of this is that when the price level is low, the real stock of money is high,

---

11. This is equivalent to the regressive expectations formula previously given, $Ex_{+1} = \alpha x + (1-\alpha 0\bar{x}_,)$ when we put $e = x$, so $E\hat{e} = Ex_{+1} - x$, and $\theta = 1 - \alpha$, since then

$$E\hat{e} = \alpha x + (1-\alpha)\bar{x} - x = (1-\alpha)(\bar{x}-x) \,^\circ_-\, \theta\,(\bar{e}-e).$$

12. This is another of those regrettable cases, like the demand and supply diagram, where economists have been careless enough to adopt a diagrammatic representation that puts what is usually the independent variable on the vertical axis.

which requires a low interest rate to persuade the public to hold it all; but then to satisfy the interest arbitrage condition and persuade investors to hold domestic bonds, they must expect a future fall in e (appreciation of the peso), which—given regressive expectations—requires that e be above its equilibrium level.

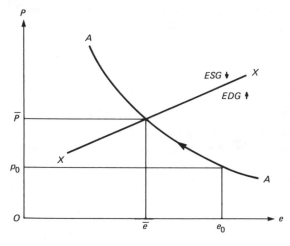

FIGURE 10–6
The Dornbusch Model of the Asset Market Approach

The second component of the model deals with equilibrium in the goods market. It is convenient to adopt again the specification that was used in the Mundell-Fleming model. Equation (10.7) showed aggregate demand as a function of e, p^*, p, y^*, and i; to this we add a variable g to represent changes in fiscal policy (or exogenous changes in investment, or any other direct influence on spending). If inflation depends on the excess of demand over the fixed output level $\bar{y}$, according to some rate of adjustment parameter δ, the result is

$$\hat{p} = \delta[\alpha\ (e + p^* - p) + \beta y^* - \gamma i + g - \bar{y}]. \qquad (10.15)$$

One may substitute for i from (10.8):

$$\hat{p} = \delta[\alpha\ (e + p^* - p) + \beta y^* - \qquad (10.16)$$
$$(\gamma/\eta)(p - h + \xi\bar{y}) + g - \bar{y}].$$

Now all the variables in this equation except e and p are exogenous: their role is that of determining the point $(\bar{e}, \bar{p})$ where the goods market equilibrium curve XX cuts AA, but they do not influence the slope of XX. To

230

determine that slope, it suffices to take deviations from equilibrium:

$$\hat{p} = \delta[\alpha(e - \bar{e}) - \alpha(p - \bar{p}) - (\gamma/\eta)(p - \bar{p})]$$
$$= \delta[\alpha(e - \bar{e}) - (\alpha + \gamma/\eta)(p - \bar{p})].$$

Thus the goods market equilibrium curve XX along which $\hat{p} = 0$ implies that

$$\frac{p - \bar{p}}{e - \bar{e}} = \frac{\alpha}{\alpha + \gamma/\eta}$$

which is positive but less than one, as shown in figure 10–6 by a line flatter than a ray to the origin. The intuitive explanation is that a rise in p reduces domestic demand in two ways: it reduces real money balances, raises the interest rate, and thus cuts aggregate demand—an expenditure-reducing effect; and it reduces the real exchange rate (cuts competitivity)—an expenditure-switching effect. The second of these effects can be neutralized by an increase in the exchange rate along the ray from the origin, but that still leaves the expenditure-reducing effect. Thus the ray from the origin must at some point take one from an area of excess demand for goods to an area of excess supply, that is, the XX curve is flatter than the ray to the origin.

Below XX there is excess demand for goods, and prices therefore gradually rise. Above XX there is excess supply, and prices are therefore assumed to fall gradually. Taking the two curves together, the model works as follows. We have a set of exogenous variables that determine $(\bar{e}, \bar{p})$. We also have a particular price level, for example, $p_0 < \bar{p}$ in figure 10–6, inherited from the past. Given that price level, the exchange rate adjusts immediately —asset markets are flexprice markets—to the point indicated by the AA curve, e_0. At the point (e_0, p_0), there is excess demand for goods, which exerts upward pressure on prices in the (fixprice) goods market. As prices rise, the exchange rate falls, this appreciation of the domestic currency compensating investors for the low domestic interest rate caused by the large real money balances. The economy moves along AA toward equilibrium as indicated by the arrow.

Consider now the effects of monetary and fiscal policy in this model. The case of a monetary expansion (an open market operation to increase the money supply h) is shown in figure 10–7A. Inspection of equation (10.16) shows that this will shift the XX curve up to $X'X'$—this is the normal expansionary effect of an increased money supply. However, a one-time increase in the money supply cannot have any permanent effect on the

231

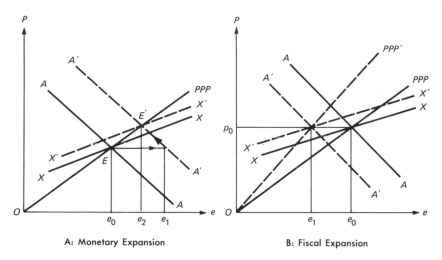

A: Monetary Expansion B: Fiscal Expansion

FIGURE 10–7
Policy Changes in Dornbusch Model

balance of payments on current account. Thus when the economy achieves its new equilibrium with no excess demand it must also be true that relative prices are restored, that is, that the original *PPP* once more holds good. Since *PPP* is represented by a ray from the origin, it follows that the new equilibrium must fall at E', the intersection of $X'X'$ and the *PPP* ray. But if *we* can deduce this from the model, then so can investors—that is the import of the assumption that expectations are rational in the sense of Muth. And if investors know that equilibrium has shifted from E to E', then the locus of points that will equilibrate the asset markets will shift to cut E', that is, the *AA* curve will shift to $A'A'$.

Suppose therefore that the economy were initially in equilibrium at E with an exchange rate e_0. There is then a sudden unexpected expansion of the money supply which pushes $X'X'$ up and moves equilibrium to E'. The market knows this and sees not only that the currency must depreciate but also that real balances have suddenly been increased by the monetary expansion and will stay that way until inflation has reversed the effect of that expansion, implying a period of low domestic interest rates. There is, therefore, a move to sell the domestic currency, which pushes the exchange rate up instantaneously to e_1, the point on the $A'A'$ curve that corresponds to the initial price level. At that point investors can see the prospect of a future appreciation to compensate them for the low interest rate involved in holding domestic bonds, so the depreciation ceases. (Note how crucial the assumption of rational regressive expectations is in generating this orderly move: if the market had no idea what was happening to e and

232

everyone tried to infer the truth from seeing what others were doing, one could easily envision much wilder gyrations of e occurring on the basis of extrapolative expectations.) From then on there is a gradual, simultaneous adjustment of p and e toward the new equilibrium E'.

The model shows that the exchange rate can be expected to *overshoot* in response to changes in monetary policy. Although the monetary expansion requires ultimately only a proportionate depreciation to e_2, the exchange rate first moves up all the way to e_1. This provides an explanation, or at least part of the explanation, as to why floating exchange rates have proved in practice to be so volatile: even credible changes in monetary policy (that is, those accepted as permanent by the market) should be expected to induce exaggerated changes in the exchange rate in the short run. Furthermore, monetary policy seldom is credible: outcomes are constantly inspected by the market to see what they can reveal about the future actions of the authorities. The result is that small changes in policy can sometimes produce large changes in market expectations, with results still more exaggerated than the overshooting that occurs with full information in the Dornbusch model.

Consider next the case of fiscal expansion shown in figure 10–7B. An increase in g also pushes XX up to $X'X'$, as can be seen from equation (10.15). From then on, however, the story is quite different. A permanent fiscal deficit requires offsetting in the new equilibrium by a permanent current account deficit financed by a permanent capital inflow. (It is necessary to suspend any skepticism about the possibility of that being permanent by remembering that we are assuming perfect capital mobility.) The price level p must, on the other hand, remain unchanged, since none of the other arguments in the demand for money function, equation (10.8), are changed.[13] Thus the new equilibrium E' must occur where $X'X'$ reaches the original price level p_0. PPP rotates to PPP′, because a lower real exchange rate is needed to avoid excess demand by generating a current account deficit that matches the fiscal expansion. Investors can see what has happened and have confidence that it will continue, so the AA curve shifts to $A'A'$. The exchange rate falls immediately to e_1, without overshooting or indeed any subsequent gradual adjustment.

Note that in most respects these conclusions are very similar to those of the Mundell-Fleming model (with perfect capital mobility). In both models, a monetary expansion leaves the current balance unchanged, depreciates the currency, and increases nominal income: the only difference is that the increase in income is real income in Mundell-Fleming and inflation in Dornbusch. A fiscal expansion has identical effects in the two models:

13. Actually, this result depends on import prices not entering the price deflator.

income is unchanged, absorption rises, the currency appreciates, and the current account goes into deficit. But the one difference is, of course, a crucial one: the Mundell-Fleming model pictures an expansionary monetary policy as a valuable instrument for increasing employment, whereas models with price flexibility suggest that it will instead tend to generate inflation.

In fact, Jeffrey Sachs (b. 1954) has shown that if we postulate that *real* wages are constant, in place of the Mundell-Fleming assumption of constant nominal wages, the traditional result is precisely reversed: monetary expansion *cannot* increase employment, but fiscal expansion *can*. In order to understand this result, consider the dependent economy model, in the form where the price of nontraded goods is equal to the wage rate ($p_n = w$) while the price of traded goods is determined by arbitrage ($p_m = ep^*$). Postulate that labor demands a given real wage v, which implies $w = vp_m{}^\alpha p_n{}^{1-\alpha} = v(ep^*)^\alpha(w)^{1-\alpha} = v^{1/\alpha}ep^*$. Since a monetary expansion simply increases e, the wage rate w rises proportionately and there are no real effects on output. In contrast a fiscal expansion leads to an incipient *increase* in p_n/p_m at the initial employment level, so output can expand to the point needed to restore w/p to v (which is the same as restoring p_n/p_m).

Although it does not seem to have been definitively proved in the literature as yet, the general conclusion suggested by these results is that fiscal expansion raises income at the expense of a bigger current account deficit but without much inflationary impulse, while monetary expansion can raise income without much payments cost but at a definite cost in terms of inflation. Hard choices have to be faced by those conducting economic policy in an environment of floating rates.

So much for the case of perfect capital mobility. Let us now take a brief look at the implications of *imperfect* capital mobility, that is, of portfolio effects. We consider a simple model due to Kouri. Suppose that investors have a portfolio choice restricted to two assets (monies) each of which has constant (perhaps zero) rate of interest. Then the opportunity cost of holding the peso is its expected rate of depreciation. Assuming that there is an equilibrium exchange rate which is known to the public and that any deviation from that equilibrium will arouse expectations of a return toward it (a regressive pattern that can as before be justified by appeal to rationality), one again has (10.13) and the relationship that a high e implies an expected future appreciation. That means that a high e will persuade investors to put a relatively large part of their portfolio into the domestic money and be satisfied with a small quantity of the foreign asset F.[14] Thus the asset market equilibrium curve AA of the right-hand quadrant of figure 10–8,

14. Note that F has now reverted to representing foreign assets, rather than liabilities.

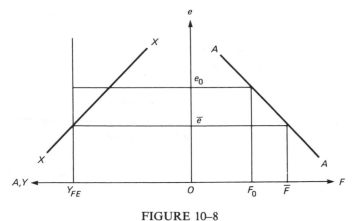

FIGURE 10–8
Kouri Model of Portfolio Adjustment

which shows the exchange rate as a function of the country's stock of foreign assets for a given money supply, is downward sloping. In the left-hand quadrant are shown absorption and output. Output is assumed fixed at full employment while absorption declines as the exchange rate rises for absorption-approach reasons, as shown by the XX schedule.

Suppose that initially the country has a stock of foreign assets F_0. To ration out this limited stock among investors, the price e of foreign exchange has to be high, at e_0. That high exchange rate implies high domestic prices and thus limited absorption, which generates a current account surplus, the excess of Y_{FE} over A. But with floating rates a current surplus implies a capital outflow, which in the present context involves an accumulation of F. Thus F gradually increases toward its equilibrium $\bar{F}$. As it does so, the greater availability of foreign exchange to investors induces a fall in e. Equilibrium is characterized by a supply of F which, given the money supply, satisfies investors to hold the two assets. In this type of model it is variations in the relative stocks of the assets rather than in their rates of return that serve to equilibrate demand and supply.

There is an important question we have commented on previously in this chapter but not as yet in the context of the asset market approach: the insulating properties of a flexible exchange rate. The basic conclusion is that *permanent* changes in either income or prices (but not interest rates) will be insulated, as in the Mundell-Fleming model, but that *temporary* changes will not be. The reason is that speculators who know that a change is temporary will realize that the exchange rate will return to normal after the temporary shock disappears and will therefore be prepared to buy (or sell) the domestic currency when it has deviated sufficiently from its equilibrium

235

value for the rebound to equilibrium to compensate them for the trouble and risk of making a portfolio shift. In practice, price level changes are typically permanent, in the sense of not being reversed; indeed, inflation is highly serially correlated. This characteristic means that inflation differentials can be effectively neutralized through exchange rate flexibility exactly as the simple models suggest. In contrast, real income has important deviations around its trend growth which are fairly clearly temporary, and the market will therefore not allow these deviations to push the rate too far away from equilibrium. This is a part of the explanation why the business cycle has remained synchronized since the adoption of floating rates, contrary to the predictions of the pre–1970s models.

The other part of the explanation has to do with the differing length of lags involved in the reaction to income changes on the one hand and to price changes on the other. The empirical evidence shows that a change in income is very quickly reflected in a change in imports, within a quarter or so, whereas we noted in chapter 8.3 that changes in competitiveness bring their effects only gradually over two or three years. This implies that it would not be possible for exchange rate adjustments to offset the impact of income changes on the trade balance in the short run as is pictured in the current balance model. Such changes in the trade balance *have* to be financed in one way or another, with a crucial question being whether speculators are prepared to provide the finance in response to a moderate shift of the rate away from equilibrium, as implied in the preceding paragraph, or whether the degree of uncertainty as to where the equilibrium rate lies (and/or the low degree of substitutability between assets denominated in different currencies) means that rates will have to swing wildly in order to generate the necessary supply of finance. In either event, however, a floating system behaves much like a fixed-rate system in regard to the synchronization of the business cycle.

10.5 Exchange Rate Policy

The debate on exchange rate flexibility was launched in the early 1950s, by two great economists of very different ideological persuasions, Milton Friedman and James Meade, arguing in favor of replacing the postwar system of (more or less) fixed exchange rates by floating rates. Friedman made two important positive arguments in favor of flexibility and one criticism of the case against. First, he argued that a floating exchange rate would give a country the freedom to choose its own monetary policy without having to be concerned about the balance of payments impact this would have: any inconsistency between its monetary policy and that of the rest of the world would be absorbed by a change in the exchange rate, rather than leading to reserve losses or gains that would feed back on the rate of monetary expansion. This was a point of crucial importance to Friedman, given his belief that a slow but steady expansion of the money supply was the key to achieving macroeconomic stability. Second, he argued that when it was necessary to achieve a change in the real exchange rate in order to adjust the balance of payments, it was much easier to do this by a single change in the nominal exchange rate rather than by revising thousands or millions of individual wages and prices in terms of national currency so as to have the same effect by changing the internal price level.

His criticism of the case against floating related to the question of destabilizing speculation, as it was then called. The Estonian economist Ragnar Nurkse (1907–59) had, during the Second World War, supervised a study of the interwar experience with floating exchange rates, in which it had been concluded that speculative pressures had time after time resulted in floating rates being violently unstable (or volatile, in the terminology used above). Friedman countered this with the simple but powerful argument that speculators who really destabilized rates, in the sense of pushing them away from equilibrium (rather than making disequilibrium rates change suddenly), must lose money! Why? Because a speculator makes money by buying something when it is relatively cheap and selling when it is relatively dear, which raises prices at the trough and reduces them at the peak, that is, *stabilizes* rather than destabilizes. A speculator who did the opposite must lose money. Since this is not what the game of speculation is supposed to be about, the key to the observed volatility of exchange rates must lie elsewhere. Ever since monetarists have been convinced that that key lies in unstable government policies (especially monetary policy).

In contrast to the laissez faire desire to minimize the role of government of Friedman, Meade's attitude was that of the technocratic manager seeking tools adequate to the job. Monetary policy was one such tool, but the analysis of chapter 8.5 (which we eventually decided in chapter 9.2 was not rendered redundant by Mundell's introduction of capital mobility) argued that it was not sufficient alone, nor in combination with fiscal policy: it needed to be combined with an expenditure-switching policy. Exchange rate policy provided the natural candidate (inasmuch as it alone does not involve creating microeconomic distortions). Meade also discussed the threat of destabilizing speculation. He did not share Friedman's confidence that this phenomenon could be ruled out on the grounds that it would be inimical to the interests of the speculators, but instead argued that it could be overcome by strong and internationally coordinated intervention policies. Although the matter is still not finally settled, the volatility of rates observed in the 1970s would suggest that Meade's fears on this score were more realistic than Friedman's confidence that it could not happen. A possible explanation is that the speculators who lose money are not the core of professionals in the market, who would surely get out of the business if they could not beat the market and make money, but a part of that large fringe of traders, tourists, and even central banks who take open positions in foreign exchange, sometimes because it is too much trouble not to, but to whom the activity is peripheral.

Opponents of flexible exchange rates developed a series of counterarguments in the years that followed, to supplement the fear that floating would mean volatility because of speculation. In the first place, they argued that this volatility would tend to make international trade and investment more risky and would therefore impede international integration. Second, they argued that removing the constraint on monetary policy provided by the need to defend a fixed exchange rate should be counted as a cost and not a benefit: countries need a discipline of that sort to prevent their political leaders engaging in irresponsible inflationary finance. Supporters of flexibility replied either that the democratic process and not the need to defend a fixed exchange rate should be allowed to decide how much inflation a country should have or that under floating inflationary finance would quickly lead to a depreciation and thus to internal inflation, which hits the public directly in a way that reserve losses do not, so that discipline would actually be more effective under floating. Third, opponents of floating argued that a fixed rate provided a built-in stabilizer: a boom or recession would draw in more or fewer imports with a fixed rate and thus tend to dampen the change in income, whereas the income expansion would be bottled up at home by a floating exchange rate, leading to inflation or slump. This effect can be seen in figure 10–2, reinterpreting the cause of the shift in *XX* as a domestic boom or recession. Supporters of flexibility retorted that this effect was crucially dependent on the assumption of no capital mobility, since a domestic boom would tend to raise interest rates and thus draw in capital rather than depreciate the currency where capital was mobile.

Two further arguments against floating were added in the 1970s, mainly by the global monetarists (who thus adopted a position on this issue opposed to that of old-fashioned monetarists). First, they argued that exchange rate changes could produce expenditure-switching effects only if there were money illusion; in its absence, a devaluation would simply induce an offset-

238

ting inflation rather than a payments improvement. This issue has never been completely resolved, but the claim is certainly not universally accepted: what absence of money illusion, *plus* the strong but usually unmentioned assumption of the uniqueness of equilibrium, jointly imply is that a devaluation *alone* will not have a lasting effect in altering competitivity. However, the sophisticated advocate of exchange rate policy envisages its use as a part of a package, not as an isolated policy instrument (remember the absorption approach) and there is no reason for believing that it cannot be useful in that context just because money illusion is absent—as it surely is. Second, it was argued that exchange rate flexibility would tend to accelerate the average rate of inflation because of ratchet effects: a depreciation would produce a proportionate inflation, whereas an appreciation would not reduce prices proportionately because of downward stickiness, so that variable exchange rates would ratchet up the price level. This sounds pretty plausible, but no decisive empirical evidence in favor of the hypothesis has yet been presented (and not for want of trying).

In parallel with the long-running debate on fixed versus floating exchange rates, there emerged in the 1960s a literature on intermediate options. One strand of this was initiated by Robert Mundell, with a paper that asked: what is the *optimal currency area*? By this, he meant the optimal area within which exchange rates should be fixed. Typically, each country has a single money, and different countries have different monies, so that exchange rates are fixed within countries but may vary between them. But is there necessarily any logic in this? Mundell argued that one should ideally have one money for each area within which factors were mobile but between which they were not, since factor mobility would make exchange rate changes redundant, while a change in the exchange rate could provide a helpful substitute for factor mobility where this was absent. Shortly afterward Ronald McKinnon (b. 1935) argued that the critical factor was the openness of the economy rather than the degree of factor mobility, since a relatively closed economy could hope to use a devaluation to promote expenditure switching, while in a highly open economy the main result would be to raise the price level. Later participants in the debate argued that the key factor was the willingness to accept the same rate of inflation. Others pointed to the necessity for a common fiscal system, in order to provide an alternative mechanism for easing interregional adjustments in the form of fiscal transfers (a criterion that suggests the normal practice of having one money per country is rational). Today, the dominant tendency is to argue that schemes for currency unification should be judged on the basis of a cost-benefit appraisal involving all these factors, rather than appealing to some single criterion to the exclusion of all others.

A second strand to the debate on intermediate options arose from the observation that there are more alternatives available than free floating and permanent fixity. For example, there are also the two other systems that have in fact been widely employed in the postwar world: *managed floating,* where there is no particular rate that the authorities are committed to defend but where they nevertheless intervene at their discretion, and the *adjustable peg,* where the authorities accept a commitment to defend the rate at the particular level where it is currently pegged, but where they reserve the right to change that rate under certain circumstances. There is also a fifth possible exchange rate regime, generally known as the *crawling peg.* This involves a country accepting a parity (or peg) for its currency but changing this gradually over time in a series of small steps rather than in the sudden discrete changes that are characteristic of the adjustable peg. Such changes may be determined according to a formal rule, for example, revalue when reserves rise and devalue when they fall, or they may be determined by discretionary decisions—either announced in advance or made as the occasion arises in response to what are considered relevant criteria. The countries that have employed the crawling peg for longest, Colombia and Brazil, both make discretionary decisions, guided in large measure by the objective of maintaining PPP with the United States so as to neutralize the effect of their high domestic rates of inflation.

The crawling peg is an intermediate regime that fits naturally into the scheme of those who see exchange rate flexibility as a technocrat's tool. It gives a country the power to reconcile any internal rate of inflation with continued external balance—as noted in the previous section, the one thing that exchange rate flexibility really can neutralize efficiently is differential inflation. This power has up to now been used to allow countries to inflate faster than the world average, but it could equally well be used as a tool to enable countries to repel imported inflation and enjoy a greater degree of price stability than the norm. Second, a crawling change in the exchange rate can be used to promote expenditure switching when this is needed. But one thing that the crawling peg cannot do is to liberate monetary policy. On the contrary, monetary policy has to be subordinated to the preservation of the interest arbitrage condition $i = i^* + E\hat{e}$: the incentive to export capital created by a known gradual devaluation has to be offset by accepting a more or less commensurate rise in the domestic interest rate if reserve losses are to be averted. Another thing it excludes is having the exchange rate do the immediate adjusting to an exogenous shock, in the manner portrayed by the jump from e_0 to e_1 in figure 10–7A. Evaluations of the crawling peg tend to depend on whether those two constraints on policy are judged to be potentially serious.

Flexible Exchange Rates

A third strand to the debate on intermediate options concerned another form of limited flexibility, known as the *wider band*. The band refers to the scope around a parity within which the exchange rate is allowed to fluctuate, even though it is pegged to the parity. In the Bretton Woods system as it prevailed up till 1971, countries agreed to hold their exchange rates within a 2 percent band, that is, within margins 1 percent either side of parity. The wider band or band proposal envisaged widening the band of 2 percent to something in the range of 5 percent to 10 percent. The main idea was to provide somewhat more freedom for contracyclical monetary policy to vary between countries. For example, a country wanting to fight a recession by low interest rates could have engineered a temporary expansion in the money supply to push the interest rate down. Its currency would depreciate toward the bottom of the band, but, so long as the market accepted that the parity would remain unchanged, there would be an expectation of a subsequent rebound of the rate toward parity which would compensate for the low interest rate and preserve the interest arbitrage condition $i^* = i - E\hat{e}$. A second aim was to make speculation on parity changes more costly and less profitable.

A new topic has become important since the move to floating exchange rates by the principal industrial countries in 1973. This concerns the exchange rate policy to be pursued by the remaining countries, who include virtually all of the developing countries. It is generally agreed that it would be unwise or even impractical for these countries to adopt floating rates: the limited scale of the market and the lack of depth of domestic capital markets preclude that option. Prior to 1973, the only question that was left was when and how to change one's parity, for example, by adopting a crawling peg. But nowadays it is necessary to decide not merely *whether* to peg but also *to what* to peg. When all the major countries were pegged to each other, pegging to the dollar meant pegging to everything else; now that the major currencies are floating, pegging to the dollar means having one's rate fluctuate in terms of everything else. These fluctuations may have some logic for the United States, but to a small country pegged to the dollar they have none whatsoever, and are pure shocks. Hence the question has arisen how the country can choose a peg—in the sense of a currency or basket of currencies to which to peg—with the object of minimizing the damage done by the exchange rate fluctuations between the major currencies. This has become known as the question of choosing an *optimal peg*. Broadly speaking, the answer is that countries should seek to stabilize their effective exchange rates by pegging to a basket of currencies. The effective exchange rate is defined as the trade-weighted geometric mean of the bilateral exchange rates with a country's trading partners and competitors. Stabilizing the effective exchange rate means that, although exchange rate changes between the major countries will still influence the competitive positions and costs of individual industries and firms, at least these effects will tend to balance out over the economy as a whole and so not disturb *macroeconomic* equilibrium. A possible disadvantage of pegging to a basket, which has to be weighed against the macroeconomic benefit, is the microeconomic risk imposed on individual traders when they no longer have a major international currency in which they can write contracts and against which their own currency is reasonably stable.

10.6 Summary

The evidence since the adoption of widespread floating in 1973 is that floating rates are volatile. Instead of the smooth and moderate adjustments that most economists had expected would prevail (largely because that was what the Mundell-Fleming model suggested would happen, and also because of the way the Canadian dollar had behaved when it was floating in the 1950s), rates have often jumped around wildly: by 2 percent or 3 percent in a single day, with cycles of well over 20 percent, and with occasional appreciations or depreciations of as much as 40 percent to 60 percent. (The extreme case is that of Britain, whose pound appreciated by over 55 percent against the dollar from its trough in late 1976 to its peak in late 1980, despite some 10 percent to 20 percent *more* inflation in Britain over the period.) Since in the short run national price levels are pretty sticky, these exchange rate fluctuations have brought with them large variations in real exchange rates. Countries suffering exaggerated appreciations have had their tradable goods sectors threatened with serious damage (for example, Switzerland in late 1978, Britain in 1980 to 1982), while exaggerated depreciations have imposed severe inflationary pressures (Britain in late 1976, the United States in late 1978, Germany in mid-1981).

How far does the theory that has been studied in this chapter go toward explaining this volatility? The following list shows factors that are capable of altering the value of a floating exchange rate:[15]

1. The equilibrium nominal exchange rate may change because of differential inflation $\hat{p} - \hat{p}^*$ to preserve PPP (maintain the real exchange rate

15. This is not the only possible way of organizing such a list. No doubt some would prefer a classification by the type of shock involved (changes in money supplies, changes in prices, etc.) rather than my classification by the channels through which shocks operate.

constant), from chapter 10.2. To that can now be added that to preserve asset market equilibrium an anticipated inflation differential must be offset by an equal interest differential ($i - i^*$) under perfect capital mobility; or by some combination of interest differential, real depreciation (remember the Kouri model), and financing through a reserve outflow under imperfect capital mobility.

2. The equilibrium real exchange rate may change for various reasons: differential productivity growth or exogenous changes in the terms of trade (chapter 10.2), changes in the underlying rate of capital inflow or permanent changes in real income (chapter 10.3). Any of these require a change in competitivity which, for given price levels, implies an exchange rate change.

3. The exchange rate may be returning to equilibrium along a correctly forecast path, having deviated because the interest rate temporarily diverged from its normal level (the Dornbusch model, or the band proposal).

4. A current imbalance may change the stock of foreign assets available and thus lead to an exchange rate change to maintain portfolio balance (the Kouri model).

5. Expectations of any of the above may change, either because of policy changes, because of news (unexpected developments that alter expectations of future policy or assessments of the value of a country's resources, or unexpected outcomes for relevant variables like the current account), or because of revisions to the assessment of previously available information. Factors of the first two sorts generate movements of the asset market equilibrium curve in the Dornbusch model and seem to go furthest toward explaining sudden jumps in the exchange rate. Revised expectations of inflation need cause no immediate movement of the exchange rate at all, provided that real interest rates remain constant. The common idea that high, even differentially high, inflation can be blamed for exchange rate volatility is wrong. (On the other hand, there is *no* exchange rate adjustment that can restore portfolio equilibrium under perfect capital mobility if the expected permanent inflation differential changes without an equal change in the nominal interest differential.)

There are some economists who believe that these models still leave one important element in the picture to be satisfactorily modeled: the phenomenon of the speculative run, of market rumors feeding on themselves to produce an exchange rate out of touch with the underlying fundamentals. It may be that under conditions of great uncertainty many market participants abandon any attempt to forecast rationally and assume instead that the fact that they observe the rate moving in a way that they had not expected must be because others are privy to information denied to them. Perhaps this goes some way to explaining why, at least within certain limits, it does seem that expectations are sometimes formed extrapolatively. And that apparent fact is at least in part responsible for the disillusionment with floating exchange rates that has been manifest by some of those economists who were previously sympathetic.

10.7 Addendum: The Large Economy

The main implication of relaxing the small country assumption relates to the Mundell-Fleming model. Two of the theorems developed in chapter 10.3 were that, with perfect capital mobility, monetary policy is ineffective under a fixed exchange rate and fiscal policy is ineffective with a flexible exchange rate. Both theorems fail in the case of the large country.

In the case of monetary policy, the analysis is obvious: a monetary expansion has a nonnegligible effect in expanding the world money supply, and therefore the national money supply increases by a nonnegligible proportion. (In the simple case of equal reserve ratios and money demand elasticities, the proportion of the monetary expansion that stays at home to reduce interest rates and increase income is equal to the country's money supply as a proportion of the world money supply.)

Similarly, a fiscal expansion by a large country will have some effect in stimulating income even with floating rates and perfect capital mobility. The reason is that the appreciation of our currency stimulates world income by a nonnegligible amount, which then exerts pressure for our currency to depreciate once again, thus stimulating our income. Equilibrium requires a higher interest rate, and higher income distributed throughout the world. Crowding out is incomplete.

10.8 Bibliography

The classic analysis of the current balance model is in R. A. Mundell, *International Economics* (London: Macmillan, 1958), chap. 17, although there were many previous, less systematic, treatments. The Laursen-Metzler effect was developed in L. A. Metzler and S. Laursen, "Flexible Exchange Rates and the Theory of Employment," *Review of Economics and Statistics,* Nov. 1950.

Cassell's major work on PPP was G. Cassell, *Money and Foreign Exchange after 1914* (London: Constable, 1922). The analysis of differential productivity growth was developed in B. Balassa, "The Purchasing Power Parity Doctrine: A Reappraisal," *Journal of Political Economy,* Dec. 1964. The international comparisons of real income made by the Pennsylvania team are reported in I. B. Kravis, et al., "Real GDP Per Capita for more than 100 Countries," *Economic Journal,* June 1978; and *International Comparisons of Real Product and Purchasing Power* (Baltimore: Johns Hopkins University Press, 1978). For the Scandinavian model of inflation, see G. Edgren, K. O. Faxén, and C. E. Odhner, "Wages, Growth and the Distribution of Income," *Swedish Journal of Economics,* Sept. 1969. Harry Johnson's formula for the impact of growth on the PPP inflation differential is in "Increasing Productivity, Income-Price Trends, and the Trade Balance," *Economic Journal,* Sept. 1954, reprinted in his *International Trade and Economic Growth* (London: Allen and Unwin, 1958). A general survey of the literature on PPP is provided by L. H. Officer, "The Purchasing Power Parity Theory of Exchange Rates," International Monetary Fund *Staff Papers,* Mar. 1976. The reference to "helicopter distribution" of additional money is to Milton Friedman, *The Optimum Quantity of Money* (London: Macmillan, 1969).

Mundell's presentation of the Mundell-Fleming model can be found in chap. 18 of his *International Economics,* while that of Fleming is in J. M. Fleming, "Domestic Financial Policies under Fixed and Floating Exchange Rates," IMF *Staff Papers,* Nov. 1962, reprinted in his *Essays in International Economics* (London: Allen and Unwin, 1972).

The asset market approach was launched in papers by R. Dornbusch, J. A. Frenkel, P. J. K. Kouri and M. Mussa to a conference in Saltsjobaden, Sweden, in 1975. They were printed in the *Scandinavian Journal of Economics,* 1976(2), and reprinted in J. Herin, A. Lindbeck, and J. Myhrman, eds., *Flexible Exchange Rates and Stabilization Policy* (Boulder, Colo.: Westview Press, 1977). The Dornbusch model presented in the chapter originates from R. Dornbusch, "Expectations and Exchange Rate Dynamics," *Journal of Political Economy,* Dec. 1976, also covered in chap. 11 of his *Open Economy Macroeconomics* (New York: Basic Books, 1980). The founding work on rational expectations is J. F. Muth, "Rational Expectations and the Theory of Price Movements," *Econometrica,* July 1961. The theorem that the effects of monetary and fiscal policy on real income are the opposite of those in Mundell-Fleming with a fixed real wage is proved by J. Sachs, "Wages, Flexible Exchange Rates, and Macroeconomic Policy," *Quarterly Journal of Economics,* June 1980.

The debate on exchange rate flexibility was launched by M. Friedman, "The Case for Flexible Exchange Rates," in his *Essays in Positive Economics* (Chicago: University of Chicago Press, 1953), and J. E. Meade, "The Case for Variable Exchange Rates," *Three Banks Review,* Sept. 1955. The "orthodox view" of destabilizing speculation attacked by Friedman was developed in a League of Nations report entitled *International Currency Experience: Lessons of the Inter-War Period* (New York: Columbia University Press, 1944). An excellent recent summary, review, and updating of the debate on fixed versus flexible rates is given by M. Goldstein, *Have Flexible Exchange Rates Handicapped Macroeconomic Policy?,* Princeton Special Papers in International Economics, No. 14 (1980). The debate on optimum currency areas was launched by R. A. Mundell, "A Theory of Optimum Currency Areas," *American Economic Review,* Nov. 1961, reprinted in his *International Economics,* was taken up in an article with the same title in the same journal by R. I. McKinnon a year later, and has recently been usefully reviewed by E. Tower and T. D. Willett, *The Theory of Optimum Currency Areas and Exchange-Rate Flexibility,* Princeton Special Papers in International Economics, No. 11 (1976). An account of the debate on the crawling peg, both in the 1960s and recently, can be found in J. Williamson, ed., *Exchange Rate Rules: The Theory, Performance and Prospects of the Crawling Peg* (London: Macmillan, 1981). The band proposal was pioneered by G. Halm, *The Band Proposal: The Limits of Permissible Exchange Rate Variations,* Princeton Special Papers in International Economics, No. 6 (1965); the most penetrating theoretical appraisal of the idea is in R. I. McKinnon, *Monetary Theory and Controlled Flexibility in the Foreign Exchanges,* Princeton Essays in International Finance, No. 84 (1971). The standard reference on the concept of the effective exchange rate is R. R. Rhomberg, "Indices of Effective Exchange Rates," IMF *Staff Papers,* March 1976. A recent survey of the literature on the optimal peg is provided in J. Williamson, "A Survey of the Emergent Literature on the Optimal Peg," *Journal of Development Economics,* August 1982.

A book that provides much material of parallel relevance to the topics of this chapter is R. I. McKinnon, *Money in International Exchange: the Convertible Currency System* (New York: Oxford University Press, 1979), which is particularly strong on the microeconomics of trade financing and exchange markets. This includes a chapter on forward markets. The interest parity condition developed in the appendix originated in J. M. Keynes, *A Tract on Monetary Reform* (London: Macmillan, 1923).

Appendix: The Forward Exchange Market

THE ANALYSIS in the chapter was conducted as though all transactions take place in the spot market, that is, the market for immediate delivery or receipt of foreign exchange. In the case of the major currencies, these spot markets are supplemented by forward markets. These are markets in which contracts are signed now to sell one currency for another on a specified future date (typically in three or six months time) at a price agreed now.

There are three types of activities that can be undertaken in the forward market. It is descriptively inaccurate but pedagogically useful to identify each of these with a distinct class of actors.

Hedging is undertaken by traders who sign a contract now in order to arrange for the future receipt or sale of foreign exchange that they know they will need or acquire, respectively, at the given date in the future. This avoids (or at least reduces—there may still be a lag before cover can be taken) exposure to exchange risk.

Arbitrage is undertaken by financiers, typically banks, in search of a riskless profit. They simultaneously sell one currency, say the peso, spot, and buy it back forward in three months time, for example. They then invest the proceeds in dollars for that three months.

Speculation is undertaken by speculators who seek to make a profit by *accepting* exchange risk—by promising to buy or sell foreign exchange at a price decided now at some future date in the hope that on that date they will be able to sell or buy, respectively, in the spot market at a rate that will leave them with a profit. Obviously this is an activity that will actually yield profits only to those who on average have a certain degree of success in forecasting the future spot rate. Speculators are in practice a diverse group: multinationals, banks, central banks, and traders who at times accept exchange risk deliberately.

Suppose that there is a single maturity in the forward market, for example, one year, for simplicity. Let the forward exchange rate—the peso price of a dollar for delivery at the end of that period—be f. Then f will be determined at the level that clears the forward market, where

$$EDH + EDA + EDS = 0,$$

where EDH is the excess demand by hedgers, etc.

It is possible to conceive of the forward market operating with only traders in the market. Every day, the value of import contracts hedged would have to equal the value of export contracts hedged. The traders undertaking these hedging operations would all be reducing their risk exposure, so there would be no reason to expect a risk premium—a systematic deviation of f from the e for the same date—to emerge. However, one would expect the rate f to be highly volatile: on a day when importers were signing a lot of contracts relative to exporters, it would be necessary for f to rise to the point where some importers were induced not to cover or not to sign their contracts after all or exporters were induced to cover more or to sell more.

The interest arbitragers would see money to be made in this volatility. Consider the case above where there is a forward discount on the peso, that is, where $f > e$. If interest rates were the same at home and abroad, it would pay financiers to sell pesos spot, invest the proceeds in dollars, and sell the dollars forward at their high price f. In general, there is an incentive to undertake this operation so long as

$$(1 + i^*)f/e > (1 + i).$$

This *covered interest arbitrage* is free of exchange risk. In the absence of effective exchange controls or different political risk at home and abroad, this means that we can rely on arbitrage to continue to the point where the inequality is replaced by an equality. At that point the forward discount $(f - e)/e$ is equal to

$$\frac{f}{e} - 1 = \frac{1 + i}{1 + i^*} - 1 = \frac{i - i^*}{1 - i^*} \approx i - i^*.$$

This is the condition of *interest parity* first derived by Keynes in 1923: the forward discount on our currency must equal the excess of our interest rate over the foreign interest rate. (In applying this formula the forward discount and the interest rate differential must apply to the same time period—one cannot compare directly a three-month forward discount with an annual interest differential.)

The interest parity condition bears a close relation to equation (10.12), the condition for equality of yields $i = i^* + E\hat{e}$. The two together imply that the forward discount is equal to the expected rate of depreciation, which is the same thing as saying that the forward rate is equal to the expected future spot rate. This is to be expected: perfect capital mobility means precisely that investors will be prepared to pursue any additional expected yield, no matter how small, even at the cost of exchange exposure. Similarly, any deviation between the forward rate and the expected future

247

spot rate implies an expected gain, which will be sought out by speculators regardless of risk under the postulate of perfect capital mobility. Risk neutral speculators are the necessary and (with rapid adjustment) sufficient condition for perfect capital mobility.

Conversely, with imperfect capital mobility f_{+1} can deviate from Ee_{+1}. If there is a preponderance of importers wishing to cover forward or if the domestic interest rate is higher than the foreign interest rate, the peso will be driven to a forward discount. As the discount widens, so speculators will enter the forward market to buy pesos cheap in the hope of being able to sell them on the spot market at a profit when their contracts mature. But the speculators have to be compensated for undertaking this risk: a risk premium $(f_{+1} - Ee_{+1} > 0)$ *is* necessary. Persuading speculators to take a greater open position, so as to finance a current account deficit or cover a capital inflow, requires that the risk premium rise.

What this implies is that the sort of analysis of macroeconomic policies undertaken in the chapter is not affected by the existence of a forward market (which is why the subject has been relegated to an appendix). Forward markets help reduce total risk (where there is two-way hedging) and permit a division of labor between traders, arbitragers, and speculators. These are valuable microeconomic functions, but they are unimportant to an understanding of the macroeconomics of exchange rates.

IV
DEVELOPMENT

THIS PART of the book considers the relevance of international factors to the process of economic development. Chapter 11 concentrates on the microeconomic aspects, while chapter 12 is devoted to mainly macroeconomic questions.

11

Trade and Development

ECONOMIC development may be defined as the process by which a traditional society employing primitive techniques and therefore capable of sustaining only a modest level of per capita income is transformed into a modern, high-technology, high-income economy. The process involves the replacement of labor-intensive subsistence production by techniques that use capital, skilled labor, and scientific knowledge to produce the wide variety of different products consumed in an affluent society. In the subsistence economy, production is essentially for own-use and exchange is marginal; in the modern economy, there is an advanced division of labor in which everyone specializes in producing goods that would satisfy only a minute part of total needs, so that production is essentially for the market and own-use is marginal.

It is clear that the indispensable prerequisite for this transformation of the nature of economic activity is the accumulation of those factors of production that are necessary to exploit scientific knowledge and utilize sophisticated production techniques. In a very broad sense, one may call those additional factors capital; but that concept must be interpreted to include not just physical capital goods but also human capital and intangible capital (relevant scientific knowledge). This question of factor accumulation forms the topic of chapter 12.

A given rate of factor accumulation may, however, have very different implications for the rate of economic growth, depending on the goods that the extra factors are used to produce. The choice of which goods will be

251

produced or of an environment in which that choice will be made by the microeconomic decision makers has come to be known as the choice of a development strategy. It is a choice that has to pay attention to various factors. In particular, it has to consider where the *markets* for the increment to output will come from, and it has to ensure access to supplies of such *intermediate goods* as may be necessary to operate the new production processes. It is because international trade can be relevant to both the development of markets for output and the acquisition of intermediate inputs that the choice of a development strategy is a part of international economics.

11.1 Alternative Development Strategies

Development typically starts (or started, since the initial steps have now been taken virtually everywhere) when a small export sector develops alongside the subsistence economy. This produces a narrow range of goods based closely on the country's resource endowment—typically plantation crops, fibers, or minerals, although occasionally peasant crops (like cocoa) are important. A monetized service sector develops to serve the export sector, parallel with the traditional services produced within the subsistence sector. Export proceeds are used to buy consumer goods, capital goods, and intermediate goods for the modern sector. To the extent that the modern sector buys consumer goods from the traditional sector, the latter also acquires money that can be used to purchase imported consumer goods.

If a country that has reached this stage begins to generate increasing supplies of the factors of production needed to expand its modern sector, the question then is where those supplies should be deployed to ensure that the resulting output finds a market and necessary supplies of intermediate goods are forthcoming. There are four alternative strategies in the literature.

Balanced Growth. When economists first began thinking of how policy could deliberately stimulate the development of underdeveloped countries, in the 1940s, a popular answer was that it was necessary to organize a simultaneous expansion of output over a wide range of industries. The Austrian-born economist Paul Rosenstein-Rodan (b. 1902) and Ragnar Nurkse became the leading exponents of what was termed balanced growth. They argued that an isolated expansion of output by one or two industries was bound to fail because there would be no increase in purchasing power elsewhere in the economy to buy the additional output; as a result only by a drastic cut in prices could an unbalanced increase in output by a particular sector be sold, which would make the expansion unremunerative. Their solution to this dilemma was balanced expansion by a large number of sectors, each thus providing additional purchasing power to help raise demand for the output of—and/or provide needed intermediate input to— all the other sectors. Thus a bold simultaneous advance might succeed where a series of piecemeal unbalanced initiatives would fail.

Although the basic insight on the nature of the problem is correct, time has not dealt kindly with the idea of balanced growth. There are two reasons. First, it is now clear that a simultaneous advance across a broad field is not practical, especially in small countries, because of economies of scale (see chap. 4). In many industries, profitable operation requires the attainment of some minimum scale of operation. But the sum of the factor requirements needed for a simultaneous expansion of the minimum efficient size in a wide range of industries will exceed the sum of the additional factors becoming available over the normal investment period of a couple of years—indeed, in small countries this excess may be very large. This would mean that a balanced expansion would have to be programmed over a longer period than the normal investment period. But no firm will be willing to start investing now when it knows that returns would start accruing only long after the investment was complete. Therefore, balanced growth would never get off the ground.

Second, balanced growth is not necessary because the international economy provides an alternative source of markets and of supplies of intermediate goods. Additional output can be sold abroad or can take over a domestic market currently supplied by imports, and the foreign exchange thus earned or saved can be used to buy intermediate goods. The alternative strategies all give a central role to the international economy in sidestepping the need for balanced growth.

Traditional Exports. An alternative is to direct the additional factor supplies to the sectors already engaged in export production, which by virtue of that fact presumably are those sectors where the country has a comparative advantage. Foreign rather than domestic markets are thus relied on to provide the additional demand, which—especially for a small country without influence on its terms of trade—they can certainly do. The proceeds of the exports can be used to purchase needed inputs abroad.

Nontraditional Exports. Another possibility is to develop new export sectors. This strategy is similar to the previous one insofar as foreign rather than domestic markets provide the addition to demand and the export proceeds finance the purchase of necessary inputs from abroad.

Import Substitution. The last possibility is to establish new industries to replace imports. The market is thus domestic rather than foreign but, unlike the first case, it is possible for import substitution to take place sector by sector. The elimination of some imports releases foreign exchange for the purchase of needed inputs on the world market, or some intermediate goods may be among those for which local production is initiated.

11.2 Historical Experience

Chapter 1 described the process of economic growth that first developed in Britain in the late eighteenth century and subsequently spread to embrace more and more countries during the nineteenth and twentieth centuries. To understand the postwar debate on the best development strategy, it is helpful to have some idea of the role of export expansion and import substitution as engines of growth in earlier periods.

The first experience of sustained economic growth, that of Britain, was fueled by an expansion of industrial exports. The technical advances that were realized in Britain made it possible for British textiles and subsequently engineering products to penetrate and indeed dominate world markets. To some extent the reductions in prices and innovations in quality served to expand total world demand. The rest came from displacing traditional supply sources, as has usually been the dominant factor in export-led growth. The effect on traditional suppliers was painful, the more so because the increased British production involved an expansion that was large in relation to the size of the world market.

The pattern was fairly similar in the next two countries to start to industrialize, Belgium and France. There was somewhat more scope for import substitution on the basis of the internal markets that had been developed by British exporters, and the impact on third markets may have been somewhat less, but the basic picture is again of manufactures produced for export constituting the leading sector.

From then on there was a major change in the pattern of development. The nucleus of a group of industrializing countries created a growing demand for raw materials and later food, which presented opportunities to other countries to come in as suppliers. The typical development strategy for the remainder of the century of peace (1815–1914) involved a central role for a traditional export sector—not always traditional in the sense of exporting products that had long been sold abroad but traditional in the sense of comprising primary products closely related to the country's natural resource endowment. Thus the United States exported cotton and later wheat, meat, and a wide range of other primary products; Japan exported silk; Canada, Australia, and Argentina exported wheat and beef; New Zealand exported butter and lamb; South Africa exported gold and diamonds; Sweden exported timber; Russia exported wheat; Brazil exported rubber and coffee; West Africa exported cocoa; India exported tea; and so on.

The above list contains some countries that had entered the ranks of the developed by 1914 (the United States, Canada, Australia, New Zealand), others that were still developing in 1914 but had certainly graduated by the 1960s (Japan and Sweden), marginal cases (Argentina, South Africa, and Russia), as well as countries that are still among the developing (Brazil, West Africa, and India). Clearly the mere establishment of a significant export sector is no guarantee that a take-off into sustained growth will be achieved. A look at what governs factor accumulation explains why some countries made the transition while others did not. For countries in close cultural contact (through geography or migration) with societies where growth had already taken root, the accumulation of human capital was relatively easy. An expanding export sector providing raw materials to the industrial center of the world economy generated demands to which the rest of the economy was capable of responding by building up import-substituting sources of supply. The export receipts, supplemented by foreign borrowing (which was feasible because the country's export performance gave assurance of ability to service its foreign debt), provided both the savings and the foreign exchange necessary to finance capital formation. Technical advances were applied in the production of food for local consumption, as well as in the modern export and import-competing sectors, so that the supply price of labor to the export sector rose. Thus the export sector avoided competing its price down to levels equivalent to a bare subsistence wage.

Things were very different in those countries where the population in general had no contact with the ways of the modern world. Without the ability to implement technical change or the entrepreneurial attitude to conceive of the possibilities, the expansion of the export sector did not set in motion other forces for modernization. Indeed, in many cases the export sector was itself the result of outside initiatives—of plantations or mines financed and managed by foreigners (typically from the colonial power) and drawing on the local economy only for unskilled labor and (the virtually free use of) natural resources. In these circumstances the modern export sector formed an isolated enclave, which generated little income locally—

not much more than the subsistence-level wages of unskilled labor. The bulk of the income accrued to the foreign owners, who either repatriated the proceeds directly or spent them on buying imports. The isolation of the exporting enclave sector from the rest of the economy was at times extreme, as when the gentlemen of Manaus (the center of the late nineteenth-century rubber boom in the Amazon region of Brazil) sent their shirts to Lisbon to be laundered.

While export-led growth was the pattern typical of the liberal nineteenth century, it was not the only pattern. It was at times mixed with, and in some cases dominated by, that of import substitution. The classic case was that of Germany. Following the formation of a customs union, the Zollverein, between the then-independent German states in 1834, the enlargement of the internal market gave a stimulus to the development of domestic industry (for reasons analyzed in chapter 5). Germany continued to follow protectionist policies following the unification engineered by Bismarck in the 1860s, and industry expanded at a rapid rate, especially in sectors like steel and chemicals. By the 1890s these industries had emerged as important export sectors. What happened was very much what the proponents of infant-industry protection had hoped and expected would occur: a temporary period of protection sufficed to establish industries to serve the home market, which then emerged as strong enough to challenge successfully the established suppliers on the world market.

Protection of the import-competing sector also played a role in the industrialization of other countries—notably the United States and Japan, also in the less-successful development efforts of Austria-Hungary and Italy, and after the First World War in the countries of recent settlement. In fact, the only countries ever to have achieved industrialization without protecting their incipient manufacturing industries producing for domestic markets are Britain and Hong Kong. The strategy of import substitution fostered by protection acquired a new importance in the interwar period. Because of the relapse into protectionism by the developed countries, especially after the onset of the Great Depression in 1929, the option of export expansion was almost closed, except for countries with oil to export. (Not completely closed, as the Japanese example showed—but Japanese attempts to expand nontraditional exports encountered strong resistance from the developed countries, and insecurity in her dependence upon world markets played a major role in propelling Japan into the imperialist expansion that culminated in the national disaster of the Second World War.) Moreover, the forced import substitution in the periphery during the First World War, when the traditional suppliers were too busy fighting each other to attend to their traditional export markets, had demonstrated that a significant measure of industrialization was a feasible option for countries that had traditionally been suppliers of primary products.

For the world as a whole the 1930s was a disastrous decade, with a collapse of income in the early years followed by hesitant recovery and a shrinkage and distortion of trade as the income changes were first reinforced and later (when income started to recover) offset by protectionist pressures. However, some individual countries managed to defy the trend and progress, in some cases more rapidly than in the generally booming 1920s. These were the countries that adopted the most protectionist and nationalist policies: newly protectionist Britain and Nazi Germany, the Soviet Union, and the larger Latin American republics that early rejected monetary orthodoxy and opted for devaluation, monetary expansion, and protection—Argentina, Brazil, Chile, Colombia, and Mexico. The countries that remained bound to the orthodoxy of fixed gold parities, the gold standard rules of the game, balanced budgets, free trade, and letting insolvent banks collapse suffered the greatest fall in real income. Until the administration of President Franklin Roosevelt took office in 1933, the leading example of orthodoxy was the United States; subsequently, the "gold bloc," led by France and encompassing Switzerland and Benelux, maintained an orthodox stance, at great cost, for another three years.

This, then, was the historical background for the great debate on development strategy which was joined in the late 1940s, following the end of World War II and the conscious adoption by the member nations of the ideals of human betterment embodied in the United Nations Charter. There had been a golden age when trade had acted as an engine of growth, and it had been possible for a country to prosper as a supplier of primary products to the booming markets of the industrial centers of the world economy. That age had, however, been supplanted by one in which trade had grown much more slowly than income and a number of countries had demonstrated the feasibility and superiority of a strategy of import substitution. It was inevitable and perfectly proper that these experiences would influence the debate on development strategy. It was not inevitable, but it was perhaps natural, that the more recent experiences should have had the dominant impact.

11.3   Import Substitution versus Export Promotion

Once the initial argument in favor of balanced growth had lost its appeal, the debate over development strategy settled into one between the relatively autarkic option of import substitution fostered by protectionism and the outward-looking option of export expansion. For the first few years the debate was dominated by those favoring import substitution. The most influential school arguing that case was based at the Economic Commission for Latin America (ECLA), in Santiago, Chile, whose dominant force was the Argentinian economist Raul Prebisch (b. 1901). Prebisch had played a leading role in guiding the rather successful heterodox policies adopted by the Argentine Central Bank in the 1930s, so that he already had a close acquaintance with a successful case of import substitution.

The principal arguments in favor of import substitution—in addition to the emotive appeal of escaping from a role often perceived as that of hewers of wood and drawers of water—ran as follows: since balanced expansion of the domestic economy was impractical, the sale of additional output required winning new markets, either domestic or foreign. Furthermore, the expansion of output required the importation of capital goods and of intermediate inputs, which meant that additional foreign exchange must be made available. The question was whether it would be more advantageous to expand the slice of the domestic market supplied from domestic sources or to win a larger share of the world market. The latter meant either starting to export additional products or expanding exports of the products that the country had traditionally supplied. Exporting additional products—developing nontraditional exports—means principally industrial products. It was argued that such an option was not viable, for two reasons: the lack of a comparative advantage in the production of such goods and the problem of incipient protection by the developed countries that were the potential importers. The interwar experience of Japan suggested that the liberal trading principles proclaimed by the West as a part of the brave new postwar world would be thrown to the winds if in fact developing countries did begin to establish a comparative advantage in the production of manufactures which might make substantial inroads into Western markets. Just how great was this pessimism of the West's unwillingness to absorb significant quantities of imports of manufactures from developing countries can be judged from a United Nations' report of 1960 estimating the growth of LDC manufactured exports over the following decade at 60 percent.

A strategy of export expansion was therefore assumed to involve putting additional resources into production of the primary products that a country had traditionally exported because of its comparative advantage based essentially on its endowment of natural resources. Despite the historical evidence that such a strategy had yielded dividends in the golden age of booming world trade prior to 1914, there were various reasons for arguing that this strategy was unlikely to offer the same advantages in postwar conditions. First, world trade had not boomed since 1914. Second, the export sectors that developing countries had previously built up had typically led to an enclave pattern of development rather than setting in motion forces leading to generalized growth. The income from additional traditional exports accrued largely to a limited class of rural (or, worse, foreign) landlords or mineowners, who lacked the interest or aptitude to invest outside their traditional activities and preferred to buy imported consumer goods rather than provide growing markets for domestic manufactures.

The third reason given has subsequently generated a substantial debate. It was argued that additional exports of primary products would turn the terms of trade against the exporting country (see the analysis of the optimum tariff in chap. 5.10). At best, this would mean that a part of the additional real income would accrue to the developed importing countries rather than to the developing exporters. At worst, where demand is price inelastic, it might lead to the phenomenon now called *immiserizing growth* (see chap. 12.6), since the terms of trade would deteriorate so much that the country actually would be worse off as a result of producing and selling more. It was asserted that these fears were not hypothetical possibilities, but that there had in fact been a historical tendency for the terms of trade of the primary product exporting countries to deteriorate as a result of supply running ahead of demand.

There was a great deal of subsequent criticism of the thesis of a secular deterioration in the terms of trade of primary producers. Critics were able to show that, by changing the period over which comparisons were made or the basket of commodities, the statistical evidence of such a deterioration vanished. (For example, consider a basket of primary commodities that includes oil and a time period that reaches 1980.) But it was also argued that such historical comparisons were missing the central point. Sir Arthur Lewis asserted that the real source of the sense of injustice felt by developing countries lies in what are technically known as the double-factoral terms of trade:[1] the enormous disparity between the manhours that have to be expended in a developing country to buy the fruit of an hour's labor in a developed country, as compared to the fraction of a manhour that has to be expended in a developed country to buy the fruit of an hour's labor in a developing country.

There was also criticism of the idea that countries should avoid activities

1. The terms-of-trade concept used up to now is the commodity or net barter terms of trade, p_x/p_m, which measures the quantum of imports that can be bought with a given volume of exports. The "single factoral terms of trade," w/p_m, measures the quantum of imports that can be bought with a given quantity of domestic labor. The "double factoral terms of trade," w/ew^*, measures the quantity of foreign labor that can be "bought" with a given quantity of domestic labor.

just because they may involve a deterioration in the (commodity) terms of trade. It was argued that any individual country could expand its exports without having a major effect on its terms of trade, given that there are few countries with much monopoly power in the supply of their exports. However, this does not really dispose of the terms-of-trade objection to the strategy of expanding sales of traditional exports. It means that an *individual* country may indeed be able to expand its export earnings by producing more but this will be at the expense of a *greater* loss in earnings for other developing countries in the (typical) case where total market demand is price inelastic. Especially where developing countries collectively supply the whole world demand for a good, as is true of all specifically tropical products, these countries *collectively* suffer when one of them increases supply to the world.

The path of import substitution seemed attractive in comparison to these perceived problems and disadvantages of export expansion. It was conceded that import substitution might be a more expensive way of relieving a foreign exchange shortage in the short run, but the infant-industry argument for protection had long provided a rationale for accepting a degree of additional short-run cost in return for the future benefits of establishing a dynamic industrial sector. Furthermore, any terms-of-trade effects would be beneficial rather than harmful, while the sector that would benefit from protection would be (it was hoped) the dynamic industrial sector that could and would reinvest the bulk of its profits in further expansion. This mixture of infant-industry, income-distribution, and terms-of-trade arguments for protection proved to have wide appeal, and in the 1950s there was a very general adoption of protectionist, import-substituting policies as concern to promote development spread to the farthest corners of what used to be known as the periphery.

The early results of the policy of import substitution appeared promising. At least in most of Asia and Latin America, where the educational system was already producing substantial numbers of trained personnel, industry responded to the chance of taking over the home market. Subsequent difficulties with import-substitution policies have, however, led to a closer examination of those experiences. It is now argued that the first stage of import substitution is characteristically easy because it involves the production of nondurable consumer goods whose production requirements are well suited to the conditions existing in countries without previous industrial experience. These goods are intensive in unskilled labor. The efficient scale of output is small. Technology is unsophisticated. There is no need for a network of suppliers of parts, components, and accessories. In short, countries with low wage levels should be able to produce economically their own nondurable consumer goods like clothing, shoes, and simple household goods, together with many of the necessary intermediates like textiles, leather, and wood.

In the early 1960s, policies began to diverge. Some countries, like India and most of Latin America, pushed on to a second stage of import substitution based on their domestic markets, involving the establishment of industries to produce durable consumer goods and more capital-intensive intermediates, like steel and petrochemicals. In some cases, especially in Latin America, an attempt was made to assist this second-stage import substitution by the formation of regional trading blocs intended to provide a wider market for the newly established industries (see chap. 5.8 for the theory and chap. 13.2 for a description of the blocs).

Other countries broke with the policy of import substitution more or less as soon as the easy first stage had been accomplished and adopted instead an outward-looking strategy that favored the growth of nontraditional exports. The leading examples, subsequently dubbed the "Gang of Four," were Hong Kong (which indeed never had an initial protective phase), Korea, Singapore, and Taiwan. Their example was partially followed in the later 1960s by some of the Latin American countries, notably Brazil and Colombia, who at that stage were already well into the second stage of import substitution in which durable consumer goods industries were established, and the import bill was pretty much down to intermediate inputs and capital goods.

The growth rates since 1960 of certain countries that have been identified as pursuing particularly outward-looking or particularly inward-looking policies are compared in table 11.1. Taiwan, which has dropped out of World Bank statistics now that the People's Republic of China has taken its membership in the Bank, would reinforce the impression that the outward-looking countries have grown much faster. Among the inward-oriented, only Tanzania has exceeded the relevant average (it is a low-income country). Among the outward-looking, the lowest performer, Ivory Coast, beats all except 7 of the 114 other countries listed in the source table for the 1960s, and all except 15 of the 115 other countries listed for the 1970s. (Of the 7 higher performers in the 1960s, 2 were oil exporters, 1 was industrial, 1 was centrally planned, and 3 were developing. Of the 15 higher performers in the 1970s, 5 were major oil exporters, 2 were centrally planned, and 8 were developing oil importers. Some, probably most, of these high performers were also outward oriented.)

The success in achieving fast overall growth recorded in table 11-1 is the main reason given for claiming success for the strategy of export promotion. In addition, however, it has been argued that income distribution has

TABLE 11–1

Average Growth of GDP of Selected Countries, 1960–79 (percentage per annum)

Country	1960–70	1970–79
Outward-oriented:		
Hong Kong	10.0	9.4
Ivory Coast	8.0	6.7
Korea	8.6	10.3
Singapore	8.8	8.4
Inward-oriented:		
Burma	2.6	4.3
Ghana	2.1	−0.1
India	3.4	3.4
Tanzania	6.0	4.9
Memorandum items:		
All low-income countries	4.5	4.7
All middle-income oil importers	5.9	5.5
All industrial market economies	5.1	3.2

SOURCE: World Bank, *World Development Report 1981* (New York: Oxford University Press, 1981),app. table 2; used by permission.

remained comparatively egalitarian. Furthermore, those pursuing the more outward-oriented policy seem to have exhibited more resilience in responding to the additional burden imposed by the oil price increase.

In order to understand this success for the strategy of promoting nontraditional exports, it is necessary to understand the disadvantages of second-stage import substitution. While the nondurable consumer goods industries that are normally developed in the first stage of import substitution are technically suited to a country with little industrial expertise, this becomes less and less true the further import substitution is pushed. The additional industries are more capital intensive and skill intensive. Economies of scale are important: the minimum efficient size of plant is large relative to the scale of the market. Supplies of parts and components become an increasingly important consideration. Thus the country finds itself trying to establish industries in which it is less and less likely to have a comparative advantage.

A useful concept that has been developed to study this question is that of the *domestic resource cost* (DRC) of saving a unit of foreign exchange. The DRC of saving a dollar by import substitution is the total value of the domestic factors of production—labor, capital, and natural resources—used in increasing the domestic output of a good that was previously imported,[2] divided by the net value of foreign exchange saved. That net value is calculated as the reduction in value of final goods imports, *less* the increase in foreign exchange payments needed to sustain domestic production—to buy imported intermediates or capital goods or to hire foreign technicians or to pay the profits of multinationals or whatever. The problem with second-stage import substitution is that it involves traveling further and further "up the staircase" represented by DRC ratios.

The concept of DRC can also be applied to export promotion. The DRC of earning a dollar through exports is the value of the domestic factors of production utilized divided by the net earnings of foreign exchange, after deducting costs of imported intermediates or other foreign exchange costs of generating exports. Clearly the normal rule should be to hold a balance between import substitution and export promotion, so as to equalize the DRC ratios on the two sides. What the supporters of an outward-oriented strategy maintain is that, once the easy first stage of import substitution has been accomplished and an initial industrial base has been established in nondurable consumer goods, the DRC ratio from exporting some of those (or similar) products is likely to be lower than that involved in further import substitution. Even if a "staircase" exists for exports, as well as import substitutes, it is much less likely to be a steep one, that is, to involve rapidly increasing DRC ratios. The reason is that the width of each stair is set by the absorptive capacity of the world market or by the domestic supply side, rather than by the limited domestic market as with import substitutes.

There are several reasons for maintaining that the DRC ratio will, after the first stage of import substitution, be lower for nontraditional exports than for further import substitution. One is that those first industries established use the factors that are abundantly available in countries lacking a past industrial history, notably unskilled labor, whereas further import substitution requires increasingly large proportions of scarce capital and skilled labor. For this reason an export-oriented strategy often creates a strong demand for the abundant factor of unskilled labor, so that the Stolper-Samuelson theorem helps explain why countries that have developed in this way have had a comparatively egalitarian income distribution. (In other cases, however, export orientation may involve emphasis on land-intensive products like soybeans, which will lead to income concentration

2. Note that if there is a good reason to suppose that the market price of some domestic factor(s) misrepresents its social value—for example, because the marginal product of labor in its alternative (subsistence sector) use is much less than the wage it will receive in the modern sector—then for the purpose of this calculation it is possible and rational to represent its social value by a shadow price that reflects the social opportunity cost.

unless the land is widely distributed among peasants.) A second reason is that an export orientation provides the chance to exploit economies of scale. There are some industries where the home market is large enough to sustain a domestic industry able to realize scale economies, but beyond some point (which seems to arise quite soon in small countries) this ceases to be true. A domestic industry limited to the home market will therefore involve the operation of a plant below the minimum economic size. In contrast, exporting enables a country to concentrate on a limited number of sectors, each of which can be large enough to exhaust scale economies. Third, even where the domestic market is large enough to sustain a plant of minimum efficient size, this is not necessarily enough. Guaranteeing the domestic market to a single supplier invites all the ills of monopoly, notably high prices and lack of incentive to ensure efficiency. The need to compete on the world market provides a potent discipline that is all too often absent in countries adopting the import substitution strategy. Thus, whether we think in Heckscher-Ohlin terms of relative factor supplies or in Krugman-Lancaster terms of differentiated products offering scale economies, the DRC ratio of nontraditional exports is less likely to rise quickly than that of import substitutes.

Advocates of import substitution have traditionally feared that making oneself too comfortable on the bottom steps of the staircase may impede subsequent efforts to climb higher. Not so, reply the proponents of an outward orientation: as a country accumulates more capital and industrial skills, it will naturally develop new industries which are intensive in the now-more-abundant factors. As comparative advantage changes, so will its mixture of industries: this is the optimistic message of dynamic comparative advantage. Attempts to drag a part of the economy prematurely up the staircase are likely to depress total income and, therefore, savings and, therefore, factor accumulation. This argument is not conclusively settled: it can be counter-argued that establishing industries with a strong demand for technical manpower will increase the salaries of such persons and thereby the incentive to acquire such skills. For this reason some economists who have been impressed by the general argument for an outward-oriented strategy might still favor the maintenance of incentives toward a broadening of the industrial base.

What policy measures are called for to implement an outward-looking development strategy? Basically, the avoidance of severe import restrictions like high tariffs, quotas, and import prohibitions, and the maintenance of a realistic exchange rate.[3] The market will then provide an incentive for

3. Some countries, like Brazil and Colombia, that had already undergone second-stage import substitution when they adopted an outward orientation, chose to maintain high tariffs and an overvalued currency and to compensate for the disincentive to nontraditional exports by subsidizing the latter. This enabled the established industries to survive, while penalizing

firms to equalize DRC ratios between imports and nontraditional exports —and, for that matter, traditional exports. With the heavy protection called for by the import substitution strategy, payments equilibrium requires that the currency appreciate to the point where the growth of both traditional and nontraditional exports is impeded. It is noteworthy that countries that have adopted a strategy of promoting nontraditional exports have also had stronger growth of traditional exports than have the import substituters.

Two other arguments advanced in favor of an outward-oriented strategy are worthy of note. The first is that an import-substitution strategy is more prone to create opportunities for bribes and corruption. Especially where the domestic market is too small to permit more than one firm and where the technology dictates that this be a multinational, the decision as to which firm will be established is essentially administrative and the temptations are evident. Furthermore, where protection is administered by quantitative restrictions rather than by tariffs, there are all the temptations that can arise from the need to distribute import licenses, as noted in chapter 5.7.

The second argument is that an export-oriented economy inherently has more flexibility to respond to shocks than a relatively closed economy, where the only goods imported are intermediate goods essential to the maintenance of domestic output and capital goods essential to the maintenance of economic growth. The existence of a margin of imports of consumer goods means that a combination of expenditure-reducing and expenditure-switching policies can adjust the balance of payments without the need to deflate output or curtail growth. This possibility still exists in a country without consumer-goods imports, but only over the longer time period needed to change the pattern of output through additional investment in the traded goods industries. This presumably explains why the "Gang of Four" seem to have experienced less trouble adjusting to the oil price increase than did less open economies, even ones on which the direct impact was smaller. However, the extra flexibility in adjustment must be bought at the cost of additional vulnerability to certain types of shock. There is evidence to suggest that the oil price increases in fact had a bigger impact on the outward-oriented, but their greater flexibility outweighed this disadvantage and enabled them to maintain growth better. But oil was not a product for which countries had been seeking to substitute imports in the 1960s. Matters may be different if the Brazilian drive to substitute home-produced alcohol for imported petroleum is successful, and there is a new oil price increase in the late 1980s.

---

the development of traditional (nonsubsidized) exports. Experience to date suggests that such caution is wiser than the precipitate and total liberalization implemented by Argentina and Chile in the late 1970s.

In fact, vulnerability to the state of the world economy remains the enduring worry about the viability of a strategy of export-led growth. The success of outward-oriented strategies in the 1960s and 1970s was possible only because the developed countries did absorb large quantities of manufactured imports from the new industrial countries (NICs). In retrospect, we know that the sluggish trade growth of the period 1914 to 1945 had given way to a new boom in trade from the early postwar period on, in which trade has expanded more rapidly than output. Instead of the 60 percent increase in LDC manufactured exports forcast in 1960 for the following decade, the actual increase was 500 percent. It should not be thought that the expected defensive reactions to limit LDC manufactured exports were absent: as will be noted in more detail in chapter 13.1, the industrialized countries resorted to a series of subterfuges to restrict their imports in those cases (like textiles) where the NICs threatened to decimate their industries. But overall the old industrial countries proved more willing to accept NIC exports and the NICs proved more capable of adapting themselves to produce goods that their customers found attractive than the economists who had thought about these things in the 1950s had believed possible. Planning for an export-oriented strategy in the future does require an element of faith that the future will prove more like the postwar period than like the 1930s.

At least in the world conditions of the 1960s and 1970s, the 1950s pessimism about the feasibility of a strategy of nontraditional export expansion proved unfounded. The combination of successful practice with the convincing theoretical reasons analyzed earlier for expecting superior performance from an outward-oriented policy has proved persuasive. The result has been to make nontraditional export expansion into something of a new orthodoxy, especially in the World Bank, where its leading advocate has long been the Hungarian-born Bela Balassa (b. 1928). Quite a number of countries have adjusted their policies in that direction in the past decade, especially in South East Asia and South America. There have been stirrings also in South Asia, with a notable liberalization by Sri Lanka in 1976. Only in Africa is the old objective of reducing the degree of integration with the world economy still dominant.

11.4 The Shadow Exchange Rate

Economists frequently use the concept of a shadow price to express the value of an extra unit of some scarce resource. Perhaps the most familiar example is the value of the Lagrange multiplier λ that emerges when one solves the standard consumer utility-maximization problem by the Lagrangean method, that is, when one maximizes the expression

$$U(x_1 \ldots x_n) - \lambda(Y - \sum_i p_i x_i)$$

with respect to the consumer demands (x_i) and λ. In this instance λ represents the value of an extra unit of the scarce resource income (Y), in adding to the objective function, utility; that is, λ is the marginal utility, or shadow price, of income.

The concept of a shadow price is far more general, but it always represents the value in terms of the objective function of a marginal increment in the availability of the resource in question. Thus the shadow exchange rate represents the social utility—which would normally be measured in terms of the availability of consumer goods—of a marginal addition to the supply of foreign exchange. Various ways of trying to measure the shadow exchange rate were developed in the 1960s; they were first drawn together in a paper by the Brazilian economist Edmar Bacha (b. 1942) and Lance Taylor.

The ideal and conceptually correct procedure is to formulate an intertemporal model representing the present production possibilities and the alternative investment opportunities confronting the economy and then to calculate the solution that would maximize whatever social welfare function is considered to represent social preferences. This may be done by dynamic programming or by use of the calculus of variations or Pontryagin's Maximum Principle, depending on whether the model is specified in discrete or continuous time. In either event, since foreign exchange availability provides a constraint on consumption and therefore on social welfare, the optimal solution will yield *inter alia* a path for the shadow price of foreign exchange or shadow exchange rate. All one needs is an adequate model of the present state and future potentialities of the economy and the computational techniques to optimize it.

Suppose that a planner had a number which told him how much domestic consumption would be equivalent to a unit of foreign exchange at a particular time. Since domestic resources can also be converted into consumption goods, he would also know the value of the domestic factors of production that it would be worth giving up to save or earn a unit of foreign exchange. This is precisely what was defined in section 11.3 as domestic resource cost! In other words, the shadow exchange rate would tell the planner the DRC which should act as a cut-off point for acceptance of dollar-saving or dollar-earning investment projects.

In reality modeling techniques are not so advanced that planners have much ground for believing that they can calculate reliable shadow exchange rates in this way. However, what can be done is to calculate a series of DRC ratios, for various actual or potential projects, list these in ascending order, and search for the cut-off point consistent with satisfying the balance-of-payments constraint. If the country is prepared to move toward the elimination of an overvalued exchange rate and the protective policies that sustained it, then that requires calculating and using as the cut-off point the equilibrium (zero- or optimum-tariff) exchange rate. Such a rate can be calculated by an elasticities-approach formula of the type examined in chapter 8.3. If the country is not prepared to move toward trade liberalization, then difficult problems of deciding which policies have to be treated as constraints in choosing the cut-off point arise.

Having selected a shadow exchange rate, planners involved in project appraisal can evaluate receipts and expenditures of foreign exchange at its shadow value rather than its market value. If this shadow value were used consistently throughout the economy, the balance of payments constraint would be satisfied in the socially most efficient way. Of course, the greater the role of profit-seeking capitalists as opposed to socially altruistic planners in making the strategic decisions that determine which investment projects are undertaken, the more important it is to maintain the market price of foreign exchange close to its shadow price (or social value).

11.5 Summary

A developing country that is succeeding in accumulating capital and skilled labor has to determine in which sectors these factors should be deployed to promote development. The relevant considerations are that new markets must be found and necessary intermediate goods must be acquired. One possible solution to this problem, balanced growth, is ruled out by the importance of scale economies. The alternatives involve international trade, either by increasing exports or by substituting for imports. Prior to 1914 peripheral countries were able to base their development on the expansion of primary product exports, for which their natural resource endowment gave them a comparative advantage, to the growing industrial markets of the center. In the Age of Crises from 1914 to 1945 this became virtually impossible owing to the sluggish growth in trade that resulted from the combination of slow growth and protectionism in the center, and the countries that prospered were those that adapted their policies to the circumstances of the times by giving protection to import substitutes. The development orthodoxy of the 1950s, assuming this world environment would continue, prescribed import substitution as the best development strategy, and this advice was widely accepted. However, world markets were far more bouyant than had been expected and gave ample opportunities for growth through the expansion of nontraditional—principally industrial—exports. Where feasible, this strategy offers many advantages in comparison to import substitution: it exploits rather than fights comparative advantage and economies of scale; it leads to more demand for unskilled labor and thus to a less concentrated income distribution; it permits the maintenance of competition and is less conducive to the creation of opportunities for corruption; and it gives more flexibility in adjustment. This strategy has therefore become a new orthodoxy and has been quite widely adopted in recent years.

Economics is notoriously subject to swings of fashion. It is therefore appropriate to close on a note of caution, despite my judgment that the new orthodoxy has been essentially correct. The first reason for caution is that the feasibility of the strategy of export expansion depends on the state of the world economy. Export-led growth was clearly the best strategy in the booming 1960s and even in the troubled 1970s. One can hope that the world economy will remain sufficiently healthy for it to remain the best strategy, but one should remain alert to the possibility that these hopes may not be realized. A second reason for caution is that exporting labor-intensive manufactures is a more attractive option when there are few other countries trying to do it rather than when everyone is, when the same problem of developing countries competing the benefits of trade away could arise as (so it was argued) exists in the case of primary product exports. Balassa has argued that this need not happen, since, as new countries start to industrialize and export the simplest labor-intensive commodities, the present NICs will have acquired the skills to move upmarket and supply the more sophisticated goods that are still the preserve of old industrial countries. (Signs of this trend can already be detected in the increasing weight of engineering products, including capital goods, among the exports of countries like Brazil, India, and Korea.) But even if this optimistic picture of dynamic comparative advantage is justified, there seems no harm in helping the process along with a modest measure of infant-industry support, which usually involves import substitution in the first instance, with the aim of building up a rounded industrial structure. The choice between export expansion and import substitution is not absolute: both may have a useful role to play in the drive to industrial maturity.

269

11.6 Bibliography

The literature on balanced growth was initiated by Paul Rosenstein-Rodan, "Problems of Industrialisation in Eastern and Southeastern Europe," *Economic Journal,* June–Sept. 1943. For an authoritative statement of the ECLA arguments for import substitution, see Economic Commission for Latin America, *The Economic Development of Latin America and its Principal Problems* (New York: United Nations Economic Commission for Latin America, 1950).

An influential early paper favoring export promotion was Santiago Macarro, "Protection and Industrialization in Latin America," *Economic Bulletin for Latin America,* Mar. 1964. The main counterrevolution in favor of export promotion was led by B. Balassa, "Growth Strategies in Semi-Industrial Countries," *Quarterly Journal of Economics,* Feb. 1970, and *The Structure of Protection in Developing Countries* (Baltimore: Johns Hopkins University Press, 1971) and by I. M. D. Little, T. Scitovsky, and M. Scott, *Industry and Trade in Some Developing Countries: A Comparative Study* (New York and London: Oxford University Press, 1970). An admirable review of the debate is provided by C. Diaz Alejandro, "Trade Policies and Economic Development," in P. B. Kenen, ed., *International Trade and Finance* (Cambridge: Cambridge University Press, 1975). Balassa has conveniently summarized his own work in his Frank Graham Memorial Lecture, *The Process of Industrial Development and Alternative Development Strategies,* Princeton Essays in International Finance No. 141 (1980).

For the debate on the secular tendency of the terms of trade of primary products to deteriorate, see Ronald Findlay, "The Fundamental Determinants of the Terms of Trade," in S. Grassman and E. Lundberg, eds., *The World Economic Order: Past and Prospects* (London: Macmillan, 1981). On the shadow exchange rate, see E. Bacha and L. Taylor, "Foreign Exchange Shadow Prices: A Critical Review of the Literature," *Quarterly Journal of Economics,* May 1971; and B. Balassa, "Estimating the Shadow Price of Foreign Exchange in Project Appraisal," *Oxford Economic Papers,* Mar. 1974.

12

Factor Accumulation in the Open Economy

THE fundamental prerequisite of economic growth is accumulation of larger stocks of the factors of production (including knowledge). If growth is to lead to higher living standards, then the factors accumulated must be factors other than unskilled labor. The topic of the present chapter is how this process of factor accumulation is influenced by the openness of the economy.

The traditional two-factor model used to analyze questions of economic growth assumes that factors of production can be aggregated into homogeneous capital and homogeneous labor. Labor growth is either assumed to be exogenous or else to decline as per capita incomes rise, representing the effect of higher income levels in raising aspirations and reducing desired family size. In either event, the key to economic progress, interpreted as raising per capita income, is to be found in capital accumulation.

12.1 Capital Accumulation in the Closed Economy

There are at least three different visions of what drives the process of capital accumulation in a closed capitalist economy. These may be identified with neoclassical, Marxist, and Keynesian schools of thought.

The neoclassical view treats investment as determined by savings and savings as the result of the intertemporal consumption decisions of households. This is, for example, the situation in the neoclassical growth model of chapter 6.4, where there is continual full employment and capital accumulation is that part of full employment output that households choose not to consume. A critical question is: what is supposed to maintain continual full employment? The only logically satisfactory answer is that this must be the result of price flexibility (including interest rate variations). The problem with the more realistic answer, that the government may adopt an active fiscal-monetary policy to maintain full employment, is that in that event the savings ratio will depend upon the necessity for, and the form of, the government's demand management policy, rather than simply reflecting household consumption preferences.

Assuming that the story of price flexibility is sufficiently convincing to make the neoclassical model worth further consideration, there are two ways in which it can be extended. One is to modify the simple assumption that households always consume a constant fraction of their income and assume instead that they make an attempt at intertemporal optimization. This has the effect of introducing wealth and interest rates as determinants of the level of savings. A consequence of this modification is to rule out certain implausible possibilities that arise with the fixed savings ratio, such as society saving too much for its own long-run good.[1] A second extension involves disaggregating goods into a consumer good and a capital good, and positing a concave production possibility curve between them. This means that any attempt to increase the rate of growth would tend to run into diminishing returns, since a cut in the output of consumption goods would not permit a proportionate increase in the output of capital goods.

The analysis of the German economist, sociologist, and philosopher Karl Marx (1818–83), the founder of socialism, centered on the process of capital accumulation. It is therefore not surprising that he presented a distinctive view on the subject. This view coincides with the neoclassical one in assuming that it is savings that determine investment but differs in identifying the main determinant of the savings ratio as the distribution of income between wages and profits rather than the consumption preferences of households. In its extreme form, the Marxist savings hypothesis says that workers spend all their income while capitalists save (and invest!) all theirs, but the qualitative flavor of the analysis is retained so long as capitalists save a higher proportion of their income than do workers.

1. This is strictly true only if individuals are infinitely longlived. Another consequence is that the possibility of the growth rate being raised by resort to inflationary finance, which is suggested by the literature on money in growth models, is reduced.

Factor Accumulation in the Open Economy

The Marxist savings hypothesis has proved popular with a number of non-Marxist economists, such as the Hungarian-born British-peer Lord Nicholas Kaldor (b. 1908) and some of his Cambridge colleagues. It also plays a central role in Sir Arthur Lewis's famous analysis "Economic Development with Unlimited Supplies of Labor." In that model, a small modern manufacturing sector is assumed to be implanted by local capitalists in a predominantly subsistence economy where the marginal product of labor is close to zero but everyone receives a subsistence income equal to the average product of labor because of the extended family system. The modern sector can therefore draw on an unlimited supply of labor at a real wage that exceeds the average product of labor in the subsistence sector by enough to tempt unskilled laborers to leave their homes and traditional way of life. The excess of the output of the modern sector over the subsistence-plus wages paid to labor constitutes a surplus for the capitalists which they plough back into expanding the size of the modern sector. Barring crises, the process of expansion of the modern sector will persist for decades, but one day the whole of the surplus labor will have been absorbed by the modern sector and real wages will start to rise, thus exerting pressure for modernization in the traditional sector as well.

A third view of capital accumulation, pioneered by the Austrian economist Joseph Schumpeter (1882–1950) but now mainly associated with Keynesian thought, sees savings as determined by investment rather than vice versa. In Joan Robinson's graphic phrase, investment is determined by the animal spirits of the entrepreneurs rather than by a passive decision of capitalists to invest all. (To be sure, Marxists also recognize the possibility that the profitability of investment may decline to the point where capitalists lose interest in investing, but then excitement at the prospective crisis leading to the demise of capitalism tends to displace further analysis.) Given investment, income adjusts to generate that level of savings, so long as income does not run into the full employment constraint. If investment exceeds full employment savings, a variety of adjustment mechanisms may come into play: interest rates may rise, thus pruning back investment and stimulating savings in a neoclassical way; prices may rise more than wages, redistributing income from wages to profits and so increasing savings according to the Marxist savings hypothesis; the government may deflate, either cutting investment or increasing savings; or inflation may develop, adding to savings through the inflation tax.

Of these three visions of what drives the process of capital accumulation, the most popular among economists has traditionally been the neoclassical view and the least popular has been the Keynesian. Unfortunately this order of popularity reflects the ease with which the respective hypotheses can be embodied in elegant and self-contained models more than their usefulness in illuminating the real world. Circumstances do exist in which the neoclassical or Marxist models can be useful, as noted above in the discussion of the various adjustment mechanisms when investment exceeds full employment savings. But one always needs to consider whether investment is constrained by the lack of incentive to invest or by a shortage of savings, rather than reasoning automatically in terms of a model which takes it for granted that only a savings constraint can exist.

12.2 Investment and the Exchange Rate

In the analysis of international investment of chapter 6, a capital inflow simply adds to the total of goods available for consumption or investment. Those goods are treated as a single homogeneous good. If the additional goods are invested, we have the case of borrowing to enhance income (see chap. 6.2); if they are consumed, we have the case of borrowing to modify the time path of consumption (see chap. 6.3).

The analysis of the preceding section suggests further ways in which the openness of the economy may influence the process of capital accumulation. The first is through the Keynesian channel of influencing the *incentive to invest*. Especially regarding the incentive to invest in the production of tradable goods, an important determinant is the expected future level of the real exchange rate. When businessmen see their currency becoming overvalued and believe that state of affairs is likely to be allowed to continue—or even if they feel great uncertainty whether it will be allowed to continue—their natural defensive reaction is to cut back on investment. Assurance of a competitive exchange rate is therefore an important element in stimulating investment.

It is also true that an *undervalued* currency can hold back investment. The reason is that an undervalued currency tends to generate a current account surplus, which reduces the savings available for domestic investment. When the level of savings is the effective constraint on investment, an increase in competitiveness, that is, a rise in the real exchange rate, will tend to reduce the level of investment. In fact, a condition for maximizing the rate of investment and therefore the rate of growth is that the real exchange rate equate the *ex ante* level of investment to full-employment savings plus the capital inflow. A higher real exchange rate will reduce the current deficit below the capital inflow and thus cut investment below its potential. A lower real exchange rate will cut the incentive to invest, and the excess potential savings will be wasted in unemployment rather than translated into more capital. Maximizing growth involves having an appropriate real exchange rate.

12.3 The Two-gap Model

Another way in which openness of the economy may influence capital accumulation is through the requirement that some part of the capital goods be imported. When capital goods and consumer goods are distinct, as in the two-good extension of the neoclassical model, the home country may be able to produce one of them only at great cost or conceivably not at all. In reality it is capital goods that are typically imported, especially by developing countries. The technology of producing capital goods is generally more complex, their production is skill intensive, and demand is smaller relative to the minimum-cost level of production, thus denying scale economies to countries that seek self-sufficiency. The result is that even the industrially more advanced of the developing countries, or for that matter developed countries, continue to import a relatively high proportion of their capital goods. The less developed of the developing countries rely on imports for the vast bulk of the capital goods they install.

In developing countries, growth is generally constrained by the lack of resources to make investments rather than by the lack of an incentive to invest. Hence the two important ways in which openness influences capital accumulation are generally through the possibility of supplementing domestic savings through foreign borrowing and via the necessity of importing a part of the capital goods invested. The interrelationship between these two influences has been formalized in the two-gap model first developed by the subsequent vice-president for development policy at the World Bank, Hollis Chenery (b. 1918), in conjunction with the Israeli economist Michael Bruno (b. 1932). The model has been quite influential in guiding the policies of the World Bank, especially with regard to the international distribution of aid flows. It derives its name from the dual role played by an inflow of foreign exchange, in reducing both the savings gap and the foreign exchange gap.

The model treats the extreme case where production requires the combination of two distinct types of capital goods in fixed proportions. One of these capital goods, K_f, is not made at home and therefore has to be imported. The other, K_d, can be made at home, although it can also be imported. Let the fixed input coefficients per unit of output be α of K_f and β of K_d. Assume also that production requires the utilization of a fixed quantity of an imported intermediate good (oil, for example), and let the import content per unit of output be m. Finally, assume that exports are limited to some fraction γ of total output, Y, because only that fraction of productive capacity has been designed to produce exportables.

According to these assumptions, one limit to total output Y is set by the availability of the two forms of capital goods (it being implicitly assumed that labor is available in unlimited supply from the subsistence sector)

$$Y \leqq \min. \ [K_f/\alpha, \ K_d/\beta].$$

If the economy is initially at full employment and the two types of capital are in appropriate balance, with neither in excess supply, then

$$Y = K_f/\alpha = K_d/\beta.$$

Any *increase* ΔY in Y will require an increase of both $\Delta K_f = \alpha \Delta Y$ and $\Delta K_\alpha = \beta \Delta Y$. Hence the savings necessary to finance growth of ΔY would be

$$S = (\alpha + \beta)\Delta Y. \qquad (12.1)$$

According to the neoclassical savings hypothesis, domestic savings S_d are a fixed proportion of income. Income is the net value of output, after deducting the import content, so

$$S_d = s(1 - m)Y. \qquad (12.2)$$

Note that (12.1) and (12.2) reduce to a simple Harrod-Domar growth formula for the case of a closed economy ($\alpha = m = 0, S = S_d$):

$$\Delta Y = S/\beta = (s/\beta)Y$$
or
$$g = \Delta Y/Y = s/\beta,$$

that is, the growth rate is equal to the savings ratio divided by the capital-output ratio. The Harrod-Domar model can in turn be regarded as a short-term approximation of the neoclassical growth model, valid over such a period of time as the capital-output ratio can be considered a constant rather than increasing with capital accumulation due to diminishing returns. Since there is little reason to expect diminishing returns to set in during the period of industrialization while the modern sector is drawing

276

labor from the subsistence sector at a constant real wage, the technological assumptions can be regarded as satisfactory for the purpose in hand.

The capital-output ratio, or strictly speaking the incremental capital-output ratio (ICOR) $\Delta K / \Delta Y$, varies considerably both between sectors and between countries. It tends to be high in utilities and urbanization and low in agriculture, with a wide range in manufacturing. Since second-stage import substitution normally involves the establishment of capital-intensive industries while an outward-oriented strategy involves the growth of labor-intensive exports, one would expect ICORs to be higher in countries pursuing a strategy of import substitution. The differences are in fact large. While a value of three used to be taken as a typical figure for an ICOR, Balassa quotes figures for ICORs for the period 1960 to 1973 that vary from 1.8 in Singapore, 2.1 in Korea, and 2.4 in Taiwan to 5.5 in Chile, 5.7 in India, and 9.1 in Uruguay.

In the open economy, domestic savings S_d may be supplemented by an inflow of capital or aid. Denote that inflow S_f. It has been customary to assume that the ratio of capital/aid inflow to income can be treated as a constant, which we may denote by ζ. The savings constraint on the growth rate then takes the form

$$\Delta Y \leq S/(\alpha + \beta) = (S_d + S_f)/(\alpha + \beta) = [s(1-m) + \zeta]Y/(\alpha + \beta),$$
or
$$g = \Delta Y/Y \leq [s(1-m) + \zeta]/(\alpha + \beta). \qquad (12.3)$$

Equation (12.3) makes excellent intuitive sense: an increase in the propensity to save or in the capital inflow raises the feasible growth rate, while an increase in the technically necessary quantity of either form of capital reduces feasible growth.

Figure 12–1 illustrates the way in which the growth rate depends on the inflow of capital or aid (as a proportion of income), ζ. Equation (12.3) provides the first constraint on the growth rate, that coming from savings. The savings constraint has a positive intercept on the vertical axis at a value of $s(1-m)/(\alpha + \beta)$: even without a capital inflow domestic savings will be sufficient to finance a certain positive rate of growth, assuming only that $m < 1$ (which had better be true, or the country would be better off producing nothing at all!).[2] It has a positive slope equal to $1/(\alpha + \beta)$: each additional unit of inflow provides enough to finance the purchase of the two capital goods in quantities that will permit output to rise by that much. Growth is confined to the rate on or below the savings constraint.

2. The condition $m < 1$ is the simplest form of what is known as the Hawkins-Simon conditions, which are necessary for an economic system to be "productive" in the sense that it is capable of producing more than it consumes.

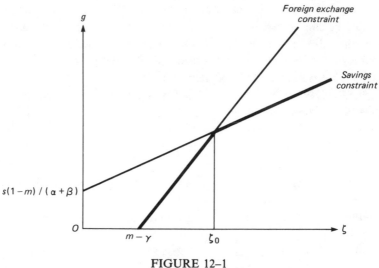

FIGURE 12–1
Savings and Foreign Exchange Constraints

So far as figure 12–1 is concerned, it would make no difference if savings were generated by a Marxist rather than by a neoclassical savings function. There would still be a determinate level of domestic savings generated at full employment, and that level could still be expected to rise more or less proportionately with the level of income. Foreign savings could still supplement domestic savings and thus generate an upward sloping savings constraint.

The second constraint on growth arises from the limited availability of foreign exchange. Ignoring changes in reserves, on the grounds that a rundown in reserves cannot be maintained long enough to boost the growth rate significantly, the balance of payments equation says that exports plus the inflow of capital/aid will equal imports of intermediate goods and final goods:

$$X + S_f = mY + \Delta K_f,$$

or
$$\gamma Y + \zeta Y \geqq mY + \alpha \Delta Y.$$

Since there is no limitation on reserve *accumulation,* this may be rearranged to express the foreign exchange constraint on growth:

$$g = \Delta Y/Y \leqq (\gamma - m + \zeta)/\alpha. \tag{12.4}$$

The foreign exchange constraint of (12.4) can also be shown in figure

278

12–1. It may intercept either axis, depending on whether $\gamma \gtreqqless m$. When $\gamma > m$, the country's exports exceed its imports of intermediate goods, so it has some foreign exchange left over to buy imported capital goods even without an inflow of capital/aid. When $\gamma < m$, exports are insufficient even to keep the economy operating at full capacity, and an inflow of capital or aid is essential to permit any growth at all. In either event the foreign exchange constraint has a slope $1/\alpha$, which is necessarily greater than that of the savings constraint $(1/(\alpha + \beta))$. Growth cannot exceed the level permitted by the foreign exchange constraint.

Considering the two constraints together, growth is limited to the area below both curves, bordered in figure 12–1 by the heavy line. The main conclusion is that up to a certain critical level (ζ_0 in the figure) an inflow of capital or aid is likely to be of strategic importance to the development process in easing a foreign exchange bottleneck. In this range the rate of return will be very high. Despite this, a country may fail to attract a capital inflow on commercial terms if it is considered to be a bad credit risk. The policy conclusion is that aid should be allocated in such a way as to fill such gaps. Once the inflow passes the critical level ζ_0, it will still permit an increase in the growth rate, but it will be less effective inasmuch as it now has to finance the purchase of *all* the additional capital goods rather than just those that cannot be produced at home.

There has been much debate about whether a foreign exchange constraint independent of the savings constraint really exists. A neoclassical view suggests that there are likely to be possibilities of substitution in production, either or both to boost the export proportion γ or to cut the import coefficient m, or even to increase β at the expense of α. Such possibilities imply that the foreign exchange constraint can be relaxed and that the only real constraint on growth is that furnished by the savings constraint.

No doubt in the long run the type of flexibility suggested by the neoclassical analysis exists. The proportion of output exported can be increased, and import substitution can reduce both m and α. But long-run considerations are not the only ones that are relevant. Nasty things can happen in the short run during which inflexibilities persist: people may starve, the people may revolt, or generals starved of new arms in the cause of reducing m may stage a coup. Relaxing the foreign exchange constraint can therefore be an important objective of policy, and it makes no sense to design policy on the assumption that no such constraint ever exists. After the sudden downward shifts of the foreign exchange constraint produced by the two oil price increases of late 1973 and 1979 to 1980, even semiindustrialized countries found the foreign exchange constraint had again become operative.

12.4 Technology

Studies of the determinants of economic growth, such as those undertaken by Edward Denison (b. 1915), have typically concluded that the largest single contributing factor is technological progress, as opposed to capital accumulation, improved education, or any other specific factor. The studies in question have, admittedly, concentrated on explaining growth (in supply) in the leading countries, especially the United States. It is in principle more difficult to separate the effect of technical progress from that of capital accumulation or education in countries that are in the phase of catching up. The essence of the growth process in that phase is that unskilled labor is drawn out of the low-productivity subsistence sector and employed, along with a mixture of suitably skilled labor, in a modern sector that is being expanded by investment in new capital goods that embody modern technology. When ample supplies of unskilled labor are available from the subsistence sector, and ample supplies of skilled labor are being produced by the educational system, this process can sustain miracle level rates of growth of upwards of 6 percent per annum. But the technological improvement is an integral part of the process of investment: while it is an indispensable condition for the growth, it is impossible to say that x percent of that growth is due to the investment and y percent to the technological advance.

Technology is analogous to capital in that resources currently devoted to investment in making technological improvements are expected to permit larger output to be realized in the future. However, there is a very important difference between capital and technology, deriving from the public-good characteristics of the latter. When a capital good is constructed, it is clear to whom it belongs and hence who is entitled to receive the income that it generates, and because of this there is an incentive to make investments whenever the projected returns outweigh the costs. When a new invention is made, on the other hand, it is rather difficult to prevent others copying it. Moreover, *given* that the invention has been made, it is undesirable to stop others imitating, inasmuch as their making use of the invention does not diminish the possibility of the inventor using it—the invention is in that sense a public good. The problem is that no one would have an incentive to invest in making inventions which could immediately be copied by everyone since the imitator would compete the price of the original down to a point that would deprive the inventor of any profits to compensate him for his costs of making the invention.

There is no universal or perfect solution to this dilemma, but societies use a variety of ways to reach tolerable compromises. One possibility is to resort to the classical solution to the public-good problem, which is to have the state provide the service in question. Hence one finds research centers and universities supported by the state, especially for pure research and for research in sectors like agriculture where productive units are so small that there are few realistic alternatives if any research at all is to be done. The problem with this approach is that research tends to be too far removed from the point of application—the researchers may be out of touch with the day-to-day problems that determine which approaches are feasible and suggest where effort would be best expended. Hence an alternative possibility, that of creating a *patent system,* may also be employed. A patent is a legal grant of the monopoly right to use a certain invention for a limited period of time (typically fifteen to twenty years). By granting a patent to an inventor, the state gives him the opportunity to recover the funds he has invested and make a profit out of the monopoly profits available during the lifetime of the patent in return for which the invention is made freely available to everyone when the patent expires. Large oligopolistic firms employing specialized technologies or selling capital goods might find it worthwhile to engage in research and development even without the protection afforded by a patent system, on the reckoning that they can keep the know-how secret sufficiently long to more than recover their costs, by continually renewing their product range and making it more attractive.

It is the public-good characteristics of technology that are responsible for the fact that present day developing countries have the chance of making the transition from subsistence economy to affluence so much more rapidly than did the first industrial countries. (Britain took perhaps 150 years to accomplish what Singapore did in the last quarter of a century.) Present-day capital goods which can be bought off the shelf embody a range of technical advances that reflect the investments in technology of some 200 years. In itself, this is an enormous advantage, but it does not mean that developing countries face no problems of access to suitable technology. There are in fact two important problems.

The first concerns the general question of what balance to strike between providing an incentive to innovate and allowing progress through imitation. Some have argued that, in view of the vast opportunities for imitation open to present-day developing countries, it makes no sense for them to invest resources in innovating or to limit the access of their firms to available technologies for the sake of stimulating local innovation. Two important points are raised in reply. First, it is argued that efficient employment of modern technology requires not just the use of potential information but also the deployment of a range of know-how that is only half in the public domain and that a patent system is important in giving multinationals the security to enter the country and bring their latest know-how with them. Second, it is argued that there is a need to encourage inventions adapted to the specific conditions of developing countries—which means in part to their generally tropical climates, but above all to their factor endowment. The idea is that the form of innovation responds to economic stimuli, so that in capital-rich countries with high labor costs the incentive is to develop labor-saving inventions, whereas capital-saving inventions would be far more useful to the typical developing country with its abundant supply of unskilled labor. According to this argument, innovation to match local conditions, rather than just taking techniques over from the developed countries, is much to be desired.

The second problem that arises in securing the adoption of appropriate technology in developing countries is that, even if suitably labor-intensive production techniques exist, it may not pay firms to adopt them. The rates of pay to urban labor may substantially exceed the opportunity cost of labor in the subsistence sector. The reasons why this distortion frequently occurs include the power of trade unions, the greater political influence of the urban proletariat as opposed to the rural poor (especially under left-wing governments), and the tendency for labor to receive its average product rather than its (supposedly smaller) marginal product in the subsistence sector.

There are lots of opinions but no very firmly established generalizations as to the relative and absolute importance of these considerations. Fragmentary evidence from Latin America suggests that local private enterprise firms tend to be more innovative in adapting northern technology to a more labor-intensive form than are multinationals, while the latter in turn exhibit more flexibility in this regard than do state enterprises. This suggests that, even though market forces may be blunted by excessive urban real wages, some market incentive to innovate nevertheless exists. It also suggests that it is naive to assume that state enterprise can necessarily be relied upon to undertake actions more in accord with social needs than those induced by private incentives.

12.5 Human Capital

The other essential element in the development process is the education of the labor force in the wide range of skills that are essential to the operation of a modern economy. One may summarize the skills needed as those of engineers, to operate the necessary technical processes, and of entrepreneurs, to perceive and exploit the opportunities of applying those processes. But in reality there are many other professions that have a role to play, including that of the economist—even if his role must at times be the negative one of trying to restrain ideologues from foolish acts like imposing marginal tax rates of 100 percent odd, or fighting inflation by cutting tax rates a mere fraction of that.

Acquisition of skills again involves a process of investment. Teachers and students devote their time to imparting and acquiring skills that will subsequently permit increased production, whereas they could be producing output for current consumption. Some twenty years ago economists started to exploit the analogy between the formation of physical capital and of human capital. Many studies were undertaken on the rate of return on investment in education, leading to the general conclusion that this is indeed a sensible form of investment yielding a competitive rate of return. Of course, none of this is to deny that education may be worthwhile for general cultural reasons quite unrelated to anything that can be measured in the GNP statistics. It demonstrates rather the reverse: that even philistines who attach no value to culture should be prepared to support a strong educational system on crude economic grounds.

The special economic characteristic of investment in human capital is that a large part of its return accrues in the form of increased earnings for the particular individual in whom the investment was made. There is no market mechanism that would permit an investor with surplus cash to decide that the best way to invest it would be in the education of the most talented (although he might decide to spend it on educating some of his family). Where markets fail, the state tends to step in; and so one finds most educational spending being undertaken or at least subsidized by the state. But this solution still leaves a large part of the returns accruing to the individuals who receive the education rather than to the society that makes the investment. The result is highly inegalitarian: middle-class children are subsidized by the population at large to enhance their own earning ability. It is something of a mystery why this inequitable arrangement is tolerated so readily, with virtually no attempt to mitigate the inegalitarian impact by financing education through loans. Even so, it may well be that state expenditure on education is less inegalitarian than many other ways of encouraging growth, like subsidizing private investment.

The international dimensions of investment in human capital are not markedly different from those of investment in physical capital, except that the import component tends to be smaller. Nevertheless, the import component is not negligible at early stages of development—foreign teachers are hired, and students go to foreign universities. Import substitution takes place in the educational sector as in any other, starting at the primary level and ending up with Ph.D. programs. Foreign borrowing can be used to invest in human capital as much as for any other purpose, either to pay for the import content or to permit imports of consumer goods that permit more domestic resources to be released for an expanded educational program. There is an opinion, apparently based largely on the experience of Korea, that the best way of telescoping the development process is to invest very heavily in education at the initial stages.

12.6 Immiserizing Growth

The key to growth is factor accumulation. But around the mid-1950s economists started finding cases in which factor accumulation and the resulting growth in output actually made an open economy worse off, or "immiserized" it.

The first example in which this can occur was produced by Jagdish Bhagwati, and arises from the possibility that increased output would turn the terms of trade against the growing country. At constant prices, the outward movement of the production possibility curve generated by factor accumulation increases the excess supply of exportables and the excess demand for importables. This will tend to worsen the terms of trade if the country is large enough to be able to influence its terms of trade at all. It is possible for this deterioration in the terms of trade to be so large as to outweigh the physical increase in output and leave the country worse off than before. On the other hand, it can be shown that this is not possible if the country is imposing an optimum tariff (see chap. 5.10). Although the large-economy assumption needed to permit immiserizing growth may rule out the possibility when considering the isolated growth of a single developing country, it cannot be ruled out when the simultaneous expansion of all the developing countries is considered.

A second case of possible immiserizing growth, demonstrated by Harry Johnson in the mid-1960s, stems from technical progress in the import-competing industry or accumulation of the factor of production used intensively in that industry. The argument is simplest in the case of technical progress as shown in figure 12–2. The diagram with the solid production possibility curve is basically the same as figure 5–1B, except that it omits details of the free trade equilibrium. Production with the tariff is at *P*, while

284

consumption is at *C.* Suppose now that there is technical progress in the *M* industry, so that the *ppc* moves up to the dotted position. Then it is clear that for a small economy, which therefore faces unchanged prices, the new production point *P'* must lie above and to the left from P. The critical question is on which side of the line *CP* does it lie. In particular, one cannot exclude the possibility that it will lie to the left-hand side, as shown, in which case it is clear that the new consumption point must lie on a lower indifference curve than *C.* [3]

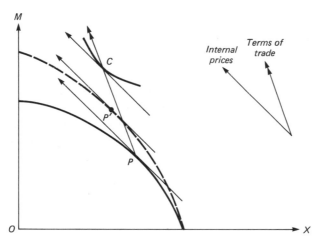

FIGURE 12–2
Immiserizing Growth with Technical Progress

The intuitive explanation of this case of immiserizing growth is quite simple. Technical progress increases potential output per head, but it also shifts resources toward the industry in which progress occurs. Where this is a protected import-competing industry, the social value of the output is less than it was in the export industry from which the resources were withdrawn. It is possible for this cost of the increased distortion to outweigh the benefit of the increase in potential output. This would not be possible if the country were employing an optimal tariff, which in this case is zero.

A third case, which has been analyzed by the Canadian Richard Brecher (b. 1951) and the Cuban-born Carlos Diaz Alejandro (b. 1937), arises when foreign capital is attracted by a national tariff. They show that immiseriza-

3. An increase in the stock of the factor used intensively in producing *M* would shift the ppc outward throughout its length, rather than leaving the intercept on the *X*-axis unchanged as in the case of technical progress. However, the Rybczynski theorem tells us that *P'* will lie above and left of *P,* so that the possibility of immiserizing growth again arises.

tion is in this case not just possible, but (admittedly on the assumption that the profits of the foreign investor are not taxed) *inevitable* over a certain range. The reason is shown in figure 12–3. P is again the original production point, and C the point of consumption. Suppose that in response to the tariff there is an inflow of capital that shifts the ppc out, and that the new point of tangency is a point P' as analyzed above. We already know that growth would be immiserizing in the case considered in the previous section where P' lies to the left of PC, so consider the case where it lies to the right as shown. That implies that if the increased capital stock belonged to domestic residents, consumption could rise to the point C' (assuming a linear income-consumption path). But in fact the foreign investors must be paid. In the absence of taxation they receive the marginal product of capital, valued at domestic prices, multiplied by the size of the capital inflow. Measured in terms of the exportable good, the increment in output due to the capital inflow is ZP' (since Z has the same value as P measured in domestic prices). But the level of consumption attainable from Z is only C'', which is less than C. Thus growth has once again immiserized and must do so unless profits taxation is high enough to leave the foreign capitalists with a sufficiently small part of their profits as to place the domestic economy to the right of PC.

Once again, immiserizing growth was possible only because of a distortion. This is in fact the common theme to emerge from these examples: that the circumstances under which growth would immiserize are not far-fetched, but they all depend upon policy creating some distortion (classify-

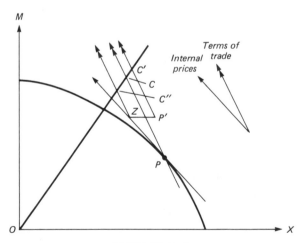

FIGURE 12–3
Immiserizing Growth with Foreign Capital

ing a deviation from the nationally optimal tariff as a distortion). Countries that follow sensible policies have nothing to fear.

12.7 Summary

Economic development depends upon capital accumulation, using that phrase broadly to cover the intangible capital of technical knowledge and the human capital of skilled manpower, as well as physical capital. The international dimension is important to the process of capital accumulation in influencing (1) the incentive to invest; (2) the availability of savings; and (3) the availability of imported capital goods. The interraction between the last two aspects is summarized in the two-gap model. But mere factor accumulation does not guarantee that a country will benefit; in the presence of sufficiently misguided policy, growth can immiserize. The ICOR statistics quoted in chapter 12.3 suggest that, even short of the case of immiserizing growth, a rational microeconomic policy is essential to making good use of the macroeconomic sacrifices that a policy of development requires.

12.8 Bibliography

The important paper of Arthur Lewis is "Economic Development with Unlimited Supplies of Labour," *Manchester School of Economic and Social Studies,* May 1954. The two-gap model was developed in H. B. Chenery and M. Bruno, "Development Alternatives in an Open Economy: The Case of Israel," *Economic Journal,* Mar. 1962, reprinted with modifications as chap. 8 in H. B. Chenery, *Structural Change and Development Policy* (New York: Oxford University Press, 1979); the clearest exposition was developed by R. I. McKinnon, "Foreign Exchange Constraints in Economic Development and Efficient Aid Allocation," *Economic Journal,* June 1964.

"Growth accounting," the attempt to decompose the (supply-side) determinants of growth, was pioneered by E. F. Denison, *Why Growth Rates Differ* (Washington, D.C.; Brookings Institution, 1967). An advanced survey of the work on human capital formation is provided by M. Blaug, "Human Capital Theory: A Slightly Jaundiced Survey," *Journal of Economic Literature,* Sept. 1976.

The papers referred to on immiserizing growth are J. N. Bhagwati, "Immiserizing Growth: A Geometrical Note," *Review of Economic Studies,* June 1956; H. G. Johnson, "The Possibility of Income Losses from Increased Efficiency or Factor Accumulation in the Presence of Tariffs," *Economic Journal,* Mar. 1967; and R. A. Brecher and C. F. Diaz Alejandro, "Tariffs, Foreign Capital and Immiserizing Growth," *Journal of International Economics,* Nov. 1977. All three are reprinted in J. N. Bhagwati, ed., *International Trade: Selected Readings* (Cambridge, Mass.: MIT Press, 1981).

V

WORLD ECONOMY

THE previous three parts of the book have focused on the interaction between an individual country and a rest of the world that was considered to be parametric. At this stage, the point of view changes. This last section of the book aims to examine the characteristics and logic of the world economic system. Chapter 13 deals with international trading arrangements, chapter 14 with the world capital market, and chapter 15 with monetary arrangements. Chapter 16 discusses proposals for reform of the international economic system—the Third World demands for a New International Economic Order. The final chapter endeavors to provide a basis for understanding how the interaction between various forces determines the evolution of the main world economic aggregates.

13

International Trading System

 HE historical account opening this book recalled how the era of free trade before the First World War gave way to unprecedented economic nationalism in the 1930s, during the Great Depression. This economic nationalism took various forms: protectionism, exchange control, bilateral trade deals, competitive devaluation. Some of the countries that took the lead in abandoning the old ideals of free, multilateral trade and exchange suffered less than most, but their gain was in part at the expense of others. Not only did this vicious competition bring economic loss to the world but it fanned the flames of a new war. The militarists who took control of Japan could appeal not just to xenophobia but also to quite rational concerns for economic security in the face of foreign protectionism, which threatened the ability to earn the foreign exchange essential to the purchase of imports of materials. Territorial expansion was in part a response to that threat, which in due course provoked the announcement of an oil blockade by the United States. Pearl Harbor was a pre-emptive strike to break that incipient blockade, not the bolt from the blue that it has customarily been painted in Western propaganda.

Fortunately Western economic statesmen were not deceived by their own propaganda but started to think about how a liberal international economic order could be restored even while the Second World War was at its peak. Their designs came to fruition in certain respects: specifically, they created the World Bank and a monetary order supervized by the IMF that more

291

or less functioned till 1971. But their ambitious plan for a comprehensive International Trade Organization (ITO) was never accepted by the United States Congress, and was allowed to lapse in 1950. What survived that wreckage was an agreement to restrain imposition of further trade restrictions and to provide a framework for negotiating reductions in trade barriers on a multilateral basis, the General Agreement on Tariffs and Trade, known as GATT.

13.1 General Agreement on Tariffs and Trade (GATT)

The General Agreement on Tariffs and Trade originated from a conference designed to bargain down tariffs and held in Geneva in 1948. This agreement was supposed to be one element in the ITO but was maintained when the latter failed to win acceptance. A modest secretariat was established in Geneva, where GATT has continued to function ever since. Some ninety countries, including all the non-Communist developed countries and most of the larger developing countries with the exception of Mexico, are now members.

The GATT obligations provide the ground rules governing commercial policy of the member nations. There are three basic rules: (1) not to *increase* tariffs; (2) not to impose quantitative restrictions (quotas); and (3) to grant "most favored nation" status to all other members of GATT. The purpose of the first rule is self-evident; there would be no point in countries going to great efforts to negotiate trade concessions if there were no obligation to maintain the concessions that were agreed. The second rule reflects the conclusion of chapter 5 that quotas are a particularly virulent form of protection, as well as the belief that they are such an effective form of protection as to be best outlawed. The third rule, the most favored nation (MFN) clause, needs more explanation. If country U grants country V MFN status, this means that U promises that no other country Z will be granted better terms for exporting to U. So if U then cuts its tariffs on imports from Z, it must also cut them on imports from V—otherwise V would be less favored than Z. The GATT obligation is to treat *all* other members as most favored, that is, not to discriminate between them.

The basic GATT rules thus serve to restrain increases in trade restrictions and to generalize liberalization that may occur. By themselves, these rules could not have secured the enormous liberalization in world trade that has taken place since 1947. The main instrument in engineering that liberalization in the early years was a series of tariff-bargaining conferences. In the early conferences, the main method of negotiation involved the principal supplier of a product to a particular market requesting a concession from the importer, who would demand a quid pro quo. If and when they agreed a bargain they judged to be mutually advantageous, the MFN rule ensured that it was generalized to all other GATT members. This procedure ensures that all participants can expect to benefit from liberalization negotiations, since there is no obligation to agree to concessions unless one expects to benefit from them, while everyone will pick up advantages on the side from other countries' concessions.

By the mid-1950s, the possibilities of such easy tariff cutting through bilateral bargains were becoming exhausted. It therefore became necessary to organize more complex bargains, with a shift from item-by-item bargaining to across-the-board tariff cuts and many concessions thrown together to form a package whose net outcome would be judged acceptable to all participants. The most recent negotiations on trade liberalization, the so-called Tokyo Round, were formally completed in 1978 after a full five years of intermittent talks, so complex has it become to put a mutually advantageous package together and deal with the complex issues of non-tariff barriers.

The underlying logic of GATT is that countries can be expected to benefit from general but not from unilateral adoption of free trade. The classic argument leading to this conclusion is the optimal tariff analysis. Each country (other than those too small to be able to influence their terms of trade at all) can benefit, at the cost of a greater loss to its trading partners, by restricting its trade and so improving its terms of trade. But if all countries restrict trade in the attempt to improve their terms of trade, there is a presumption that they will all lose, as compared to the free trade situation.

That is only a presumption. It is logically possible (if empirically unlikely) for one country (or more) to gain by imposing optimal tariffs, even after optimal retaliation, as compared to free trade. But even in that case, the world as a whole is worse off: one country's gain is more than outweighed by another's loss. Many other social contexts exhibit the possibility of "negative sum" acts (for example, throwing litter or entering a traffic intersection one cannot leave), where one party can gain by imposing a larger loss on others. A well-organized society deals with such situations by passing a law, or promulgating a social obligation,[1] designed to induce

1. One might identify a well-integrated society as one where the promulgation of a social obligation will suffice to induce a general willingness to modify actions in the light of their impact on third parties.

behavior that takes account of the spillover costs on third parties. GATT represents the attempt of the international community to reap the potential gain from mutual forbearance in restricting trade, by creating a set of rights (notably MFN treatment) that are available only to countries that accept corresponding obligations with regard to the treatment of other members.

While the optimal tariff argument is the clearest reason for believing that a country can gain by participating in a mutual trade liberalization even though it might lose through a unilateral tariff reduction, it is not the only reason. Another stems from the transitional effects of trade liberalization. A unilateral tariff reduction will tend to lead to a fall in demand, a payments deficit, and industrial dislocation, as well as a deterioration in the terms of trade. It is, of course, true that all these effects (except that regarding the terms of trade) are temporary, and that in the long run the economy will tend to return to equilibrium with higher real income (ignoring the terms-of-trade effect). But political decision makers tend to have a very short time horizon, either because of the need for policies to be seen as successful before the next election or because nondemocratic methods of changing governments may also involve summary (and typically more unpleasant) penalties for those whose policies are judged unsuccessful. Hence participation in a multilateral tariff reduction, which allows the rise in export demand to compensate the increase in imports so far as the income, payments, and terms-of-trade effects are concerned (and which will also reduce the dislocation caused by liberalization where the trade expansion is intraindustry as analyzed in chapter 4), will be politically more attractive than unilateral tariff reduction.

A third reason why a country may find it advantageous to join a pact for mutual self-restraint with respect to commercial policy relates to its possible use for anticyclical purposes. Protection is a potential method of expanding income in a recession, but it acts at the expense of other countries—it is a beggar-my-neighbor policy for remedying unemployment, in Joan Robinson's phrase. In the absence of any international restraints, countries would consider whether to use trade restrictions or fiscal-monetary policies to combat recession purely on the basis of their national interests (usually interpreted in a very short-run sense), and would presumably sometimes choose the former as happened in the 1930s. Given the stylized fact that the business cycle is highly synchronized between countries, this will typically intensify the conjunctural problem of other countries. An international prohibition of the use of commercial policy obliges countries to turn instead to the use of fiscal-monetary policies, which generally have positive spillover effects on other countries (despite the qualifications under floating rates noted in chapter 10). There is a general international interest in avoiding the use of policies that work against efficient global demand management.

Thus there are strong reasons for having an international agreement along the general lines of the GATT. Moreover, if one looks at the general record of trade liberalization since GATT was founded, it is impressive. Quota restrictions on trade were endemic, outside the dollar area, in the late 1940s: now only a minority of LDCs use them as a major policy instrument. Tariffs have fallen from average levels of 30 percent, 40 percent, 50 percent, or even more at the end of World War II, to averages as low as 4 percent or 5 percent for the main industrial countries. Trade has multiplied some seven times since 1950. Developing countries have been able to adopt a strategy of export-led growth. For all this, GATT can take much credit.

So much for the good news. The bad news is that that is far from being the full story. There are a half-dozen important industries—textiles, footwear, steel, automobiles, shipbuilding, and electronics—where trade has once again become heavily regulated. The admirable GATT principles are riddled with exceptions, and GATT is not very effective in preventing any determined country from adding to them.

1. Particular success in import penetration has provoked importers into demanding "voluntary" export restraints from the exporters. The concept of voluntarism here is that familiar from military practice: it is made clear that failure to volunteer will result in even more severe restrictions, however illegal those might be under GATT rules. Initially the main "volunteer" was Japan, but the NICs soon came under pressure too, especially to limit their textile exports. By the early 1960s there was such a network of bilateral voluntary restraints on exports of cotton textiles that they were replaced by a multilateral agreement, which was in turn succeeded by the Multi-Fiber Arrangement in 1974. This is a multilateral agreement which allows unilateral action to limit quantitatively all forms of textiles imports. It is used to limit exports from the developing to the developed countries. More recently voluntary export restraints have been demanded and implanted in other areas where Japan and the NICs have built up substantial exports—footwear, steel, and electronic products in particular. In addition, Japan is periodically obliged to limit its exports of cars.

2. Most trade in agricultural products is not carried out under GATT rules. This constitutes an important limitation on the effectiveness of GATT.

3. GATT has allowed developing countries to become members and benefit from the trade concessions extended by developed members without demanding anything much in the way of their accepting the obligations and disciplines of membership. While there is a reasonable case for allowing

295

developing countries to afford infant-industry protection in specific cases, an argument can be made that this blanket exemption was unwise and against the interests of the developing countries themselves. In particular, it has deprived the LDCs of the ability to cite the need to respect international obligations as a weapon for combating their own special interest protectionist lobbies—not least the multinationals they host.

4. Countries are permitted to limit imports by quantitative restrictions (QRs) if the IMF certifies that they are suffering from a serious balance-of-payments problem. This does not matter much in practice, because QRs are too drastic a weapon for major countries to want to use them for balance-of-payments purposes.

5. There are also exceptions to the nondiscrimination provision. When GATT was created, members were allowed to maintain existing preferences. This was perceived as a great British victory, which permitted the maintenance of Imperial Preference—the system by which members of the British Empire and Commonwealth used to extend tariff preferences to one another—whose abolition was a principal United States aim in the ITO negotiations. In fact those preferences were heavily eroded through the 1950s and 1960s, and finally disappeared following British accession to the European Community in 1972. (In retrospect it is difficult to understand the passions that this issue aroused on both sides of the Atlantic in the 1940s.) A second exception to the nondiscrimination rule permits members forming customs unions and free trade areas to discriminate in favor of one another: without such an exception, the formation of such trade blocs would have been illegal. The third exception concerns a set of limited tariff preferences in favor of developing countries that has been introduced by developed countries: the generalized system of preferences (GSP), as these limited preferences are known.

13.2 Trading Blocs

GATT rules permit discrimination in favor of other countries that are fellow members of a customs union or free trade area, including a bloc in process of formation where internal tariffs have still not been completely abolished. In principle it is only full unions, involving the ultimate complete abolition of internal tariffs, that are permitted. In practice GATT has not only tolerated some projected unions that created preferential arrangements by internal tariff reductions and then ceased to advance at even a snail's pace, but it has also acquiesced in the classification of preferential trading arrangements between the European Community and its associated states as "free trade areas."

A brief idea of the constitution and achievements of the various trading blocs that have functioned since the early 1960s follows.

EUROPEAN ECONOMIC COMMUNITY (EEC)

The EEC is based on the 1957 Treaty of Rome and started to cut tariffs in 1958. The initial members were Belgium, France, Germany, Italy, Luxembourg, and the Netherlands, with headquarters in Brussels. The Rome treaty provided for the establishment over a ten-year transitional period of a customs union in industrial products: that is, internal free trade and a common external tariff (set at the average of the previous tariffs of the members). It was also planned to create a common, though controlled, market in agricultural products, and this was duly done. Details vary from one product to another, but the typical pattern is that the Community sets each year a minimum support price at which it acts as residual buyer, while preventing producers in the rest of the world benefiting from this price by imposing a variable levy on imports to the Community equal to the excess of the support price over the foreign supply price. When support prices are set high enough to induce an excess of EEC supply over demand, the excess is put into stock (forming a "butter mountain," or a "wine lake," etc.) and eventually dumped on the world market for whatever price can be obtained, to the not-surprising indignation of competitive suppliers. In addition to the basic plan for a common market in industrial and agricultural products, the Treaty of Rome provided for free internal movement of labor, a coordinated antimonopoly policy, ambitions toward monetary union (see chap. 15.6), and absorption of the existing Coal and Steel Community and the projected Euratom within the umbrella of the European Community.

There is no doubt that the common market in industrial products was a great success. In a world where trade in general was expanding at 8 percent per annum in real terms, it was estimated that EEC intratrade in manufactures grew some 50 percent more than would otherwise have occurred in the decade following the Rome Treaty. Although the orthodox triangles (of consumer's and producer's surplus) analysis of the welfare implications of trade liberalization is dismissive of the benefits of even such a large expansion of trade, some reasons were given in chapter 5.8 for believing that the orthodox analysis is seriously incomplete, and there was certainly a widely shared perception in Europe that the EEC was a major factor in promoting the prosperity of the 1960s. The common agricultural policy was less of a success, the main problem being that the farm lobby managed to set and maintain support prices too high, with a consequent chronic tendency to induce wasteful excess supply. Common policies were put in place on other issues as well, with results that varied from the marginally useful to the mildly comic.

The early success of the EEC led Britain to regret her initial decision to stand aside, and twice during the 1960s she applied for admission, only to be rejected by de Gaulle's France. A third application submitted after de Gaulle's retirement and death was successful, and in 1972 the EEC was enlarged by the entrance of Britain, Denmark, and Ireland. Although the expansion of intratrade among the original members showed signs of slowing down in the 1970s, trade involving the new members grew sharply. This benefit was, however, somewhat overshadowed by the general stagflation and disputes about payments into the EEC budget (mainly used to finance agricultural subsidies), so that the EEC no longer exuded that dynamism that it had done in its first decade. Despite that, it has attracted new applicants for membership: Greece acceded in 1981, and Portugal and Spain are negotiating to join as this is written.

EEC ASSOCIATION

The European Community has concluded association agreements with a large number of countries. These fall into two categories: a common agreement with a large number of small developing former colonies (under what is known as the Lomé Convention, in honor of the Togo capital where the agreement was negotiated), and a series of ad hoc individual agreements, initially with Mediterranean countries and subsequently with EFTA members. The Lomé Convention gives preferential access to the European market for certain products, typically tropical produce rather than manufactures, from the fifty-odd African, Caribbean, and Pacific associates. These preferences are undoubtedly overwhelmingly trade diverting in their impact, at the expense of Latin America and to some extent Asia and the Middle East. The Lomé Convention also provides for a flow of aid from the EEC and for price support for certain exports of the associated states.

Other association agreements are individually negotiated, providing for preferential access to the EEC market of specified quantities of various goods. Most countries bordering on the Mediterranean, from Algeria and Morocco to Israel and Turkey, have concluded such agreements. These used to provide that the associates would grant preferences in their markets for imports of certain goods from the EEC, but under pressure from competing suppliers these reverse preferences have now been dropped. Only with EFTA members, with whom the EEC now has virtual free trade in industrial products, do reverse preferences still exist.

EUROPEAN FREE TRADE ASSOCIATION (EFTA)

When Britain found to her surprise in 1958 that the six original members of the EEC were in earnest about creating a common market from which she would be excluded, she retaliated by trying to organize most of the excluded European countries into a free trade area. This was the origin of EFTA, whose members, besides Britain, were Austria, Denmark, Finland, Iceland, Norway, Portugal, Sweden, and Switzerland. Despite its anomalous shape, EFTA proved quite successful in promoting intratrade in manufactures, although there is evidence that a much higher proportion of this (perhaps 50 percent as against 25 percent in the case of the EEC) represented trade diversion—overwhelmingly at the expense of the EEC. The intuitive reason for expecting a higher percentage of trade diversion in the EFTA case is that the EFTA economies were more heterogeneous in resource endowments and income levels than the EEC economies, so that there were relatively more opportunities for changing the source of what had to be imported anyway than there were for importing what was primarily produced at home. EFTA has continued to exist even after the withdrawal of Britain and Denmark and now enjoys virtual free trade in industrial goods with the EEC.

LATIN AMERICAN FREE TRADE ASSOCIATION (LAFTA)

Stimulated by the example of the EEC and by GATT pressure to withdraw former ad hoc tariff preferences that contravened the MFN principle, ten Latin American nations (Argentina, Bolivia, Brazil, Chile, Colombia, Ecuador, Mexico, Paraguay, Peru, and Uruguay) signed the Treaty of Montevideo establishing LAFTA in 1960. This called for free trade among members by 1980. In the early days some quite useful tariff concessions were made, but further liberalization ran into resistance from domestic producers threatened by import competition from partners. The process of liberalization petered out far short of free trade. In 1980 the members acknowledged the failure of the original ambitions but reaffirmed their commitment to a measure of Latin American integration, replacing LAFTA by the Latin American Integration Association, which officially adopted preferential tariffs for partners (thus breaching GATT openly where the previous violation had been unofficial). Most of the increase in intra-LAFTA trade was in food and raw materials rather than manufactures. And this rise in primary commodity trade only reestablished 1950s levels of regional trade (the period prior to the emphasis on import substitution).

CENTRAL AMERICAN COMMON MARKET (CACM)

Five small Central American republics—Costa Rica, El Salvador, Guatemala, Honduras (which withdrew in 1968) and Nicaragua—formed a common market in 1960. Their aim was unequivocally that of providing a market large enough to sustain a viable program of import substitution, and trade expansion among the members has been primarily in manufactures. Despite the difficulty of maintaining a balance in the location of the import-substituting industries established, a recent study has concluded that all of the members benefited, with a total gain in 1972 estimated at some 3 percent or 4 percent of their combined GNP. This estimate included attempts to quantify the benefits accruing from economies of scale, from foreign exchange savings, and from the employment of additional labor at a real wage above its social opportunity cost, as well as the traditional welfare triangle benefits of trade creation and costs of trade diversion. Political troubles have caused this promising experiment to languish for the last decade.

ANDEAN GROUP

Dissatisfaction with the slow progress of LAFTA led a subgroup composed of Bolivia, Colombia, Chile, Ecuador, Peru, and, subsequently, Venezuela to found the Andean Group in 1960. The primary aim was again that of promoting import-substituting industrialization, complementing tariff liberalization with industrial programming and a common policy toward inward direct investment. Once again, the initial experience involved a useful rise in intratrade, but in due course tensions about the distribution of new investment plus the withdrawal by Chile after the ideological shift following Pinochet's coup led to a loss of momentum.

ASSOCIATION OF SOUTHEAST ASIAN NATIONS (ASEAN)

In 1967 Indonesia, Malaysia, the Philippines, Singapore, and Thailand agreed to establish ASEAN to promote regional cooperation in the economic, social, cultural, and technical fields. After a slow start, ASEAN became an effective mechanism in the mid-1970s and resolved *inter alia* to work toward gradual economic integration. Intra-area trade liberalization was initiated in 1976, with a view to working toward establishment of a free trade area. The motivation was encouragement of import substitution on the basis of production for a regional market, within the context of a generally export-oriented development strategy. Southeast Asia is currently the most rapidly industrializing area in the world, but the modest growth of intratrade in manufactures realized thus far is not a major element in this.

COUNCIL FOR MUTUAL ECONOMIC COOPERATION (COMECON OR CMEA)

The members of COMECON, which was founded in 1949, are those Communist states that look to the Soviet Union for political leadership: Bulgaria, Cuba, Czechoslovakia, East Germany, Hungary, Mongolia, Poland, Romania, and Vietnam, as well as the USSR itself. The aim is not to free trade, which is neither possible nor desired given that trade is a state monopoly in each of the member countries, but rather to plan production on a joint basis and seek to ensure that the resulting trade flows balance. For some reason that is incomprehensible to a Western economist, COMECON seeks to establish *bilateral* trade balance between each of the member states rather than simply requiring that each be in overall balance and then transferring claims between them in some convertible currency. A requirement of bilateral balance is virtually guaranteed to lead to inefficiency, since only by coincidence would the trade pattern that emerges from each country maximizing its overall utility subject to a single constraint of balanced trade (or a given level of imbalance) also satisfy the additional constraints imposed by the requirements of bilateral balance. Perhaps this explains why COMECON has not been a great success, as manifest by the preference members display for selling to the West (where they earn convertible currency) rather than selling to their partners.

OTHERS

There is a common market, known as CARICOM, between some of the small former British colonies in the Caribbean. An East African Common Market embracing Kenya, Tanzania, and Uganda was inherited from colonial days but broke up under the twin pressures of Tanzanian and Ugandan resentment at Kenyan success in attracting the bulk of the induced import-substituting industrialization, and sharply differing political ideologies. This has now been succeeded by a larger Preferential Trade Area of Eastern and Southern African states covering 18 countries, but the impact of this arrangement appears to have been minimal as yet. A West African Economic Community (WAEC) was also preserved from colonial days, consisting of the francophone West African states and has continued to function. A larger but looser Economic Community of West Africa (ECOWAS), comprising sixteen French-, English-, and Portuguese-speaking countries in West Africa, was founded in 1975, but has not had much success in stimulating intra-trade as yet. Some Asian countries (initially Bangladesh, India, Korea, and Sri Lanka) extended preferential tariff cuts among themselves under the Bangkok Agreement, which went into effect in 1976. Finally, the Arab world has often debated the establishment of an Arab Common Market, but this has not yet been achieved. The major form of economic integration between the Arab countries takes the form of *factor* mobility: of flows of capital from the capital-surplus countries with large oil revenues and small populations to those in a reverse situation and of labor flows in the reverse direction.

William Cline (b. 1941) has provided a convenient comparative summary of the impact of six integration projects on the intratrade of their members (see table 13–1). It can be seen that in every case integration had a significant effect in stimulating intratrade relative to total trade during the first decade, but that subsequent progress was generally slower and that there were cases of retrogression (notably CACM and WAEC). The great success stories were the EEC, where the initial level of intratrade was already high, and CACM, where the common market was almost certainly a major element in the degree of industrialization achieved in the 1960s.

TABLE 13–1

Intra-trade as a Percentage of Total Exports for Six Integration Groupings

Group	1960	1970	1976
EEC[a]	34.6	48.9	51.8
LAFTA	7.7	10.2	13.5
Andean Group	0.7	2.0	5.0
CACM	7.5	26.8	20.2
CARICOM	4.7	7.3	8.3
WAEC	2.0	9.1	6.1

SOURCE: W.R. Cline, "El interés de America Latina en la integración económica," *Integración latinoamericana*, Oct. 1981, p. 23.
NOTE [a]. EEC of 6, 1960–70; EEC of 9, 1976

13.3 Generalized System of Preferences (GSP)

By the 1960s, world trade arrangements were becoming distinctly lopsided. Trade among the industrial countries had been very substantially liberalized, and there was even talk of a North Atlantic Free Trade Area. In contrast, imports of the traditional manufactured exports of the developing countries were encountering new restrictions, mainly in the form of pressure to adopt voluntary export restraints, plus the restrictions on textile imports allowed under the Multi-Fiber Arrangement. Admittedly these restrictions were not as fierce as those that many LDC economists had feared would emerge at the first sign of LDC success in developing exports of manufactures, but they were a far cry from the near free trade that had developed among the industrial countries. (See Paul Krugman's explanation in chapter 4.3 of the dichotomy between acceptance of trade liberalization among the industrial countries versus resistance to liberal importing from the NICs: the fact that the former involves intraindustry trade, which promises gains to everyone, while the latter involves Heckscher-Ohlin trade, which threatens the interests of one factor in the industrial countries.)

The rapid growth in NIC exports of manufactures that occurred despite Northern protectionism reflected in part a willingness of the developed countries to allow some increase in their imports of the restricted goods over time. Even the Multi-Fiber Arrangement accepts the goals of expanding textile trade, reducing barriers to such trade and providing for a substantial increase in LDC export earnings from textiles, although the emphasis given to these objectives has steadily decreased. More importantly, however, the increase in manufactured exports of the NICs reflects their success in expanding the range of products they supply to the world market far beyond the traditional LDC staples of textiles and footwear. The big NIC success has been in developing nontraditional exports, in the fullest sense of that term. And the developed countries have a generally good record in terms of having helped this process along.

The imbalance in the commercial policy of the developed countries was becoming evident at the same time as the Third World was turning its attention to economic issues. Until the early 1960s, the struggle for political independence had pushed economic questions into the background except in Latin America. But after the decolonization of Africa (around 1960) economic development became the top priority. Discontent with existing trade arrangements led to pressures to create a new organization, and the first meeting of the United Nations Conference on Trade and Development (UNCTAD) was accordingly convened in 1964.

In practice UNCTAD has operated in parallel with, rather than in competition with, GATT. Whereas GATT annual meetings are humdrum business occasions that the press never notices, the triennial UNCTAD meetings are month-long diplomatic wrangles full of rhetoric and marked by North-South confrontations that fill countless column-inches of the more serious newspapers. Whereas the GATT secretariat does research that is more likely to appear in an academic journal than to inspire a political initiative, the UNCTAD secretariat has operated as a think-tank for the Third World (a role that has not endeared it to the laissez faire ideologues of the economics profession). Whereas GATT has a set of rules that it is supposed to police as best it can, UNCTAD tries to change the rules of other organizations.

Other reforms that UNCTAD has pressed will be reviewed in chapter 16. For the present, there is just one of these that is relevant, which happens to be the first issue on which UNCTAD was successful in getting a major change in the rules: the question of the tariffs applied by developed countries to imports from developing countries. The EEC gave preferential access to its market for certain imports from signatories of the Lomé Convention and other associates, and this led to the exclusion of competitive products from Latin America and other areas not eligible for associate status. UNCTAD argued that the principle of allowing preferential access for the exports of developing countries was right, but that the practice of restricting such concessions to a limited number of developing countries and thus diverting trade was wrong. Such tariff preferences should be generalized to apply to all developing countries.

After much negotiation, a limited scheme for generalized preferences, the GSP, entered into force in 1971. This scheme provides for each of the

TABLE 13–2
Import Coverage of the GSP, 1976

Country	Total Value	Under GSP Value	Under GSP Percentage of total
Austria	647	126	19
Australia	1268	179	14
Canada	2031	303	15
EEC	15155	4446	29
Finland	415	21	5
Japan	12314	1789	14
Norway	556	22	4
Sweden	1247	145	12
Switzerland	1042	257	25
USA	24499	3154	13
TOTAL	59174	10442	18

Nonfuel Merchandise Imports from Developing Countries (in millions of dollars)

SOURCE: World Bank, *World Development Report 1981* (New York: Oxford University Press, 1981), table 3.5; used by permission.

304

developed countries—with the EEC acting as a single country in this respect, as in other questions of commercial policy—to draw up its own
individual list of the products in which it will make tariff concessions on
imports from "all" of the developing countries. The word "all" is in
quotes, because when a country has too much success in building up a
large volume of exports, it may find its name withdrawn from the list of
beneficiaries for the product in question. Given that the quantity of imports that is going to be accepted on preferential terms is limited, there is
in fact a certain logic in excluding countries that have successfully established themselves as exporters of a particular product. This enables the
scheme to act as a stimulus to infant exporters, and so helps in the first
critical stage of launching nontraditional exports on the markets of the
industrial countries.

The main criticism of the GSP is its limited scale of operation. Table 13–2
shows that less than 20 percent of LDC exports to industrial countries (even
excluding petroleum) enter on preferential terms under the GSP.

13.4 Primary Products

Unlike trade in industrial products, which are generally sold in fixprice
markets, most primary products are traded in flexprice markets. Of course,
neither proposition is universally true: the markets for certain intermediate
products of the chemical industry appear to be essentially flexprice, while
bananas are bought and sold by the United Fruit Company or Fyffes in a
markedly fixprice way. (The price paid for bananas in Central America once
remained unchanged for nearly twenty years!) Nevertheless, the bulk of
world trade in primary products, excluding fruit and iron ore, is conducted
on the basis of prices determined in organized commodity markets, in which
the price fluctuates from day to day and hour to hour to clear the market.

These commodity markets are mainly located in London, New York, and
Chicago. There are active markets for metals like aluminum, copper, gold,
lead, mercury, platinum, silver, tin, and zinc; for fibers like cotton, jute, and
sisal; for lumber and plywood; for rubber; for beverages like cocoa, coffee,
and tea—and frozen orange juice; and for foodstuffs (for animals and/or
people) like cattle, chicken, corn, eggs, fishmeal, oats, pigs, potatoes, pork
bellies, soybeans, soybean meal, soybean oil, sugar, and wheat. By no means
all the trade in these products is carried out on the basis of contracts
concluded on those markets, but since the prices agreed in contracts signed

off-market are strongly influenced by ruling market prices, one can with a good conscience use the economist's favorite model, of supply and demand, to analyze these markets.

The outstanding stylized fact about the markets of most primary commodities is that both demand and supply tend to be distinctly inelastic with respect to price in the short run. Once again, this is not true of all primary commodities: demand for those which form the basis for luxury consumption, like cattle, gold, orange juice, and silver, may well be price elastic. But by and large demand is inelastic either because primary products provide the basic staples of life or because their cost is only a small fraction of the total cost of production while their input coefficient is pretty much determined technologically. And supply is usually inelastic in the short run because of technological factors: once the mines are sunk, the trees are planted, or the crops are sown, there is not much scope for varying output in response to a change in price.

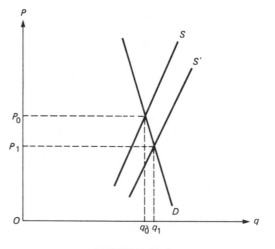

FIGURE 13–1
Market for a Typical Primary Product

Figure 13–1 shows a competitive market for a typical primary product, with inelastic demand and supply curves. Initial price is p_0 with the corresponding equilibrium quantity q_0. Now suppose that the supply curve shifts right, to S', perhaps because of unusually favorable weather conditions. There is no contradiction between the hypothesis of inelastic supply and the hypothesis that supply may be subject to big shocks: one refers to movements along, the other to shifts of, the supply curve. The new equilibrium is characterized by a lower price p_1 and a higher quantity q_1, but, because the demand curve is inelastic, the total revenue (pq) *falls* as a result of the increase in supply.

Shifts in demand produce even more violent variations in the incomes of primary producers, since price rises a lot because of the inelasticity of supply, while, to the extent that quantity does vary at all, it reinforces rather than counters the effect of the increase in price. (Imagine a rightward shift of the demand curve in figure 13–1.) Once again, such shifts in demand are in no way inconsistent with inelasticity of the demand curve, and in fact the demand for many primary products does fluctuate. Specifically, a cyclical boom in the developed countries strengthens demand for basic materials, especially metals, and thus leads to big increases in the value of primary product exports. Conversely, world recession leads to a sharp fall in the value of exports of primary products, and therefore in the export receipts of the typical developing country.

Thus shocks to either demand or supply can create fluctuations in the receipts of primary-product exporting countries. The aggregate analysis presented above might suggest that the demand shocks would produce the more violent fluctuations, inasmuch as a supply shock involves an increase (decrease) in quantity to at least partially compensate the fall (rise) in price. However, that compensation applies only to the particular country that experiences the supply shock. For example, when frosts in the south of Brazil reduce the world coffee crop and so raise the price of coffee, both Brazil and the aggregate of all coffee exporters experience a fall in quantity that, at least in part, compensates the rise in price. But the other sixty-odd coffee-exporting countries do not: they enjoy a rise in price and, to the extent that their supply is elastic at all, a *rise* in quantity, just as under a demand shock. Thus a finding that fluctuations in the prices of primary commodities are principally the result of supply shocks rather than of demand shocks does not necessarily go very far toward laying to rest the fears of the consequences of instability in commodity prices.

There is, of course, an important influence in many primary product markets that has not yet been mentioned: speculation. With any storable commodity, as with currencies (see chap. 10.4), one should expect to find people attempting to profit by buying when the product is relatively cheap and selling when it is dear. To the extent that they succeed, they will perform the social service of financing a carryover of stocks from periods of plenty to those of scarcity, in the process diminishing the fluctuations in price that provide the incentive to speculate.

Speculation does indeed occur in the markets for the storable primary commodities. Nevertheless, judging by the price swings that continue to occur, it is not very successful. There is no reason to give credence to populist beliefs that speculators try to *amplify* price movements—it requires either a monopolistic ability to corner the market or some market pathology[2] to make money that way. But, equally, the evidence hardly dictates awe at the collective omniscience of the speculators.

Not unnaturally, those whose foreign exchange receipts depend heavily on sales of a few primary commodities with volatile prices have tended to regard the present organization of the primary product markets as unsatisfactory. There have in fact been a number of attempts to manage markets with a view to reducing the volatility of prices and income. These have taken two general forms: limitations on supply and the establishment of buffer stocks.

Supply limitations are difficult to administer. The same reasons that make supply curves inelastic serve to give an incentive to individual suppliers (whether peasants, companies, or countries) to avoid their share in the necessary total cutback in supply. Since a limitation on supply in weak periods does nothing to raise supply in periods of strong demand, the average rate of return rises and attracts new entrants, further compounding the difficulty of limiting supply. The leading historical example of supply limitation was that unilaterally practiced by Brazil in the 1930s, when she had a near-monopoly of the supply of coffee. Burning coffee made sense from a national if not from a cosmopolitan Pareto standpoint—at least in the short run. But new entrants flooded in, and in the long run Brazil lost her near monopoly.

The alternative is to establish a buffer stock, which is an attempt to do through official channels what the private speculators have failed to do satisfactorily: to buy when the price is low and sell when it is high to reduce the swings in prices. Figure 13–2 illustrates the principle. Given that you know (at least approximately) the average position of the demand and supply curves over the long run and can therefore estimate the average equilibrium price p_e, you set a ceiling price above that level and a floor price below. If the supply curve shifts right and the demand curve shifts left to the point where the price falls to the floor, the buffer stock comes in as residual buyer to prevent any further price decline. Conversely, a combination of a positive demand shock and/or negative supply shock such as to threaten to raise the price above the ceiling leads the buffer stock to act as residual seller. Price is therefore constrained to the range between the floor and ceiling, with a reduction in the fluctuations in export receipts.

2. Such a pathology is just conceivable in the foreign exchange market, due to the lags that provide the foundation for the J-curve, as I once showed ("Another Case of Profitable Destabilising Speculation," *Journal of International Economics,* February 1973). But no one has yet provided a plausible rationale for supposing there could be a comparable pathology in the commodity markets.

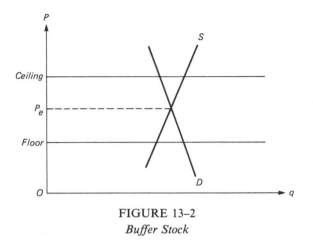

FIGURE 13–2
Buffer Stock

Buffer stocks have functioned off and on for several commodities since the 1920s, most especially for tin and cocoa. Sometimes they have operated as intended, for a while. But sooner or later they have usually either run out of their commodity, at which point the price has shot above the ceiling, or run out of money, at which point the price has dropped through the floor. One could always avoid the latter problem by giving the buffer stock manager more money, but there is a point at which those putting up the money (especially when these are the consumer nations) wonder whether they are making a sensible investment. A buffer stock which delayed the initiation of adjustment in response to a fall in the equilibrium price by holding prices artificially high for a while could in the end magnify the adjustment problem for the producers as well. The fact is that a successful buffer stock needs much the same forecasting abilities as a successful speculator in the private sector, and the basic problem is simply that the world is not that forecastable. Many economists nevertheless intuitively feel that it must be possible to do better than in the past, but even a sympathizer has to admit that at the present time this conviction seems to be sustained more by hope than by evidence.

13.5 Petroleum

The most important commodity entering world trade is crude oil. Petroleum, together with its manufactured derivatives, accounted for about 25 percent of the value of world trade, or about 5 percent of GWP, in the period 1980 to 1981.

From the time that the oil trade started, around the turn of the century, until the early 1970s, the trade in oil was conducted overwhelmingly on an intracompany basis. With the exception of the United States, which had its own oil companies, the countries where major oil discoveries were made lacked the technology necessary to exploit them. They therefore granted exploration and production rights to one of the major oil companies—the Seven Sisters, as the seven principal oil multinationals[3] are known. The company produced (normally in a very enclave-economy way, with minimal impact on the rest of the local economy), transported, refined, distributed, and sold petroleum products in the consuming countries. Marginal (though increasing) quantities of oil were sold by one oil major to another or to the independent refiners that began to emerge, but the typical pattern was one in which the first and only market transaction that petroleum experienced was at the gasoline pump.

Given the enclave-economy production pattern, the main impact of the oil industry on the economies of the exporting countries stemmed from the royalties received by their governments. Although these were rather modest, they were still sufficient to make the low-population oil exporters the aristocrats of the developing world. Their governments became unhappy, however, when competition between the Seven Sisters led to a fall in the price of crude oil and therefore in their royalty receipts, as happened in the late 1950s. The main oil exporters decided to form a producers' association to prevent further erosion of their receipts, and in 1961 the Organization of Petroleum Exporting Countries (OPEC) came into being. Currently, and for some years past, OPEC has had thirteen members: Algeria, Ecuador, Gabon, Indonesia, Iraq, Iran, Kuwait, Libya, Nigeria, Qatar, Saudi Arabia, the United Arab Emirates, and Venezuela.

For the first decade of its existence, no one except specialists had heard of OPEC. It succeeded in the initial aim of preventing further erosion in royalties. Although the oil price continued to edge down even in nominal terms through most of the 1960s, the oil companies agreed to pay royalties on the basis of a fictional posted price rather than on the price they were using in intracompany transactions. The low and declining real price of oil energy led to a rapid growth in demand which the oil companies succeeded in satisfying with a vast program of exploration and development. The world became increasingly dependent on oil and, in particular, on Arab oil. "Expert analysts" happily extrapolated these trends into the future, and plans for economic growth were accordingly based on the assumption of the continued availability of cheap energy. By the early 1970s the producing

3. Exxon, Gulf, Mobil, Standard Oil of California, and Texaco of the United States, Royal Dutch Shell of the Netherlands and the United Kingdom, and British Petroleum of the United Kingdom.

countries were already nationalizing the activities of the oil companies in their territory, but these were regarded as problems for the oil companies rather than for the oil-importing countries.

This fool's paradise came to an abrupt end following the Egyptian-Israeli war of 1973. To pressure the West to lean on Israel following the fighting, the Arab oil exporters decreed a cutback in oil exports. OPEC took advantage of the prospective supply shortage to quadruple the price of oil within three months. Milton Friedman had the courage of his longstanding conviction, that all markets could be analyzed as though they were perfectly competitive, to proclaim that once the partial Arab oil embargo had ended, the OPEC cartel would break up and the price of oil would fall back to its previous level. His convictions notwithstanding, the real price of oil remained fairly steady until 1979 (except for some erosion in 1977) and then took another upward bound.

The global macroeconomic consequences of the two increases in oil prices are analyzed in chapter 17.4. Our purpose here is to comment on the nature of the oil market, which has changed radically since the days when the Seven Sisters traded oil in intracompany transactions. The process of nationalization was quickly completed following the act of OPEC self-assertion in 1973. Since then, oil has been produced by companies owned by the producing countries; these companies contract foreign technicians and technical services as necessary, including those of the old oil majors. It is sold by the producers in major part under contract to the oil companies of the importing countries, who are nowadays much less dominated by the seven majors. An increasing though still minor proportion of oil is sold on a competitive flexprice market, located in Rotterdam.

There are three stories about the correct way to characterize the post-1974 oil market. A first is to picture it as a cartelized market. According to this view, which has been the dominant one in the oil-importing countries, the competitive price is more or less that which prevailed (in real terms) up to 1973. The fact that the real price has been much higher since then is attributable to the success of OPEC in organizing the producers into a cartel that holds the price above the competitive level and persuades producers to supply less than they would choose to on the basis of calculations of nationally optimal supply levels, so as to sustain the cartelized price.

A second version treats the oil price as being set on the basis of calculations of intertemporal optimization by the holders of an exhaustible resource. A basic theorem about the pricing of an exhaustible resource says that its price should rise over time at a rate equal to the rate of interest, so as to make holding the resource in the ground as attractive an investment as any other. The *height* of the price path should be such as to ration out the supply of the resource over time, avoiding both unduly rapid depletion, which would leave the world short of an essential resource before a satisfactory substitute was developed, and unduly slow use, which would delay development in the short run to an extent that outweighs greater availability of the resource in the more distant future. Naturally, the oil exporters tend to take this view of the oil market, arguing that the pre-1973 price was unduly low and therefore induced wastefully rapid depletion. According to this point of view, the question that demands explanation is not so much why the oil price was so high after 1974, but why it was so low before. One suggested answer is that the oil companies that previously controlled the oil supply realized they would be nationalized before long and therefore lacked the incentive that property rights bring to avoid unduly rapid depletion. Another possible reason is simply that no one realized the extent of potential monopoly power.

The third story about the oil market argues that the increase in the oil price could be maintained because the supply curve of oil is backward bending. Prior to 1973, the producing countries had to pump all the oil they could in order to earn enough cash to finance the imports they wished to buy. After the price rise, however, they were able to satisfy all their import needs and still have cash left over. Rather than invest it all in the paper assets issued by the importing countries, it made sense to invest some in larger stocks of oil in the ground—that is, to reduce the supply they placed on the world market. Adherents of this story point to the fact that in the 1979–80 oil price increase it was the price on the Rotterdam free market that *led* the rise, with OPEC raising its price every few months toward the free-market level. This is hardly consistent with the story of a cartelized market, since a cartel typically dictates a price rise and then spends its time policing those of its members who cheat by offering discounts.

It is probably too simple to imagine that any single one of these stories adequately characterizes the oil market. There are surely elements of truth in both the second and third models. Whether there is also truth in the cartel story or whether that is important mainly in understanding North-South diplomacy rather than the functioning of the oil market is being tested for the first time as this book goes to press.

13.6 Summary

Trade in industrial products has been substantially liberalized in the postwar period under the twin influences of GATT and a series of trading blocs and by the mid 1970s was probably freer than at any time in history. This generally impressive record has been marred more recently by the new protectionism, a series of restrictions on those exports of the NICs that have had particular success and threatened the survival of the competing industries in the old industrial countries. The NICs have succeeded to a remarkable degree in circumventing these restrictions through export diversification, assisted in a minor way by the GSP.

Trade in primary products is generally conducted on the basis of prices set in flexprice commodity markets. Because demand and supply are generally price inelastic, the incomes of primary producers tend to be volatile. Neither private speculation nor intergovernmental buffer stocks have an impressive record of reducing this instability.

Trade in petroleum was for many years conducted as intracompany trade by the oil multinationals, but since the early 1970s the producing ends of the companies have been nationalized by the host countries. There is not yet a consensus as to whether the world oil market is best viewed as cartelized, as dominated by rational intertemporal optimization by the producers, or as characterized by a backward-bending supply curve.

13.7 Bibliography

A detailed though now somewhat dated discussion of the functioning of GATT is contained in K. W. Dam, *The GATT: Law and International Organization* (Chicago: University of Chicago Press, 1970). The GATT *Annual Report* is worth consulting to keep up to date with developments. A factual account of all the existing international economic organizations is contained in M. A. G. van Meerhaeghe, *A Handbook of International Economic Institutions* (The Hague: Martinus Nijhoff Publishers, 1980). GATT is covered in chapter 3, while commodity agreements are covered in chapter 4, COMECON in chapter 7, the European Communities in chapter 8, EFTA in chapter 9, and the smaller regional integration arrangements in Part 4 of the Introduction.

A useful series of papers on the EEC, including a review of attempts to measure its impact on trade, can be found in B. Balassa, ed., *European Economic Integration* (Amsterdam: North-Holland, 1975). A painstaking attempt to evaluate the trade impact of EFTA was made by the EFTA Secretariat, *The Effects of EFTA on the Economies of Member States* (Geneva: EFTA, 1969).

The most comprehensive investigation of trade integration among developing countries relates to the Central American Common Market: W. R. Cline and E. Delgado, *Economic Integration in Central America* (Washington, D.C.: The Brookings Institution, 1978). For an overview of Latin American experience with trade integration, see W. R. Cline, "El interés de América Latina en la integración económica," *Integración latinoamericana,* Oct. 1981. On ASEAN, see J. Wong, *ASEAN Economies in Perspective* (London: Macmillan, 1979). A calculation of the potential gains from economic integration in West Africa is to be found in S. R. Pearson and W. D. Ingram, "Economies of Scale, Domestic Divergences, and Potential Gains from Economic Integration in Ghana and the Ivory Coast," *Journal of Development Economics,* Oct. 1980.

There is a vast though scattered literature on instability in the export earnings of primary producers and international commodity agreements. A useful review of the econometrics of the topic can be found in F. G. Adams and J. R. Behrman, *Econometric Modeling of World Commodity Prices* (Lexington, Mass.: D. C. Heath, 1978). See also Behrman's chapter in W. R. Cline, ed., *Policy Alternatives for a New International Economic Order: An Economic Analysis* (New York: Praeger, 1979). An important pioneering study of commodity price stabilization is D. M. G. Newberry and J. E. Stiglitz, *The Theory of Commodity Price Stabilization* (Oxford: Oxford University Press, 1981).

14

World Capital Market

THERE ARE two polar idealizations of how a world capital market might function. One involves a centralized international market in which participants from the various national markets place their excess funds or relieve their cash shortages by borrowing. The other involves the series of individual national markets being linked together through the residents of one country participating in the markets of other countries, by lending or borrowing. From the point of view of the real effects of capital flows (see chap. 6) or their payments implications (see chap. 9), it makes little difference which of these institutional forms the international capital market takes. But from the point of view of understanding the functioning of the market, it is useful to start off by recognizing this distinction.

In reality the world capital market contains important elements of both forms. The Euromarkets, alternatively referred to as the offshore markets, are not completely centralized, but they nevertheless approximate the first form, inasmuch as they consist of an international meeting place for the participants from different national markets. Parallel to these, there exist a number of ways in which the residents of one country can deal in the financial markets of other countries—through overseas bank branches, through bond flotations in foreign markets, through the purchase of equities or bonds in foreign markets, through the issue of export credits, through shifting bank deposits (especially through the accounts of multinationals), and so on.

Another important distinction is whether capital moves through the public or the private sector. The critical criterion in distinguishing between the two relates to the identity of the *lender* rather than the borrower; a large part of what are normally classified as private international capital movements involve loans made to public-sector borrowers. What are considered public-sector international capital movements involve aid given, or loaned, by governments, and loans made by the development finance institutions (like the World Bank).

14.1 Eurocurrency Markets

About 70 percent of all Eurocurrency deposits are denominated in dollars. Next in importance come the deutsche mark (DM) and the Swiss franc, followed by the Japanese yen, the pound sterling, the French franc, the Dutch guilder, the Belgian franc, the Italian lire, the IMF's SDR (see chap. 15.5), and perhaps small quantities of some other currencies as well. It will be convenient to speak of Eurodollars in the analysis that follows, but an equivalent analysis can be performed for any of the other currencies with an active Euromarket.

A Eurodollar deposit is simply a bank deposit denominated in dollars on the books of a bank outside the political jurisdiction of the country that issues dollars, namely the United States. They are called Eurodollars because the first banks to accept such deposits were located in Europe and that is still where the bulk of the market is. London remains the leading center, with about a third of all deposits, but its dominance is declining. Other important European centers are Amsterdam, Brussels, Frankfurt, Luxembourg, Milan, Paris, and Zurich. The market has, however, extended to the Middle East, Asia, and the Caribbean. The main center in the Middle East used to be Beirut, but the Lebanese civil war and competition from the Persian Gulf has now led to Bahrain becoming preeminent. The Asiadollar market is centered in Singapore, with Hong Kong also important. The main Caribbean centers are the Bahamas, Barbados, Bermuda, Panama, Cayman Islands, and the Virgin Islands.

Eurodollar deposits are time deposits, not demand deposits. Their term may be very short—a few days, or even overnight—but it is not possible to withdraw on demand or to use them as a medium of circulation to write cheques. Accordingly, it is appropriate to exclude Eurodollars from narrow measures of the money supply (M_1-type). Typically terms are for a month or less, three months, or six months, which suggests that in principle Eurodollar deposits should be included in wide (M_3-type) measures of the world money supply.

Banks that accept Eurodollar deposits typically use those funds in order to extend loans, which are also denominated in dollars, and hence are referred to as Eurodollar loans. Borrowers normally wish for loans with maturities longer than the few months for which lenders are prepared to deposit their funds. The banks responded to this inconsistency between the preferred maturities on the two sides of their balance sheets by inventing the *rollover loan* with a *floating interest rate*. A borrower receives what is in form a six-month credit, but with a guarantee that it will be renewed—rolled over—at the end of that period, and at the end of every subsequent six months for the de facto life of the loan, which is anything up to eight years and may on occasion range up to ten or twelve years. Each six months the interest rate is adjusted, according to a formula, in order to keep it in line with the market interest rates that the bank is having to pay on its deposits. In this way the risks of maturity transformation—as the normally risky process of borrowing short to lend long is known—are kept down to what the market practitioners claim is a safe level.

The normal formula for a floating interest rate is:

$$\text{Interest charge} = LIBOR + \text{spread.}$$

LIBOR stands for the London interbank offer rate. This signifies the rate that the Eurodollar banks charge on the loans that they extend to one another—a large proportion of the deposits placed in the market are shuffled around between the banks, before coming into the hands of a bank that needs the funds to extend a loan to a final borrower. LIBOR is determined competitively day by day, as the banks borrow or lend in order to balance their books without carrying excess liquidity. Banks normally aim to pay something less than LIBOR on the deposits they take from non-banks. The LIBOR element of the interest charged on a rollover loan for a six-month period is typically the average value of LIBOR over the month preceding renewal: this means that in a period of rising interest rates a bank may have to pay more than it receives for a while, but the danger of losing out seriously is minimal.

The spread is a charge specific to each loan. It is set at the time the loan is granted. It covers the administrative costs of the bank, as well as its gross profits, including compensation for the risk inherent in lending. Banks' perception of risk is, in fact, a principal determinant of the spread charged. Risk can be broken down into two elements: (1) country risk—the risk that borrowers from a particular country will have to interrupt debt-service payments because of a government decision, usually motivated by balance-of-payments problems; and (2) borrower risk—the risk of bankruptcy of the

317

borrower. Since the Euromarket usually lends only to blue-chip borrowers, country risk is in practice the dominant element in determining whether the spread is a fraction of 1 percent or over 2 percent.

Depositors in the Euromarkets consist of commercial banks that have more cash than they can advantageously deploy in their domestic markets, central banks (though the central banks of the leading financial powers in the Group of Ten[1] long ago accepted a self-denying ordinance to not increase their deposits), other government units, multinational corporations, and large national companies or even wealthy individuals from countries with liberal exchange control regulations. Geographically, depositors are very widely spread, with about 50 percent of deposits coming from Western Europe and with OPEC also much overrepresented in proportion to its weight in the world economy. However, there are also depositors from the other areas, including the developing countries and the Communist countries. The latter are reputed to have played a crucial role in the creation of the Eurodollar market in the late 1950s, when the Soviet Union and other East European countries were anxious to hold dollar deposits but also anxious to avoid holding them in the United States where they would have been vulnerable to freezing by the United States government. Friendly London bankers resolved the problem, by accepting dollar deposits in London banks, and the Eurodollar market has never looked back.

Borrowers in the Euromarkets consist of commercial banks that want to increase their domestic lending (see the Frenkel model in chap. 9.4); occasionally governments; much more often, state enterprises; multinationals; and large private companies of individual countries. Geographically, borrowers are also widely spread, with Western Europe again accounting for about half the market. The middle-income developing countries and the Communist countries are heavy net borrowers, while OPEC and Switzerland are the heavy net lenders. OPEC uses the Euromarkets to recycle a substantial part of the oil surplus (see chap. 17.4), while Swiss banks use it to recycle a substantial part of the funk money placed in anonymous bank accounts from who-knows-where.

Eurobanks normally hold small working balances with New York banks. These are used for making payments to the bank's customers when someone who has received a loan wishes to draw it down or when someone whose deposit has matured wishes to call it. These working balances are normally a very small proportion of total deposits, perhaps 1 percent or 2 percent. This observation gave rise to a debate about whether or not there was a

1. The members of the Group of Ten are Belgium, Canada, France, Germany, Italy, Japan, the Netherlands, Sweden, the United Kingdom and the United States. Switzerland is an honorary member. See chap. 15.4.

Eurodollar multiplier at work whose operation could explain the rapid growth of the Eurodollar market through the 1960s and 1970s.

One school of thought argued, by analogy with domestic monetary theory, that, if working balances were only 2 percent of Eurodeposits, there must be a money multiplier of 50.[2] However, it was soon pointed out that the traditional formula applies to a *closed* banking system, in which it can be assumed that every recipient of a loan and everyone who receives payments from him will redeposit the proceeds of the loan in a bank that is a part of the system. This certainly does not describe the Eurodollar system. A few recipients of loans may redeposit their receipts in Eurobanks or pay multinational corporations who deposit there, but in general a recipient of a Eurodollar loan uses the funds to switch into his domestic currency, since this is what he normally needs in order to make payments. Those funds will then get fed back into the Euromarket only to the extent that the central bank of the country of the borrower chooses to deploy its extra reserves in the Euromarket rather than elsewhere. In other words, there is a very high leakage of funds from the Euromarket—and such leakages form a *second* element that enters the money multiplier formula. In fact, with a redeposit ratio α, the money multiplier formula becomes[3] $1/[1 - \alpha(1 - \phi)]$, which is $1/\phi$ for the closed monetary system where $\alpha = 1$, but falls to unity for a completely open monetary system where $\alpha = 0$. The general view nowadays is that leakages from the Euromarkets are sufficiently high to ensure that the multiplier is not much above unity, and also that it is variable as a result of instability in the size of the leakage.

A multiplier equal to 1 implies that any expansion in the size of the market occurs only because someone decides to switch more funds to hold there, rather than because of the internal dynamics of the market itself. It is a fact, illustrated in table 14–1, that the Eurocurrency market has grown very rapidly ever since its inception in the late 1950s; today the total net[4] size of the market is approximately 12 percent of the value of the money supply[5] of the industrial countries. If this rapid growth cannot be explained by a multiplier process, the question arises as to how it can be explained.

2. Remember the money multiplier formula introduced in chap. 7.5, $k = 1/\varphi$, where φ is the reserve ratio of the commercial banking system.

3. Proof. Consider an initial deposit B_0, which initially expands the monetary base by that amount. The bank receiving the deposit then increases its loans by $(1-\varphi)B_0$, which leads to a secondary expansion of deposits of $\alpha(1-\varphi)B_0$. Banks then loan $\alpha(1-\varphi)^2 B_0$, which leads to a tertiary rise in deposits of $\alpha^2(1-\varphi)^2 B_0$; etc. Summing the geometric series, the final increase in deposits is $[1/(1-\alpha(1-\varphi))]B_0$.

4. The "net" size refers to the netting out of interbank transactions; when Chase London receives a $100 million deposit which it lends to the Luxembourg branch of Deutsche Bank, which lends it to ENI, that adds only $100 million to the size of the Eurodollar market.

5. On a wide concept of the money supply, covering the IMF's measures of money and quasi-money, plus Eurodeposits.

TABLE 14–1

*Estimated Net Size of the Eurocurrency
Market
(end of year, in billions of dollars)*

1964	9
1967	18
1970	57
1973	132
1976	247
1979	475

SOURCE: Bank for International Settlements,
Annual Report, various years.

Why should there have been a continuing shift of portfolio preferences toward holding an ever-larger proportion of liquid assets in the Euromarkets, over a period of more than twenty years?

Various answers have been given to this question. In the early years, potential users were discovering the market for the first time, and so it was natural that there should be a portfolio shift as the attractions of the market became more widely known. These attractions include such factors as: the convenience of being able to hold short-term dollar deposits in a bank in the same continent, and especially the same time zone, as one's business; the freedom of the market from bank regulations, which enables the banks to offer relatively more attractive interest rates since they do not need to tie up a part of their portfolio in holding noninterest earning reserves; the absence of tax withholding on interest income; and the freedom from fears of freezing and of capital controls by the United States authorities. From 1963 to 1974, another factor promoting the expansion of the Eurocurrency market was the attempt of the United States to cure its balance of payments deficit through a program restricting capital outflows United States banks were (with certain exceptions) forbidden to lend abroad from their domestic branches. This tended to raise interest rates abroad, including in the Euromarkets, relative to those in the United States. But foreign corporations (in particular) were not prohibited from switching their dollar deposits from United States banks to Eurobanks, which they naturally did to take advantage of the higher interest rates available there. ("Money is fungible," as critics of the United States capital controls used to say.)

After 1974, a new factor came into play. Some of the wealth-owners who had already decided to hold a substantial part of their portfolio in Eurodeposits were the central banks of OPEC countries. With the sudden emergence of a large OPEC current-account surplus in 1974, the financial wealth of these countries grew far more rapidly than before; the redistribution of wealth, with given portfolio preferences on the part of each holder, led to an expansion of the Euromarket. Indeed, the same factor has probably been operating, if in a less graphic way, ever since the 1950s: that part of the world economy that is likely to think of placing a part of its liquid assets in the Euromarkets—notably the multinationals but also the more entrepreneurial central banks (typically of OPEC and NIC countries)—has been expanding relative to the rest.

In fact, the Euromarkets played a key role in recycling the oil surplus after 1974. An example of how this recycling occurs can help one understand the operation of the Euromarkets. Consider the case of a Brazilian oil deficit with Iraq. A particularly simple case would occur if Brazil settled its debt by drawing down its holdings of United States Treasury bills to get the dollars to write a check on a New York bank; if Brazil paid this check to Iraq, which then deposited it in the Euromarket; if the Eurobank made a loan to a Brazilian state enterprise, which then converted its borrowing into cruzeiros with the Brazilian central bank; which could then complete the circle by using its dollar receipts to buy United States Treasury bills. Obviously one does not expect that the circle will usually be closed in this way, but the example serves to illustrate the important principles. In particular, the Euromarket creates reserves (for Iraq) and acts as a financial intermediary for passing Iraq's savings on to Brazil, which can thus finance its current-account deficit without losing reserves and avoid the cutback in investment or consumption that would otherwise be necessary.

There has been much debate about whether the Euromarkets pose a threat to financial stability. One fear is that the Euromarkets manufacture additional liquidity, outside of any national control, which may have inflationary consequences. We have already examined, and rejected, one theory that often underlies this view—namely, that there is a high Eurodollar multiplier. But even those who accept that the Eurodollar multiplier is little different from unity need to recognize that a switch of dollar deposits to the Euromarket will have a net expansionary impact on global liquidity, due to such factors as the absence of reserve requirements against Eurodollar deposits. The policy question is whether that effect is sufficiently important to justify an attempt to regulate the Euromarkets, for example, by imposing reserve requirements against Eurodeposits, or whether it can be ignored in the same way that the liquidity-creating potential of nonbank financial intermediaries is customarily ignored in the formation of national monetary policy.

The main fear is that the Euromarkets are vulnerable to a financial panic. Since the banks lend extensively among themselves, especially in the London interbank market, the worry is that default by an important borrower could trigger a chain of bank failures. In a national market, a central bank would step in to lend to a bank suffering liquidity difficulties or would even bail out a bank faced with insolvency, if this were judged advisable, and so prevent a default leading to a general collapse. But there *is* no central bank that takes a clear responsibility for administering the Euromarkets—in part because the central banks of the countries where the market is physically located fear that attempts by them to control the market would simply drive it away to other centers. However, countries have now tightened prudential supervision of the loans extended by their own banks, including their foreign branches, in an attempt to ensure that default by a single borrower could never threaten bank solvency. Moreover, the principal central banks have agreed in the course of their discussions at the Bank for International Settlements in Basel on the basis of a formula to determine which of them would be responsible for giving aid to the Euromarket as lender of last resort should that some day prove necessary. Most bankers seem convinced that these measures are sufficient to minimize the threat of collapse.

14.2 Other Private Markets

While the Euromarkets are the best-known part of the international capital market, they are not in fact the quantitatively dominant part: less than one-half of international bank lending is undertaken by the Eurobanks. Instead, for example, Citibank (New York) may make a loan—almost always expressed in dollars—directly to a foreign borrower, which may well be one of its own subsidiaries. In the latter case, the local branch of Citibank acquires additional funds with which it can expand its loan portfolio in the borrowing country, as analyzed in chapter 9.3. It is the initial foreign borrower—which in the example just mentioned is the local foreign branch of Citibank—that takes the exchange risk, for which it will normally expect to be compensated (as was hypothesized in the Frenkel model of chapter 9.3).

Under certain ideal circumstances it makes no difference at all whether a deposit is placed in a Eurobank or a United States bank. If the regulations applying to Euro- and United States banks were the same, if they both held their reserves at the Federal Reserve, and if the managers of the two sets of banks had identical behavior patterns, it would make absolutely no difference whether Iraq placed its newly acquired funds in a Eurodollar bank in London rather than in New York. In the latter event, the New York bank could just as easily extend a loan to Brazil as the Eurobank did in the example at the end of the last section.

Conversely, the process of intermediation will be affected if the various *ceteris paribus* assumptions made above are violated.

Differing Regulations. The most important way in which regulations differ between the United States market and the Euromarket is in respect to reserve requirements. There are no reserve requirements on Eurodeposits, whereas the Federal Reserve imposes a 3 percent reserve requirement against time deposits held in United States banks. This means that an Iraqi decision to hold deposits in New York rather than London would increase the demand for base money and reduce the sum available for lending and raise the interest rate that a bank lending to Brazil would charge.

Different Reserve Holdings. The major United States banks hold their working balances (as well as required reserves) at the Federal Reserve whereas Eurobanks hold their working balances at United States commercial banks. This provides a second reason why an Iraqi decision to place its deposits in New York rather than London would increase the demand for base money and exert a relatively contractionary effect on the global money supply.

Different Behavioral Patterns. It is a fact that the proportion of loans made to non-United States borrowers by Eurobanks is far higher than that for loans made by United States banks. For example, the latter have about 4 percent of their portfolio in loans to nonoil developing countries, as opposed to over 12 percent of the portfolio of Eurobanks. However, this in itself is not necessarily very important. It is surely true that California banks lend more of their portfolio to California farmers than do New York banks, but no one would conclude from that that a switch of deposits from California banks to New York banks would squeeze the borrowing ability of California farmers. The reason is that the United States capital market is so integrated that funds would be promptly arbitraged back from New York to California to permit the distribution of final loans to remain determined by considerations of economic efficiency. Similarly, a switch of Iraqi deposits from London to New York would not deprive Brazil of access to bank credit, even if New York bankers were entirely incapable of visualizing making loans to Brazil (which they are not), so long as there were no capital controls separating the United States market from the Eurodollar market. An incipient rise in the Eurodollar interest rate relative to the New York interest rate would encourage the funds to be arbitraged back to London for lending to Brazil. One may conclude that, given the current absence of capital controls by the United States, differences in lending patterns by particular groups of banks will not influence significantly the result of the intermediation process.

A second form in which national capital markets are interlinked involves the bond market. An international capital market dominated by bank lending is, in fact, a historically recent phenomenon. In the previous great age of international lending, prior to World War I, the dominant instrument was the bond. A company, typically a utility, or a government, would issue a fixed-interest bond denominated in the currency of the lender, and sell it in the lender's market. Local individuals (or companies, though institutions like pension funds were unimportant in those days) would buy the bonds, and the borrower would switch the cash into his national currency to finance investment or use it directly to pay foreign bills.

International capital flows through bond issues revived earlier than the expansion of international bank credits, though on a much smaller scale. A factor that has contributed to limiting the size of the bond market in recent years is uncertainty over future inflation. Any certain future rate of inflation can be allowed for by a corresponding increase in the nominal interest rate. But *uncertainty* of the future inflation rate creates a problem: an interest rate that would provide a minimal real return to the lender with 15 percent inflation would prove a crippling financial burden to the borrower if inflation turned out to be 5 percent. The bankers largely circumvented this difficulty by inventing the rollover loan with a floating interest rate. An equivalent technique in the bond market, the *floating rate note* whose interest yield is adjusted in line with market rates, has until now proved less popular, although its use is growing. Another apparent solution to the problem, the use of index-linked bonds, has also been ignored to date. Hence the bond market remains relatively small: net new international bond financing was about $29 billion in 1980, as against $165 billion of net new international bank lending. Moreover, the bond market is largely restricted to maturities no longer than those of bank credits, in contrast to the twenty or thirty years that were commonplace prior to 1914.

Capital mobility can also result from investors buying bonds in foreign markets, though this is not common. The issue of equity in a foreign market is also possible—and unusual. Most international flows of equity capital involve investors entering foreign markets. The increasing importance of institutional investors, for whom the transactions costs involved are acceptable, is tending to promote international flows of equity capital. The different risk pattern characteristic of equities issued in different countries provides a strong incentive for international diversification of equity portfolios.

Export credits involve bank loans either to exporters who then grant extended credit to their foreign customers or direct to the foreign importers.

Their distinctive characteristic is that the availability of the loan is conditional on purchase of goods in the country granting the credit and normally limited to the value of the exports involved. Exports of capital goods are typically financed by medium-term export credits of up to eight or ten years: indeed, it would be difficult to sell capital goods internationally without credit attached. Export credits were an important form of LDC capital import in the earlier postwar period, but they have now been dwarfed by regular bank credits. At times countries have competed for exports by offering low-interest export credits, but the OECD now sponsors an agreement among its members providing for minimum rates of interest on such loans.

The final form of capital mobility that merits mention is that of shifting bank deposits. Anyone—or, more relevantly, any company—with bank accounts in more than one currency can shift money from one account to another. Obviously this is used mainly for short-term speculative capital movements. Indeed, in the presence of exchange controls, most forms of capital mobility can be impeded, but it is difficult to prevent leads and lags —accelerated payment of bills denominated in a currency that is expected to rise in value and delays in the payment of bills denominated in a currency that is expected to fall in value. The companies in the best position to evade exchange controls through leading and lagging are the multinationals, who indeed can switch funds directly between their bank accounts in different currencies and within wide limits justify this by choosing which of the various trade credits between their branches are being settled.

There are, of course, other channels through which capital movements can and do occur: "money is fungible."

14.3 Aid and the Development Banks

Aid consists in the donation of financial or real resources by one country to another without the expectation of an equivalent payment in return. In fact, pure—or grant—aid involves a donation, for which nothing is expected. For other aid, the grant element is calculated as the excess of the sum donated over the present value of the repayment obligations, where that present value is calculated using a conventional discount rate, customarily 10 percent.

Aid provided by the United States through the Marshall Plan to Western Europe, in the sum of about 2.5 percent of the donor's GNP, played a vital role in securing European recovery from World War II after 1948. As the European Recovery Program achieved its objectives, in the 1950s, there was an international move to redirect the flow of aid to support the cause of development and to enlist the newly recovered rich nations of Europe—and subsequently Japan and Australia as well—as donors. The United Nations adopted targets for donor countries' aid: the most famous was that each donor was supposed to aim at a total net resource flow to the developing countries of at least 1 percent of GNP. Since virtually anything could be included in this total—export credits, direct investments, or loans on commercial terms—that target has in general been achieved (see table 14–2), but at the same time it does not really mean very much, since the bulk of what it includes is not really aid at all. The more serious target is that 0.7 percent of GNP should be denoted as official development assistance (ODA). The OECD Development Assistance Committee (DAC), which has tried to goad its members into living up to their responsibilities, further prescribed that ODA should have a grant element of at least 80 percent. That last target has been achieved in recent years, but the total level of ODA has fallen far short of the 0.7 percent target, as table 14–2 shows.

TABLE 14–2
The Aid Record

| Year | OECD (DAC members) | | OPEC |
	(Net resource flow)/GNP	*ODA/GNP*	*ODA/GNP*
1960	0.88	0.51	n.a.
1965	0.77	0.49	n.a.
1970	0.78	0.34	n.a.
1975	1.17	0.36	2.59
1980	1.04	0.37	1.36

SOURCE: World Bank, *World Development Report 1981* (New York: Oxford University Press, 1981), app. table 16; used by permission. Organization for Economic Cooperation and Development, *Development Assistance,* 1971, and *Development Assistance Efforts,* 1980.

In fact, the only OECD donor countries that have achieved the 0.7 percent target are Denmark, the Netherlands, Norway, and Sweden. The countries at the bottom of the ODA league table in 1980 were Italy (0.17 percent), Austria and Finland (0.22 percent), Switzerland (0.24 percent), and New Zealand and the United States (0.27 percent). The most generous donor countries nowadays are in fact not the traditional DAC countries at all, but rather certain of the OPEC members: countries like Kuwait, Qatar, and the United Arab Emirates have been donating over 3 percent, and at times over 10 percent of their GNP (which amounts to a far higher proportion still of their net national product, for reasons explained in chapter 6, note 3). There has recently been an endeavor, led by the World Bank, to redirect the flow of aid—of real, concessional aid—to the poorer countries, who have not in general developed the ability to attract capital on commercial terms from the market.

Aid is distributed both bilaterally and multilaterally. Bilateral aid is, as the name implies, a payment made directly by one government to another country—typically to the government of that country. It is frequently used as an instrument of foreign policy, so that the recipients tend to be those whom the donor wishes to promote, usually out of ideological or religious sympathy.

Multilateral aid is channeled through the development finance institutions (DFIs), of which the leading example is the World Bank. The International Bank for Reconstruction and Development (IBRD), to use its official name, was created as a sister institution to the IMF following the Bretton Woods conference of 1944, with the object of providing a flow of long-term finance to substitute for the then-vanished private capital market. Its resources proved inadequate to the task of playing a major role in postwar reconstruction, in which capacity it was overwhelmed by the Marshall Plan, but it emerged subsequently as a significant source of development finance. The Bank itself raises money by issuing bonds on commercial terms, and lends these funds to developing countries, so that the only element of aid provided is the Bank's ability to borrow on somewhat better terms than individual developing countries could—a possibility helped by the guarantee that the developed countries provide on the Bank's borrowings. However, in 1960 the Bank established an affiliate, the International Development Association (IDA), to provide highly concessional assistance (fifty-year loans with a zero interest rate and a substantial grace period) to the poorest countries. This is financed with funds specifically provided by the donor countries: negotiating IDA replenishments to keep IDA in business is a perennial diplomatic problem.

Since the funds provided by the World Bank and, even more, by IDA, are on concessional terms, there is, not surprisingly, a potential excess demand for such loans. As always, some rationing mechanism is needed to choke off the excess demand. In the case of the World Bank, this takes the form of limiting lending to the foreign-exchange component of approved projects.[6] There is really no compelling economic rationale for only provid-

6. It is true that in the late 1970s the Bank supplemented its traditional "project lending" with "structural adjustment lending" to provide general balance of payments support to countries that were willing to negotiate a package of policy reforms, but the former remains quantitatively dominant (some 90 percent of lending).

ing foreign exchange to finance particular projects nor for refusing to finance the local currency cost. After all, foreign borrowing is basically needed to provide additional real resources to sustain a higher level of investment overall, and it is entirely possible that the most efficient way of accomplishing that is to import more intermediate goods to produce more consumer goods to enable labor to be redeployed to an investment project with a zero component of imported capital goods. But insisting that only project loans are eligible has the administrative advantage of restricting demand to a part of the cost of those projects for which a serious economic case not only can be made but actually has been made, which requires much bureaucratic effort and thus provides a rationing mechanism. There is a second advantage to insisting on project lending: it requires the technocrats of the borrowing countries to keep up to date with the latest thought on project appraisal, as well as giving the World Bank's staff opportunities to undertake detailed studies of the borrowers' economies, and in these ways contributes to the Bank's educational role in the world.

There are other development finance institutions besides the World Bank: the regional development banks (the African Development Bank, the Asian Development Bank, and the Inter American Development Bank); the International Fund for Agricultural Development sponsored by the Food and Agriculture Organization of the United Nations; the Islamic Fund for Economic Development, the Kuwaiti Fund, and the Arab Fund. Most of these follow policies broadly modeled on those of the World Bank, in the sense that they seek to make project loans rather than to give general balance of payments finance.

14.4 An Evaluation

The underlying purpose of a capital market is to transfer funds from savers to investors, in a way that provides a mixture of assets that matches the preferences of the savers and allows investment to be undertaken at the points where it promises to yield the highest return. It is the latter aspect that is traditionally accorded prime importance in judging the efficiency of a capital market—the phrase "perfect capital mobility" is interpreted as referring to a situation in which capital flows so as to equate expected risk-adjusted rates of return in all uses. However, the role of capital mobility in reducing risk to savers, through diversification, is also important from a welfare point of view.

How adequately does the present international capital market serve these two welfare functions? The mere fact that it makes sense to pose this question at all marks an enormous shift from the early postwar period when capital flows were quite marginal and each country was effectively limited to the savings (and the assets) generated at home. Today one can indeed think in terms of a world capital market. Nevertheless, it remains an imperfectly integrated market, for three reasons.

The first of these is *exchange risk.* Even when there are no administrative obstacles to capital flows, someone has to accept an exchange risk when there is net lending by the residents of one currency area to those of another.[7] Given the stylized fact of risk aversion, increasing exchange exposure will need to be compensated by a higher expected rate of return. This means that, especially with flexible exchange rates, there will be scope for —and, indeed, a need for—differences between expected rates of return in different currency areas. The empirical evidence indicates that this is an important factor: capital mobility between different currencies is far from perfect.

The second reason for imperfect integration of the world capital market relates to *creditworthiness* of countries. Within a unified monetary system, a lender has to base his evaluation of creditworthiness—the risk that he may not get repaid—only on the prospects of the borrowing enterprise. With an international loan—and, especially, with a loan between currency areas, which is almost the same thing—there is a second consideration to be taken into account. This is the risk, called "sovereign risk," that the borrower's country will act in a way that prejudices repayment, for example, by imposing exchange control, by changing the exchange-control rules to limit remittances, or even by default. Normally such actions are prompted by balance of payments problems, which is why it is significant whether a loan is between currency areas. The fact of national sovereignty means that there is always some risk that the borrower's government may intervene to impede repayment in a manner inconsistent with the lender's laws. There is no question but that creditworthiness doubts are an important factor in restricting international capital mobility, especially in limiting the sums that can be borrowed by the poorer countries.

In fact, no outright debt repudiation of the form practiced by the Soviet Union after the First World War has occurred for many years. Similarly, debt moratoria of the type declared by many hard-pressed borrowers in the 1930s were absent until the Mexican crisis of August 1982. Debt defaults —formal declaration by the lending banks that they have not been paid their

---

7. A forward market permits the redistribution of exchange risk, but it cannot *eliminate* the risk involved in net lending between currency areas (see the appendix to Chap. 10).

due—have been restricted to Cuba in 1962 and Iran in 1979 (following the United States action in freezing Iranian assets). Instead, what has happened in debt crises is that debt arrears have piled up and new credit has evaporated, until finally countries have entered into negotiations to reschedule their debts. Official debt is normally dealt with first, by a group of creditor governments acting jointly in the so-called Paris Club. The Paris Club requires the debtor country to reach agreement on a high-conditionality program with the IMF. It then reschedules official debt, by stretching out maturities but not (in general) by giving concessional interest rates that would reduce the present value of the debt, while ensuring uniform treatment among the official creditors and insisting that other creditors not receive more favorable treatment. Those other creditors, in the form of the commercial banks, then seek to negotiate their own rescheduling, again insisting on uniform treatment among themselves, as well as avoiding postponement of payments of interest. Critics charge that these arrangements are unfair to borrowing countries, since the banks are almost automatically bailed out even when they have tempted countries into contracting excessive debt.

The third source of imperfections in the world capital market is actual *exchange controls.* Such controls can often be evaded where the stakes are very high, as they are when an imminent step devaluation is anticipated (see chap. 9, n. 2), but they are effective enough in impeding perfect capital mobility. These controls have now been substantially abolished by a number of the industrial countries, notably the United States, Germany, the United Kingdom, Switzerland, and Canada, as well as by a number of oil-exporting countries, notably the surplus states of the Persian Gulf. Other countries, like Japan and Chile, have significantly liberalized in recent years. Beyond that there is a gradation from the industrial countries that still maintain exchange controls, like Belgium, France, Italy, and the Scandinavians, through middle-income developing countries like Brazil, ASEAN, and Korea, to the poorer developing countries afraid that liberalization could only mean outflow, and the ideologically autarkic like Algeria, Libya, Tanzania, and the Communist states.

While the boundaries between the groups are not precise, it is useful to classify countries into three groups with respect to their relation to the world capital market. At the core are the group of countries without exchange controls, plus the Euromarkets. Capital mobility within this area is quite high, though nowhere near perfect, apparently mainly because of the existence of separate currencies and the consequential presence of exchange risk. Residents of these countries are able to reap the benefits of capital mobility both as investors, in supplementing domestic with foreign savings when interest rates are lower abroad, and as savers, through diversifying their portfolios and lending abroad when returns are higher there. The price paid for these advantages is a severe limitation on the ability to pursue a macroeconomic policy at variance with that in the rest of the world, or, at least, in the rest of the core area. Under fixed rates, a monetary policy inconsistent with that of the rest of the core area is quickly overwhelmed by reserve movements; under floating rates, by exchange-rate swings so sharp as to undermine price stability (when a country tries to expand more than the group) or to threaten deindustrialization (when it tries to expand less).

Beyond this core group, there are a large number of countries that participate actively in the world capital market in a more limited way, usually mainly as borrowers. They retain exchange controls, either in the belief that their withdrawal would prompt a large capital outflow or in the attempt to retain a measure of autonomy in conjunctural policy. However, the controls are operated in such a way as to permit a controlled measure of foreign borrowing; therefore, investors are able to enjoy the benefits of access to foreign savings. In contrast, savers are denied most of the chances to pursue higher returns abroad and to diversify (though they often endeavor to circumvent the restrictions through a black market). The quid pro quo is that these countries retain more independence in their conjunctural policies.

The third group consists of those countries that are at best marginal participants in the international capital market. These are most of the low-income countries, plus some of the Communist countries (not all— Poland is the best known example of a heavy borrower). They are not significant borrowers because they are not considered creditworthy. And they are not lenders (apart from deposits of official reserves) because their governments fear that their citizens would take the same view of their creditworthiness as foreign bankers do, and therefore the governments impose stringent exchange controls to prevent capital outflows. These are the countries that are almost entirely dependent on foreign aid and the loans of the DFIs to supplement their domestic savings.

14.5 Summary

The international capital market has come a long way since its reestablishment, mainly in the form of offshore banking known as the Euromarkets, in the 1950s. Real resources have been channeled in substantial quantities in the broad direction that economic logic would dictate, from the capital-abundant industrial countries and more recently the capital-surplus oil exporters, to the capital-poor developing countries and the capital-hungry primary producers like Canada and Australia. Nevertheless, it is possible to get too euphoric about these developments. It is very doubtful whether the flow to the middle-income developing countries, let alone to the low-income ones, is anywhere near as large as would be needed to equate expected marginal rates of return internationally. There may also be considerable unexploited scope for increasing the welfare of savers through greater international diversification. And, furthermore, it may be argued that the price for capital market integration, in the form of the loss of freedom over conjunctural policy, is substantial.

14.6 Bibliography

Two useful introductory works on the Euromarket are R. I. McKinnon, *The Eurocurrency Market,* Princeton Essays in International Finance No. 125 (1977), and G. W. McKenzie, *The Economics of the Euro-currency System* (London: Macmillan, 1976). A more comprehensive treatment of international banking is provided by B. J. Cohen (in collaboration with F. Basagni), *Banks and the Balance of Payments: Private Lending in the International Adjustment Process* (Montclair, N.J.: Allenheld Osmun, 1981). The most authoritative econometric study is R. J. Herring and R. C. Marston, *National Monetary Policies and International Financial Markets* (Amsterdam: North-Holland, 1977).

For factual material, see the Bank for International Settlements quarterly and annual reports (especially on the Euromarkets), and the World Bank's annual *World Development Report* and its quarterly *World Debt Tables.* A review of the LDC debt position as of 1981 can be found in B. Nowzad, R. C. Williams, et al., *External Indebtedness of Developing Countries* (Washington, D.C.: International Monetary Fund, 1981). For a discussion of LDC (specifically, Latin American) participation in the world capital market, see R. Ffrench-Davis, ed., *External Financial Relations and their Impact on the Latin American Economies* (London: Macmillan, forthcoming).

15

International Monetary Arrangements

A TRADITIONAL classification distinguishes three functions of money: providing a unit of account, medium of exchange, and store of value. All three roles contribute toward eliminating the inconvenience of barter and permitting the division of labor that Adam Smith first recognized as the basis of a modern economy. Indeed, the phrase "monetized sector" is virtually a synonym for "modern economy." Without a monetary unit to provide a common basis in which to express values, a monetary medium against which exchanges can be made, and a medium that can be held to permit desynchronization of sales and purchases, the division of labor simply could not be carried very far.

International monetary arrangements have a similar purpose at the international level. They enable transactions between the residents of different countries to be carried out without the need to ensure that the accounts between countries are always, continuously, and bilaterally balanced. One can distinguish three requirements that must be satisfied in one way or another for that to be possible. First, there must be an *exchange-rate regime* which determines the rate of exchange at which one money is exchanged for another, so as to permit monetary (rather than barter) international transactions. Second, there must be a *reserve regime* defining the assets that will be transferred in settlement of residual surpluses or deficits when transactions are unbalanced. Third, while it is inherent in the nature of money that agents can escape from the need to maintain continuous and and bilateral balance, it would ruin the incentives to microeconomic efficiency if they could escape from the need to maintain long-run and overall (multilateral) balance. That implies that an international monetary regime also involves *adjustment obligations,* covering both its requirements as to when imbalances should be adjusted rather than financed and who is to take what actions when adjustment is called for.

Naturally an evaluation, as well as a description, of those arrangements is of interest. A first test of a monetary system concerns its efficiency in facilitating microeconomic transactions. Does it permit financing all Pareto-improving sets of transactions? Does its operation cost more than is necessary? Does it intermediate efficiently between borrowers and lenders? Does it avoid exposing transactors to unnecessary risks?

The second test of a monetary system involves its compatibility with macroeconomic stability. Microeconomic efficiency advantages of abandoning barter in favor of a monetary economy are bought at a cost, which is the possibility of macroeconomic instability. For example, Say's Law holds in a barter economy, so that there cannot be Keynesian unemployment. Equally, there is no such thing as inflation in a barter economy. But both unemployment and inflation are possible in a monetary economy as a result of individual decisions not summing to a total consistent with the macroeconomic constraints. The extent to which a monetary system accommodates such inconsistency and thus permits macroeconomic malfunctioning is self-evidently important.

It is the same with international money: the cost of the convenience of transactions that are unbalanced (in the short run) is the danger that the set of national policies will no longer add up to consistency with a global constraint. Individual countries can escape from the need for income to equal absorption by running current-account imbalances, but the world cannot. Individual countries can all try to gain reserves, but, if the supply of reserves is not elastic, they cannot all succeed. Individual countries may be able to cut unemployment and inflation simultaneously by tightening monetary policy and loosening fiscal policy and so engineering an appreciation of their currency, but this is not an option for the world as a whole.

This issue has arisen in various guises and received various names in the literature on international monetary economics. It has been called the n-1 problem, on the ground that in a system with n countries or exchange rates or balances of payments, there are only n-1 degrees of freedom. Once n-1 countries have adopted policies to determine their payments position, for example, the payments outcome of the nth country is determined as a residual, and any attempt by that nth country to seek a different outcome would threaten to generate conflict. It has also been called the *redundancy* problem, on the ground that the nth country's policy instrument is redundant—a terminology that denies the possibility that the nth country will not be content to accept the residual outcome and that international conflict will ensue as a consequence. Perhaps the best term is that of Benjamin Cohen (b. 1937), who calls it the *consistency* problem.

15.1 The Pre–1914 Gold Standard

Since every country on the gold standard defined its currency in terms of gold, the ratios between each pair of currencies—exchange rates—were essentially fixed. The only scope for variations arose from the costs of shipping gold between central banks, which allowed rates to fluctuate within what were known as the "gold points."

A country on the gold standard allowed its residents to ship gold abroad to finance a payments deficit, and the central bank stood ready to buy or sell gold with its currency. Thus gold served as the principal reserve asset. In the later years of the system, some countries began holding reserves in the form of currency (mainly sterling).

The gold-standard rules of the game specified adjustment obligations and provided an adjustment mechanism. Loss of gold signified an obligation to accept monetary contraction, and a gain of gold implied an obligation to expand. These policies did promote adjustment, as analyzed in chapters 8.1, 8.6, and 9.4—if not always through the price-specie-flow mechanism as conceived by David Hume, then through some combination of interest-rate effects on capital flows, of Ohlin's income effects, and of Triffin's terms-of-trade effects on the periphery (see chap. 8.1).

In retrospect, the operation of the gold standard was idealized as a golden age in international monetary relations. The system certainly promoted microeconomic efficiency: trade could be financed without unnecessary restrictions or expense and there was a thriving international capital market intermediating funds mainly from British and French savers to investors in the lands of recent settlement and elsewhere. It has also been credited with solving the consistency problem. Gold provided a world monetary base whose redistribution among countries would cause some to expand and others to contract without imposing any net pressure for world inflation or deflation. Critics have pointed to the fact that financial panics occurred at irregular intervals even in the principal countries and that these panics usually brought sharp (though short-lived) recessions in their train. They have argued that current-account adjustment tended to operate by the wasteful method of high unemployment. Triffin argued that the system worked comparatively well for the center countries only because they were able to export a large part of the burden of adjustment, through inducing changes in their terms of trade, to the primary producers of the periphery. Golden ages are, perhaps, relative.

15.2 The Gold-Exchange Standard of the 1920s

Convertibility of their currencies into gold was suspended by all the belligerents except the United States during the First World War. Paper currencies were exchanged for one another on the basis of floating rates. All countries inflated, though some much more than others. Once the war was over, the dominant aim became that of reestablishing prewar normalcy, though Germany and several East European countries went through the traumatic experience of hyperinflation before dedicating themselves to the task of normalization.

In the monetary context, the normal was interpreted as the gold standard. There was, however, an obstacle to revival of the prewar gold standard: the shortage of gold that resulted from the wartime inflation, given the determination of the United States and the United Kingdom to maintain and to restore, respectively, their prewar gold pars.[1] A world economic conference held in Genoa in 1922 decided to solve this problem by two steps: encouraging nations to withdraw gold from circulation and recommending that countries other than the main financial centers hold their reserves in the form of gold-convertible currencies rather than gold itself. A system with the latter feature is known as a "gold-exchange standard." It came into being formally in 1925, when Britain reestablished the gold convertibility of the pound at its prewar par and most other independent countries soon followed, many holding a part of their reserves in currencies like sterling and the United States dollar.

The exchange-rate regime of the gold-exchange standard was in principle

1. A par, or par value, is the official central rate declared for a currency in terms of the system's unit of account, or numeraire. A parity is the ratio of two par values, the official central rate of one currency in terms of another.

336

the same as that of the gold standard, a system of fixed rates. However, there was a difference in that the world had just undergone the experience of seeing fixed rates abandoned under pressure. The insistence on returning to the old prewar pars may have been intended to promote confidence in the fixity of those rates, but—as often happens with the attempt to establish confidence by clutching at symbols instead of creating objective conditions that merit confidence—if so, it was counterproductive: the overvaluation of the pound sterling (in particular) bred nervousness as to how long Britain would be prepared to continue paying the price involved in keeping its exchange rate fixed. Confidence was further undermined when the French franc was stabilized at an undervalued level.

The reserve regime was now officially a gold-exchange standard rather than a pure gold standard, so that leading currencies, as well as gold, were held in reserves. In practice, the change from prewar days was not all that sharp, since some countries were already building up foreign-exchange reserves before the war while others proved reluctant to accept the recommendation of the Genoa conference that they run down their gold holdings.

Adjustment obligations were in principle unchanged. In practice, however, governments were in full retreat from the laissez faire philosophy that had allowed them to play by the rules of the game, and were embracing instead (with varying degrees of competence and enthusiasm) the commitment to internal balance. In particular, the Federal Reserve sterilized the flow of gold into the United States so as to avoid worsening United States inflation.

At the microeconomic level, the system worked well enough, except perhaps for the failure to resume large-scale capital flows toward the developing countries. However, the coherence that enabled the gold standard to function reasonably satisfactorily at the macroeconomic level had been destroyed. There were two problems. One was that there was no longer any assurance of adjustment with fixed exchange rates, both because of the tendency to abandon the rules of the game and also because of the growing downward inflexibility of wages. The second was the fact that any decision by central banks holding reserves in foreign exchange to exercise their right to convert them into gold would result in a net destruction of gross reserves (since the converting central bank simply changed its reserve composition, while the reserve center suffered a reserve loss), thus exerting asymmetrical contractionary pressure on the system. Add to that the recent reminder that exchange rates were not immutable and the financial incentive that any central bank holding foreign exchange has to shift out before a devaluation of its reserve currency occurs, and a crisis was inevitable sooner or later. It came as part of the Great Depression (which is indeed one of the factors that gave it the adjective "great"). The Wall Street crash of 1929 led to a virtual cessation of United States capital exports, which had previously been a major source of the money used by Germany to pay reparations. Reinforced by the cut in United States imports caused by the depression and the ultraprotectionist Smoot-Hawley Tariff Act of 1930, Germany stopped making reparations payments, which undermined the fragile structure of intra-European credit. The French had already cashed in their sterling deposits for gold, and others were restrained from following their example only by solemn British assurances of the immutability of sterling's link to gold. Then in 1931 came the crash of the Austrian bank Creditanstalt, and a wave of bank runs spread over Europe. In due course this caused a run on sterling and, on September 21, 1931, Britain "went off gold."

15.3 The Monetary Chaos of the 1930s

That decision ushered in the monetary anarchy of the 1930s. Countries coalesced into currency blocs: a sterling bloc based on Britain and the Commonwealth (except for Canada) plus a number of other countries with close historic and financial links to London; a dollar bloc based on the United States; and a gold bloc of south and west Europe headed by France. The ideologically autarkic—Germany, Japan, and the Soviet Union—stood alone.

Some currencies floated, with intervention by the central banks of the countries involved. Others remained pegged to gold, though their gold pars no longer carried much assurance of fixity; the dollar was devalued in the period 1933 to 1934, while the gold bloc held out till 1936. Others pegged to intervention currencies. Many countries welcomed depreciation as a method of stimulating aggregate demand. Only with the Tripartite Agreement of 1936 between Britain, France, and the United States was a minimal measure of agreement to restrain competitive devaluation achieved even amongst the leading currencies.

Foreign exchange reserves were largely liquidated in the crisis of 1931, so that, although the members of currency blocs continued to hold working balances in dollars and sterling, gold became once again the dominant reserve asset. The value of gold reserves was much increased by the devaluation of the dollar in 1933 to 1934.

Countries acknowledged no obligations with respect to when or how they should adjust, although they remained subject to a reserve constraint, which

338

implied that they had to initiate adjustment when they ran short of reserves. A powerful new instrument, exchange control, was invented with the deliberate purpose of enabling countries to avoid the traditional adjustment mechanism, by rationing scarce foreign exchange rather than reducing the demand for it through deflation or devaluation. Commercial policy, as well as devaluation, was used as an expenditure-switching weapon in attempting to increase output relative to absorption at a time when there was an acute global deficiency of demand.

The international monetary arrangements of the 1930s were an unmitigated disaster in terms of both microeconomic efficiency and macroeconomic consistency. Trade fell drastically in the Great Depression and failed to regain earlier trends even when output recovered in the mid-1930s. Not only was trade reduced in volume, but it was diverted from its previous and efficient pattern by a web of preferential tariffs and bilateral payments agreements. The international capital market ceased to function. The countries that came closest to prospering were those that were most ruthless in pursuing their national advantage without concern for the repercussions on others. The arrangements contained no inducements to countries to eschew such beggar-my-neighbor arrangements in favor of policies that would help to relieve the shortfall of global aggregate demand. The lack of international monetary organization must therefore be assigned a share of the blame for the disasters of the 1930s.

15.4 The Bretton Woods System

Negotiations between Britain and the United States on postwar economic planning started almost as soon as the United States entered the Second World War at the end of 1941. Although the phrase was not used, there was a clear intention of creating a new international economic order. Despite occasional British hesitations, from no less a figure than the chief British thinker and negotiator, Lord Keynes, among others, the conscious aim was that of creating a liberal, multilateral order that would be the polar opposite of the restrictions and bilateralism of the chaotic 1930s. As conceived, this new liberal order would be supervized by a triad of new international economic institutions: the International Trade Organization (ITO), whose premature death was noted at the beginning of chapter 13; the World Bank, whose functioning was examined in chapter 14.3; and the International Monetary Fund (IMF).

Having first achieved a substantial measure of bilateral agreement on the basic issues, Britain and the United States invited the other wartime allies to a conference to draft the Articles of Agreement of the World Bank and the IMF. This conference met in July 1944 in the mountain resort of Bretton Woods in New Hampshire—a township that thereby lent its name to the international financial order planned for the postwar world. This order, and the principal controversies surrounding its design, can again be described under the headings of the exchange-rate regime, the reserve regime, and adjustment obligations.

Exchange rates were normally to be fixed, except for a margin of ± 1 percent to emulate the old gold points and provide an incentive for commercial-bank clearing of most exchange transactions. The par values of all exchange rates were to be expressed in terms of gold. A par value could, however, be adjusted if the country so requested and the IMF agreed that a change was necessary to correct a "fundamental disequilibrium." This concept was never formally defined, but it was intended to refer to a situation in which a country was unable to maintain external balance over the trade cycle as a whole without a significant departure from internal balance or from its obligations with respect to the maintenance of liberal trade and payments. By allowing devaluation (or revaluation, though that was not an option in anyone's mind in 1944) but only subject to international approval, the negotiators hoped they had found a middle way between countries being forced to sacrifice their internal economies to the defense of a fixed exchange rate, as had happened to Britain in the 1920s, and the dangers of a repeat round of competitive devaluations, as had occurred in the 1930s.

In the early Anglo-American discussions on postwar financial planning, Britain had proposed the Keynes Plan for creating a radically new reserve regime. In place of the IMF, there would have been an International Clearing Union (ICU) which would have acted as a central bank for central banks. Each central bank would have had an account at the ICU in terms of a new international money called "bancor." Countries could have acquired bancor balances by depositing gold or by receiving bancor from deficit countries—which they would indeed have been obliged to accept in settlement of deficits. Each member country would have had a right to a certain overdraft, related to the size of its trade, which would thus have provided leeway for deficit countries to finance their deficits. The proposed overdrafts were on the generous side (the European overdrafts would have come to much the same total as Marshall Plan aid finally did), so the United States rejected the idea as a British plot to soak the surplus countries, which they automatically equated to themselves. The British therefore had to be content with the main outlines of the White Plan, named after the chief

United States negotiator Harry Dexter White (1892–1948), later hounded as a supposed Communist. This plan merely proposed creating a pool of gold and currencies in the hands of the IMF, which could be lent to countries suffering a temporary deficit to supplement their holdings of the existing reserve assets. Those existing reserves were still overwhelmingly gold, with sterling and dollars—in that order—as reserve currencies.

The Keynes Plan included a provision whereby countries would have had to pay interest not only on their borrowing from the ICU, but also on excessive *credit* balances. The purpose was to spell out the obligations of *both* deficit *and* surplus countries as to when they should adjust and to provide an incentive for them to respect those obligations. This idea was another early casualty of the bilateral Anglo-American negotiations. Nevertheless, the Bretton Woods agreement (the IMF Articles) did contain an endorsement of the idea that surplus countries had a responsibility to play a role in promoting adjustment. A scarce currency clause enabled the Fund to declare a currency scarce if its holdings of that currency were becoming exhausted as a result of many countries borrowing it (to settle deficits with a chronic surplus country), whereupon Fund members would have been authorized to discriminate against imports from that country. (The clause was never invoked and has now been abolished.) Deficit countries were still subject to the discipline imposed by limited reserves, ameliorated by loans from the IMF if the Fund saw fit. Although no one worried much about the United States becoming a deficit country, it is worth noting that there was no suggestion that the special position accorded the United States dollar in the Bretton Woods agreement would limit the United States responsibility for initiating adjustment. This special position consisted of the United States defending the dollar by buying and selling gold, while other countries defended their currencies by buying and selling dollars. However, if surplus countries had used all the dollars acquired in intervention to buy gold from the United States, the United States would have been exposed to the same pressure to adjust when in deficit as any other country.

Bretton Woods did not spell out very explicitly how countries were supposed to adjust when adjustment was called for. The general principles implicit in the system were that a high priority should at all times be accorded to the preservation of internal balance; that temporary imbalances should be financed rather than adjusted; that modest but persistent imbalances should be met by trimming fiscal-monetary policy as long as this did not involve a major departure from internal balance; and that large and persistent imbalances not due to deviations from internal balance could be met by exchange rate changes. It was accepted that destabilizing capital movements could be suppressed by exchange controls.

341

The Fund was formally created in 1946, but it accomplished little in its first decade primarily because the limited resources with which it had finally been endowed were insufficient to make any impact on the main issue of the day—postwar reconstruction and its counterpart, the chronic European payments deficit. The problem of an acute shortage of dollars (the dollar problem) was finally resolved by Marshall aid. (This, by a nice historical irony, might never have been necessary had the United States accepted the Keynes Plan, in which case the United States could have lent what eventually she gave away.) To keep some control over who was receiving what, it was agreed that countries receiving Marshall aid would not also draw from the IMF. That left the Fund with the responsibility of approving devaluations, of which by far the most important was the round of 1949 devaluations of most of the nondollar currencies that laid the basis for the end of the dollar shortage, and the role of making loans to its Latin American members. These provided the testing ground for the principles of Fund conditionality and the stimulus for the emergence of the Fund's version of the monetary approach to the balance of payments (see chap. 8.6).

The Fund began to emerge from the twilight in 1956, when Britain and France needed bailing out from the financial consequences of their Suez escapade. But by two years later a fundamental change in the world economy had become manifest: the dollar shortage had vanished and been replaced by a dollar glut. (In those two years the phrase "dollar problem" came to mean an excess supply of, instead of an excess demand for, dollars.) The Europeans at last declared their currencies convertible at the end of 1958, thus accepting the obligations that brought the Bretton Woods system into operation. The United States sought to adjust its balance of payments, but without devaluing or doing anything else that might hurt too much. Until the hoped-for adjustment took effect, it sought to persuade other countries to hold their dollars instead of converting them into gold.

In terms of microeconomic efficiency, the Bretton Woods system of the following decade was an unbridled success. Transactions costs fell, many restrictions disappeared, risks were low, trade flourished, and the reborn international capital market expanded dramatically.

In terms of macroeconomic consistency, the record was more mixed. From a short-run standpoint, the early 1960s were highly satisfactory. Keynesian demand management was in its heyday, with the efforts of countries to "fine tune" demand to match capacity being internationally coordinated, to take account of spillover multiplier effects, by the OECD (see chap. 17.2). Inflation, though modest, provoked attempts to design incomes policies to reduce it still further without sacrificing employment targets. It was an era of relatively noninflationary full employment with rapid real growth and modest payments imbalances.

The great question was whether this prosperity was sustainable in the longer run. At the domestic level, the issue was whether maintenance of high levels of employment through active demand management would not stimulate accelerating inflation (a doubt clearly formulated by economists in 1967 with the work of Friedman and Phelps). At the international level, analogous doubts about the sustainability of the system had been formulated much earlier, even as the Bretton Woods system was moving into its golden age at the end of the 1950s.

The main prophet was Robert Triffin. He argued that the growth in dollar reserves being generated by the United States payments deficit and not being converted into gold was necessary if world economic expansion were to be maintained; countries needed growing reserves as trade expanded if a given degree of trade liberalization was to be maintained, and there was no other significant source of reserve growth. (Commercial demand for gold was fast catching up with supply at the official, supposedly eternal, price of $35 per ounce that had been set by President Franklin D. Roosevelt in 1934.) However, if the short-run dollar liabilities of the United States continued to expand while its gold assets remained constant or even shrank, it was only a matter of time before the credibility of the commitment to sustain the $35 gold price was called into question. At that point central banks would rush to convert dollars into gold, just as had happened to Britain in 1931. Thus the system faced a dilemma, quickly dubbed the *Triffin Dilemma:* either the United States would succeed in curing its payments deficit, in which case world growth would be strangled by the emergence of a progressively more acute liquidity shortage; or its deficit would continue, in which case a crisis of confidence would sooner or later be inevitable. The system as constituted was inherently incapable of solving simultaneously what later analysts called the *liquidity problem*—how to ensure that reserves grow at an appropriate rate—and the *confidence problem*—avoiding crises of confidence.

Another problem with the Bretton Woods system was termed the *adjustment problem.* This referred to restoring and maintaining payments equilibrium (where equilibrium should be interpreted as external balance in the sense of chapter 9.2). Until about 1960, the Bretton Woods system had had a functioning adjustment mechanism, in the form of progressive trade liberalization by Europe and Japan; a tendency toward excessive surplus was exploited to take another step toward fulfilling paper obligations of freer trade and payments. But by 1960 those obligations were being fulfilled,

343

and thus there remained no further scope for differential trade liberalization to be exploited as an adjustment weapon. Nothing else took its place. Fiscal-monetary policy was ruled out, except to the most marginal extent, by the near-universal commitment to full employment. Exchange-rate policy was being ruled out by a reinterpretation of the rules of Bretton Woods, which were read as implying that devaluation was an ultimate weapon whose use was a national disgrace—a reinterpretation generated by the need to prop up confidence by denying that you were about to devalue, which naturally created an interest in not breaking one's word. So the only *adjustment mechanism* left was a Mundellian manipulation of the fiscal-monetary mix, which is really a means of financing rather than of adjustment, and as such is at best a temporary solution (see chap. 9.2).

In the short run the situation was viable. Payments imbalances were not particularly large, so that the lack of an adequate adjustment mechanism was not too pressing an issue. And most other central banks (with the exception of the Banque de France during de Gaulle's presidency) were willing to go along with the United States in financing its deficit by mainly holding rather than converting dollars, at least for a time. Once the official world had been convinced that there was a problem of long-run viability of the system, negotiations on international monetary reform got under way (see sec. 15.5). The dominant view was that measures like restraint in converting dollars into gold were buying time until a reform could be negotiated. The main problem was, of course, the lack of a consensus as to the desirable direction of reform, which in the event prevented adequate changes being negotiated before the crisis finally broke.

The beginning of the end came in 1967, with the devaluation of the pound sterling, following repeated denials that this would occur and a period of five and a half years in which no major currency had changed its par value. This had the predictable effect of eroding confidence in the United States commitment to defend the gold price, resulting in a run from the dollar into gold in early 1968. A hastily convened conference in Washington decided to create a two-tier gold market, with the price on the private market left free while the official price for transactions between central banks remained $35 per ounce. Since Bretton Woods had never involved an official commitment to trade with the private sector in gold, this did not change the formal rules of the system. But in fact it brought Gresham's Law into play and virtually drove gold out of active circulation as a reserve asset, as well as making it clear to central banks that extensive recourse to their right to demand gold from the United States Treasury would almost surely provoke a withdrawal of that right. Since other countries de facto accepted that situation, the world came very close to being on a dollar standard.

The following years were marked by a series of speculative crises, of ever greater force, involving in particular runs from the French franc (1968–69) and sterling (1968), into the DM (1968–69), from the Belgian franc (August 1969) and into the Belgian franc (October 1969), and into the Canadian dollar (May 1970). Politicians prated about how they would never devalue or revalue a few weeks before doing it, thus devaluing political assurances about financial policy. Eventually the long-feared run out of the dollar got under way, at least on the part of the private sector, following a notable easing of United States monetary policy in 1971. By August there were signs of uneasiness on the part of official holders as well. This combined with a growing conviction in Washington that the de facto dollar standard had not been serving United States national interests, in particular by allowing the dollar to become seriously overvalued. On August 15 President Richard Nixon's administration closed the gold window, as part of an effort to get other countries to revalue against the dollar. Most economists mark the death of Bretton Woods from that date.

The United States suspension of gold convertibility left the other major countries with little alternative but to float, which they did with great reluctance. Accordingly everyone agreed that negotiations to construct a new international monetary system to succeed the defunct Bretton Woods system were an urgent necessity. The first step in this reconstruction was agreed to be the reestablishment of a new structure of pegged exchange rates. This was accomplished at a conference held in the Smithsonian Institution in Washington in December 1971, involving a small (8 percent) devaluation of the dollar in terms of gold and some revaluation of the stronger currencies. This agreement started to unravel a mere seven months later, when a run on the pound led to a British decision to let sterling float again. The next February came more speculative runs, leading to a new wave of currency realignments, which this time lasted only a couple of weeks before being overwhelmed by further speculative pressures. The adjustable peg had, quite patently, become unworkable, and the major countries finally accepted that fact by moving to a system of generalized floating. At that point, all that remained of Bretton Woods was the IMF.

15.5 The Reform Debate

Triffin's diagnosis of the dilemma facing the gold exchange standard led him to a prescription for its reform. He argued that a mechanism was necessary for creating additional international reserves which would both bring the total growth of reserves under purposive international control and avoid progressively undermining confidence. Triffin proposed a solution somewhat reminiscent of the Keynes Plan, involving an expansion of the IMF into a deposit bank for central banks. Each member would have undertaken to hold a certain proportion of its reserves as deposits at the IMF, while the Fund could have expanded reserves by granting loans (medium or long term) or by buying securities.

Promulgation of the Triffin Plan initiated a wide-ranging and long-running debate on reform of the international monetary system. It started off with academic economists inventing rival plans, and the official world brushing aside all these suggestions with assurances that revolution was unnecessary because a satisfactory process of evolution was already under way. The academics retorted that such "ad hockery" was not enough, and in the surprisingly short time of about three years the official world came around to their view and initiated discussions on the desirable nature of reform. Academic participation was not invited, to the annoyance of the leading academics, who thereupon set up their parallel Bellagio group with the aim of clarifying the issues. It was the first report of this group that classified the problems of the Bretton Woods system into the triad of adjustment, liquidity, and confidence already used in the last section. Subsequently the academics and officials made their peace, and the Bellagio group was broadened into a meeting place between the two sides, in which the academics could keep up to date with the evolving issues and the officials could draw on the fruits of academic analysis. The interaction of theory and practice that characterized the reform debate owed much to these meetings.

At least five reasonably distinct schools emerged during the debate. The first was that inspired by Triffin. The essential underlying idea was that the world reserve stock provides a world monetary base that has to grow at an appropriate rate if harmful inconsistencies in national policies are to be avoided. If the stock of reserves grows too fast, countries in general are enabled or encouraged to pursue overexpansionary demand policies, and inflation results. If reserves grow too slowly (or, even worse, if they fall because of a switching of reserve currencies into gold in the course of a confidence crisis), the result is likely to be deflation, competitive devaluation, and/or rising protectionism. The program of action suggested by this vision was that of creating a new reserve asset and limiting the supply of alternative forms of reserves to bring the total supply under purposive control. This was the dominant view inspiring official negotiations through the 1960s and right up to the failure of the reform exercise in 1974.

A second school looked to markets to solve most problems, including those of adjusting balances of payments and producing consistency between the policies adopted by different countries. For these purposes, they wanted to allow exchange rates to float. This school was much more influential among academics than among officials, although there was some sympathy in this direction in the Nixon administration.

A third school wanted to reinstate gold, starting off by increasing its price. The hard members of this school, headed by de Gaulle's confidant the French economist Jacques Rueff (1896–1978), wanted to go back to the classical gold standard, including reliance on the monetary mechanism of adjustment to solve the adjustment problem and reliance on the symmetry of that mechanism to ensure policy consistency. France espoused these views during de Gaulle's presidency, while global monetarists began to endorse them in the 1970s. There was also a soft version of the school, which thought that Bretton Woods could be revitalized by increasing the gold price, since no one would want to shift from dollars into gold once the prospect of a gold price increase in the near future were banished. They also argued that this would resolve the consistency problem, which they perceived as arising from competition to generate current-account surpluses. They expected a higher gold price to generate a net inflow of gold into reserves, which would have enabled the world as a whole to generate a net current-account surplus.[2]

A fourth school favored a dollar standard, a system under which the dollar is the basic reserve asset, convertible into nothing else. Other countries peg to the dollar, and if they do not like their payments outcome, they adopt adjustment policies, while the United States treats its balance of payments with benign neglect. This provides a resolution of the consistency problem, since one country allows its balance of payments to be determined as a residual, which it is in a financial position to do in view of the willingness of other countries to hold its currency. This school was dominated by United States academics and found a fair measure of sympathy in the Nixon administration prior to August 1971.

The fifth school believed that one needed *both* control of the reserve supply *and* limited exchange-rate flexibility, especially a crawling peg. The former was envisaged as necessary to resolve the liquidity problem, while the latter would provide a solution to the adjustment problem without undermining confidence. Consistency in aims would have been provided by control of the reserve stock as in Triffin's model, while that consistency

2. This arises from an accounting asymmetry. The gold producer counts gold exports as a normal commodity, while the country importing gold puts it in the monetary account. This enables the sum total of world current accounts to be positive.

could have been translated into action through the existence of a usable adjustment mechanism.

Negotiations on international monetary reform started in earnest among the ten major financial powers constituting the Group of Ten in 1965, after the United States endorsed (at least pro tem) the Triffinesque orthodoxy of the first school. Despite French opposition based on de Gaulle's support for the alternative of a revived gold standard, the negotiations to create a new reserve asset were brought to a successful conclusion at the IMF's Annual Meetings in Rio de Janeiro in 1967. The new reserve asset was called a Special Drawing Right (SDR), the oddness of the term being a linguistic attempt to mollify the French for having lost out on the substance of the argument. The SDR was defined as having a value of 1/35 of an ounce of gold, the same as the value of the dollar at that time. It carried an interest rate of 1.5 percent per annum. It was to be used in much the same way as gold, to be sold by a country in deficit to a strong-currency country in exchange for currencies that would be usable in intervention in the exchange markets. The IMF would designate which strong-currency country would receive SDRs, while the use of SDRs was restricted to countries in deficit to avoid adding to the confidence problem.

SDRs were created by allocating them to members in proportion to their quotas in the Fund; that is, on a given day the Fund simply credited the accounts of participants with a certain number of SDRs, which they were thenceforth able to use to finance deficits. They did, however, accept the obligation to pay interest on their past allocations, so that the system was self-financing. How new allocations of SDRs should be distributed between participants was, naturally, a controversial question. Initially the industrial countries had thought of limiting the issue of a new reserve asset to themselves, on the ground that countries receiving an allocation were taking responsibility for guaranteeing the asset, which would make sense only if restricted to highly responsible countries. The developing countries countered by a proposal that became known as "the link,"[3] under which they would have received a disproportionate portion of allocations, partly on the ground that that would enable the industrial countries to run a collective current-account surplus just like gold inflows would and partly on the ground that, if there was "seigniorage"[4] around, it should go to the most

3. The "link" was initially a part of the phrase "a link between reserve creation and development assistance," signifying that newly created reserves would have accrued in a way that financed development programs, but the phrase has now been abbreviated.

4. "Seigniorage" originally (in the Middle Ages) referred to the profit the crown reaped on minting metal into coins, but it has now been broadened to refer to the profit that accrues to the first spender from the ability to issue money in any way.

needy. The compromise of basing allocations on IMF quotas was supposed to be distributionally neutral, which it would be if quotas were a good index of average reserve holdings.

The first SDRs were allocated on January 1, 1970, after everyone had argued themselves into more or less believing that there was a liquidity shortage developing and therefore a need to relieve it by creating SDRs. But even as that was being done, United States monetary policy was easing. There was a vast outpouring of dollars in the following years, which, in the attempt to prop up the fixed exchange rates of Bretton Woods, were absorbed by the central banks of other countries. (Reserves rose by 61 percent in the period 1970 to 1971 alone, as opposed to 22 percent in the whole of the 1960s.) Hence when the Bretton Woods system collapsed, the perception of the Triffin school, which included the European-Japanese bloc in the IMF, was that the essential step was to restore a workable convertibility-type discipline to the United States so as to limit further reserve creation to the level judged internationally desirable. That provided their basic objective in the reform negotiations that ensued.

Other countries had different views of what the reform negotiations should be achieving. The United States had by this time lost sympathy with the Triffin school, having been partly seduced by the prestige and convenience of having the world on a dollar standard and partly convinced by the advocates of exchange-rate flexibility. On the other hand, the United States negotiators realized the importance that other countries were attaching to a restoration of convertibility in some form or other. Given the tensions between these mutually contradictory positions, the United States showed considerable ingenuity in fashioning a set of reform proposals. Their centerpiece was a system of reserve indicators, under which each country would have had a normal level of reserves and been expected to take adjustment action as necessary to keep its reserves within specified margins about its norm. This looked ironically like Keynes' proposals for penalizing countries whose bancor holdings deviated too far from zero in either direction, which the United States had summarily rejected almost thirty years before. These reserve indicators were to be accompanied by a restoration of dollar convertibility, essentially into SDRs rather than into gold, for countries that stayed suitably close to their reserve norms. Thus there was a limited restoration of convertibility to placate other countries; a limit on that convertibility to safeguard against the United States being subject to excessive pressures of a sort that the dollar standard had eliminated; and reserve indicators that would more or less oblige countries to change exchange rates when adjustment was necessary.

349

The third major group of countries in the negotiations consisted of the developing countries. The fact that they were included at all was noteworthy, given that the industrial countries had previously dominated the crucial negotiations on monetary issues. In 1972, it was agreed that the attempt to design a successor system to Bretton Woods would be done by a committee whose composition would parallel that of the IMF Executive Board, which gave nine of the twenty places to the developing countries. Their general position was sympathetic to a structured system, with pegged exchange rates and the SDR as the principal reserve asset. They also used the occasion to pursue their own distinctive interest in a system that would promote a transfer of real resources to themselves: the principal mechanism that they sought to give effect to that objective was the link.

The Committee of Twenty (C–20), as the committee charged with designing a reform was termed, held periodic meetings during the years 1972 to 1974, where it discussed the various reform proposals at great length. There was, however, no meeting of minds on the basic shape that a reformed system should take, and there was no hegemonic power with the ability to force its will on the others in the absence of their voluntary assent. Accordingly, the Outline of Reform that expressed the results of the committee's deliberations was largely limited to recording the general principles on which all had agreed—an "effective and symmetrical adjustment process," "cooperation in dealing with disequilibrating capital flows," "better international management of global liquidity, with the SDR becoming the principal reserve asset," etc.—and a host of alternative mechanisms for effecting those principles on which they had not agreed. Even in the rare case where there was supposed to be agreement, this tended to be unrealistic, as in the case of the resolve to restore "stable but adjustable exchange rates"—the very system that broke down during the committee's deliberations and that even its original supporters were recognizing to be unrealistic by 1974.

In that year, the oil price increase provided a convenient alibi for declaring the reform to be postponed, and the committee turned its attention to more immediate issues before abolishing itself. It approved three specific decisions.

First, the value of the SDR was redefined to make it equal to the value of a basket of the sixteen major currencies.[5] Some such step was essential to enable the SDR to function effectively in a world of generalized floating, since the value of gold, the previous measure, no longer had an unambigu-

5. The basket consisted of 33 percent US dollar, 12.5 percent Deutschemark, 9 percent pound sterling, 7.5 percent each French franc and Japanese yen, 6 percent Canadian dollar and Italian lira, 4.5 percent Netherlands guilder, 3.5 percent Belgian franc, 2.5 percent Swedish krona, 1.5 percent each Australian dollar, Danish krone, Norwegian krone, and Spanish peseta, and 1 percent each Austrian schilling and South African rand. The composition of the

ous meaning. Defining the SDR as equal to a basket of currencies enabled it to serve as a unit of account equal to an average of the major currencies. Allied to this change was a decision to raise the interest rate on the SDR about half-way toward a market rate. A second decision involved the promulgation of a set of guidelines for floating exchange rates—a code of good conduct for the authorities of countries with floating rates, encouraging them to intervene to smooth out erratic fluctuations while proscribing aggressive intervention to promote competitive depreciation or appreciation. The third decision involved the creation of a high-level committee, modeled on the C–20 itself, to meet about twice a year to supervize the IMF. It was envisaged that this might some day be a formal council with executive powers, but for the moment it remains an informal Interim Committee with advisory powers only.

Matters could not be left where they were at the end of the C–20, however, since all the major members of the Fund were in transgression of the IMF's Articles, which prohibited floating rates. Furthermore, the major holders of gold were dissatisfied with the extent to which gold had been immobilized. The private gold price had risen far above the official price, but central banks were forbidden to sell above the official price—making their gold totally unusable except through elaborate deals in which it served as collateral for borrowing. There then followed eighteen months of haggling to find a form of words that would recognize the facts of life and legalize what everyone was doing or determined to do. Agreement was finally achieved at a meeting of the Interim Committee in Jamaica in 1976.

15.6 The Present Nonsystem

The nonsystem that had come into being in March 1973 was legalized by the Interim Committee decisions at Jamaica in January 1976. It is called a nonsystem because it makes no attempt to subject countries to obligations or to impose any order, as the gold standard and Bretton Woods had done. A description of present arrangements under the same three headings previously used to characterize earlier regimes will make this clear.

The revised IMF Articles allow countries to float or to peg. If they float,

---

sixteen-currency basket was subsequently updated so that it continued to contain the currencies of the sixteen countries with largest exports. It was then simplified to the five major currencies on January 1, 1981, with shares of 42 percent for the US dollar, 19 percent for the Deutschemark, and 13 percent each for the French franc, Japanese yen, and pound sterling.

they are supposed to be subject to IMF surveillance, but since the Fund has failed to specify any norms more specific than those in the original guidelines, this has not amounted to much in practice. If they peg, they can peg to anything they like—except gold! This includes not just the possibility of pegging to a single currency but also to a basket or to the SDR or for a number of currencies to peg to each other. There are no limits on the margins within which pegged exchange rates are allowed to fluctuate, and no rules as to whether pegs should be changed in large steps, as under Bretton Woods, or small steps, as under the crawling peg.

Countries in fact employ a wide variety of exchange arrangements. In general the currencies of the major industrial countries are allowed to float, though the central banks intervene to attempt to smooth out fluctuations —with the United States usually having been less disposed to intervene than the others. There is a group of EEC countries, however, that peg their currencies to each other (while they float against other currencies). This mutual pegging evolved from the so-called snake[6] into the European Monetary System (EMS) in March 1979, and now covers all members of the EEC except Britain and Greece. About fifty currencies are still pegged to the dollar—virtually all of Latin America and the Communist bloc, plus countries scattered over Africa, the Middle East, Asia, and Oceania. Fourteen francophone African countries remain pegged to the French franc and a handful of other currencies are pegged to other single currencies, normally of the former colonial power. Some thirty currencies are pegged to a basket and about fifteen to the SDR. Most of the pegged currencies still change their pegs according to the old Bretton Woods practice of making substantial changes at infrequent intervals, but close to ten operate a crawling peg. A number of those that claim to peg to a basket announce neither the composition of their basket nor when they are changing the peg, so that it is difficult to know what they actually do.

The reserve regime is equally anarchic. There are no rules on what countries may hold as reserves or where they may hold them nor on

6. It started off in 1972 as the "snake in the tunnel," when the EEC countries agreed to limit the deviations in their cross-rates to less than was possible given their intervention points against the dollar. (The object was to move toward European monetary union.) The dollar intervention points provided the "tunnel," and the European currencies snaked around together within those limits, hence the term. (The Benelux currencies kept closer still, a relationship dubbed the "worm in the snake.") Then, in March 1973, the snake broke out of its tunnel, but it held together and even collected Norway and Sweden for a while. Membership fluctuated somewhat, but by 1978 was reduced to the DM and Germany's small Benelux and Danish neighbors. Then came the wild exchange rate movements of 1978, which gave rise to a new initiative to stabilize intra-EEC exchange rates: it is this which became the European Monetary System (EMS). Incidentally, both the snake in its later years and the EMS have sought to avoid the speculative pressures that killed the adjustable peg by keeping realignments small, operating a semicrawling peg.

permitted levels of reserves, such as were sought in the C–20 negotiations. The dominant reserve asset, constituting about 75 percent of total liquid reserves, is foreign exchange. About three-quarters of these exchange reserves are still held in United States dollars, although since 1978 there has been a strong tendency for the holdings of other reserve currencies to increase. The other currencies with a significant reserve role are now the DM, the Japanese yen, the Swiss franc, the pound sterling, the French franc, and the Dutch guilder. An increasing part of foreign-exchange reserves, especially of developing countries, are held in the Euromarkets. The other components of liquid reserves consist of the reserves created by the operations of international organizations, the IMF and the European Monetary Cooperation Fund (the agent of the European Monetary System). The IMF creates SDRs, as already described, and members also gain reserve positions in the Fund, which count as an element of reserves, when other countries borrow their currencies from the Fund. The European Monetary Cooperation Fund accepts deposits of reserve currencies and gold from members in certain quantities, and issues European Currency Units (ECUs) in return. The composition of the reserve stock is shown in table 15–1.

In addition to the foregoing elements of reserves, central banks still carry gold on their balance sheets as though it were a reserve asset. In fact it long ago ceased to merit that classification according to the standard definition of a reserve asset, which is an asset unconditionally available at short notice to support a country's currency in the foreign exchange market. But since central banks have still not brought themselves to reclassify gold as the speculative commodity that it has become, but like to show it in their balance sheets as a reserve asset, a concession is made to their feelings by including it as a nonliquid asset in table 15–1. The penultimate row shows

TABLE 15–1

Official Reserves
(in billions of SDRs at year's end)

	1970	1975	1980
Foreign exchange: US dollars	35.2	116.8	173.0
other	10.2	20.5	68.3
Reserve positions in the Fund	7.7	12.6	16.8
SDRs	3.1	8.8	11.8
ECUs	—	—	52.2
Total liquid assets	56.2	158.7	322.1
Gold: at SDR 35 per ounce	37.0	35.6	32.8
Gold: at London market price	39.5	121.9	433.5

SOURCE: International Monetary Fund *Annual Reports.*

the value of gold holdings at the old official price of SDR 35 per ounce, which was abolished at Jamaica. The final row shows the value at the price prevailing in the London gold market, which is a price that has now become somewhat relevant because it was also agreed at Jamaica to abolish the prohibition against selling at the market price. It is only "somewhat" relevant, however, because if any major central bank tried selling a significant part of its gold on the market it would bid the price down, and central banks do not like depressing the book value of their assets. This is one of the factors that still makes gold an illiquid asset (though more liquid than prior to Jamaica). But, even if an illiquid speculative asset, and despite two major price declines, gold was a great speculative success over the 1970s as a whole, as the contrast between the last two lines of table 15–1 shows. The developing countries, who hold little gold, feel a sense of grievance at the contrast between the way the developed countries allowed their own gold holdings to be revalued and the way they rejected pleas for the link.

The nonsystem is also permissive in its specification of adjustment obligations and adjustment mechanisms. Even the old discipline of limited reserves has been much eroded by the international capital market, which allows most of the major countries (though not the poorer developing countries) considerable latitude to finance current-account deficits by going into debt. There are no agreed rules, or even conventions, as to the mix of exchange-rate policy, monetary (credit) policy, and fiscal policy that countries should adopt. In practice policy in the major countries has become dominated by the attempt to secure a preannounced rate of growth of the money supply as recommended by Friedmanian monetarism.

At the microeconomic level, the current nonsystem has clearly been inferior to its predecessor. Transactions costs have risen: buy-sell spreads in the foreign exchange markets are now typically about four times what they were, though they remain small as a percentage of the value of transactions. Exchange rates have proved extremely volatile, on any measure. Exchange risk has increased in consequence, and deviations of real exchange rates from PPP have widened rather than being reduced, as many advocates of greater exchange-rate flexibility had expected. Nevertheless, markets have continued to function: there has been no seizing-up of trade or capital flows. Some economists believe that the greater uncertainty being generated by volatile exchange rates must be having bad effects, like discouraging trade, ratcheting up the rate of inflation, and bankrupting businesses in countries with overvalued currencies. To date, however, there is not much hard evidence to support these conjectures.

In terms of macroeconomic consistency, there is once again a lack of consensus at this stage. The optimists argue that flexibility in interest rates and exchange rates is capable of establishing a satisfactory world equilibrium. If there were inconsistent national ambitions toward current-account surpluses, for example, then interest rates would be bid down until some countries were tempted into borrowing more and others into wanting to lend less. The pessimists point out that there are other variables that may adjust besides interest rates, notably income and employment. How one assesses these contending positions depends to a large degree on whether one believes the post-1974 unemployment to have been a price that the world had to pay to secure a deceleration of inflation and an acceptance of slower growth in real incomes arising from supply-side factors. Those who adopt this view tend to be sanguine that market forces will continue to secure consistency without the need for conscious policy harmonization. In contrast, those who believe that inflation was boosted more by fluctuations in real exchange rates than it was damped by high unemployment judge the present nonsystem to be a dangerous failure.

In view of the ideological predisposition of President Reagan's administration toward free markets, no major agreed changes in existing arrangements seem very likely in the near future. What is perhaps more probable is further development of European arrangements. A move to complete monetary union—a single European money—has been much debated, and a three-stage plan to achieve that objective by 1980 was endorsed in the early 1970s. The first stage of this plan, which involved the narrowing of intra-European exchange-rate margins to create the snake in the tunnel, was actually introduced in 1972. But in due course Britain, France, and Italy all dropped out, and the plan was quietly shelved. European concern over large exchange-rate misalignments led to a revival of interest in the topic in 1978, and the result was the establishment of the EMS in early 1979. This is still little more than an enlarged snake, and may well not be extended (for example, to involve a real reserve pool and an integrated monetary policy) until there are further political changes in Europe, involving *inter alia* full British participation in the EMS. But it is perhaps more likely that major changes may come in this way than through an agreed worldwide reform.

15.7 Summary

The world has experienced a variety of international monetary regimes over the past century. On most criteria, the most successful regimes were the two that were most structured, the gold standard and Bretton Woods.

However, neither could be restored at this stage. Incidentally, it has been argued that their success was due to the existence of a hegemonic power able to enforce rules—any rules—more than to any inherent logic in the rules themselves. Present world arrangments bear more resemblence to the free-for-all of the 1930s than to anything else, but the consequences have not, to date, been anywhere near as damaging. The main source of complaint has been the size of variations in real exchange rates, and their deviation from medium-term equilibrium levels. It seems doubtful whether dissatis-faction on this score, important as many believe it to be, will prove suffi-ciently acute to push the world into a renewed attempt at a major overhaul of its monetary arrangements in the foreseeable future.

15.8 Bibliography

A lucid and fairly detailed account of international monetary history is to be found in L. B. Yeager, *International Monetary Relations: Theory, History, Policy*, 2nd ed. (New York: Harper & Row, 1976), pt. 2.

On the gold standard, see A. T. Bloomfield, *Short-Term International Capital Movements under the Pre-1914 Gold Standard*, Princeton Studies in International Finance No. 11 (1963); P. H. Lindert, *Key Currencies and Gold, 1900–13*, Princeton Studies in International Finance No. 24 (1969); and R. Triffin, *The Evolution of the International Monetary System: Historical Reappraisal and Future Perspectives*, Princeton Studies in International Finance No. 12 (1964). For a monetarist interpretation, see D. N. McCloskey and J. R. Zecher, "How the Gold Standard Worked, 1880–1913," in J. A. Frenkel and H. G. Johnson, eds., *The Monetary Approach to the Balance of Payments* (London: Allen and Unwin, 1976).

On the interwar period, see League of Nations, *International Currency Experience* (Geneva: 1944), and W. A. Brown, *The International Gold Standard Reinterpreted, 1914–1934* (New York: National Bureau of Economic Research, 1940).

A very readable account of the negotiations that led up to Bretton Woods is contained in R. F. Harrod, *The Life of John Maynard Keynes* (London: Macmillan, 1951), chap. 13. More detail is provided in R. N. Gardner, *Sterling-Dollar Diplomacy*, 2nd ed. (London: McGraw Hill, 1969). An official history is contained in J. K. Horsefield, *The International Monetary Fund 1945–65* (Washington, D.C.: International Monetary Fund, 1969).

Triffin's diagnosis of the weaknesses of the Bretton Woods system and his proposals for reform were contained in R. Triffin, *Gold and the Dollar Crisis* (New Haven: Yale University Press, 1960). The adjustment-liquidity-confidence classification was introduced in F. Machlup and B. G. Malkiel, eds., *International Monetary Arrangements: The Problem of Choice* (Princeton: International Finance Section, 1964). A brief history of the Bretton Woods system is provided in chap. 1 of J. Williamson, *The Failure of World Monetary Reform, 1971–1974* (New York: NYU Press, 1977), the rest of which is centered on an account of the C–20 negotiations. A useful recent analysis of the problem of world monetary reform is provided by B. J. Cohen, *Organizing the World's Money* (New York: Basic Books, 1977).

Some immediate reactions to the birth of the international monetary nonsystem were provided in E. Bernstein et al., *Reflections on Jamaica*, Princeton Essays in International Finance No. 115 (1976). A variety of views appraising its functioning were presented at a conference whose proceedings are contained in J. Dreyer, G. Haberler, and T. D. Willett eds., *The International Monetary System: A Time of Turbulence*, (Washington, D.C.: American Enterprise Institute, 1982).

16

Proposals for a New International Economic Order

THE international economic order described and analyzed in the last three chapters had its origins in allied planning during the Second World War. The objective was that of creating a liberal order, and to a significant degree this objective was achieved. Supporters of a liberal order argue that such a system is in the general interest and cannot legitimately be characterized as an instrument for advancing the interests of some at the expense of others. That is a claim that has traditionally excited more sympathy among the haves than among the have-nots. And so it has proved internationally in the last twenty years.

The growing diplomatic power of the Third World, and especially its dominance of the United Nations organs, was exploited in the early 1970s to vent this dissatisfaction with the international status quo. On May 1, 1974, a Special Assembly of the United Nations expressed by an overwhelming majority its "determination to work urgently for the establishment of a new international economic order," and adopted a Program of Action for the Establishment of a New International Economic Order (NIEO). This set in motion a train of negotiations that included general conferences of UNCTAD in Nairobi in 1976 and in Manila in 1979; of

357

UNIDO (the United Nations Industrial Development Organization) in Lima in 1975; and the Conference on International Economic Cooperation that met sporadically in Paris from December 1975 to June 1977. Many other international negotiations were influenced by the call for a NIEO. A North-South summit meeting was held at Cancún, Mexico, in 1981, but this proved to be a diplomatic occasion where world leaders spent most of their time discussing the favorite topic of diplomats—namely, the forum where future negotiations should take place—rather than economic substance.

This chapter is devoted to outlining and analyzing the economics of the proposals for redesigning the international economic order that have been presented by the South in the course of these negotiations. In addition, the South has striven for increased power and influence in the process of international economic decision making, for example, in the IMF, the World Bank, and GATT.

16.1 Perceptions and Positions

The stereotype of the Southern position, as this tends to be expressed in the resolutions that the Southern coalition drives through the United Nations and its specialized agencies like UNCTAD and UNIDO, is antimarket and prointerventionist. Laissez faire is treated as an ideology propagated by the rich to rationalize the status quo. Governments and coalitions of governments acting through international institutions have the duty to temper corporate power, plan for the general good, stabilize what is harmfully volatile, and redistribute income. It is time for these principles to be applied at the international level. The greater Northern reluctance to implement these reforms, the more essential it will become for the South to fall back on collective self-reliance.

The stereotype Northern position, as this tends to be expressed by the ministers of the major Western powers in North-South negotiating sessions, is that the existing liberal order has served everyone well, including the developing countries. No one is forced to participate in international exchanges if they do not wish to, hence the system must be helping everyone to achieve Pareto-preferred positions. The South's proposals for change tend to be either foolish, in threatening to destroy the liberal order that gives them their chance to progress, or else self-serving. Moreover (though this is not said in public), they often serve the interests not of the Southern masses but of the political elites who run those countries. These perceptions result in a negotiation with the South being treated as an occasion to educate the adversary or, where this is not possible, to stall. Changes should be accepted only to the minimum extent necessary to avoid diplomatic unpleasantries.

These stereotypes are, of course, surrounded by a wide range of opinions on the issues in question, in both the developing and the developed countries. In both cases, there are significant elements of opinion that adopt a more pessimistic evaluation of the adversary than the mainstream. In the developing countries, these tend to be Marxists who see the industrial countries as engaging in unequal exchange and so profiting from the poverty of the South. They may even charge the North with complicity in conspiring to keep the South poor. In the North, the extremists are generally conservatives who not only exclude those of a different race from the scope of the welfare function but also believe the South to be dedicated to their destruction.

The polar opposite of those confrontational views is the belief that the true interests of North and South are harmonious and that the lack of agreement on major changes therefore represents diplomatic failure. This view dominates where South and North routinely work together, as in the World Bank, or where their distinguished representatives have labored to produce a joint report, as in the Brandt Commission.[1] Adherents of this group typically accept that, in general, a liberal order is good for efficiency but recognize that its consequences for the distribution of income are capricious. Accordingly, North and South ought to be jointly searching out ways in which liberal principles can be more fully applied, while the North ought to be willing to make concessions to the South designed to go at least a small way toward redistributing income. Those who take this view will be termed the *liberal internationalists*.

16.2 Manufactures

At its 1975 conference in Lima, UNIDO set a target of locating 25 percent of global manufacturing in the developing countries by the year 2000. This Lima target of 25 percent compares with some 7 percent in the 1960s, which had risen to only 9 percent by 1977.

1. The Independent Commission on International Development Issues, consisting of eighteen distinguished elder statesmen from around the world and chaired by Willy Brandt of Germany, deliberated in 1978–79 on the steps that should be taken to promote North-South cooperation.

However, in the absence of policy instruments, setting targets does not get one far. The important questions are what policy changes have been proposed to further the ambition of industrializing the South, rather than what dreams have received endorsement by which United Nations organs. The South has raised three topics relevant to this area: trade policy, the regulation of multinationals, and creation of a new financial intermediary.

The principal Southern demand is for reduced Northern protectionism against Southern manufactures. Although a part of the drive has been for preferential access to Northern markets, as embodied in the GSP considered in chapter 13.3, the South has also called for trade liberalization, in greater intellectual accord with the stereotype Northern than the stereotype Southern position. Naturally the liberal internationalists are behind the South on this issue and indeed tend to be critical that these demands are not given higher priority by the South. They argue not only that liberalization of the Multi-Fiber Arrangement, or an international obligation on countries introducing restrictions to pay compensation, would be worth more than any number of United Nations resolutions, but also that the North's hypocrisy toward its own professed philosophy in restricting Southern exports would make this a favorable ground on which to do battle. In fact the net tendency in recent years has been toward more rather than less Northern restrictions on the imports of Southern manufactures. The broadening of the GSP by some countries and the benefits that LDCs drew from the Tokyo Round concessions by developed countries have been more than offset by the new protectionism—the ad hoc introduction of import restrictions and demands for voluntary export restraints, on the products exported by the South.

A second area where the South has sought changes in the international rules concerns the regulation of multinationals. The objective here is less that of promoting the Lima target than of redistributing power—away from the North and the corporate sector toward the South and the public sector. It is not surprising that LDC governments feel uneasy in their dealings with multinationals, which frequently have larger turnovers than their budgets. Moreover, there are respectable enough liberal precedents, like the United States antitrust acts, for not leaving large companies to their own devices and for harmonizing national policies toward the corporate sector, like the EEC rules on regional aid. The liberal internationalists tend to sympathize with the attempts of the United Nations to improve the existing OECD code dealing with anticompetitive and antisocial business practices, although the more squeamish sometimes shudder at the rhetoric. The North originally argued that the voluntary code of good conduct already adopted by the OECD was sufficient, but its position mellowed in the course of discussion.

The sort of United Nations code that now appears probable would specify the type of information that MNCs will be expected to publish and provide guidelines on foreign exchange operations, transfer pricing, and anticompetitive practices. In return the good conduct of host governments will be spelled out in terms of such questions as confidentiality in their dealings with multinational corporations and nondiscrimination between multinational corporations and national companies.

A third area where the South has sought a new initiative related directly to the Lima target is in proposing that UNIDO have an industrial financing unit, to be called the International Fund for Industrial Development (IFID). This would raise money on the world capital market and lend it to developing countries in support of industrial projects. Northern blessing for this venture has not been forthcoming, at least not yet.

16.3 Primary Products

Even excluding oil exporters, over 50 percent of developing country exports remain primary products. This is a much lower figure than it was —as recently as 1960 the figure was over 80 percent. But the success in exporting manufactures has been largely restricted to a limited number of NICs, while the great majority of LDCs remain overwhelmingly dependent on primary product exports to generate foreign exchange. The World Bank's low-income LDCs still earn some 70 percent of their export receipts from primary products. Hence proposals on this subject are at the heart of the drive for a reform of the international economic order.

Indeed, the success of the OPEC countries in increasing their export receipts through collective action to raise the price of petroleum in 1973 was one of the major stimuli to the drive for a NIEO in 1974. Many developing countries that were badly hit by the oil price increases refrained from criticism of their oil-exporting fellows, hoping that the time had at last come when they would be able to exploit commodity power and swing the terms of trade in their favor. There were indeed certain actions of other producer groups to exploit their market power in the period 1974 to 1975: bauxite producers levied greatly increased taxes on output, export quotas were maintained by the parties to the International Tin Agreement, the banana exporters levied new export taxes, and the copper producers introduced quotas first on exports and subsequently on production. In the short run those steps met with a measure of success in raising export receipts and generated a certain amount of Northern concern at the threat to security of supply. Suggestions were made that Southern guarantees of access to supplies could be traded against Northern concessions of reduced protectionism.

However, these hopes and fears proved a flash in the pan or at least premature. Primary product prices fell in the 1975 recession, and some of the countries that had initially benefited from restrictions (most notably Jamaica, which led the move to tax bauxite) found themselves short of markets. Oil, it seemed, was a special case: in virtually all other commodities there were either too many potential suppliers or too much substitutability on the demand side to hold out much prospect of the suppliers redistributing income to themselves through joint actions independently of the buyers.

In fact, the proposals presented by the South for reforming trade in primary products were not ostensibly directed toward raising commodity prices—although many Northerners undoubtedly believed that this was the real motive. The proposals advanced were called the Integrated Program for Commodities. They envisaged investment in the production, processing, and marketing of primary products and the establishment of buffer stocks for eighteen storable commodities. This program would have been financed by a Common Fund, with the idea that it needs less cash to sustain a series of buffer stocks of goods whose prices are imperfectly correlated than to support that same set of buffer stocks with equal insurance levels from a set of individual bank accounts. The intuitive explanation is that one commodity tends to be in short supply and thus generating revenue when another is at its floor price and being bought. It can in fact be shown that this pooling of funds will reduce costs for a given level of security provided only that the price fluctuations of different commodities are less than perfectly correlated, which is a very weak condition.

The Integrated Program for Commodities and its associated Common Fund generated a great deal of academic polemic and diplomatic wrangling. Mainstream Northern opinion was distinctly hostile, on grounds both of the interference with the market mechanism that would be involved and of the fear that this organization of the market would pave the way to subsequent cartelization. A number of arguments were advanced for believing that commodity price stabilization—as opposed to cartelization that succeeded in raising average prices—would be against the interests of the developing countries. First, it was argued that *price* stabilization might easily *increase* rather than decrease income instability, as in the case where it was primarily shocks to supply rather than to demand that were the cause of price fluctuations (see chap. 13.4). Second, it was argued that more stable prices might mean lower average prices, to the extent that supply was discouraged by price variability. Third, it was argued that even if price stabilization did have the effect of stabilizing incomes without reducing the average, that was not necessarily a blessing: according to the permanent income hypothesis, greater income fluctuations will tend to raise the savings ratio. Finally, it was asserted that even if buffer stocks could be made to work this time, against past experience (see chap. 13.4), and even if they did stabilize income without reducing its mean level or the savings ratio, the money that would be necessary to finance the buffer stocks could be much better used in other ways, like in providing aid.

The developing countries were not moved to change their position by this torrent of criticism. They pointed out that some of these arguments, notably those relating to whether producer incomes would be destabilized or reduced by successful price stabilization, are sensitive to the particular assumptions employed. They also argued that the important incomes to stabilize are not those of producers as a group but those of individual countries and that successful price stabilization in the face of supply shocks would just as surely stabilize the incomes of those producers who did not experience those shocks as it would in the face of demand shocks (see chap. 13.4).

The liberal internationalists have been divided on the merits of the Integrated Program for Commodities. Some, like the Brandt Commission, have endorsed it; others, like the World Bank, have been skeptical. (The World Bank has perhaps been particularly emphatic in arguing that there are better uses for the money!)

The LDCs first presented their program at the UNCTAD conference in Nairobi in 1976. Three years and much diplomatic effort later, the North agreed to a scaled-down version of the Common Fund. Expectations that this will have a major impact on future trade in primary products are not currently very high.

A second Southern demand is for reduced Northern protection of agricultural products, most notably sugar and beef. The arguments are very similar to those adduced in relation to trade in manufactures, although Northern governments are if anything even more obdurate in refusing to live up to their proclaimed liberal principles.

16.4 Resource Transfer

The *transfer of real resources* to a country is defined as its deficit on goods and nonfactor services. Thus a country is enabled to finance a larger resource transfer by aid, by capital inflows, or by lower debt service payments.

All three channels have figured in proposals for the NIEO. In addition to those proposals discussed here, there have been schemes for using monetary devices to finance resource transfers (discussed in the next section).

The most enthusiastic supporters of increased aid tend to be the liberal internationalists rather than the LDCs. According to the philosophy of the liberal internationalists, what is wrong with the world (in economic terms) is basically the distribution of income, and the traditional way to change that is to tax the rich to give to the poor. Indeed, there is a large literature on excess burdens which says that such redistributive taxation is better than methods that produce allocative distortions, like encouraging poor producers to form cartels to raise the price of their products. Thus the Brandt Commission Report called (as its predecessor the Pearson Commission had done a decade earlier) for a move toward the 0.7 percent of GNP target for ODA by the donor countries, and the World Bank never ceases to preach the need for more aid.

This school of thought sees virtue in making aid commitments more automatic. Donor countries should be persuaded to treat the 0.7 percent target as a commitment. Better still, one should seek out possible revenue sources that could provide income directly to an appropriate development finance agency, so as to escape from the vagaries of democratic budgetary processes. The Brandt Commission urged that international levies should be organized on such bases as international trade, arms production or exports, international travel, and the global commons—a term that usually covers the oceans, Antarctica, and outer space, that is, areas not included within existing national frontiers under international law. The commission proposed creating a new international institution, the World Development Fund, in large part to receive and administer the revenues generated by such international taxes.

The revenue source that has attracted the most attention from economists is the oceans. Richard Cooper urged that the high seas and the seabed below them be treated as the common heritage of mankind, rather than the territorial property of the coastal states. An international seabed authority should charge users the appropriate economic rents when the oceans were used for offshore oil production, fishing, and the mining of manganese nodules from the ocean floor. He estimated that such charges could yield a sum of perhaps $4.5 billion per annum by 1985 (in 1976 dollars), as well as eliminating the economic loss that is presently occurring as a result of over fishing due to the lack of property rights to ocean fisheries.

While the developing countries remained in favor of more aid, it did not constitute a major demand of the NIEO. Perhaps this was simply because the LDCs wrote aid off as a lost cause. Or perhaps it is because the more powerful and successful among them were ceasing to benefit much from aid as a result of the reorientation of aid programs in favor of the most needy that was begun in the 1970s. Or perhaps appealing to the conscience of the rich, as opposed to demanding rights, was out of tune with the spirit of the times. Whatever the reason, the donors remained rather niggardly through the 1970s and this provoked comparatively little criticism from the developing countries. In the early 1980s, President Reagan's budget cutters were sympathetic with that part of the intellectual spectrum that had long argued aid to be counterproductive on the ground that it normally accrues to a corrupt and inefficient government sector that is thereby enabled to bid scarce resources away from the comparatively efficient private sector, so they made aid one of their first targets.

Capital flows, unlike aid, continued to thrive through the 1970s. This did not, of course, prevent calls for yet more to be done. There were various Southern initiatives for massive transfers, none of which came to anything.

What received much more attention in the early LDC proposals was debt relief. Instead of the ability to contract new loans, it was urged that existing debts be cancelled, thus increasing the ability to finance resource transfers by eliminating debt service charges. Some of the early appeals were for a general debt cancellation, covering all developing countries and both private and official debt. However, the creditworthy middle-income countries that were planning to borrow more in the future quickly disavowed their desire to participate, thus revealing one of the important interest cleavages within the LDC group. For these countries, the present value of expected future borrowing clearly outweighed the value of having their existing debt cancelled; they could only suffer by suspicions that their debts might be at risk, which would simply serve to worsen the terms on which they could borrow. Before long, therefore, it was being made very plain that the request for debt relief was confined to official loans to low-income countries.

This reduced, though it did not entirely eliminate, the three standard objections to debt relief. The first is that the benefits of debt relief are distributed capriciously, to those who happen to have borrowed most in the past. Some might want to add that the costs are distributed capriciously, too, to those who have lent most in the past. The second is that if it encourages borrowers to believe that debt relief may happen again, it will destroy the incentive to make prudent calculations of costs versus returns and stimulate irresponsible attempts to overborrow. The third is that if it encourages lenders to believe that debt relief may happen again, it will destroy their incentive to lend and cut the flow of capital below the optimal level.

Although there was no generalized debt relief, a number of donor coun-

365

tries did decide to cancel the official debts owed to them by the poorest countries. The incentive effects of such circumscribed debt relief were, after all, unlikely to be profound. Moreover, since the donor countries counted such relief in their bilateral aid programs, they could compensate for distributional inequities by adjusting the volume of new aid going to different countries. In this strictly limited role, there is something to be said for debt relief. It is not tied to the purchase of goods from the donor country—a mercantilist practice that still survives from the days of chronic payments crises and can reduce the value of aid to the recipient significantly. It does not require the borrower to expend manpower drawing up projects that he thinks will appeal to the donor or incur costs in providing on-site inspection tours.

Or are those advantages? There is a strand of opinion in the North, which includes even some of the liberal internationalists, that is critical of giving the recipients too much freedom to use resource transfers as they please. Members of this school point to the money that has been wasted on prestige projects, the corruption of many Third World governments, their lack of concern with human rights, and their propensity to pursue policies that benefit the local elites, rather than those that meet basic needs, to justify retaining donor control over the way that money is spent. It can be retorted that such ills are not unknown in the other Worlds, even the First World, and that in any case one does not build up the responsible local decision making that is necessary to combat such ills by excessive supervision. The argument is not one that economists are in any position to settle, but they should be aware of the sort of political tensions that run just below the surface in many North-South confrontations.

16.5 Monetary Affairs

Doctrinally, the South has favored a structured international monetary system, with pegged exchange rates and a principal reserve asset outside national control, in the debates of the past decade. Sweeping denunciations of the international monetary nonsystem are a regular part of the rhetoric. Such attitudes have a free run at occasions like the South-North Conference on the International Monetary System and the New International Order, held at Arusha, Tanzania, in July 1980. This denounced the loss of legitimacy of the IMF and demanded a United Nations Conference on International Money and Finance to create a new international monetary order "capable of achieving monetary stability, restoring acceptable levels of employment and sustainable growth . . . ," as well as "supportive of a process of global development. . . ."[2] But when it comes to Third World governments dealing in the fora where actual decisions are made, attitudes have usually been a lot more pragmatic. Demands for the North to adopt and abide by rules have not prevented demands for freedom from rules that might prove irksome to themselves, and the greatest effort has been invested in securing ad hoc concessions.

Consider the C–20 negotiations. The developing countries strongly supported the maintenance of "fixed but adjustable" exchange rates, and establishment of the SDR as the principal reserve asset. But they were unwilling to discuss the possibility of limitations on their freedom to switch reserves from one currency to another or to place their reserves in the Euromarkets, even though it was difficult to see how the SDR could emerge as the central reserve asset without such restrictions. One can recognize that the Euromarkets are a part of the present nonsystem that works to the advantage of the LDCs, mainly by acting as a useful source of borrowing, and therefore understand why they should seek to fend off proposals to slap controls on the Euromarkets. But agreement on a structured system would inevitably have required concessions from all parties, which the South showed itself no more willing to make than the North.

The principal aim of the LDCs in the C–20 negotiations was, as noted in chapter 15.5, the introduction of a link between reserve creation and development assistance. Specifically, they proposed a change in the formula whereby newly created SDRs would be distributed among participants giving all developing countries a share larger than they are entitled to on the basis of quota and giving the least developed[3] a larger share still. They also resisted proposals to raise the interest rate on the SDR, a step argued to be necessary in order to make the SDR an attractive asset to hold in comparison with alternatives, since this inevitably reduces the value of receiving SDR allocations because SDR use becomes more expensive. Once again, a question of the consistency of their position arises: was it realistic to think that an SDR system could be brought into being, especially if allocations were to be skewed toward themselves so that the average industrial country would have to be a net holder of SDRs, if there were no restrictions on reserve composition and subeconomic interest rates?

The developing countries found it easy to head off talk of restrictions on the Euromarkets, delayed the move to raise interest rates on the SDR (which finally reached a full commercial rate at the beginning of 1981), and

---

2. "The Arusha Initiative," published in *Development Dialogue* 1980 (2), p 18.
3. For a list of the countries currently classified as "least developed," see chap. 17.1.

failed to win acceptance of the link. By the time of the C–20, most of the industrial countries had decided that the link would be an acceptable concession in return for LDC acceptance of the rest of a package, if such could be negotiated, but Germany and the United States held out against even that. The LDCs have continued to demand a link since but have met with no more sympathy than before.

While the link has continued to be rejected, the *demand* for it has had some spin-off. The developed countries have felt obliged, or felt it expedient, to occasionally temper their negative stance on the main issue by offering concessions on other aspects of the Fund's operations. There are three such issues on which significant concessions were won by the developing countries during the 1970s: establishment of the Extended Facility, liberalization of compensatory financing, and sale of Fund gold to establish a Trust Fund.

The Extended Facility emerged from the concluding stages of the C–20, as an attempt to pacify the LDCs for rejection of the link. It is extended in the senses that it provides loans paid out over a longer period, with a longer maturity, and on a larger scale relative to a country's quota, as compared to the Fund's regular facilities. The intention is to be able to help a country undertake an adjustment program that requires structural adaptation and not just demand restraint. In terms of the analytical categories of chapter 8, this type of program requires expenditure switching in order to combine external adjustment with the preservation of internal balance, but the supply structure is so inelastic as to preclude expenditure switching independently of new investment to implement structural change.

The Compensatory Financing Facility had been established back in the mid-1960s as one of the first fruits of LDC efforts to improve their financial environment. Its purpose is that of providing semiautomatic (low conditionality, in the jargon) financing to a country whose receipts from primary product exports decline due to factors outside its own control. This may mean either crop failures or other negative supply shocks or else a deterioration in the terms of trade. The IMF has a formula which determines the maximum amount that a country can draw, based on how much export receipts in the given year fall short of the estimated five-year moving average. (This is an estimate, because it involves forecasting export receipts for the last two years of the period.) Drawings are also limited by reference to the size of a country's quota, and it was primarily those regulations that were liberalized as a part of the Jamaica accords in early 1976. Considerable use was made of the increased borrowing possibilities afforded by liberalization in 1976, but there is some doubt as to whether the facility has in fact done much to stabilize foreign exchange receipts. One problem is that repayment is on a fixed schedule rather than dependent on ability to pay, so that a country may be required to reimburse the Fund when it is even shorter of cash than when it drew. In any event, the LDCs have not accepted compensatory financing as a substitute for commodity price stabilization.

Until the end of the 1960s, IMF members paid a quarter of their quota subscriptions in gold. (The rest was paid in their national currency.) This meant that when gold ceased to be a reserve asset and became a lucrative speculative investment instead, the IMF was holding a lot of gold—almost a tenth of total official gold stocks, in fact. The French—still gold bugs, despite de Gaulle's death—proposed that this be returned, or "restituted," to the members who had paid it to the Fund. The LDCs saw this redundant gold as a possible source of development finance. The compromise struck at Jamaica was to restitute one-sixth of the Fund's gold to members, to sell another sixth on the private market and use the proceeds for development finance, and leave the remaining two-thirds with the Fund for disposal as might be decided in the future. Accordingly, a sixth of the Fund's gold was auctioned off over the following years, and the profit—the excess of the sum realized over the value of SDR 35 per ounce at which the gold was valued in the Fund's books—was channeled into establishing a Trust Fund. This made very low interest loans (on essentially IDA terms) subject to minimal conditions to the poorest of the Fund's members, provided they could show a balance of payments need.

Another area in which the developing countries have pressed for IMF reform in recent years involves *conditionality*—the conditions that the Fund has been accustomed to impose on drawings from its high-conditionality facilities.[4] As noted in chapter 8.6, programs in this category designed to secure payments adjustment have normally involved limits on domestic credit expansion (DCE). The Fund has adopted the practice of treating these DCE limits as *performance criteria*, which means that a country exceeding the agreed limits ceases to be eligible for further drawings. Other performance criteria often involve limits on government borrowing, requirements of payments liberalization, and restrictions on foreign borrowing.

There are two complaints against these arrangements. One is that they involve unnecessary supervision of borrowing countries, and the other that

---

4. Fund lending is divided into three categories: unconditional (the SDR scheme and the reserve tranche, which essentially corresponds to what a member has put into the Fund); low-conditionality (the first credit tranche, the compensatory financing facility and the oil facility of 1974 to 1976); and high-conditionality (the remaining three credit tranches, the extended facility, and enlarged access). Low-conditionality involves not much more than a demonstration that a country has a payments deficit and a declaration that it will cooperate with the Fund in finding solutions to any payments problems it may have.

the programs called for by the Fund frequently require unduly severe deflation and/or devaluation. The developing countries have therefore called for Fund lending to be based on more automatic criteria and subject to less onerous conditions. A thoughtful UNCTAD report published in 1979 suggested that the principle underlying the Compensatory Financing Facility needed to be explicitly recognized and then consistently and comprehensively applied. The basic principle, it argued, was that countries should automatically be entitled to a measure of help from the international community when they encountered balance of payments problems as a result of factors outside their own control. The Fund's practices might be appropriate where a country had brought on its own problems as a result of irresponsibly expansionary policies, but this was not the only nor (more arguably) the main cause of payments deficits.

The Fund has not accepted the arguments for general access to low-conditionality finance where exogenous shocks occur, but it has extended compensatory financing to cover temporary excesses in the cost of cereal imports. For a time the Fund also loosened the conditions attached to drawings from the high-conditionality facilities, but these were tightened again in 1981 following the misgivings voiced by the Reagan administration. One argument in favor of maintaining relatively strict terms is that these are needed so that the IMF's approval can reestablish a country's creditworthiness with the private market. Should conditionality cease to imply an assurance that the country's policies have changed enough to promise a payments recovery, the process of reestablishing lost creditworthiness could become much more difficult and painful.

16.6 Summary

The political emergence of the developing countries in the two decades up to 1965 was followed by a desire for an economic situation of greater equality with the developed countries. There was a wide range of views regarding the extent to which the international economic system could be held responsible for LDC poverty, from Marxists who interpreted the system as deliberately exploitative to orthodox Northerners who argued that the system gave every country the chance to better its position. LDC rhetoric tended to come closer to the Marxist position, but the practical steps proposed were often closer to the liberal philosophy. Northern rhetoric also had its share of humbug: even those who were indignant at Northern restrictions on textile imports drew the line at poor Southern workers being allowed to migrate freely to the North.

The original hopes, and fears, that OPEC marked the beginning of a new order have by now largely vanished. The system has continued to evolve, and the direction of that evolution has surely been influenced by the diplomatic pressures of the South. The South has in fact made modest gains on a wide variety of specific issues—but there is no sign of that revolution in power relationships and the distribution of income for which the South originally called. If the subtitle of the Brandt Commission's report—"A Program for Survival"—is justified, the outlook for humanity is bleak.

16.7 Bibliography

On unequal exchange, see A. Emmanuel, *Unequal Exchange* (New York: Monthly Review Press, 1972).

The report of the Brandt Commission was published as *North-South: A Program for Survival* (Cambridge, Mass.: MIT Press, 1980). The proceedings of a 1976 conference devoted to consideration of the NIEO debate were published in J. N. Bhagwati, ed., *The New International Economic Order: The North-South Debate* (Cambridge, Mass.: MIT Press, 1977). Some of the papers presented to a conference held at Refsnes Gods, Norway, to consider the relevance of "accepted Western economic theories" to the negotiations for a NIEO are contained in G.K. Helleiner, ed., *For Good or Evil* (Toronto: University of Toronto Press, 1982).

Another useful collection of papers, again from a predominantly "liberal internationalist" perspective, is W. R. Cline, ed., *Policy Alternatives for a New International Economic Order: An Economic Analysis* (New York: Praeger, 1979). Useful discussions of many North-South issues, from a World Bank perspective, can usually be found in the *World Development Report,* now an annual publication of the World Bank.

For a hostile Northern view of foreign aid, see P. T. Bauer, "Foreign Aid and the Third World," in P. Duignan and A. Rabushka, *The United States in the 1980s* (Stanford, CA: Hoover Institution, 1980). For a hostile view of the whole idea of a NIEO, see K. Brunner, "Economic Development, Cancun and the Western Democracies," *The World Economy,* Mar. 1982.

On monetary questions, an overall liberal Northern view is provided by W. R. Cline, *International Monetary Reform and the Developing Countries* (Washington, D.C.: Brookings Institution, 1976). For a radical Southern view, see I. S. Abdalla, "The Inadequacy and Loss of Legitimacy of the International Monetary Fund," *Development Dialogue,* 1980 (2), and the other papers from the Arusha meeting gathered there. The "UNCTAD proposal" for a right to low-conditionality finance for deficits outside a country's control is to be found in S. Dell and R. Lawrence, *The Balance of Payments Adjustment Process in Developing Countries* (New York: Pergamon Press, 1980). For contrasting discussions of International Monetary Fund conditionality, see S. Dell, *On Being Grandmotherly: The Evolution of IMF Conditionality,* Princeton Essays in International Finance No. 144 (1982); B. Nowzad, *The IMF and Its Critics,* Princeton Essays in International Finance No. 146 (1981); and J. Williamson, *The Lending Policies of the International Monetary Fund* (Washington, D.C.: Institute for International Economics, 1982).

17

Global
Macroeconomics

THE TWO leading macroeconomic theorists of the twentieth century, Keynes and Friedman, both constructed their principal theoretical analyses for closed national economies. An unfortunate legacy of that framework is that analysis of macroeconomic phenomena, like activity, inflation, and growth, all too often still pays insufficient attention to the international dimension, despite the best efforts of many international economists over the years. It is to be hoped that the reader will understand the errors of closed-economy thinking and realize that the business cycle is a world phenomenon, that inflation cannot diverge much among countries that maintain fixed exchange rates, that the possibilities of translating savings into growth depend on the receptiveness of the international environment to export expansion, and so on.

However, recognizing that unemployment, inflation, and growth in the open economy depend on the state of the world economy is not enough. We also need to understand what drives the evolution of the world economy. Although the world economy is closed, the straightforward application of traditional closed-economy models is not possible. The division of the world into nation states, with their individual commercial policies, their distinct legal systems, their own monies, and their individual command of fiscal instruments, sees to that. A distinct type of analysis is needed to understand how the evolution of the global economy results from the sum of the policies pursued in individual countries.

All macroeconomic modeling rests on the use of certain aggregates as analytical categories. Most global macroeconomic modeling has in practice used certain country groupings as aggregates. It is important to understand how and why countries are customarily aggregated for purposes of presenting data and analyzing global macroeconomic developments.

There are three issues that have dominated concern about global economic management since 1960. In the 1960s, the great issue was the international interaction of demand management policies and the business cycle. In the early 1970s, this was overshadowed—though not displaced—by the problem of the simultaneous worldwide explosion of inflation. The first oil price increase superimposed a new dominant problem, the oil deficit, on continuing worries about the level of activity and inflation. These issues are treated in this chapter within the context of a description of relevant historical developments.

17.1 Aggregates

The four main country groupings to be found in most data presentations or analyses are the industrial countries, the centrally planned economies, the oil exporters, and the developing countries. The names given to these groups and the boundaries between them differ somewhat, depending both on the analytical purposes and the political sympathies of the user. The groupings may also be disaggregated.

The following brief discussion of the names and country composition of each of those four groupings, of their common characteristics and of ways in which they are frequently disaggregated should be read in conjunction with table 17–1, which provides leading statistical data on all the larger countries (defined as those with a population estimated at over 5 million in mid-1979). Countries are allocated among the four groups, with a further disaggregation between middle-income and low-income developing countries, and listed alphabetically within each group. Distribution of marginal cases between the groups has been undertaken on the basis that seems most natural to me.

The data shown for each country (where available) in the table are as follows. The first column shows the conventional estimate of GNP per capita in 1979 (the most recent data available), calculated by taking the estimate of per capita GNP in local currency and converting to dollars at the average dollar exchange rate for the year. As noted in chapter 10.2, this

TABLE 17-1
Summary Statistics of Larger Countries

	1979 GNP per Capita (Exchange Rate Basis: US dollars)	1975 Index of Real GDP per Capita (USA = 100)	1975 GNP per Capita (Exchange Rate Basis: USA = 100)	Average GDP Growth 1970–79 (% per annum)	Population 1979 (millions)	Imports/ GNP 1979	Average Export Growth 1970–79 (% per annum)
Industrial countries							
Australia	9120	—	—	3.2	14.3	0.13	4.2
Austria	8630	69.6	69.8	3.7	7.5	0.31	7.2
Belgium	10920	77.7	87.8	3.2	9.8	0.56	5.2
Canada	9640	—	—	4.2	23.7	0.23	4.6
Denmark	11900	82.4	104.5	2.8	5.1	0.30	4.4
France	9950	81.9	89.6	3.7	53.4	0.20	7.1
Germany	11730	83.0	94.7	2.6	61.2	0.22	6.0
Italy	5250	53.8	47.9	2.9	56.8	0.26	7.3
Japan	8810	68.4	62.3	5.2	115.7	0.11	9.1
Netherlands	10230	75.2	84.5	3.1	14.0	0.47	5.7
Spain	4380	55.9	41.0	4.4	37 0	0.16	10.8
Sweden	11930	—	—	2.0	8.3	0.29	2.6
Switzerland	13920	—	—	0.2	6.5	0.32	4.2
UK	6320	63.9	57.6	2.1	55.9	0.29	8.2
USA	10630	100.0	100.0	3.1	233.6	0.09	6.9
Centrally planned economies							
Bulgaria	3690	—	—	6.2	9.0	0.26	11.2
Cuba	1410	—	—	6.0	9.8	0.34[b]	3.9
Czechoslovakia	5290	—	—	4.8	15.2	0.18	6.6
East Germany	6430	—	—	4.5	16.8	0.15[b]	7.6
Korea (north)	1130	—	—	6.2	17.5	0.05	—
Hungary	3850	49.6	29.6	5.3	10.7	0.21	8.6
Poland	3830	50.1	36.0	6.1	35.4	0.13	7.3
Romania	1900	33.3	24.3	10.6	22.1	0.26	4.7
USSR	4110	—	—	5.1	264.1	0.05	7.3
Vietnam	—	—	—	—	52.9	—	—
OPEC							
Algeria	1590	—	—	5.8	18.2	0.29	0.0
Ecuador	1050	—	—	8.3	8.1	0.23	8.2
Indonesia	370	—	—	7.6	142.9	0.14	6.5
Iran	1648	37.7	22.1	—	37.0	0.16	−4.6
Iraq	2410	—	—	10.5[a]	12.6	0.23	2.5
Nigeria	670	—	—	7.5	82.6	0.22	−0.3
Saudi Arabia	7280	—	—	11.1	8.6	0.39	5.6
Venezuela	3120	—	—	5.5	14.5	0.21	−10.3
Developing countries— middle income							
Angola	440	—	—	−9.2	6.9	—	−7.9
Argentina	2230	—	—	2.5	27.3	0.11	10.7
Bolivia	550	—	—	5.2	5.4	0.34	−1.6
Brazil	1780	25.2	16.0	8.7	116.5	0.09	7.0
Cameroon	560	—	—	5.4	8.2	0.28	0.5
Chile	1690	—	—	1.9	10.9	0.23	10.7
Colombia	1010	22.4	7.9	6.0	26.1	0.13	0.9
Dominican Rep.	990	—	—	7.5	5.3	0.20	5.6
Egypt	480	—	—	7.6	38.9	0.20	−2.1
Ghana	400	—	—	−0.1	11.3	0.22[b]	−7.2

	1979 GNP per Capita (Exchange Rate Basis: US dollars)	1975 Index of Real GDP per Capita (USA = 100)	1975 GNP per Capita (Exchange Rate Basis: USA = 100)	Average GDP Growth 1970–79 (% per annum)	Population 1979 (millions)	Imports/ GNP 1979	Average Export Growth 1970–79 (% per annum)
Greece	3960	—	—	4.9	9.3	0.26	12.3
Guatemala	1020	—	—	5.9	6.8	0.22	4.5
Hong Kong	3760	—	—	9.4	5.0	0.91	8.3
Ivory Coast	1040	—	—	6.7	8.2	0.29	5.2
Kenya	380	6.6	3.4	6.5	15.3	0.28	−0.5
Korea (south)	1480	20.7	8.1	10.3	37.8	0.36	25.7
Malaysia	1370	21.5	10.9	7.9	13.1	0.44	6.5
Mexico	1640	34.7	20.4	5.1	65.5	0.11	10.9
Morocco	740	—	—	6.1	19.5	0.25	1.3
Peru	730	—	—	3.1	17.1	0.18	1.7
Philippines	600	13.2	5.2	6.2	46.7	0.24	6.2
Portugal	2180	—	—	4.5	9.8	0.28	−0.3
Senegal	430	—	—	2.5	5.5	0.32b	−0.8
South Africa	1720	—	—	3.6	28.5	0.18	8.1
Syria	1030	25.0	10.0	9.0	8.6	0.38	7.4
Thailand	590	13.0	5.0	7.7	45.5	0.28	12.0
Tunisia	1120	—	—	7.6	6.2	0.41	4.8
Turkey	1330	—	—	6.6	44.2	0.08	1.7
Yemen Arab Rep.	420	—	—	8.4	5.7	0.62	—
Yugoslavia	2430	36.1	23.2	5.9	22.1	0.26	4.7
Zambia	500	10.3	6.9	1.5	5.6	0.27	−0.7
Zimbabwe	470	—	—	1.6	7.1	0.28	—
Developing countries— low income							
Afghanistan	170	—	—	4.5	15.5	0.26	3.0
Bangladesh	90	—	—	—	88.9	0.19	−4.1
Burma	160	—	—	4.3	32.9	0.06	−0.3
China	260	—	—	5.8	964.5	0.07	—
Ethiopia	130	—	—	1.9	30.9	0.14	−2.7
Guinea	280	—	—	3.6	5.3	0.23	—
India	190	6.6	2.0	3.4	659.2	0.07	4.6
Madagascar	290	—	—	0.3	8.5	0.26	−1.0
Malawi	120	4.9	1.9	6.3	5.8	0.58	4.6
Mali	140	—	—	5.0	6.8	0.19	6.7
Mozambique	250	—	—	−2.9	10.2	—	−16.6
Nepal	130	—	—	2.7	14.0	0.14	—
Niger	270	—	—	3.7	5.2	—	11.7
Pakistan	260	8.2	2.6	4.5	79.7	0.20	−0.9
Sri Lanka	230	9.3	2.6	3.8	14.5	0.43	−3.0
Sudan	370	—	—	4.3	17.9	0.18	−4.4
Tanzania	260	—	—	4.9	18.0	0.23	6.6
Uganda	290	—	—	−0.4	12.8	0.06	−7.0
Upper Volta	180	—	—	−0.1	5.6	0.25	3.1
Zaire	260	—	—	−0.7	27.5	0.08	−1.1

SOURCES: Columns (2) and (3) from I. B. Kravis, et al., "New Insights into the Structure of the World Economy," *Review of Income and Wealth*, Dec. 1981. Other data: World Bank, *World Development Report 1981* (New York: Oxford University Press, 1981); used by permission.
NOTES: *a.* For period 1970 to 1978.
   b. Import figures are for 1978, not 1979.
   —Not available

procedure is grossly inadequate. Hence the next column shows in index form the most recent estimate (relating to 1975) of real GDP per capita from the University of Pennsylvania project for real income comparisons, which uses a conceptually appropriate basis for such comparisons. While a large part of the differences between the first two columns reflects the inadequacies of the conventional method of making real income comparisons, there is also a significant part that stems from the fact that the two columns relate to different years: hence the next column shows the index of GDP per capita for 1975 using the conventional exchange-rate conversion technique.

The remaining columns of the table are straightforward. Column 4 shows average real GDP growth during the 1970s. Column 5 shows mid-1979 population. Column 6 shows the ratio of imports to GNP in 1979: this is the most common measure of the openness of an economy. Column 7 shows the average rate of growth of export volume in the 1970s, as a measure of countries' recent success in developing export markets.

INDUSTRIAL COUNTRIES

The industrial countries, industrialized countries, or developed countries, as we have referred to them, are also called the industrial market economies (by the United Nations and World Bank) or the advanced capitalist countries (by those with Marxist sympathies). The fourteen core members of the group are Belgium, Canada, Denmark, France, Germany, Italy, Japan, Luxembourg, the Netherlands, Norway, Sweden, Switzerland, the United Kingdom, and the United States. Some or all other members of the OECD may be included in the group, most regularly the high-income ones, like Australia, Austria, Finland, Iceland, and New Zealand, and usually Ireland and Spain. The other OECD members in southern Europe, namely Greece, Portugal, and Turkey, as well as Yugoslavia, are more often grouped with the middle-income developing countries. Israel and South Africa are also occasionally placed among the industrial countries, although the latter is difficult to justify on economic grounds unless one is implicitly treating the white minority (which does enjoy industrial-country living standards) as a separate nation from the black majority.

The common economic characteristics of the industrial countries are that they have relatively high per capita incomes, that they have completed the transformation from a subsistence economy to a modern economy, and that they have broadly market-oriented (capitalist or mixed) economic systems.

The core members of the group now all have liberal-democratic systems of representative government.

The most frequent disaggregation involves picking out some of the large economies, notably the United States, Japan, and Germany, and quite often all seven of the large economies (which involves adding Canada, France, Italy and the United Kingdom). The remaining small industrial countries may be treated as a group. Alternatively, the industrial countries may be disaggregated into North America, Europe, and Japan (plus Australia). The EEC may also be treated as a subaggregate.

CENTRALLY PLANNED ECONOMIES

The centrally planned economies, as they are referred to by the United Nations, may also be called the nonmarket economies, the Communist countries (usually by capitalists), or the Socialist countries (usually by Communists). The core group consists of Bulgaria, Czechoslovakia, East Germany, Hungary, Poland, and the Soviet Union. Romania, the poorest European member of COMECON, is also usually included, though the World Bank now lists it and all other countries with Communist governments among the developing countries. The non-European members of COMECON, that is, Cuba, Mongolia, North Korea, and Vietnam, are also usually included. The other obvious candidates are Albania (probably the world's most closed economy), China (the most populous country), Kampuchea (formerly Cambodia), Laos, and Yugoslavia. Other Third World countries with Marxist-oriented governments have customarily been left in the category of developing countries, presumably because their regimes have not looked sufficiently securely entrenched to merit the trouble of reclassification.

The obvious common characteristics of the countries in the group are that they all have governments that call themselves Socialist-Communist-Marxist and look fairly permanent; they have all undertaken a major socialization of the economy; and they all rely on central planning rather than the price mechanism for important economic decisions. Per capita incomes range down, from the maximum in East Germany about equivalent to that in one of the poorer industrial countries like the United Kingdom, to levels typical of low-income LDCs.

The centrally planned economies are too closed to have much impact on the evolution of economic events in the rest of the world, so for some purposes it is convenient to absorb them into one of the other aggregates.

377

The natural candidate is the middle-income developing countries, to which they are similar in respect to their relationship to the world capital market.

OIL EXPORTERS

Since the 1973 oil price increase it has become customary to treat some group of oil-exporting countries as a separate aggregate. The simplest basis for drawing this distinction is to select the thirteen members of OPEC (Algeria, Ecuador, Gabon, Kuwait, Indonesia, Iran, Iraq, Libya, Nigeria, Qatar, Saudi Arabia, United Arab Emirates, Venezuela). The objection to this procedure is that membership in OPEC is not a particularly good indicator of the importance of oil to a country's economy. Some OPEC members have quite large, diversified economies to which oil is, while more than marginal, fairly minor. Others provide only a tiny fraction of the world oil supply. On either criterion, some non-OPEC members are now stronger candidates for inclusion than some OPEC members.

These considerations have led to rival alternative classification schemes. First, those countries with economies dominated by oil, and few alternative productive resources, and which therefore had payments surpluses on current account throughout the period from 1974 to 1981, are called the *low-absorbing* or *capital surplus* oil exporters. These are the core oil exporters, which are always placed in this category: Kuwait, Libya, Qatar, Saudi Arabia (the dominant member of the group), and the United Arab Emirates, with Iraq a marginal case (at least until the Iraq-Iran war). Second, the IMF now calls the *oil-exporting countries* those whose oil exports comprise more than two-thirds of their total exports *and* more than about 1 percent of total world supply: as compared to the membership of OPEC, this has the effect of excluding Ecuador and Gabon and including Oman. Third, one might list the countries that are actually net oil exporters: this would give a list comprising all the above plus Bahrain, Bolivia, China, Congo, Egypt, Malaysia, Mexico, Norway, Peru, Romania, Syria, Trinidad and Tobago, Tunisia, the United Kingdom, and the USSR. But then one could of course ask: why only oil, why not recognize that Dutch gas has the same effect as Norwegian oil? Or why only hydrocarbons, why not all forms of energy? Or why only energy, why not other forms of mineral wealth? As usual, there is no perfect basis for aggregation.

DEVELOPING COUNTRIES

All countries not included in one of the preceding aggregates are put in the category that has in recent years usually been referred to as the develop-

378

ing countries. They started off being called the poor countries, a term progressively modified to underdeveloped, less developed (from which the LDC acronym still sticks), and then developing, in an attempt to find a term that would not offend national pride. But, given that the major criterion for inclusion is in fact per capita income rather than its rate of increase, the nomenclature leaves much to be desired. The World Bank has recently started to split the developing countries into two groups, on the basis of per capita income: middle-income and low-income countries. This is a commendable step—despite the continued use of naive exchange-rate conversions to compare per capita incomes and draw the dividing line—which is followed in table 17–1.

The main thing the developing countries have in common, apart from low per capita incomes, is their dissatisfaction with the international status quo. This is manifest in their frequent joint action in fora like the United Nations, UNCTAD, and the Group of Seventy-Seven—a pressure group originally formed by the 77 LDC participants in the first UNCTAD conference, which retains its original name although it now has over 100 members.

The middle-income countries had 1979 per capita incomes (measured by exchange rate conversion) ranging from $375 up to about $4,000. The majority of these countries now has significant access as *borrowers* to the international capital market, though not many of them allow their residents to *lend* extensively. An important subcategory is the semiindustrial countries or NICs or major exporters of manufactures: the World Bank lists Argentina, Brazil, Colombia, Egypt, Greece, Hong Kong, Israel, Mexico, Philippines, Portugal, Romania, Singapore, South Africa, South Korea, Spain, Turkey, Uruguay, and Yugoslavia in this category. In general it can be seen that these are the richer of the developing countries, although a problem arises in classifying the larger countries like Egypt and India, which have manufactured exports that are *absolutely* quite substantial but small *relative* to the domestic economy.

The low-income countries as defined in table 17–1 are those with a per capita income (using exchange-rate conversion) of under $375 in 1979. Most of them have very little creditworthiness with the private market. All except China, India, and Indonesia are overwhelmingly exporters of primary products. An important subcategory, characterized by both very low *per capita* income and the absence of any significant modern sector, are the least developed. The current United Nations list comprises Afghanistan, Benin, Bhutan, Burundi, Central African Republic, Chad, Ethiopia, Guinea, Haiti, Laos, Lesotho, Malawi, Mali, Nepal, Niger, Rwanda, Somalia, Sudan, Tanzania, Uganda, Upper Volta, Yemen A.R., and Yemen P.D.R. The United Nations has urged the international community to make special efforts to help these countries and has to that end recently established a separate aid target for them, involving donors giving at least 0.15 percent of their GNP to the group.

17.2 Demand Management in the 1960s

The 1930s provided graphic evidence of the international interdependence of economic activity. The lesson was not forgotten in the early postwar years, when people used to talk of how "Europe would catch pneumonia if the United States sneezed," meaning that any United States recession would spread to, and have magnified effects in, Europe. Then came 1958 and the most severe postwar recession prior to the oil price increase, from which Europe recovered rapidly while President Dwight Eisenhower's caution sent the United States into a new recession almost as soon as recovery had started. That served to lay to rest the worries about European dependence on the United States.

It did not, however, lead decision makers to the false conclusion that demand-management policy should be treated as a purely national problem. It so happened that the Organization for European Economic Cooperation (OEEC) had just worked itself out of a job, with the successful completion of postwar reconstruction in Europe and the winding up of the European Payments Union. However, one can never abolish a bureaucracy, especially an international bureaucracy, so it was necessary to find it a new job. The solution adopted was to enlarge it (to include the United States and Canada, then Japan, and subsequently Australia and New Zealand), change its name (to OECD), and charge it with the task of coordinating economic policy. Although OECD has concerned itself with myriad aspects of economic policy over the last twenty years, from fisheries to technology to pollution to energy to trying to get its members to bully one another into stepping up aid, a central part of its work has always been the coordination of conjunctural policy.

In the 1960s, this was conceived as a topic that was relevant only to the industrial countries. The others were regarded as having neither any significant degree of policy autonomy capable of influencing the course of the world economy nor any worthwhile expertise to offer to those who had. Consequently, it was deemed natural and appropriate to discuss conjunctural coordination within the limited confines of what outsiders dubbed the rich men's club. This became the province of the OECD's Economic Policy

Committee and its Working Party No. 3, whose terms of reference committed it to supervision of the process of balance of payments adjustment. Senior civil servants converged on Paris every six or eight weeks to scrutinize one another's policies with regard to demand management and payments adjustment. It was not possible to divorce discussion of the two topics because, as noted in chapter 15.4, the Bretton Woods system after about 1960 had no adjustment mechanism other than the trimming of demand-management policy to the needs of external balance (apart from the last-resort technique of exchange-rate changes).

The spirit of the 1960s, especially the early 1960s, was overwhelmingly Keynesian. It was taken for granted virtually throughout the Atlantic Community (a geopolitical concept that came to include Japan) that it was possible and desirable to manipulate monetary and especially fiscal policy with a view to pursuing those targets that we have been calling internal balance and external balance. Policy was not confused by the parallel existence of financial targets like preordained growth rates of the money supply or balanced budgets (usually three years in the future), as it was in the 1970s. If unemployment rose above target, the government raised its spending, cut taxes, and since monetary policy was generally dedicated to maintaining the interest rate constant, financed part of the resulting increase in the budget deficit by monetary expansion. If the economy showed signs of becoming overheated, those policies were put into reverse. A payments deficit induced similar reactions, though with a greater component of monetary restriction thrown in (a reflection of Mundell's argument about manipulating the fiscal-monetary mix). A payments surplus tended to induce some easing of policy, though rarely enough to deflect sermons being delivered in Paris about the responsibilities of surplus countries.

In retrospect, one looks back on the 1960s as a "belle epoque" when governments wielded their policy instruments in a rational way and achieved an impressive measure of success. At the time, however, the problems looked real enough. And, indeed, one can now see that the failure to meet some of those problems at the time—especially those of inflation and the United States payments deficit—undermined the continued viability of the belle epoque.

Richard Cooper, the major analyst of the "economics of interdependence" of the period, diagnosed three general problems. The first was an insufficiency of instruments. The second was a possible inconsistency in targets. The third was dynamic inefficiency when policy instruments with strong international spillovers were adjusted by national policy makers in an uncoordinated way. All three were problems which, although they had always existed to some degree, were magnified in importance by the dramatic increase in interdependence within the Atlantic Community after 1958.

The two instrument insufficiencies that most worried observers related to the balance of payments on the one hand and inflation on the other. Demand-management policy was preempted for an internal balance target, interpreted as a particular level of employment. Given the unwillingness to use exchange-rate changes or commercial policy, and the inadequacy of merely financing rather than adjusting current imbalances, there was one instrument too few to achieve the external balance target. The desire to remedy this deficiency provided one of the bases for advocacy of greater exchange-rate flexibility. Similarly, the employment target was thought of as implying a particular outcome for the inflation rate (by the Phillips curve). Opinion divided as to what to do when that outcome was unacceptable. The Germans[1] argued that priority should be given to combating inflation, if necessary by adjusting the employment target to a rate consistent with price stability. This argument eventually triumphed among the Anglo-Saxons as well, after Phelps and Friedman had called the implied employment target "the natural rate of unemployment" and experience had demonstrated that there was something in the idea that attempts to hold unemployment lower would lead to accelerating inflation. But there was another reaction, as well, which at the time was more influential within the OECD. That was to search for another policy instrument, capable of reconciling full employment and price stability. That was the birth of the search for incomes policies. It is a search that has not been conspicuously successful to date. Nevertheless, the pressures that motivated the search are greater today than they were then (estimates of the natural rate of unemployment are now around 7 percent in both the United States and the United Kingdom), so it will be surprising if the search is not resumed in the future.

The second general problem was that of target inconsistency. The inconsistencies that caused concern were those regarding the balance of payments —the n-1 or consistency problem again. We already discussed in chapter 15.5 how one of the arguments in favor of creation of a new reserve asset was the desire to be able to increase the stock of reserves to reconcile reserve accumulation objectives that might otherwise be inconsistent. The solution to the n-1 problem was, therefore, that of providing an nth degree of freedom to the system. But there was another type of inconsistency in payments objectives to which the solution was not so easy: objectives for the current account of the balance of payments. Cooper (1968, pp. 156–57) records that in 1962 all the major industrial countries were simultaneously

1. Supported by other German-speakers (including the Dutch, who can all speak German, too).

wishing to increase their current-account surpluses or decrease their deficits. True, they could have accomplished that if the rest of the world had correspondingly increased its current-account deficit, and this was indeed one of the arguments deployed in favor of the link (see chap. 16.5). But that solution did not prove to have much appeal to the OECD countries, which instead settled down to years of debate in OECD as to how they should divide up between themselves the total current-account deficit that the rest of the world could finance. Critics regarded this debate as rather sterile, inasmuch as the countries did not actually wield any policy weapons capable of accomplishing much effect of any sort, including harm to the system, if they set about pursuing inconsistent targets.

The third problem was that of dynamic inefficiency when policy instruments with strong international spillovers were adjusted by national policy makers in an uncoordinated way. The fact that international spillovers are significant is illustrated by the estimates shown in table 17–2. These come from simulation exercises undertaken on the OECD model called INTER-LINK, which is a model that consists of thirty-one submodels (of twenty-three OECD countries and eight non-OECD regions) linked together through a world trade model. All estimates refer to the first-year impact of an exogenous fiscal expansion equivalent to 1 percent of GNP by the country listed in the first column. (The figures for the smaller countries are not shown in the table.) The second column then shows the domestic multiplier; for example, a fiscal expansion equal to 1 percent of GNP in the United States would increase US GNP by 1.47 percent. Note that this

TABLE 17–2

OECD Estimates of International Demand Spillovers

Country Expanding Demand (1)	Domestic Multiplier (2)	OECD Multiplier Domestic Multiplier (3)	Effect on OECD (4)
USA	1.47	1.23	0.74
Japan	1.26	1.46	0.21
Germany	1.25	1.90	0.23
France	1.21	1.68	0.18
UK	1.17	1.98	0.13
Italy	1.24	1.96	0.09
Canada	1.27	1.83	0.10
Netherlands	0.73	2.69	0.04
TOTAL OECD	n.a.	n.a.	2.04

SOURCE: *The OECD International Linkage Model,* Organization for Economic Cooperation and Development Occasional Studies, January 1979, table 8.

includes the foreign repercussion of chapter 8.9. There is clearly a tendency for the domestic multiplier to decline as the economy becomes smaller and more open, reaching values less than unity in three cases, of which the lowest is the 0.73 for the Netherlands. The third and critical column shows the ratio between the multiplier for the whole of the OECD area and the domestic multiplier. Even for the relatively closed United States and Japanese economies, it is estimated that the multipliers for the whole OECD are almost a quarter and a half larger, respectively, than the domestic multipliers. The ratios are higher for other countries: almost double for the other large countries, and ranging up to three times as large for the small countries. If one had an estimate of the world multiplier rather than the OECD multiplier, the spillover would be relatively more important still.[2]

The final column shows the estimated percentage effect on OECD GNP of a 1 percent fiscal expansion in each country. Obviously this effect is larger in the bigger countries: thus a 1 percent United States fiscal expansion is estimated to raise OECD GNP by 0.74 percent, while a 1 percent fiscal expansion by the Netherlands would raise it by only 0.04 percent (despite the fact that, dollar for dollar, Dutch expansion is actually more effective than United States expansion). The last line of that column shows that the total OECD multiplier is just over 2, that is, a 1 percent fiscal expansion in all the OECD countries simultaneously would increase OECD GNP by an estimated 2.04 percent.

Why should this interdependence constitute a problem for policy? Given that the national policy makers control sufficient instruments and that the targets they are pursuing are mutually consistent, there is no reason to suppose that the system would not in due course approach equilibrium just because the policy instruments are wielded without conscious coordination. The situation is analogous to that which arises in the case of Mundell's assignment problem illustrated in figure 9–2: there the policy instruments were wielded by independent agencies within a single country, whereas here instruments are controlled by policy makers in different countries. But no one has ever suggested that there is any danger of an assignment of domestic full employment and national payments equilibrium to the authorities of each country turning out to be unstable.[3] Hence those who are convinced by Mundell's analysis should presumably reject Cooper's concerns. But it will be recalled that in chapter 9.2 we argued that it made little sense to have the economy pursue a zig-zag path from its initial position at E_1 to its

2. The figures cited include an estimate for the increase in OECD income that comes about because of the induced rise in the rest of the world's income, but the figures do not include an estimate for that increase in the rest of the world's income.

3. Assuming, at least, that the targets are consistent.

desired equilibrium at E (in figure 9–2B), as is implied by uncoordinated manipulation of fiscal and monetary policy by the Treasury and central bank, when coordination between the two would let them guide the economy straight to E. Coordination of policy instruments is, in other words, intended to reduce the time the economy spends away from the desired equilibrium.

Cooper argued that exactly the same thing was true in the international context. A lack of policy coordination could be expected to delay the achievement of policy objectives (as well as increasing the need for international reserves to finance the payments imbalances that would arise on the path to equilibrium). Moreover, he showed that the costs of a lack of coordination, in terms of delays in achieving objectives and increased reserve needs, increase with the degree of interdependence. For example, suppose that Europe were at internal balance when the United States ran into excessive demand pressures and therefore decided to deflate. Then the higher the United States import propensity, the greater would be the impact of United States deflation on European income, and therefore the greater would be the need for Europe to embark on prompt reflationary measures if undesired unemployment were to be averted.

The OECD consultations on coordination of economic policy therefore involved swapping experiences of attempts to widen the range of instruments available, attempting to secure consistency in national policy objectives (mainly with respect to the balance of payments), and ensuring that demand management policies for the OECD area as a whole added up to a stance consistent with a satisfactory level of activity for the area as a whole. The task that involved the most continuous monitoring was the third of these. In principle, it covered the pursuit of external, as well as internal, balance, but in view of the insufficiency of policy variables, it was the latter that was important. In the 1960s governments had no qualms about using fiscal-monetary policy in pursuit of an employment target. And in general the OECD area did stay close to full employment, though it is not clear to what extent policy coordination contributed to that success.

One potential danger of coordinating demand policies is that exhortations to expand or contract, issued because of the state of the world conjuncture, will induce parallel policies in most countries. Given that all demand policies act with a substantial lag, it is entirely possible that the business cycle might be amplified rather than reduced. It was indeed argued that this happened in the early 1970s, when the urgings to expand out of the 1971 recession led to the synchronized world boom of 1973, and the restrictive actions induced by that boom magnified the simultaneous recession of 1975. The conclusion drawn from these experiences by the OECD was the need to foster cyclical desynchronization. That gloss has been one factor modifying the policy recommendations of the OECD in recent years. But a far more important factor has been the problem of inflation.

17.3 The Outbreak of World Inflation

Although the world never returned to price stability after the Second World War, it got close to it in the 1950s. The IMF's world average of the rate of increase of consumer prices was a mere 0.3 percent in 1950 and 1 percent in 1955. Even the United Kingdom recorded an inflation rate as low as 0.6 percent in 1959, while actual price falls were recorded for about 13 percent of industrial-country years in the 1950s (excluding the Korean War years). Inflation expectations were near zero; indeed, few economists were aware of the concept.

The uneven, gradual, but persistent acceleration of inflation from the mid-1950s through to 1974 is shown by the figures presented in table 17–3. When concern about the persistence of inflation started to mount in the late 1950s and early 1960s, it was viewed as a series of national problems. The dominant theory of inflation at the time was the simple Phillips curve.

TABLE 17–3
World Inflation, 1950–80
(percentage per annum increase in CPI)

	World	Industrial Countries	USA	Japan	Germany	France	UK
1950	0.3	0.1	−1.3	−7.1	−6.1	8.0	2.7
1951–52	6.8	6.7	5.1	10.8	5.0	14.8	8.1
1953–55	1.1	0.7	0.3	4.0	0	−0.2	3.4
1956–59	3.7	2.6	2.2	1.0	2.0	6.2	2.7
1960–64	3.5	2.2	1.2	5.4	2.3	4.0	2.6
1965–69	4.8	3.6	3.4	5.3	2.5	3.8	4.3
1970–72	5.9	5.2	4.5	6.1	4.7	5.8	7.6
1973	9.6	7.7	6.3	11.8	6.9	7.4	9.1
1974	15.3	13.3	10.9	24.3	7.0	13.7	16.0
1975	13.4	11.1	9.2	11.9	5.9	11.7	24.2
1976	11.1	8.3	5.8	9.3	4.3	9.6	16.5
1977	11.4	8.4	6.5	8.1	3.6	9.4	15.9
1978	9.8	7.2	7.5	3.8	2.8	9.1	8.3
1979	12.1	9.2	11.3	3.6	4.1	10.7	13.4
1980	15.5	12.0	13.5	8.0	5.5	13.3	18.0

SOURCE: *International Financial Statistics,* 1981 Yearbook.

Inflation occurred because governments were pursuing ambitious employment targets, and it was faster in countries like Britain and France which gave a greater weight to low unemployment than it was in other countries like Germany or the United States that gave a higher priority to combating inflation. The monetarist view at that time was not very different: monetarists preferred to argue straight from monetary policy to inflation rather than recognize the intervening effect on employment, but, given that they thought of monetary policy as money-supply policy and regarded that as under national control, they still thought of inflation as a series of national phenomena. When national policies proved incompatible to the point of jeopardizing external balance, both schools accepted that the country that was out of line should change its exchange rate to restore PPP.

This view of inflation was challenged by two fundamental analytical developments in the late 1960s. Monetarists played an important role in both, while many Keynesians resisted both. The fact that events soon demonstrated that both contained substantial elements of truth perhaps did more than anything else to undermine the credibility of Keynesianism and entrench monetarism, despite the fact that the logical link to the rest of the monetarist creed is not particularly strong.

The first new development was of course the Phelps-Friedman accelerationist theory, or the vertical long-run Phillips curve, already sketched in chapter 8.5. This amounted to reinterpreting the Phillips curve as representing the net balance of desired *relative* price changes. To deduce the corresponding actual rate of price change, it is necessary to add the expected rate of inflation. Then, if you add the adaptive expectations hypothesis (see chap. 10.4) according to which expected inflation will adjust toward the rate actually experienced, one can conclude that any attempt to hold unemployment below the natural rate will generate accelerating inflation—such as the world experienced from the mid-1950s to the mid-1970s.

Taken by itself, the natural rate hypothesis would suggest that each individual country would experience an acceleration of inflation that depended on how close it was operating to full employment. But in fact the inflationary acceleration was more uniform across countries than that could have explained. This is where the second analytical innovation entered: the view that under a fixed exchange-rate system (such as the world largely retained till 1971, or even 1973) inflation was a single global phenomenon, rather than a series of national phenomena.

Monetarists advanced two main analytical grounds for this assertion. The first is that price levels are kept in line internationally by arbitrage. We already encountered this global monetarist claim in chapter 9.4 and concluded that the empirical evidence strongly refutes the extreme version of the hypothesis. But that is not to dismiss it altogether. Empirical price equations typically do find a role for foreign competitors' prices, as well as for domestic costs (with the former, quite plausibly, being more important in explaining export prices than domestic prices, and more important in small countries than in large ones). This implies that inflation will spill over from one country to its trading partners and hence that inflation rates will tend to move in parallel internationally.

The second principal channel that monetarists argued must maintain parallel inflation rates within a fixed exchange rate area is the spillover of money through the balance of payments. An expansion in domestic credit in one country will tend to flow out through an increased payments deficit, on current or capital account or both, which will swell the reserves and—in the absence of complete sterilization—the money supplies of its trading partners. Thus monetary expansion gets spread around the world and generates inflation more or less equally everywhere so long as exchange rates remain fixed. The central question in understanding world inflation then becomes understanding how the world money supply is determined. Chapter 15.1 demonstrated how under a gold standard the world money supply is determined in large measure by the stock of gold reserves and that the reserve gain and consequent expansionary impulse in the surplus countries is offset by the increasing pressure to reverse their expansionary policies in the credit-creating deficit countries. However, the world was not on a symmetrical gold standard in the late 1960s but on a somewhat asymmetrical gold-exchange standard that came close to being a totally asymmetrical dollar standard after creation of the two-tier gold market in 1968. This has strong implications for the world money supply process, as the Swiss economist Alexander Swoboda (b. 1939) has analyzed most extensively. Since dollars that flow out through a United States payments deficit were added to other countries' reserves rather than depleting the stock of United States reserve assets, the United States could afford to—and did—sterilize its deficit completely. Meanwhile those dollars provided high-powered money that generated monetary expansion in other countries. Thus under a dollar standard United States monetary policy provides the motive force driving world monetary expansion.

This analysis suggests that the key event in igniting world inflation was the superimposition of the Vietnam War on President Lyndon Johnson's ambitious Great Society social programs in the United States. Given the absence of an external payments constraint, it was all too easy to finance a good part of the resulting fiscal deficit by monetary expansion. In due course the United States payments deficit exploded, and other countries imported inflation. The abandonment of pegged exchange rates in early

1973 was, in this view, a consequence of the unwillingness of countries like Germany and Switzerland to continue importing inflation. Floating against the dollar gave them the option of appreciating instead of buying dollars and thus permitted them to secure a lower rate of inflation—which is precisely what they proceeded to do.

Economists in the eclectic mainstream accept the basic notion that inflation rates within a fixed exchange-rate area cannot diverge very far, but they tend to argue that the monetarist version goes too far in some respects and not far enough in others. It goes too far when it argues that price levels are rigidly pegged together through arbitrage, that countries cannot inflate themselves into uncompetitiveness, that devaluation cannot improve competitiveness, and that inflation can be brought down to the international norm without the threat of a drastic departure from internal balance simply by pegging the exchange rate. But it does not go far enough when it concentrates attention on arbitrage and money spillovers as the *only* channels tending to keep inflation rates in line internationally. One other channel that is certainly important in practice is the direct cost-push effect of increased prices of imported raw materials and intermediate goods. Another is the demand-pull effects that are generated by increased exports and import substitution when a country becomes more competitive as a result of foreign inflation not neutralized by an exchange rate change. It is even possible—and was seriously suggested in the late 1960s, when the French Events of May 1968 were followed by increased labor militancy in other European countries—that a successful union wage push in one country can induce emulation in others.

An adequate theory of inflation needs to recognize the existence of a series of proximate sources of inflationary pressure. These include the pressure of domestic demand; domestic cost pressures (stemming, for example, from the attempts of labor to achieve collectively more real income than is available); imported inflation, stemming from foreign price rises; quasi-imported inflation, arising from exchange depreciation—which has similar effects, though not causes, to foreign price rises; and inflationary inertia, arising from inflationary expectations or indexation. If one wishes to think in Phillips curve terms, one would say that the first factor determines the position on the Phillips curve, while all the others influence its position. Thus an upward shift of the short-run Phillips curve is produced by increased inconsistency of real income claims, higher foreign inflation, depreciation, increased inflationary expectations, or, where indexation is present, higher past inflation. There is no inconsistency between this eclectic view of the proximate sources of inflationary pressure and recognition that in the long run inflation in a closed economy will stay close to the growth rate of the money supply. Nor is

389

this eclectic view in any way inconsistent with recognition that in the long run inflation in an open economy with a fixed exchange rate will stay close to inflation in the rest of the world. The eclectic view does, however, suggest that recognition of such long-run truths does not by itself furnish an adequate basis for policy formation, since the transitional consequences of antiinflationary policy are critically important and can be profoundly influenced by the antiinflation strategy that is adopted.

While certainly not dismissing the significance of the inflationary financing of the Vietnam War, an eclectic interpretation of the origins of the inflationary explosion of the early 1970s would suggest that there were other important reinforcing factors at work. First, there appears to have been a tendency in at least some countries for real income aspirations to run increasingly far ahead of what the economy could generate. The outstanding examples were the French Events of May 1968 and the British wage explosion of autumn 1969. Second, there were adverse supply shocks, particularly in the form of the failure of the Soviet grain harvest in 1972 and the disappearance of the anchovy from the Peruvian coast due to past overfishing in 1973. Third, the cyclical expansion of 1973 was probably the most synchronized the world has ever seen. In the short run, GWP grew by almost 7 percent in the year, a record. But the cost was to bid up the prices of raw materials in a commodity boom unprecedented since the Korean War and thus add yet another reinforcement to the inflationary momentum. What was a cost-push effect from the viewpoint of each individual country was a clear example of demand-pull at the global level.

The explanation for the breakdown of the exchange-rate system of Bretton Woods offered by the mainstream view is not very different to the monetarist interpretation already noted. Even with fixed exchange rates, countries could experience faster or slower inflation than their partners for a while. But if they did not ratify such a discrepancy by an exchange-rate change, the pressures to drag them back into line multiplied. Countries with above-average domestic inflationary pressures found themselves with overvalued currencies, and therefore confronted with a threeway choice between devaluation, chronic current account deficit, and unemployment. Countries that succeeded in curbing domestic inflation found themselves in the converse situation, forced to choose between revaluation, increasing external surplus, and importing inflation. As long as world inflation remained generally low, most countries found the common rate of inflation dictated by fixed exchange rates tolerable—although even before 1973 there were occasional changes in exchange rates caused mainly by some combination of differing cost-push pressures and differing determination to resist inflation.

But, as inflation accelerated, both countries like Britain, that had allowed their internal inflationary momentum to get out of hand, and those like Germany, that resented having to import the common rate of inflation, found the situation intolerable. Agreed international monetary reforms relevant to the situation (like general crawling to allow inflation differentials to be accommodated or a restoration of dollar convertibility to discipline United States monetary policy) not being forthcoming, exchange rates were allowed to float from March 1973.

Floating allows inflation rates to diverge, which they have duly done since 1973 (see table 17–3). It also has profound repercussions on the nature of international spillover effects. Under fixed rates, an expansion of demand in one country increases demand in its trading partners and therefore has an inflationary impact involving a shift along the Phillips curve. In contrast, under floating a demand expansion—at least if engineered by monetary policy—causes the domestic currency to depreciate and hence foreign currencies to appreciate, which will help to counter their inflation, by shifting the Phillips curve. (It was also traditionally argued that a monetary expansion in one country would lead to a demand contraction in its partners, but this inverse transmission of the business cycle presupposed an absence of capital mobility and does not in fact occur.)

Floating also changes the terms of policy trade-offs. In particular, monetary expansion comes to imply depreciation rather than a loss of reserves. As noted in chapter 15.5, there has been an inconclusive debate as to whether this is likely to erode or to accentuate the discipline to avoid inflationary policies. In the case of the United States, however, where payments deficits had ceased to involve reserve losses under the dollar standard, there is a presumption that the move to floating strengthened the incentive to avoid inflationary monetary policies. In fact the industrial countries showed themselves willing to pay a high price, in terms of acceptance of higher levels of unemployment, in the attempt to bring inflation down. Despite that, it stayed stubbornly high through the 1970s. Two reasons can be suggested for this. One is that many countries largely limited antiinflationary policy to adoption of a restrictive monetary policy, under the influence of the prevailing monetarist belief that the only factors relevant to the determination of inflation are the exchange rate, excess demand, and expectations. (The more successful countries, like Austria, Germany, and Japan, made a broader-based attack, not neglecting incomes policy.) The second reason is that the problem of inflation was much aggravated by the oil price increases—a new page of history, with the additional problems that emerged in 1974.

17.4 The Oil Deficit

In the last quarter of 1973 the price of the most important commodity in world trade quadrupled, thus transferring some 2 percent of GWP from the importers to the exporters of oil. The immediate consequences included a further boost to the already rapid world inflation and the creation of historically unprecedented imbalances on current account. More fundamental still, the Great Boom finally petered out, to be replaced by an epoch of stagflation that was far more difficult and uncertain to everyone except the oil exporters.

Unlike demand management in the 1960s or the inflationary explosion of the early 1970s, no one could interpret the oil shock as a matter of exclusive concern to the developed countries. In the first place, the change was a consequence of the success of OPEC in increasing the price of oil. A group of nonindustrial countries used their economic muscle to effect a major redistribution of income in their favor. Second, the victims of the oil price increase were not just the developed countries but included the oil-importing developing countries. Indeed, it is now clear that the area that suffered most was sub-Sahara Africa. Third, the middle-income developing countries exploited their newly established creditworthiness to adopt a strategy of debt-led growth. This had a significant effect in limiting the North's recession and quickly transferred the whole of the oil deficit—the counterpart to the OPEC surplus—away from the developed countries (see table 17–4). In short, global macroeconomics had become truly global: one could no longer hope to understand the evolution of the system by studying a limited part of it.

There are six ways in which the oil price increase had a significant impact on the evolution of the world economy, apart from the obvious effect of increasing potential income in the OPEC gainers and reducing it for the oil importers.

1. Higher oil prices gave a direct impulse to costs of production and thus to the rate of inflation. They also reduced the total available real income in the oil-importing countries, thus intensifying the inconsistency in real income claims that was already generating inflation in many countries and so made it more difficult and costly to reduce inflation through conventional policies of demand restraint.

2. Since the oil exporters lacked the inclination, not to mention the physical capacity,[4] to spend a large part of their extra income in the short run, the world propensity to save rose. This had a contractionary effect on

4. Limited port capacity constituted a real constraint on the expansion of OPEC imports.

TABLE 17–4

Global Balance of Payments Summary 1972–80
(in billions of dollars)

| | Current Balance | | | Capital Balance | | | Monetary Balance | | |
|------|Industrial Countries|OPEC|LDCs|Industrial Countries|OPEC|LDCs|Industrial Countries|OPEC|LDCs|
	Industrial Countries	OPEC	LDCs	Industrial Countries	OPEC	LDCs	Industrial Countries	OPEC	LDCs
1972	9.2	2.0	−13.6	−12.2	1.4	18.2	n.a.	n.a.	n.a.
1973	11.3	6.2	−8.7	−13.2	−1.9	19.0	10.1	4.3	10.5
1974	−9.6	66.7	−42.9	−5.3	−23.7	39.5	21.8	43.1	−0.3
1975	19.4	35.0	−51.3	−19.6	−15.0	43.1	8.3	20.1	2.0
1976	−0.5	40.0	−32.9	−4.6	−31.3	41.4	25.6	8.8	17.1
1977	−4.6	31.1	−28.6	3.6	−20.8	41.3	78.1	10.3	11.5
1978	30.8	3.3	−37.5	−18.1	−13.3	53.8	77.1	−10.0	15.3
1979	−7.8	68.4	−57.6	32.4	−54.4	67.5	−2.4	14.0	10.3
1980	−44.1	112.2	−82.1	51.3	−92.5	80.3	56.2	19.7	4.2

SOURCES: International Monetary Fund, *Annual Reports,* 1974, 1976, 1980, 1981.
NOTE: There is an element of ambiguity in distinguishing capital outflows from reserve accumulation in some OPEC members. There is an important accounting asymmetry in Euromarket operations, since a reserve placement at a Euro-bank permits a capital-account inflow to the country that borrows from the Eurobank. This is the principal explanation of the regular world surpluses on both capital and monetary balances.

world demand. In association with the restrictive fiscal-monetary policies that had been adopted in most of the leading industrial countries to combat inflation, it pushed the world into the 1975 recession, the most severe since the Great Depression, at least until 1982.

3. The increase in the value of oil exports, without a corresponding short-run rise in the value of OPEC imports, resulted in unprecedented imbalances on the current account of the balance of payments (see table 17–4). The OPEC surplus necessarily had as its counterpart a corresponding[5] current account deficit distributed between the other two groups—the so-called oil deficit. In 1974 (as again after the second oil price increase in 1979 to 1980) this was indeed split between the two groups, but the contrast between the contractionary policies of the industrial countries and the attempt of the LDCs to resist a major slowdown in growth soon led to the whole of the oil deficit being carried by the LDCs. This was, of course, possible only because of their success in tapping the world capital market, which succeeded in recycling petrodollars from OPEC to the deficit countries, as analyzed in chapter 14.1.

5. This neglects two factors: the centrally planned economies (which ran deficits of up to $10 billion per annum) and timing asymmetries. These were large in some years, especially when oil prices rose, since the oil exporters then included the value of their oil exports at the new high prices while the oil importers were still recording in their import statistics the cheap oil that had set to sea some weeks before.

4. Over time, the OPEC countries started to use their increased earnings to buy more imports and hire more foreign workers. This was the major reason for the near-disappearance of the oil surplus in 1978, when only the low absorbers remained in significant current-account surplus. It provided an especially important cushion for countries close to the main OPEC markets, especially the nonoil Arab countries, but also India and Pakistan. Naturally the oil importers faced a transfer problem in switching resources to meet the increased OPEC demand, but in fact the transfer process encountered no difficulties.

5. The rise in the relative price of oil created incentives to modify production techniques and consumption patterns to economize on the use of petroleum and energy in general and also to exploit more fully alternative sources of energy. This effect was tempered after the first oil price increase by uncertainty as to whether the higher energy prices were going to stick, but preliminary evidence suggests there was significantly more response after the 1979 to 1980 increases. As of mid-1981, it appears that energy consumption in the industrial countries is about 15 percent below what it would have been on the basis of pre-1973 trends.

6. The increased relative oil price has decreased the rate of growth of potential output of the world economy. The qualitative effects are shown in figure 17–1. First, some previously installed energy-intensive capital goods must have become uneconomic at the higher oil prices, thus leading to a one-time decline in potential output as shown by the downward step in the growth path. Second, a part of investment was diverted from sectors like manufacturing with a relatively low ICOR to the production of alternative forms of energy or to economizing on energy, which are much more capital-intensive activities. This reduced the increase in output that resulted from a given level of investment and thus the growth rate of potential output, as shown by the shallower slope of the new growth path in figure 17–1. The growth accountants like Edward Denison reckon that this factor explained a fall of perhaps 0.3 percent annum in the rate of growth of United States potential output after the first oil shock, out of a total decline of about 1.5 percent per annum. In other words, while it would be quite wrong to dismiss the effect of the oil price increase, there were other and more important factors at work in bringing the rapid expansion of the Great Boom to an end.

One major factor was the approach to technological maturity. By the early 1970s both Western Europe and Japan had largely eliminated the stock of labor in low productivity and subsistence sectors, whose transfer to the modern sector had been at the root of their rapid growth from the end of postwar reconstruction to about 1970. Perhaps the most impressive

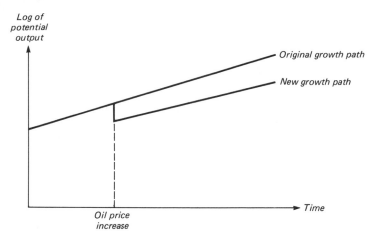

FIGURE 17–1

Impact of an Oil Price Increase on Potential Output

evidence for believing this to be the major explanation is the fact (docu-
mented in table 17–5) that in the 1970s Japan slipped from being the
fastest-growing to the slowest-growing of the capitalist economies of East
Asia. It is not easy to think of an explanation that can account so naturally
for such a striking change in ranking, except that Japan has closed the
technological gap with the West while the rest of the region still has much
leeway that it is making up.

TABLE 17–5

Growth Rates of GNP/GDP of Capitalist East Asia

	(% per annum)	
	1960–70	*1970–79*
Hong Kong	10.0	9.4
Indonesia	3.9	7.6
Japan	10.5	5.2
Korea	8.6	10.3
Malaysia	6.5	7.9
Philippines	5.1	6.2
Singapore	8.8	8.4
Taiwan	9.2	7.7[a]
Thailand	8.2	7.7

SOURCES: World Bank, *World Development Report 1981 (New York: Oxford University Press, 1981),* app. table 2; used by permission. For Taiwan, Johns Hopkins University Press, *World Tables* (Baltimore, 1980).
NOTE *a.* For period 1970 to 1977.

395

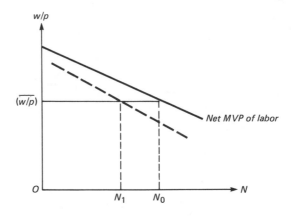

FIGURE 17–2
Impact of an Oil Price Increase on Employment

A second major factor, which has been much emphasized by Bruno and Sachs, is real wage rigidity. The higher oil price decreased the real income available to share between labor and capital; that is, it reduced the net marginal value product of labor at any given level of employment, as shown by the leftward shift of the schedule to its dashed position in figure 17–2. If labor resists a fall in the real wage from its initial value of ($\overline{w/p}$), the effect is to reduce employment from N_0 to N_1. And if governments attempt to expand employment back to N_0 by Keynesian demand expansion, the result is explosive inflation.

Even without the oil price increase, therefore, the 1970s would probably have been a decade of stagflation—of slowing output as opportunities for easy growth were exhausted in the developed countries, of continuing inflation as real income aspirations remained ahead of the collective possibilities, and of increasing unemployment as governments sought to combat unemployment in the lopsided ideologically fashionable way which excluded any attempt to maintain equilibrium real wages through incomes policy. These problems were accentuated rather than caused by the oil price increase.

The massive current-account imbalances superimposed on a stagflationary world economy were, in contrast, a direct result of the oil price increase. Those imbalances provoked fears on two distinct scores.

First, there were renewed worries about a possible inconsistency in current-account targets of the same sort that caused concern in OECD in the 1960s but on a much bigger scale. In place of the division of a collective *surplus* of $5 billion to $10 billion among the OECD countries, the problem was how to divide up a collective *deficit* of $30 billion or $40 billion among the oil importers. There were fears that countries might refuse to accept their fair share of the oil deficit and that the attempt to adjust deficits away more quickly than OPEC was increasing its imports would drive the world into renewed protectionism, competitive devaluation, or cumulative deflation. The only one of these that would have cut the OPEC surplus, as opposed to shifting it around, was deflation, but this would have been an extremely costly solution—elimination of the OPEC surplus of perhaps 0.5 percent of GWP would have required a cut of between 10 percent and 20 percent of GWP.[6] Some economists therefore recommended that the IMF should get into the business of developing sensible rules of thumb that would enable it to allocate consistent current-account targets to its member countries. As usual, the forces of inertia prevailed, and the fact that the rise in protectionism was limited, that there was no sign of competitive devaluation, and that the nonsystem muddled through were adduced to demonstrate the wrongheadedness of those who called for a more active IMF role.

The second fear was that countries might be unable to finance the current-account deficits that they were willing to accept: that is, the fear that the recycling process might break down. This fear reached its peak in the second half of 1974, following the failure of the Herstatt Bank in Germany and of the Franklin National Bank in the United States. The fear was reinforced by the specter of a major industrial country—Italy—unable to borrow more from the private market and forced to use its gold as collateral to raise a loan from Germany in order to finance its current-account deficit. There were subsequent crises of overindebtedness in countries like Peru, Turkey, and Zaire, which were overcome only after the countries involved adopted severe measures of economic retrenchment under the tutelage of the IMF. There was, however, no general breakdown in the process of recycling. And by 1978 there seemed grounds to hope that the dangers were past: the OPEC surplus had been whittled down, the industrial countries were back in comfortable current-account surplus (and with the prospect of a reasonable balance among them), and the LDC deficit was down close to a sustainable level. Then came the Iranian revolution, the consequential cutback in oil supplies, the new oil price increases of 1979 to 1980, and the resulting transfer of a further 2 percent of GWP from the importers to the exporters of oil. The oil deficit reemerged and with it new worries as to the sustainability of the recycling process.

Although Southern growth held up much better than did Northern growth after the first oil shock, it nevertheless declined. This was the first reversal of the acceleration in the trend of LDC growth since World War

6. In round numbers, oil provided 50 percent of energy requirements, OPEC provided 60 percent of the oil, and OPEC's surplus was a third of its receipts. Thus, assuming a constant oil price, GWP would have had to fall by 10 percent if other forms of energy were available and perfectly substitutable for oil and by 20 percent if substitutability were zero.

II. Moreover, there are signs that after the second oil shock many LDCs concluded that the strategy of debt-led growth was no longer viable, because their indebtedness was straining their creditworthiness. Encouraged by the international community in the form of the IMF, the tendency in 1981 was for the developing countries to seek to adjust their deficits by curtailing growth. This portends a further reduction in the momentum of development. Thus a slowdown in Southern growth, rather than a major financial panic, seems the likely outcome of present (1981) trends.[7]

What sort of impact would a slowdown in Southern growth and a curtailment of Southern deficits have on the North? The main effect will be to reduce the prop that Southern demand provided for Northern income and employment in the second half of the 1970s. In the Keynesian era, one would have argued that this would have induced the North to take expansionary action to limit unemployment. Such a reaction can no longer be taken for granted, although, insofar as lower demand really does serve to cut inflation, the ultimate effect will be similar: less Southern demand will mean lower Northern inflation, which will increase real money balances (given fixed monetary growth rates), which will expand Northern demand.

There are, of course, those who doubt the strength or even the existence of the link from the pressure of demand to the rate (or acceleration) of inflation. This line of thought was influential in President Jimmy Carter's administration and the OECD in the second half of the 1970s. It led to calls for a coordinated economic expansion to get the world economy out of the 1975 recession and the subsequent period of sluggish growth. First the three major countries in strong payments positions (the United States, Japan, and Germany) were likened to locomotives that would be able to pull the world out of recession without causing payments problems for each other if they expanded jointly. Then, when a number of other countries were in stronger payments positions, the locomotive approach was supplanted by the convoy approach, under which a convoy of countries was supposed to expand demand simultaneously. The idea was again to relieve countries of the dangers of an isolated expansion, in terms both of bigger current-account deficits and of currency depreciation leading to an acceleration of inflation. In the event, Germany and Japan agreed to adopt more expansionary policies only in mid-1978, in the course of a summit conference in Bonn, but by that time the United States was already suffering from a recrudescence of the problems of deficit, depreciation, and inflation, which were aggravated by the fact that its previous expansion had been isolated.

7. After this book went to press Mexico declared a temporary moratorium on debt service and the world found itself in the most serious financial crisis since the Great Depression. As of December 1982, however, there seems no need to revise the judgement in the text.

The same type of analysis that supported the case for a concerted OECD expansion from 1976 to 1978 suggests that a resumption of Northern growth is what is needed to pull the South back on to a higher growth path and reverse the trend toward increasing indebtedness. Some economists, like Nicholas Kaldor, argue that increased Northern demand would meet an elastic Southern supply of manufactures. Others, like Lance Taylor, view the world economy in structuralist terms, as driven by the interaction between a Keynesian (demand-constrained) North that produces manufactures and a neoclassical (supply-constrained) South that produces primary products. Higher Northern demand, generated by deficit spending by Northern governments or livelier animal spirits on the part of Northern entrepreneurs, would raise the demand for (but not the supply of) primary products and so shift income toward the South. Conversely, a Northern decision to fight inflation by demand restraint reduces the relative price of the South's output: to the extent that it succeeds in curbing inflation, it does this by squeezing Southern incomes and so relieving the inconsistency of Northern real-income claims. Not surprisingly, the South tends to think that the North should find other solutions to the problem of reconciling inconsistent claims to real income.

The view that faster growth by one part of the world economy will necessarily have positive spillover effects for other areas is not, however, universally accepted. The most striking alternative hypothesis was one that emerged in 1979, when the oil price was being bid up by the competitive scramble of the oil importers to ensure access to supplies. It was suggested that the supply of energy was so inelastic that world output was effectively limited by an energy constraint, rather than by the level of productive capacity. An expansion of world output would at some point lead to a bidding up of energy prices that would continue until the redistribution of income to the high-saving oil exporters cut back demand. This hypothesis would imply that the oil importers were engaged in a zero-sum game among themselves: higher output by one could be sustained only if output elsewhere fell and so reduced the demand for energy to the available supply. In such a world, developed countries would have no incentive to ease the LDC payments constraint by liberalizing their imports, increasing aid, or sustaining the recycling process.

These worries are out of fashion at the moment. There is, at least temporarily, an oil glut, but the story still provides a useful warning of what could happen if energy economy were allowed to lapse. The worries of the hour are those of a mix of expansionary fiscal and contractionary monetary policy in the United States leading to a major overvaluation of the dollar, thus inducing monetary restriction in other countries and an inappropriately low rate of growth of the world money supply. But the dominant concern will no doubt be different by the time this book is used. It will have served its purpose if it helps the reader to analyze current problems as they evolve.

17.5 Summary

Global economic interdependence has long since reached the point where study of world economic developments is essential to understand the prospects of individual countries. In the 1960s, the international community developed efforts to influence the policies adopted by the major countries with a view to improving the performance of the system as a whole. However, the combination of insufficient instruments and overambitious employment targets in some of the central countries of the system led to the outbreak of inflation, which was generalized to the world as a whole by the attempt to preserve a fixed exchange-rate system. The adoption of floating allowed inflation rates to diverge, but it transformed rather than eliminated the problem posed by economic interdependence: deflation by one country came to threaten its trading partners with increased *inflation* (as its currency appreciated and theirs depreciated). The oil price increases magnified the problems of slower growth and stagflation that would in any event have troubled the 1970s, while creating new concerns regarding the proper distribution of payments deficits and the sustainability of the LDCs' debt-led growth. Despite the importance of the issues, economists have not yet paid much attention to building formal models in this area, so perhaps it is not surprising that coherent attempts at international coordination have not been much in evidence.

17.6 Bibliography

Richard Cooper's book on the logic of policy coordination was called *The Economics of Interdependence: Economic Policy in the Atlantic Community* (New York: McGraw Hill, 1968). The outbreak of worldwide inflation was analyzed in L. B. Krause and W. S. Salant, eds., *Worldwide Inflation: Theory and Recent Experience* (Washington, D.C.; Brookings Institution, 1977). A good statement of the monetarist interpretation is contained in Swoboda's chapter. For his work on the determinants of the world money supply under fixed exchange rates, see A. K. Swoboda, "Gold, Dollars, Euro-Dollars, and the World Money Stock under Fixed Exchange Rates," *American Economic Review,* Sept. 1978. An authoritative statement of mainstream reactions to the economic difficulties of the mid-1970s is to be found in the McCracken Report: P. McCracken et al., *Towards Full Employment and Price Stability,* A Report to the OECD by a group of independent experts (Paris: OECD, 1977). Analyses of the first oil shock can be found in E. R. Fried and C. L. Schultze, eds., *Higher Oil Prices and the World Economy* (Washington, D.C.: Brookings Institution, 1975), and W. M. Corden, *Inflation, Exchange Rates, and the World Economy* (New York: Oxford University Press, 1977). The most accessible source of the Bruno-Sachs thesis regarding the failure of the real wage to adjust is J. Sachs, "Wages, Profits, and Macroeconomic Adjustment: A Comparative Study," *Brookings Papers on Economic Activity,* 1979, pt 2. A critical discussion of the arguments for coordinated economic expansion was written by W. M. Corden, "Expansion of the World Economy and the Duties of Surplus Countries," *The World Economy,* Jan. 1978, to which I replied in the same journal in Oct. 1978. Kaldor's views on global growth are contained in "Capitalism and Industrial Development: Some Lessons from Britain's Experience," *Cambridge Journal of Economics,* 1977 (pt. 2), reprinted in his *Further Essays on Applied Economics* (London: Duckworth, 1978). Lance Taylor's model is in L. B. Taylor, "South-North Trade and Southern Growth," mimeographed (Cambridge, Mass: MIT, 1981), a revised version of which will appear as chapter 10 "Trade Patterns and Southern Growth," in his *Structuralist Macroeconomics: Applicable Models for the Third World* (New York: Basic Books, 1983).

Notation

The notation used is in most cases standard throughout the book, although it can be seen that a few letters serve double duty, often for closely related concepts. So far as possible symbols have been chosen to conform with customary usage.

A	Absorption
AA	Asset market equilibrium
B	Base money
C	Consumption
D	Demand; domestic credit
D_1	Central bank component of domestic credit
D_2	Commercial bank component of domestic credit
E	Equilibrium
F	Foreign liabilities (usually); foreign assets (on occasion)
G	Government expenditure
H	Money supply (the use of H to represent money originated from the term "high powered money," for which we use base money)
K	Capital stock
L	Labor
M	Importable good; imports; composite traded good
N	Nontraded good
O	Origin
P	Production point
PPP	Purchasing power parity
Q	Quantity; quality
R	Reserves
S	Supply; savings
T	Taxation
TB	Trade balance; current-account balance
U	Our country, "us;" unemployment
V	Value marginal product; a small trading partner country
W	The other (large) country; the rest of the world
X	Exportable good; exports
Y	Output; income, nominal or real, depending on context
c	Cost; marginal propensity to consume
d	Differential
e	Exchange rate (units of domestic currency per unit of foreign exchange)
f	Forward exchange rate
g	Rate of growth
i	Nominal interest rate
k	Capital/labor ratio
l	Input of labor per unit of output

m	Marginal propensity to import
n	1 . . . n, the number of something
p	Prices; general price level
ppc	Production possibility curve
q	Quantity
r	Real interest rate
s	Marginal propensity to save
t	Time
v	Real wage
w	Nominal wage rate
y	Output per capita
ϵ	Elasticity of supply
ζ	Capital inflow/income ratio
η	Elasticity of demand
κ	Money multiplier
λ	Rate of population growth
μ	Export subsidy
ξ	Quota
π	Purchasing power parity, PPP
ρ	Rate of productivity growth
σ	Standard deviation
τ	Tariff rate
ϕ	Reserve ratio of commerical banking system
*	Foreign variables (for example, $Y^* =$ income in W)
.	Rate of change (for example, $\dot{Y} = dY/dt$)
^	Rate of growth (for example, $\hat{Y} = \dot{Y}/Y$)
the dollar:	country W's currency
the peso:	country U's currency

Index

Index

Fund holdings of, 369; speculation in, 353–54

gold-exchange standard, 336–38; Bretton Woods system, 8–9, 12–13, 241, 339–45, 390; and reform debate, 345–51

gold standard, 338; adjustment mechanism, 138–41; basic features of, 6, 138; discontinuation of, 141, 181–82; establishment of, 6–7; and reform of Bretton Woods system, 347; pre–World War I, 335–36; post–World War I, 8

government expenditure in national income accounts, 131–32

Great Depression, 8, 141, 256, 339

Group of Ten, 318, 318n1, 348

Group of Seventy-Seven, 379

growth: comparative advantage and, 264; constraints on, 275–79; export-led, 254–55; immiserizing, 259, 284–87; and labor growth, 52–54; neoclassical model of, 113–17; and technology, 280–82; trading blocs and, 297–98, 300

guidelines for floating, 350–51

GWP (gross world product), 3, 3n1; measurement of, 3n1; 1960 to 1973 growth of, 10; petroleum in, 13, 309, 392, 397; post–1974 growth of, 13–14

Gylfason, T., 203n12

Haberler, Gottfried, 35, 55, 146

Harrod, Roy, 142

Harrod-Domar model, 276

Heckscher, Eli, 31, 54, 55, 74

Heckscher-Ohlin model, 31–58, 70–71, 84, 85, 264; bibliography on, 59; described, 38–41; Leontief Paradox and, 44–47, 54; paradoxes of, 60–61; Rybczynski theorem and, 52–54, 56; Stolper-Samuelson theorem and, 47–52; summary on, 54–55

Heckscher-Ohlin theorem, 42–44

hedging, 246

Helliwell, J. F., 203n12

Heston, A., 3n1

Hicks, Sir John, 65

homothetic tastes, 23n2

human capital, see labor

Hume, David, 138–41, 166, 172, 335

ICOR (incremental capital-output ratio) 14, 94–95, 277, 394

IMF (International Monetary Fund), 9, 159–60, 163, 166, 168; Bretton Woods system and, 340–42; oil price increases and, 397–98; in plans for reform of monetary system, 346; present system and, 351–55; proposals for monetary system reform, 366–70; Special Drawing Rights and, 348–51, 352, 367, 369; stabilization programs, 159, 163, 168, 369–70

immiserizing growth, 259, 284–87

imports: in balance of payments accounting, 126, 127; in elasticities approach to devaluation, 147–56; licenses for, 93, 94–95; in multiplier analysis, 143, 144; prohibition of, 75; quantitative restrictions (QR) on, 296; see also quotas; tariffs

import substitution, 254, 256–57; arguments for, 258, 260; and domestic resource cost (DRC), 262–63; in education, 284; vs. export expansion, 257–66; first stage of, 260–61; second stage of, 261, 262–63; see also trading blocs

income distribution: export subsidies and, 90–91; tariffs and, 52–56, 84–85

incremental capital-output ratio (ICOR), 14, 94–95, 277, 394

industrial countries, 376–77; characteristics of, 376–77; disaggregation of, 377; statistics on, 374; see also specific countries; OECD

industrialization: impact of colonialism on, 7; early British, 4–5, 254; protection in process of, 256–57; spread of, 5–7, 254–55

Industrial Revolution, 4–5, 254

infant industry protection, 80–81, 83, 87, 91, 98–99, 295–96

inflation: balance of payments accounting and, 126–27; current monetary system and, 354–55; in elasticities approach to devaluation, 155–56; expectations of, 387; fixed vs. flexible exchange rates and, 238–39, 387–89, 391; gold standard and, 7; increase in, 12, 386–92; post–1974, 13–14, 392–400; oil prices and, 13, 392–400; Phillips curve, 160–61, 169, 174, 227, 382, 386–87, 389, 391; productivity growth and, 214–15; purchasing power parity and, 212–17; Scandinavian model of, 214–15; serial correlation of, 236; taxes and, 159; unemployment and, 160–61, 169, 174, 227, 382, 386–87, 389, 391; post–World War I rates of, 216

intangible property, defined, 118

Index

Machlup, Fritz, 142, 146, 158

manufactures, trade in, 60–73; bibliography on, 73; by developing countries, 258, 266, 359–61; economies of scale and, 61–65; monopolistic competition and, 68–72; product cycle model and, 72; role of demand in, 65–68, 71–72; summary on, 72–73; trading blocs and, 296–302

Marshall, Alfred, 146

Marshall-Lerner condition, 140, 151–53, 155, 172, 175, 208

Marshall Plan, 325, 327, 340, 342

Marx, Karl, 272

McKinnon, Ronald, 239

Meade, James, 160–65, 174, 179, 182, 197, 236–38

mercantilism, 20–21, 137–38

Metzler, Lloyd A., 55, 209n1

migration, 6, 12, 15

monetary accounts, 133–35

monetary approach, 165–70, 175, 197–204, 387–89; arbitrage and, 168–70; balance of trade and, 172, 173; and capital mobility, 197–204; Polak model of, 167–68

monetary base, 134, 139n1

monetary policy: asset market approach to exchange rate and, 231–34; effect of, with floating exchange rates, 210–11; and fiscal policy, 185–86, 188; and fixed vs. flexible exchange rates, 236–42; inflation and, 387–88

monetary system, international, 333–56; basic requirements of, 333–34; bibliography on, 356; Bretton Woods system, 8–9, 12–13, 241, 339–45, 390; chaos in, in the 1930s, 338–39; current status of, 351–55; gold as basis of, 6–7, 335–38; reform of, 345–51, 366–70; summary on, 355–56

money supply: components of, 134–35; gold standard and, 138–41; in the Polak model, 167–68; *see also* monetary approach

monopolistic competition, 68–72; tariffs and, 85

most favored nation (MFN) status, 292–93, 294

Multi-Fiber Arrangement (1974), 295, 303, 360

multinational corporations (MNCs): direct investment by, 11–12, 117–19, 128, 130, 180–81; exchange controls and, 325; proposals for regulation of, 360–61; resource exploitation by, 67; Seven Sisters,

310, 310n3, 311; technology spread and, 281–82

multiplier: in the Eurocurrency market, 319–20, 321; Lagrange, 267; money, 134–35, 194–95, 319n2

multiplier analysis, 142–46, 171–72, 209

Mundell, Robert, 166, 184–86, 210–11, 217, 237, 239, 381, 384

Mundell-Fleming model, 217–24; asset market approach and, 225–28, 233, 235; assumptions of, 217; capital mobility in, 218–24; inadequacies of, 225

Mussa, Michael, 197

Muth, John, 228, 232

national income accounts, 131–33

natural resources: Leontief Paradox and, 46–47; multinational exploitation of, 67

Neary, Peter, 49–50

new classical macroeconomics, 201–2, 272

new industrial countries (NICs), 379; exports of, 14–15, 266; trade liberalization and, 71; *see also* developing countries

New International Economic Order, 357–58, 361, 364, 366

Nixon, Richard, 345, 347

n–1 problem, *see* consistency problem

nontariff barriers, 75–76, 293

Nurkse, Ragnar, 237, 252

OECD, *see* Organization for Economic Co-operation and Development

official development assistance (ODA), 326

offset coefficient, 196

offshore markets, *see* Eurocurrency markets

Ohlin, Bertil, 31, 55, 74, 142n2, 172

oil, 10, 11, 309–12, 361, 362; early trade in, 310; income of producers of, 111–12; inflation and, 13, 392–400; 1973 price increase of, 13, 392–94; post–1974 market for, 311–12, 392–400; OPEC control of price of, 310–12, 392; trade in, 309–312

oil-exporting countries, 378; oil deficit and, 392–400; statistics on, 374; *see also* Organization of Petroleum Exporting Countries

oligopolistic competition, tariffs and, 85

opportunity cost, 26

optimal currency area, 239

optimal peg, 241

Index

413